THE POSTMODERN WORKER

EXPOSED

UNMASKING AN UNDER-ACHIEVING WORKFORCE

JAMES R. FISHER, JR., PH.D.

Table Of Contents

For Thomas L. Brown

The very notion that millions of workers displaced by the re-engineering and automation of agricultural, manufacturing, and service sectors can be retrained to be scientists, engineers, technicians, executives, consultants, teachers, lawyers and the like, and then somehow find the appropriate number of job openings in the very narrow high-tech sector, seems at best a pipe dream, and at worst a delusion.

—Jeremy Rifkin, *End of Work: The Decline of the Global Labor Force and the Dawn of the Post-Market Era*, 1995.

The acceptance of corporatism causes us to deny and undermine the legitimacy of the individual . . . The result of such a denial is a growing imbalance which leads to our adoration of self-interest and our denial of the public good. Corporatism is an ideology which claims rationality as its central quality. The overall effects on the individual are passivity and conformity in those areas which matter and non-conformism in those which don't.

—John Ralston Saul, *The Unconscious Civilization*, 1995.

FORWARD

A Positive Expose

Alas, the masses need not be asses.

Ken Shelton

Spoiler alert: As you pick up a book with the word "exposed" in the title and "unmasking" in the subtitle, you should expect to find *the naked truth*, Rated R for its *Revealing* portrayals and portraits, in this case of working professionals, along with their managers and leaders in the milieu of modern organizational mania and madness.

However, here author James R. Fisher, Jr. is not publishing pornography nor writing a lurid tell-all autobiography; rather, he is crafting *lithography* in which the image to be printed is ink-receptive and the blank area ink-repellent. Ergo, in reading his words, you will either be receptive or repellent to his ideas and images, depending in part on your own life experience and point of view.

Warning: In this book, Jim is not shooting blanks but live bullets, meaning you could be injured or influenced. Indeed, he aims both for the mind and the heart, and, in the end, he wants you to take action.

My Take on Jim Fisher

Having known Jim Fisher for at least two decades, having read much of what he has written, and having published more than a score of his commentaries on this and related subjects for my *Leadership Excellence* magazine, I can attest: he is a prolific word machine, but not because he is vain and verbose but rather because he is a rare *Renaissance man* of ideas and ideals, motived by his diminishing time in mortality to share them more widely. In this sense, he serves like James, the apostle of Jesus, as a "fisher of men".

This "expose" provides further evidence of his excellence, as he aims to expose the plight of the postmodern professional worker (most of us). This is not easy reading. You may well toss this book across the room (or delete it from your screen), and that's fine, as long as you then pick it up again. Fisher is an acquired taste, as he is not writing like Norman Vincent Peale, in public relations mode to "win friends and influence people"; nor illustrating nostalgic notions like Norman Rockwell; rather, he writes more like Norman Lear, to reveal discrepancies and expose hypocracies and paints word pictures like Vincent Van Gogh, the Dutch post-modern impressionist known for his bold colors and dramatic, impulsive and expressive brushwork.

With his deft brush, Fisher calls out the worst sins of corporate leaders and silent killers in managment waste bins. But along with the description of the problem, we also find here real solutions, such as the healing balm to loneliness and isolation—*being your own best friend.*

In reading this book, I hope you gain the same kind of respectful relationsnip with Jim and his writings as I have: I deeply respect this man and applaud his messages. Clearly, he is a man who is comfortable in his own skin and skull, skillful in sketching out manuscript skeletons and then fleshing out ideas. He is both a technician and artist, writing as much for the craft as for change. He is not seeking entertainment or recreation but attainment and re-creation. He asks his readers not only to think but also to act; not only to transition but also to transform.

While Jim is a stanch Catholic, he appears to be writing to refine organizational theology and reform management/leadership idealogy. He is a *Saint James*, and yet he writes in the style of Martin Luther and John Calvin, as he too is bold in publishing his grievances.

As a professional, Jim is the rarest of breeds: a company man who succeeded in many organizations but always as his own man, perhaps because his answers are as valuable as his questions. For example, while working in *Human Resources at Honeywell,* even when he saw that the Honey was all about the Money, his well of resourcefulness never ran dry.

My Take on This Book

Like Joseph Conrad, James Fisher is writing his own *Heart of Darkness,* as one who has penetrated the mind and soul of managers and leaders. He finds that "executive excellence" is at best a humorous contradiciton and at worst a heinous oxymoron, with an emphasis on *ox* and *moron*—the executive elites who exploit the professional expendables.

While Jim pumps out paragraphs, he is full of powerful one-liners. For example, in *Work Without Managers: A View from the Trenches*, he writes: *"Take charge of your work! It is the best way to take charge of your life. Damn the torpedoes! We don't need managers. They need us!"*

Real power, he notes, has shifted dramatically from management to the worker domain, *"But workers behave as if management still possesses the power.*

The organization waffles like a rag doll in the wind. Uncertainty reigns supreme, and power is falling between the chairs."

In *The Worker, Alone! Going Against the Grain!*, Jim argues that nothing changes at work until working professionals change. *"Games of trendy themes like empowerment continue. It is now urgently up to workers to put this house in order. Neither house cleaning nor finger pointing will do. Professionals must get off the dime and boldly take charge of work, their work, which is the path to taking charge in life."*

In *Six Silent Killers: Management's Greatest Challenge*, Jim writes: *"Termites destroy a person's home with no one the wiser until irreparable damage is done. And social termites, the six silent killers of the infrastructure, are eating away the hand that feeds them. Social termites choose to deny reality; to become inauthentic to themselves; and to become obsessively negative to others. Social termites look for what is wrong, not right; for what they can get; not give; for what they don't have, not possess; and the glass for them is always near empty. Social termites develop amazing political cunning, displaying an incredible facility to manage, influence, and manipulate colleagues and superiors indiscriminately. They conveniently choose to see themselves as victims of a system that fails to appreciate them or satisfy their needs.*

"Without knowing it, they are seduced by the six silent killers; behaviors that can kill a career before it is underway; undermine all that they could become; and destroy the enterprise for which they work. Organizations plagued with these social termites find management preoccupied with damage control without dealing with the source of the problem. Managers, as manic monarchs, take ownership of the wreckage, while the social termites treat the workplace as their merry madhouse. It is like the plague all over again, a disease that contaminates everyone and everything, but no one seems to recognize the source."

In *Be Your Own Best Friend*, Jim writes: *"No greater taboo exists than the one that prevents us from being our own best friend. Tragically, instead of cultivating loyalty, trust and belief in ourselves, we elevate the opinions of others above our own; trust experts rather than cherishing our own experience; search for heroes to worship, rather than celebrating our own lives.*

"We yearn for outside approval, while it is within us. Widely, we are counseled about the critical importance of self-knowledge, while popular culture incessantly promotes self-indulgence. Self-help books feed this self-indulgence by the devious ploy of inferring that personal progress comes at the expense of self-rejection. This rejection feeds self-doubt. Ironically, the more self-conscious we are, the less genuine we are with ourselves, eventually leading to a desperate search for self by avoiding personal self-responsibility and positive change."

And in *Corporate Sin: Leaderless Leadership and Dissonant Workers*, Jim writes: *"Management is not leadership. It has opted for pyramid climbing by always campaigning for the next position never having time to do the job paid to do. Now that the pyramid is collapsing and with it, its position power, the workplace has become dysfunctional to the extreme. Why, then, should there be any surprise when those that climb to the top can't lead?"*

While Jim has his research and references, this work is mostly in-search and reflections. His arguments appeal to both reason and passion, and his is a tough love: *"Life's hard rule is that everyone is responsible for their own actions, and to learn from the consequences of those actions. Everyone gets a report card on their performance every day of their life."*

Jim's Closing Argument

Jim admits this attempt is *"a risky analysis of a complex problem"* since *"there is no way such an analysis can be made without stepping on some toes and the hands that feed me."*

A first step, he says, is *"to recognize that the 'management of things' and 'management of people' are discretely different functions. That managers and consultants must realize that listening is more powerful than telling; that framing the problem is more important than generating solutions; that we are on the threshold of a wonderful tomorrow if we can 'let go' of all our precious false assumptions of the past, and allow a little reality to guide our way."*

He notes that while *"happy ignorance"* rules the head if not the heart of most workers, there is a rapidly building movement against the grain. *"The focus of this natural fault is apparent — the worker, alone! Were we only to pause a moment we would realize we come into the world alone and we leave the world alone. What transpires between the coming and the going is our own individual affair as we are in the constant company of ourselves."*

"Minds that can make technology soar are not minds without the capacity for self-mastery. The plunge into chaos has been a gratuitous retreat into self-indulgence. Instead of changing their ways and taking matters into their own hands, professional workers have allowed themselves to be treated as interchangeable parts in a giant economic machine, gravitating to the pathetic role of victims of circumstances. Professional workers have all the power, but they act as if they have none. They could stop this manic drift with a simple statement, 'Hell, no, I won't go!' People still count for more than robots, that is, if they can see themselves as counting more."

In his *"happy intelligence"*, Jim cries out: *"We need each other more than we need money. By ignoring our biological and spiritual programmed needs, and substituting artificial material needs, we risk physical and mental distress."*

Jim, I salute you for your courage in exposing sins and explaining solutions, and I invite all to read your insightful writings and heed your warnings.

Ken Shelton is CEO of Executive Excellence, LLC, author of Beyond Counterfeit Leadership, and editor-publisher of Leadership Excellence magazine for 30 years.

Introduction

The Author's Journey to this Collection

Everything changed after World War II especially with *Corporate American Society*, which was reasonably under control, despite the excesses of the *Robber Barons* of the late 19th and early 20th century. With *'The Great Depression'* and collapse of the world economy in the 1930s followed by the most devastating war in human history, only the continental United States was spared the detritus of war enabling American industries to surge 24/7 to meet the demands of a decimated world.

MAD MONARCHS OF THE CORPORATE MADHOUSE

Corporate American capitalism proved to be benign when it was unchallenged and draconian when it was. The brutal union strikes of the 1930s were but a memory by 1945. But during the 1930s, American workers sued for decent wages and better working conditions by striking. *Corporate America* met this challenge with *strike busting tactics* often hiring thugs to crash strike barriers to allow scabs to work in its places of employment.

THE POSTMODERN WORKER EXPOSED

Unmasking An Under-Achieving Workforce

Dr. James R. Fisher, Jr.

Question: Why have professional workers failed to deliver on their great promise?

Answer: In a collection of penetrating essays, Dr. Fisher supplies the answer —a startling and blunt indictment.

Post-World War II massive unemployment was now a thing of the past with an actual glut of jobs for unskilled and semi-skilled workers in the burgeoning economy. The manufacturing centers of Detroit, Pittsburgh, Philadelphia, Chicago, Cleveland, St. Louis, and Kansas City across the rust belt of the nation were booming.

At the time, everyone across the globe wanted to "buy American." These were halcyon days for American workers. It was the "Golden Age" of employment and upward mobility for the working class. It was also an idyllic period of unbridled hope that would however last only fifteen years or until 1970. Then everything would start to unravel with few having a clue as to what was happening or why.

British political economist David Ricardo wrote in 1819, *"The amount of employment in an economy was of no consequence, as long as rent and profits, out of which flowed its new investment, were undiminished."*

Italian historian and economist Simonde de Sismondi echoed these sentiments during the same period:

"Wealth is everything, men are absolutely nothing. What? . . . In truth, then, there is nothing more to wish for than that the king, remaining, alone on the island, by constantly turning a crank, might produce, through automata, all the output of England."

So, it is not new for *Corporate America* to treat its indigenous workers ambivalently irrespective of their basic needs or prevailing requirements. Over the last 200 years, workers have been treated as interchangeable or replaceable parts in the giant *Corporate American machine* in the name of *progress*.

The monarchs of the world understand this insolent attitude. But they no longer reside at the pentacle of hierarchical power in Europe or elsewhere. They do however reside in the *Corporate America hierarchy of the United States*. Corporations have taken the place of kings, turning the crank at their discretion that sets into motion the mechanical, electrical, and electronic automata that provide the goods and services to the nation and the world.

The only difference today with the past is that the 1 percent of *Corporate America* that controls 80 percent of the market and service economy enjoys a degree of infallibility and dominance never before experienced by monarchial empires.

The New Cosmopolitan Elite

The new cosmopolitans are *Corporate America's executive class.* In 1953, or eight years after World War II, executive compensation was the equivalent of 22 percent of corporate profit. By 1987, it had risen to 61 percent. In 1953, CEOs in the United States earned 10 to 20 times that of the average factory worker; by the 1990s, it was well over 100 times and rising. In 1960, when John F. Kennedy was about to assume the office as *President of the United States*, CEOs of the *Fortune 500 companies* were earning $190,000 a year; by 1990, they were earning $1 million a years; today, the majority are earning between $10-20 million a year. There are some 200 top American executives, however, who earn between $50-100 million a year, while their counterparts in other countries are likely to earn between $2-6 million a year.

Meanwhile, the growing gap in wages and benefits between top management and the rest of the American workforce has created a deeply polarized and divided nation, or the equivalent of an island populated by a small group of corporate elites isolated from an increasingly impoverished nation of unemployed or underemployed workers, many with first-rate academic credentials but crippled with the dual daggers of joblessness and staggering student loan debt.

To put this in a human context, less than 1 percent of all United States companies employ more than 500 workers, but these firms often considered "too big to fail" employ more than 41 percent of all the workers in the private sector. This gives you some idea of the mad rush of many workers to the safe harbor of the public sector that lacks the profit motive and cruel reality of a "profit & loss" balance sheet.

Into this entropic dystopian maelstrom, wanders the consensus savior, re-engineering. This discipline treats the human tragedy of employee displacement and disruption as if failing parts of a giant inanimate machine.

Corporate America & America Individualism

The mania for re-engineering has come to affect the middle echelons of the corporate community, more specifically *middle management*. Middle managers clearly have no role in the future scheme of things. But this was obvious thirty years ago, and yet excellent engineers and scientists gave up their professional acumen for managerial roles, going back to school to earn pointless MBAs in management and then to assume a role they would prefer to have avoided, and all for the sake of money!

These middle managers are people who live in affluent suburbs and have excellent professional credentials, but are being laid off in droves. Literally tens of thousands of these laid-off middle managers and executives find themselves at home, waiting for a text message with a potential job offer. Most of them, sadly, will wait in vain.

Corporate guru Peter Drucker says, *"The managerial class is beginning to feel like slaves on an auction block."* Blue collar workers have been on this auction block seemingly forever, and would most likely say with a bit of sarcastic bitterness, *"Welcome to the club."*

Drucker's underlying message is that individualism is now fully subjected to the demands and needs of *Corporate America;* demands quite apparent in *corporate speak*. This message is also apparent in the rhetorical voice of many social science academics. It is "the group that counts," not the individual. It is "the team that makes a difference," not the person.

Corporate speak refers to the organization "as family" with the CEO and his or her direct reports as the parents, while promoting "group think," which is an oxymoron.

There is no need to register surprise at how smoothly our American universities have fitted into the structure of *Corporate America*. Its approach in education is to teach the mechanistic skills required to perform specific tasks at the expense of developing habits of thought that are essential to creative thinking. To put it another way, a *corporate managed society* scoffs at liberal education with universities aligning themselves with specific market forces in an effort to create a conforming society of passive inclined specialists.

With such an obsessive focus of aligning basic education on current job needs in the marketplace, this attention could prove illusory if students display sophisticated skills in technology alone – with computers and artificial intelligence for example – producing graduates who have never developed the ability to think outside the box while possessing what will eventually be obsolescent skills. Reacting with notable acumen to a machine, is not thinking but the passive response to a valuable but limited programmed tool.

The previous century saw an explosion in all types of management. Our entire education system is still ironically creating managers of every description. Yet, it is *the managerial class* that is dying a slow death while weighing down our economy.

With management, there is no due process when thousands of workers are made redundant; when job categories and disciplines are summarily erased from the employment board; when plants close and relocate; when the *Board of Directors* bumps up the salaries and the bonuses of its executives.

The denigration of the democratic individual worker from the very beginning of the rise of Corporate America has been strangely unopposed.

Corporate speak has been successful in selling its capitalistic ideology along with the idea of progress through market dominance as its most important product. Corporate jargon that has become familiar includes such expressions as "downsizing," "outplacement services," "re-engineering," "reacting to the changing demands of the marketplace," "creating a lean organization," "pursuing cutting edge technology," and of course the fallback positions when everything goes awry of "mergers," "acquisitions," and "hostile takeovers."

The central core to this jargon is "downsizing" and "creating a lean organization" through "re-engineering." The problem is that cuts do not produce growth, prosperity or effectiveness. Nor do they promote risk taking or creativity. Instead, they result in employee anxiety and plummeting morale and productivity. Such actions are however natural to corporate society in a state of panic.

Alas, mega-corporations are no longer propelled by leadership, but by management and re-engineering. Corporate management, in any case, is not a creative but an administrative function. Creativity frightens the administrative mind and so it has a negative influence on innovation. So, when power and control wane due to the lack of leadership, there is a furtive attempt to restore corporate viability by purchasing innovation and creativity from small creative companies where these qualities thrive.

Mergers, acquisitions and takeovers are often the penance workers endure for the sins corporations commit through lethargic leadership. It is always a short term fix for the corporation, but a long term traumatic shock to workers who are given a pink slip after several years of dedicated service, "and they have done nothing wrong."

After World War II, once *Corporate America* was in power, discretion and modest demands commenced to unravel as pointed out earlier, while the concert of individual workers who were equitably participating in the economic boom suddenly disappeared in the 1970s. Double digit inflation and double digit unemployment then crippled workers, but not *Corporate America*.

Corporate America in order to thrive requires group norms and general acquiescence in support of its authoritative agenda and protocols. Individualism in order for it to thrive requires participation, meaning it cannot be bogged down by gender issues, race and religion bigotries, ideologies, or anything but the work at hand; in other words, political correctness issues or corporate propaganda has no place in the equation.

Corporate America has used prestidigitation to persuade workers that what they have in common counts; that it is where legitimacy lies; that workers exist primarily as a function of management, not as individuals; that corporate legitimacy lies with group connections, not the individual worker's requirements.

What I am describing here is the essence of the corporation where there is no room for the individual.

16

Yet, individualism was on display with Steven Jobs, Steven Wozniak, and Bill Gates, among many others, who have had the temerity to reject the stultifying corporate security and conforming corporate blanket of such storied giants as IBM, GM, T&T, Xerox, and Wall Street, to create the modern era of *information technology*. Indeed, the true cultural norms of American society since its inception have been those of individualism, a status now in danger of disappearing more quickly than man being replaced by robotics.

Corporate America by reducing human individuals to measureable value, as if machine parts or pieces of property, has resulted in massive conformity, apathy and general passivity among workers whatever the skill level or professional qualifications. This will be apparent in excerpts from the books discussed in this presentation.

One of the great tragedies of the mid-20th century is illustrated when workers gave up their power, which was the control of work, for *Corporate America's* promised goodies. This once vibrant class of industrial blue collar workers won World War II with their industry and worker pride. David Halberstam touches on this accomplishment in *"The Next Century"* (1991):

With our great assembly lines and our ever expanding industrial core (and protected as we were by two great oceans in an age when weaponry could not yet cross an ocean), we became the industrial arsenal for the mightiest war efforts. In 1942 and 1943 America alone produced almost twice as many airplanes as the entire Axis. In 1943, and 1944 we were producing one ship a day and an airplane every five minutes.

Today that power has shifted from brawn to brains, from *position power*, which *Corporate America* enjoys, to *knowledge power*, which is now in the hands of individuals who are scientists, engineers, computer specialists and in many other disciplines. Yet, these professionals behave as if they are working in the ambience of 1945 with management still in undisputed control. The focus of *The Postmodern Worker Exposed* is on this 21st century dilemma along with the challenges and opportunities. Let us now look at what happened to worker power in the *labor union movement*.

Labor Unions Capitulation

While the professional class of workers seems frozen in the headlights of the on rushing future, labor unions did a disservice to union workers, and workers in general, when they enjoyed premiere bargaining power immediately following World War II. Admittedly, workers in the trenches have seldom been aware of their clout, and now when they are being replaced by "thinking machines," they are unable to launch a counterattack as they lack the psychological disposition to do so.

Labor unions waffled on the issue of automation after World War II only to cast their lot with management to the detriment of their own worker community. During the early postwar period, Norbert Weiner, the "Father of Cybernetics," warned of the dangers of widespread and permanent technological unemployment:

"If these changes in the demand for labor come upon us in a haphazard and ill-organized way, we may be well in for the greatest period of unemployment we have ever seen."

Weiner anticipated in mid-20th century that the cybernetic revolution *"will undoubtedly lead to the factory without employees."* Clearly, his words were not heeded. Instead, labor union management through the persons of Walter Reuther of the *United Auto Workers* (UAW) and George Meany of the *AFL-CIO* capitulated.

Behind closed doors, despite rhetoric to the contrary to the public and their workers, the UAW and the AFL-CIO, fearing being branded as *Luddites*, that is, opposed to new technology and new ways of working, assumed the defensive in collective bargaining when they held all the deciding cards.

Now, seemingly, so absurd in retrospect, ten years after World War II or 1955, the UAW issued a ringing endorsement of automation. Having boxed itself into a corner, the UAW made a hasty retreat, shifting their collective bargaining demands from *the issue of control over production and work processes*, which were fundamental to workers' best interests, to accepting corporate management's proposal of *job retraining, salary and benefit concessions, and retirement packages.*

This total retreat from worker power to the role of workers with little economic or political clout hangs like an ominous shadow over these two unions but also over tens of thousands of highly trained but anxious professionals who have no idea what role they may have in the future.

With the aborting of the control of work and the active participation in the economic benefits of technology in favor of retraining and compensation concessions, the *union movement* lost much of its effective bargaining power. Collective bargaining agreements from the 1950s on would celebrate increased compensation and entitlement concessions until the union movement would be reduced to the marginal status that it experiences today.

Had control issues remained a strong priority, labor might have successfully negotiated collective bargaining agreements with management that would have ensured labor's participation in productivity gains brought on by automation. Then some of the profits would have gone to workers improving their security and job stability, while possibly changing the entire landscape of American enterprise to resemble something approaching economic parity; or if not that, something at least much different than what it is today.

Shortsighted labor capitulated with defensive passive agreements that provided job security for older workers. *Corporate America*, which never totally bought into the fig leaf proposition of *worker retraining*, suffered little blowback for such an omission. Instead, all eyes were focused on compensation which continued to rise for all union workers during the boom years of 1945 through 1970.

The Decline of Middle Management/Dawn of the Professional Class

Books profiled in this collection that will follow, were written over the past thirty years, and were meant to energize the professional class of workers to face the fact that leadership and executive power had shifted to them; that position power was anachronistic and that knowledge power, which they now possessed, needed to be harnessed for American economic life to prosper and grow; that professionals were in the driver's seat and must assume the controls with accountable leadership; and that they must avoid the errors of the labor union movement.

But alas, my efforts were not heeded as narcissistic self-indulgence in the workforce had already set in with professionals desiring the trappings of position power without the risks, responsibilities or requirements; without the stress and strain; indeed, without the sacrifices or possibilities of failure.

Workers since 1945, professionals and blue collar workers alike, went from the security and comfort of the home to the comfort and complacency of the workplace with management the surrogate parent calling all the shots reducing workers to reactive conforming adults to management's commands. This has resulted in workers being suspended in terminal adolescent and learned helplessness with the organization (i.e., the workplace) responsible for these workers' total well-being. Consequently, the corporate workplace is saddled with 70 years of counter dependence at a time when it is a luxury the corporation can least afford.

From the time we are born, we are programmed to follow orders, and if we do, we won't get into trouble. Why? Because corporate society expects us to behave to its authority; at home, at school, at church, at work and in the community. Our primary obligation is loyalty to the demands of corporate society: to be an obedient student at school; a safe hirer at work; and to bring no undo attention to oneself.

This brings to mind corporate life as Swiss psychotherapist Carl Jung describes it: *"Is that gentle and painless slipping back into the kingdom of childhood, into the paradise of parental care."* Jung continues, *"Why, because all mass movements slip with the greatest of ease down the inclined plane made up of large numbers. Where the many are, there in security; what the many believe must of course be true."*

Corporate America has killed democracy in the workplace, where there is no place for the individual, and it did so because of its lust for power and control. Now, workers, whatever their pedigree are culturally and psychologically damaged with a toxic inclination to passively conform to the dictates of Corporate America no matter how idiotic the corporate policy.

20

Given this tired apathetic situation, Corporate America remains reluctant to turn the crank one turn in acknowledgement of the change in power and control or to admit the deep hole it has created for American enterprise.

Truly, *Corporate America* continues to manage, motivate, and manipulate work, workers and the workplace as if it is still 1945, failing to recognize that 90 percent of the jobs of unskilled or semi-skilled blue collar production workers have disappeared being replaced by a contingent of 80 percent college trained professionals competent in all phases of organizational life including science and technology.

The service economy, which has taken on significance in recent decades, is manned by more than 50 percent of these professionals who are teachers, lawyers, doctors and government employees as well policeman, salespeople and franchise managers of business, sporting and entertainment emporiums, as well as professors and administrators of colleges and universities and other service facilities.

Since the 1970s, or when the American economic boom approached economic bust with the *Vietnam War*, the *OPEC embargo*, the *Cold War*, the *Watergate Scandal* and several other societal embarrassments, *Corporate America* could be seen to create with one hand a manufacturing kingdom of cutting edge technology and a full service private sector and to take away with the other hand when it felt a little economic crunch time.

The service sector grew on the back of the typewriter and telephone; shrank under the impact of the Xerox machine and the mail order catalogue; was reinvigorated with the computer and subsequent information technology. Through all these iterations, *Corporate America* could be seen sitting securely at the controls on its paradise island, turning the crank at its whim while the automata would go to work.

With no more fanfare than this, automatic, robotic and computer moving mechanical devices, made in imitation of human beings, commenced to replace workers and managers, first slowly than as if an avalanche eliminating workers whatever their credentials or level of scientific and technological acumen. Job security summarily ended for tens of thousands, even millions across the nation as they were now at the mercy of the *Mad Monarchs of the Corporate Madhouse*.

One person who saw the title chosen for this book, quipped, it should be, *"THE POSTMODERN LOAFER EXPOSED!"* Indolence is not the problem with America's workers, taking control of work is.

The Incomprehensible "Third Industrial Revolution"

We are now feeling the destabilizing effects of the *Third Industrial Revolution* and have little comprehension as to what to do about it other than to submit to its momentum. If this seems irrational, we only have to look back to the precedence set by the *labor union movement.*

s we have attempted to show, when labor controlled the workplace, and had the power to negotiate with management in the dawn of automation, robotic and computers in the 1950s, it flittered away that power by conceding the control of work, workers and the workplace to management. *Industrial revolutions* have always embraced the new for something lost never to be experienced again. James Burke and Robert Ornstein in *"The Axemaker's Gift"* (1997) explore this phenomenon in a brilliant compression of human history.

The First Industrial Revolution was the era of steam power. Steam was used to mine ore, produce textiles, and manufacture a wide range of goods while the steam ship replaced the sailing schooner and the steam locomotive replaced the horse driven wagon.

The Second Industrial Revolution occurred between the *American Civil War* and *World War I.* Oil now competed with coal, and electricity was effectively harnessed for the first time. City could be lit 24/7 while the steam engine gave birth to the railroad industry with oil and electricity replacing animals as beast of burden.

The Third Industrial Revolution emerged immediately after *World War II,* and now is effectively influencing society, the meaning of life and work, and what is the function of being a human being.

The introduction of "thinking machines" has clouded what it is to be human as these machines are increasingly capable of performing conceptual, managerial, and administrative work functions once thought the domain of man. They have already erased jobs in every category of work making the concept of what is thought to be a factory, school, shopping mall, office building, hospital, playground, sports arena, or church to fade in recognition.

Indeed, the role of wholesalers and jobbers, farmers and fishermen, workers and managers are either changing dramatically or disappearing. Meanwhile, the once bloated ranks of middle management have been replaced by the process flow of information up and down and across levels of the corporate organization without a person involved.

We are seeing a chaotic and somewhat complacent mass of people clamoring to get into the United States at the Mexican border. Crime and low intensity violence are but an irritating preview of the potential calamity expected at mid-21st century when national borders will be meaningless. Economist Jeremy Rifkin envisions worldwide unemployment and increased polarity between the rich and the poor to continue to scale upward. He writes:

As machines increasingly replace workers in the coming decades, the labor of millions will be freed from the economic process and the pull of the marketplace. Unused human labor is the central overriding reality of the coming era and the issue that will need to be confronted and addressed head-on by every nation if civilization is to survive the impact of the Third Industrial Revolution.

High-tech savants remain unconvinced that trouble lies ahead (Ramez Naam's *"The Infinite Resource,"* 2013). Surrounded by sophisticated technological hardware capable of performing stupendous feats, the emerging knowledge class imagines a world of near utopian grandeur and overflowing abundance with the "power of ideas."

These optimistic savants have set about building a wall between themselves and reality creating a sense of artificial well-being. History offers a different vision. The French aristocracy, gentry and business leadership were never more satisfied with themselves than the few decades before the *French Revolution*. Likewise, the elite of the *Roman Empire* were in constant expansion and filled with a sense of their own importance, as emperor after emperor was assassinated and provinces were being lost to invaders. More recently, the Russian aristocracy two decades before *World War I* were comfortably in a state of euphoria with traditional leadership and the new emerging business class happily in control before the complete collapse of the Russian monarchy in the *Bolshevik Revolution.*

A Most Dangerous World

Technology displacement and increasing unemployment have led to a dramatic increase in crime and random gratuitous violence. We have seen mass indiscriminate killings of the innocent at schools and in parks; at shopping malls and workplaces; at places of worship such as churches, temples and mosques; and at entertainment festivals. Then, there are gang members killing each other and often innocent children at play in drive by shootings. We have also seen an increase in the pointless burning of homes, workplaces, cars and boats and places of business. Whatever the motivation, these societal deviancies are omens of more troubling times ahead.

Studies show a disturbing correlation between increases in unemployment and the rise of violent crime. In the *Merva and Fowles study*, researchers found in the United States a one percent rise in unemployment results in nearly a seven percent increase in homicides; a better than three percent increase in violent crimes; and two plus percent increase in property damage crimes. Other major violent crimes include burglary, aggravated assault, and murder; the property crimes of robbery and larceny, and motor vehicle theft.

Technology displacement and the loss of job opportunities have affected the nation's youth most of all, spawning a violent new criminal subculture with tens of thousands in city gangs across the United States. As the "American Dream" of hope for a better future has collapsed, many young people, not only in metropolitan areas, but in the suburbs of the nation are carrying guns to school, or are turning to a life of crime and violence.

The unintended consequences of television's nightly news reporting of these criminal acts is to stoke the fire of malcontents living on the edge with psychologically damaged personalities who become instant if infamous celebrities. People of all ages appear to delight in shocking others on the various outlets of the Internet. Can this sick behavior not be laid at the door of "displacement technology"?

Jeremy Rifkin writes in *"End of Work"* (1996): *We are rapidly approaching a historic crossroad in human history. Global corporations are now capable of producing an unprecedented volume of goods and services with an ever smaller workforce. The new technologies are bringing us into an era of near workerless production at the very moment in world history when population is surging at unprecedented levels. The clash between rising population pressures and falling job opportunities will shape the geopolitics of the emerging high-tech global economy well into the next century.* We see that they already have. The transition into a *Third Industrial Revolution* throws into question many of our cherished beliefs about the meaning and place of progress in the scheme of things. This collection of excerpts from my various books is offered for the reader to ponder that question and the role of professionals in this new century.

For many the world is filled with dread, not hope, with growing rage, not anticipation. Many feel the world is passing them by and suffer a sense of being powerless to intervene. They feel as if outcast in the global village

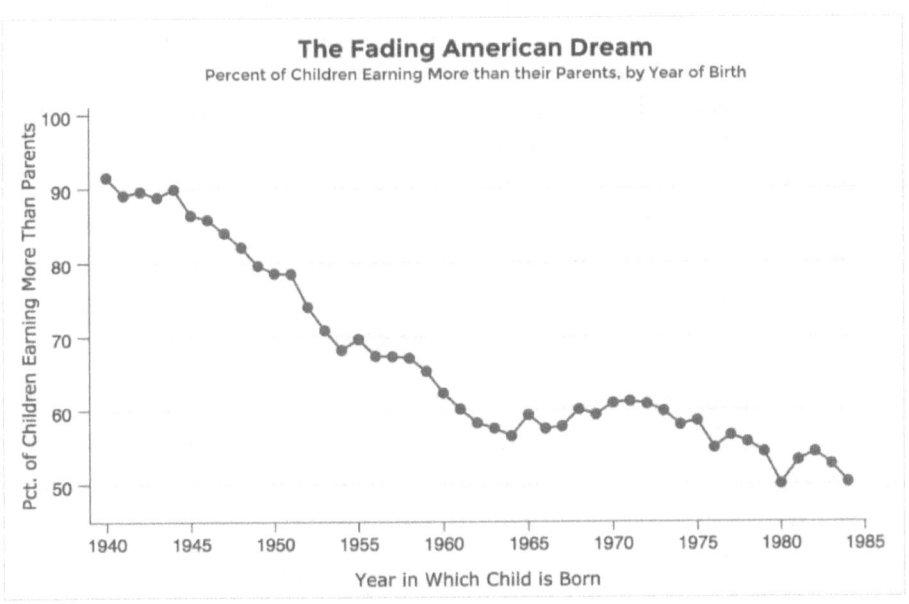

The Fading American Dream
Percent of Children Earning More than their Parents, by Year of Birth

languishing on the periphery of human existence in a cauldron of despair sensing the postmodern world has made them invisible.

In the face of this, *Corporate America* with its utopian zeal straddles the very dystopian world of this majority who languish in rife and peril as they are replaced by machines.

Corporate America sold the nation on the promise of progress squeezing more and more profits out of productivity indifferent to how that might impact working Americans. We have now had three quarters of a century of what that "cut & control" philosophy has derived. Yet, the downside of progress has been missing in the discussion as many people have been too busy being busy to notice, until now. This is similar to the union movement's surrender of control of work to *Corporate America* for a few pieces of silver. What will professionals do in the face of the "thinking machine"?

Over the past thirty years, I've asked myself that question, wondering what it will take for professionals to get off their duffs, take charge, and go against the grain of *Corporate America*. It could not be a better time for professionals to take the economic crank out of *Corporate America's hands*, who still operate as if they enjoy the *"Divine Rights of Kings,"* and establish some democratic sense to America's economic enterprise.

The monarchy and feudal system were once sacrosanct. This was also true of the *Protestant Reformation* and the birth of *capitalism*. Now, *Corporate America capitalism* is regarded as equally sacrosanct. As with the eventual fate of European monarchies, *Corporate America capitalism's* excesses place it now at the door of entropy. Yet, the next system is yet to appear. The challenge of the professional class is to create this nexus before man becomes a nonfactor.

A final aside, author philosopher Charles D. Hayes once wrote in *"The Rapture of Maturity"* (2004): *"Life is full of contradictions. My friend and fellow author James R. Fisher, Jr., provides an interesting example. He is an expert on organizational psychology but has never found an organization where he fits in."*

This is true and the reason also is quite simple. I've never been in an organization that has had room for the individual.

The Author's Memorable Journey to This Collection

During the 1970s, I was a contract consultant for *The American Management Association* (AMA) where I conducted *Management Development Seminars* for public sector executives across the continental United States. For that association and *The Public Safety Institute* (PSI), I conducted organizational development (OD) interventions for police organizations along the East Coast of the United States from New Haven, Connecticut to Miami, Florida.

Among those interventions, I was embedded for nine months in the *Fairfax County Police Department* of Fairfax, Virginia after a white police officer shot and killed a 27-year-old black man at a *7&11 Convenient Store* in Herndon, Virginia in which a major riot followed. I would write a Master's Thesis on this experience: *"A Social Psychological Study of the Police Organization, The Anatomy of a Riot."*

An even more bizarre OD intervention followed in Raleigh, North Carolina where 550 sworn police officers threatened to walk off the job in a mutinous rebellion against the *Chief of Police* with whom they said they could not work. Embedded for three months in this police organization as PSI's "people person," we were able to uncover the chronic disturbance, a misunderstanding that grew animus between the chief and these line officers. Once the composition of this was exposed, these police officers resumed their duties without penalty.

During this period, I was a mature graduate student pursuing a doctorate in *social, industrial/organization psychology*. At the same time, I was an adjunct professor to several colleges and universities teaching in the MBA programs at the *University of South Florida, Nova University, Florida Institute of Technology, St. Leo University, Golden Gate University, Biscayne University* and *St. Petersburg College*. Students were mainly engineers, program managers, chemists and teachers looking to enhance their careers.

In 1980, I joined a client as a *Management & OD Psychologist* for *Honeywell Avionics* in Clearwater, Florida. Avionics was a *Department of Defense* (DOD) hi-tech subcontractor for specific military instrumentation for the *United States Navy* and the *United States Air Force*.

This was during the peak hysteria generated by *Japan, Inc.'s* major invasion into once sacrosanct American markets: e.g., automobiles, radios, electronics, light fixtures, televisions, kitchen appliances, portable air conditioners and farm equipment. *Japan, Inc.* was doing this with statistical quality control and *Quality Control Circles* (QCC), technology borrowed from the United States that had been largely ignored by U.S. companies who considered it largely unneeded.

Not Avionics. It had, at the time, the largest QCC program in the United States for its 4,000 workers. One of my functions as an OD psychologist was to direct the QCC program; another was to conduct training seminars for professionals; still another was to write papers to be presented at various engineering conferences on work related issues; while asked to give keynote speeches on subjects relating to QCC and other OD topics.

Given the economic disruption caused by *Japan, Inc.* and other *Southeast Asia nations* with American markets at home and abroad, academics in the disciplines of sociology and management came to weigh in on the problem creating a litany of enticing rhetorical slogans such as *"Work Centered Management," "Lifetime Employment,"* and *"Participative Management,"* to name a few.

Fad consciousness was at its peak with seemingly a mad rush to duplicate *Japan, Inc.'s* approach to manufacturing across the nation while forgetting that Japan was a *group norm society* while the United States was established on the basis of *individualism* (see Robert E. Cole, *"Japanese Blue Collar,"* 1971 and *"Work, Mobility & Participation: A Comparative Study of American and Japanese Industry,"* 1979).

Peter Drucker, Rensis Likert, W. Edwards Deming, J. M. Juran, Fredrick Hertzberg, Saul Gellerman, Douglas McGregor, Robert Blake & Jane Mouton, Kenneth Blanchard & John Hersey, among many others got into the act prescribing the correct "leadership style" or "situational leadership" to enhance organization health and productivity.

One of the reason I wanted to be totally embedded in the organization, full time, was to see how my recommendations and those of others actually worked in the long term. You lack that perspective as a consultant. Alas, discovering that these proposed faddish interventions by celebrated

28

academics and consultants did not have staying power put me on this long journey of research, reflection and publication.

The problem with these well tensioned strategies was that they were expected to benefit workers without workers' involvement and participation in the discussion and so nearly all of them were eventually abandoned.

That was my experience with *"Participative Management"* as a full time OD psychologist at *Honeywell Avionics*. *"Participative Management"* had no impact because it had no teeth. It was a toothless tiger as workers still had no control or power to change anything other than cosmetically (e.g., workplace design, lighting, etc.). Conversely, in clear evidence of passive aggression, workers retreated into blatant and often juvenile contemptuous behavior in this workplace.

It was in this climate that I was asked to give the keynote speech for Avionics' *Contracts Administrative Services* (DCAS), which was hosting this conference of some one hundred military and civilian personnel working for the *Department of Defense* and the *United States Navy* and the *United States Air force* in March 1984.

The title of my speech was, *"Participative Management: An Adversary Point of View."* *Avionics Technical Publications* printed and bound some 100 copies of the speech. I mention this because immediately following the speech they disappeared in a matter of minutes.

That said, a number of senior managers at Honeywell Avionics took exception to the speech, which resulted in my being put on the equivalent of "house arrest," unable to give any speeches, write any monographs or produce any papers for professional conferences, while ordered to turn my engineering notebooks in every Friday for review, knowing that I was an extensive note taker.

The notebook collection lasted only two weeks as my boss and mentor, the late Dr. Francis Xavier Pesuth, confessed he couldn't read my handwriting. I continued to write on this subject to which the volume grew to some forty notebooks, all on the subject of work, workers and the workplace with the working title, *"Work Without Managers."*

This was continued through 1984 to early 1986 when I was released from "house arrest" to be promoted to *Director of Human Resources Planning & Development* for *Honeywell Europe, SA.* Prior to that, in 1985, I penned an article and gave a speech at a conference for *Professional Women at Honeywell* in early 1986. Subsequent to that, I was invited to give a speech on the same subject at *The American Human Resource Conference* in Dallas, Texas and to give a speech and paper on the *Technical Education Program* that I co-initiated at *Honeywell Avionics* at *The World Conference of Continuing Engineering Education* at Orlando, Florida.

During the two years that followed (1986-1988) that I worked at *Honeywell Europe's* headquarters in Brussels, Belgium, I was writing on this book, gaining greater perspective on postmodern work, the worker and the workplace from a European perspective.

In 1990, I retired from Honeywell and looked for a publisher in both Europe and the United States for this work without success, deciding to form a publishing company with my wife, Betty, called *The Delta Group Florida*, publishing the book in the fall of 1990 with a 1991 copyright.

The national reaction to its publication was immediate. The periodical *Industry Week* named it *"one of the ten best business books of 1991,"* with the caution that it appeared an angry book; *The Book Review Journal* gave it an extensive review naming it *"one of the four best books in its genre of social psychology"*; *National Public Radio* (NPR) featured it on its radio broadcast; and hundreds of calls came in from across the country on the landline of *The Delta Group Florida.* Eventually, *The National Productivity Review Journal, The Journal of Organizational Excellence, Quality & Participation Journal, Executive Excellence, The Human Resources Journal*, and newspaper such as *The Wall Street Journal* and *The Dallas Morning News* included critiques or commentaries on *Work Without Managers.*

This was five years before the publication of economist Jeremey Rifkin's "End of Work."

Once this seed was planted some thirty years ago, themes common to it have been expanded in the books that appear in this collection, but only in excerpts, mainly to show the continuity of this endeavor and to, once again, assert that the dye has been cast and that we must deal with that reality.

James R. Fisher, Jr., Ph.D.

Tampa, Florida

Work Without Managers

"We live today in a globally interconnected world, in which biological, psychological, social, and environmental phenomena are all interdependent. To describe this world appropriately we need an ecological perspective which the Cartesian world view does not offer. . . What we need, then, is a new paradigm — a new vision of reality; a fundamental change in thoughts, perceptions and values."

Fritjof Capra, Austrian-born American physicist

"The man who embraces a new paradigm at an early stage must often do so in defiance of the evidence provided by the problem solving. He must, that is, have faith that the new paradigm will succeed with the many large problems that confront it knowing only that the older para-digm has failed with a few. A decision of that kind can only be made on faith."

Thomas S. Kuhn, American physicist and philosopher

We Have Been Here Before

As Americans struggle to make sense of a series of uncomfortable economic changes and disturbing political developments, a worrying picture emerges; of ineffective politicians, frequent scandals, racial backsliding, polarized and irresponsible new media, populists spouting quick economic remedies, growing suspicion of elites and experts, frightening outbreaks of violence, major job losses, high profile terrorist attacks, anti-immigration agitations, declining social mobility, giant corporations dominating the economy, rising inequality, and the appearance of a new class of super-empowered billionaires in finance and technology-heavy industries.

These are the opening remarks of Professor of the Humanities Walter Russell Mead of Bard College in an article in *Foreign Affairs* (May/June 2018), an issue devoted to the topic: *Is Democracy Dying? A Global Report.*

What professor Mead is describing is not today, but the 35 years after the American Civil War (1865 – 1900). These were the years between President Abraham Lincoln in 1865, when he was assassinated and that of President William McKinley in 1901 when he was likewise assassinated. Dr. Mead writes:

(The years between Lincoln and McKinley) *were among the least inspiring in the history of U.S. politics. As reconstruction proved unsuccessful and a series of devastating depressions and panics roiled the economy, Washington failed miserably to rise to the challenges of the day.*

If you remember any of your American history, you know this dark period led in only a matter of two decades to the United States becoming the largest and most advanced economy in the world.

It was a combination of happenstance with the momentum of the *Industrial Revolution* and the arrival of such men as Thomas Edison (1847 – 1931) who invented the electric light bulb, and then compounding that success by creating the public utility so that metropolitan centers need never experience the darkness of night; John D. Rockefeller (1839 – 1937) who invested in railroads that would soon stretch from the Atlantic to the Pacific ocean, then adding to his colossal wealth by turning petroleum from a substance of no commercial value into gasoline to fuel the new automobile of Henry Ford (1863 – 1947), who developed assembly line manufacturing of his vehicles. This made them affordable to his workers, who he awarded with a pay increase of 500 percent from the national norm of a $1 per day to $5 per day, reducing the work week to five days and the work day from 10 to 8 hours. Ford also created a retirement fund for his workers to insure the stability of the workforce. In doing so, he initiated what would become knowing as the working middle class.

Other entrepreneurs born in the 18th century that added to this workplace revolution after the *American Civil War* were Andrew Carnegie (1935 – 1919) who was a magnet in the steel industry, and with a generous bequest, creating the American Public Library system so that ordinary citizens would have access to books not otherwise available to them.

Men of a particular genius, also born in the 18th century, would have had impact which is likely to be felt well into the 21st century and beyond. Albert Einstein (1979 – 1955) is in this company with his discovery of relativity and the explosive power of his equation on mass: $E = MC2$. Then there are the mysteries of electricity revealed by the futurist electrical engineer Nikola Tesla (1856 – 1943). He envisioned an invisible grid or electrical connection across the globe that we now have as the Internet.

Then there are those who attempt to take us out of our woes and doldrums such as Dale Carnegie (1888 – 1955) and *How to Win Friends and Influence People* (1936) and Napoleon Hill (1883 – 1970) and *Think & Grow Rich* (1937). It is no accident that these books were published at the height of the Great Depression (1929 – 1945).

The Great Inflation of the 1970s. It's the 1970s, and the stock market is a mess. It loses 40% in an 18-month period, and for close to a decade few people want anything to do with stocks. Economic growth is weak, which results in rising unemployment that eventually reaches double-digits.

The prevailing belief as promulgated by the media has been that high levels of inflation were the result of an oil supply shock and the resulting increase in the price of gasoline, which drove the prices of everything else higher. This is known as cost push inflation.

The Great Inflation. The term "stagflation" was first coined during a period of inflation and unemployment in the United Kingdom. The United Kingdom experienced an outbreak of inflation in the 1960s and 1970s.

The Great Inflation of the 1970s. It's the 1970s, and the stock market is a mess. It loses 40% in an 18-month period, and for close to a decade few people want anything to do with stocks. Economic growth is weak, which results in rising unemployment that eventually reaches double-digits.

Real and nominal price of oil, 1968–2006. The 1970s energy crisis was a period when the major industrial countries of the world, particularly the United States, Canada, Western Europe, Japan, Australia, and New Zealand, faced substantial petroleum shortages, real and perceived, as well as elevated prices.

1973 oil crisis. The 1973 oil crisis began in October 1973 when the members of the Organization of Arab Petroleum Exporting Countries proclaimed an oil embargo. ... By the end of the embargo in March 1974, the price of oil had risen from US$3 per barrel to nearly $12 globally; US prices were significantly higher.

In October 1973, in retaliation for the West's support of Israel in the Yom Kippur War, the Arab members of the Organization of Petroleum Exporting Countries (OPEC) cartel stopped supplying the US and Western Europe with oil. ... Oil prices quadrupled in a very short period of time, contributing to a deep global recession.

Managers! Who Needs Them?

Likely it seems far-fetched at first glance, a workplace absent of managers. After all, who among us has experienced a workplace without this all-important class of working professionals? And they seem to be multiplying, not diminishing in numbers. Everyone wants to be a manager, and the B-Schools are flourishing. We're sold on management actually. Yet, the more management is emphasized and the more managers we have, the less successful and fulfilled we seem to be as a society and as individuals. Ominously, our institutions and corporations are continuously teetering on the brink of ruin.

Something doesn't add up. Could it be that management as a field is not the panacea we have been led to believe? Perhaps managers do not have the answers we all thought they did.

Why Work Is Not Working Like It Ought To

We've all experienced it. Our employers seem to expect something quite different from us than what we expect of ourselves; that we know we are capable of doing. Their expectations of us are in fact quite low in terms of our standards of behavior and the quality of our work.

Our performance is constantly judged, micro-measured in fact, but what is judged and measured seems to have little to do with what we feel ought to be important to an employer. While we may have as much or more education and experience than managers above us do, we are treated like school kids. And therein lays the problem.

We are no longer dependent on adults as we once were for guidance, discipline and ideas. We are adults. We like our work and we're full of ideas and energy. We are ready to be tapped, to be activated, but with trust and acceptance.

Evidently, managers do not know this; do not understand the huge potential sitting right under their noses. How do we tell them? Well, we don't because we think they should already know this. We're the audience. Remember, that is our dutiful programmed role. And we have passively accepted this role for a long time; too long. In fairness, the threat of termination, rarely stated, is always inferred in every exchange between managers and the managed. Speaking up is death, as it were. Call it bullying if you wish.

Further, the environments, organizations and cultures in which we work are hard to fathom. They seem designed to be ineffective. We're told our job is one thing, but the culture and the organization seem to conspire against our doing the job properly. Our work is simply not very important to the managers we needed to be supporting us. They seem too busy to even notice us at times. Yet, we know our work is important; they told us it was. When we inform our manager about these inconsistencies, they accuse us of being the problem. We shut up. The organization continues chaotically along, while conflict and political maneuvering steadily siphons vital energy out of the enterprise and us.

So, let's recap. What do we have? We have a highly trained and motivated workforce of professionals who are assumed by their employers and managers to be unmotivated, undisciplined and even unintelligent. We have managers who believe their job is to train, direct, correct, manipulate and motivate these professional employees, when these workers know as much or more about the business climate and company challenges, and what needs to be done, now.

To compound the problem, the workplace environment is structured, unintentionally we must suppose, to frustrate the efforts of professional workers to create and deliver their work. As problems arise, they are dealt with as localized disturbances or dismissed as the misunderstandings of simple-minded workers. What could be more absurd?

To state this unequivocally, I am serious about a workplace without managers. We need not be constrained by the past, as we now are. We are free to discard our outdated and unexamined assumptions about work, workers and workplaces. And, most excitingly, we're ready to harness the vast dormant potential embodied by the best educated, most well-intentioned and informed workforce that has ever existed. At the same time, we'll be releasing the potential of our companies and institutions to excel in their own right to serve the common good.

The Bigger Picture

We have been flummoxed. The present became the future, without warning. A spate of books, not long ago, sought to ease our discomfort by 'explaining away' the apparent contradictions. We've read Alvin Toffler's "Future Shock" and Dennis Gabor's "Inventing a Future" and Barbara Ward's "Lopsided World," as well as C. P. Snow's "Two Cultures." They were all reasonable books, but changed nothing.

To be fair, these books thoroughly described the fundamental dislocations of society and the broad trends. What they failed to do was explain why and thereby increase our understanding of where we were going, how we'd get there, and why we ought to be going in that direction.

Work Without Managers: A View from the Trenches published more recently, attempted to answer these important questions. Some reviewers found the book "angry" others reacted favorably. These were respected publications, like *Industry Week* (named *WWMs* one of the ten best business books of 1991*), The Business Book Review Journal* (one of the four major works of 1991 in its category), and NPR radio's *All Things Considered* said:

This is not casual corporate bashing; Work Without Managers is premeditated capital punishment of standard managerial systems that Fisher thinks have outlived their prime, and may not have been useful even then.

Tellingly, it touched a nerve in certain quarters. That nerve has spread as if the organization had the shingles. Among other things, Work Without Managers argued that the First Industrial Revolution was over in 1945:

"A shocking look at American business; <u>why</u> it operates in '1945 nostalgia,' as <u>six silent killers</u> threaten to destroy it; and <u>how</u> only American Leadership can still save the day!"

About the same time this was being published, control theorist Russell L. Ackoff proposed that the world was going through a *Second Industrial Revolution*. He wrote:

"Since World War II, we have entered into a period, which will be to the future what the Renaissance was to the past. We have moved into a new age that is fundamentally different from the age, which we have come, an age that began with the Renaissance and ended essentially with World War II."

Ackoff's ideas align with sociologist Pitirim Sorokin's hypothesis. He published *Social and Cultural Dynamics* (1937), scores of years before the Ackoff thesis. Sorokin postulated the theory that we were at the end of a 600-year "Sensate Day." His "Sensate Day" commenced with the high Renaissance of 1500 A.D. in Italy, and ended with the First Industrial Revolution. Thus, we are living in Ackoff's Second Industrial Revolution, and are entering Sorokin's 600-year "Ideational Day" of the glorious tomorrow.

Remarkably, two theorists, generations apart, envisioned the same phenomenon, the end of one historic era and the dawn of another, differing only in their descriptive nomenclature.

The Paradox

We have departed the Old Machine Age and have entered the New Machine Age, characterized by microprocessors, satellites, software, robotics, and cyberspace. You may know it as the Information Age. Regardless, it's all very new and exciting, liberating in fact. Yet this New Machine Age is encumbered with some troublesome remnants of the past, principally a devotion to *reductionism*.

Reductionism is a method that seeks to reduce complex systems, to collections of parts, in order to understand and manage them efficiently. Each part is then small enough to be understood and managed independently. The disciples of reductionism, who are legion, fervently believe it to be the one and only way to understand and manage complex systems. For the most part, no one even questions this methodology. In truth, it is not often spoken of as reductionism. It's taken for granted and mostly goes unrecognized.

It's ironic that reductionism is so ubiquitous in the computer age. As a method of analysis and control it has been popular for well over a century, applied in virtually every field: atoms in physics, cells in biology, indices in economics, and Freudian elements of personality (id, ego and superego) or Skinner's conditional stimulus and response behaviorism in psychology.

Societal Reflex Thinking

Although some disciplines have moved away from reductionism, our cultural reflex is still to default to reductionism. It is evident in our susceptibility to simplistic solutions, particularly to stubborn complex problems. It is also the strongest indication that management in general is "out of sync" with the workplace of our times. Management loves simplifications; in fact it runs from complexity, while it vociferously denies this practice.

Although narrow logic dominated Machine Age Thinking, and the limits of linear logic in this non-linear age are increasingly apparent, these limits have not been sufficient to discourage their dominance. Like the limits of linear logic in this non-linear age, causation has not always proven reliable.

During the First Machine Age, the concept of environmental stewardship was unimaginable. People lived in "closed systems" obedient and unquestioning of dogmas that drove the workings of industrial society; a world of discrete parts with no explanation provided to workers about how they all worked together.

People came to understand and to be constrained by the notion that the whole could never be greater than the sum of its parts. Today, we know that is not true, but oddly, we do not usually act on that knowledge.

Mistaken Certainties

Machine Age thinking also relied on a process called "analysis," which was similarly governed by reductionism. To explain something, such as the workings of a large organization, it was first reduced to its elemental parts, figuratively and actually. These parts were analyzed, optimized and then given their own goals. Consistent with the linear logic of Socratic thinking, these components were explained in the context of a particular problem. Management called it "cutting the problem down to size." Meanwhile, in the world of psychology, the structure of behavior was reduced to the phenomena of discrete syndromes.

Realistically, most problems don't respond to this breakdown because it is not meant to deal with complexity, myriad interactions of parts and people. The result is that the problems solved are generally not the problems faced. "Paralysis by Analysis" is the term given to this absurd occurrence, where the original problem is forgotten in the process. We still do this, more often than not.

HR Reductionism

Reductionism in the office, among professional knowledge workers, has been a disaster. How can you break down knowledge work into independent specialized functions and then reassemble the work performed, expecting reasonable "results"? Incredibly, managers believe it can be done. On paper, the *expected* vs. *achieved results* appear to correlate, but in reality there is only too frequently a large gap.

Consider the Machine Age concept of "Management by Objectives" (MBOs) championed by Peter Drucker, a master of reductionism. He introduced MBOs as a rationally ordered way to achieve corporate goals. His intentions were good, but the concept was not. Widely adopted by corporations, it soon became simply a ritualistic exercise, eventually fading away.

This has happened with numerous, rational sounding, corporate management theories, appropriate for factory-like operations, treating people as products with standardized expectations. For instance, the infamous Performance Appraisal System (PAS) was meant to be a coaching, counseling, guiding and directing mechanism to improve workers' performance. Instead, it reinforced management chain-of-command control of professionals who were confined to a labyrinth of cubicles, while managers dispensed modest pay increases and, for the effort, stifled professional development.

From the mid-twentieth century on, fad theories continued percolating as to how to assess this changing workforce and gauge their problem solving contributions. These fads included the value of symbols, charismatic management, cosmetic interventions, communication schemes, leadership style paradigms and finally, engineering cybernetics.

That is, the workplace was recognized as a "system" consistent with control theory, which provided a template for evaluating and accepting or rejecting these previous theories.

Unconscious Incompetence

Today, unconsciously, most organizations, de facto, are still committed to Machine Age thinking, and reductionism, but ironically, in a rather more vigorous way.

These organizations, private and public, for profit and non-profit practice reductionism by reducing the system to discrete autonomous elements: that is, departments, divisions, functions, and technologies. Ackoff cautions this is a self-defeating strategy if this is not understood:

The performance as a whole is affected by every one of its parts. That is a basic characteristic of a system. If you think of a corporation as a system, this means that every department (division, technology, function) can affect the performance of the corporation. That is the first condition of a system. If you have a department, which has no effect on the performance of the corporation, the one thing you can be sure of is that it is not a part of the corporation.

A second characteristic of a system is that the way that any part affects the whole depends on what one other part is doing. No part of the system has an independent effect on the whole. What this says is that the way marketing affects corporate behavior depends on what other departments do, and vice versa.

Now the third condition is the most complex. If you take these elements (components) and group them in any way, they form subgroups. These subgroups will be subject to the same first and second conditions as the original elements were, that is, each subgroup will affect the performance as a whole and no subgroup will have an independent effect of the performance of the whole.

Ackoff argues this is the difference between an indivisible part and an indivisible whole in which the roots of the current Intellectual Revolution lay.

Standing Back

Systems Thinking is the new approach to the problem solving and organizational effectiveness. It means moving from a preoccupation with parts of things to a new concentration on the whole and on the wholes of which they are a part, or a shift from analysis to synthesis.

With analysis, if you wanted to explain a problem, you took it apart, explained the parts, then put it back together again, explaining the problem in terms of the parts.

In synthesis, if you wanted to explain a problem, you did exactly the opposite. You didn't look at the problem to be explained as a whole to be taken apart, but as a part of a greater whole. You explain the whole of which it is a part, and then extract an explanation of the thing you started with from an explanation of the whole.

If this sounds confusing, it is because of our conditioning. It may seem to be counterintuitive thinking, which often comes into play in OD work. Ackoff comes to our aid:

If you consider a system and take it apart to identify its components, and then operate those components in such a way that every component behaves as well as it possibly can, there is one thing of which you can be sure. The system as a whole will not behave as well as it can. The corollary is this, if you have a system that is behaving as well as it can, none of its parts will be. Consider some advantages of counterintuitive thinking:

It nullifies the practice of interdepartmental competition and validates the synergistic power of cooperation.

It abhors the idea of comparing and competing in a drive to excellence as it cheapens a central focus and instead becomes a second hand imitation of an excellent company as model. Unequivocally, with a central focus, people in the company realize they are sitting on acres of diamonds.

It acknowledges the workplace isn't working like it used to work. Counterintuitive thinking may not have been critical to Machine Age thinking, but is essential to *Systems Thinking*.

The Cure is Known

Ackoff's theorems, as you see, have special significance to *Work Without Managers*. In my more than forty years working in corporations at every level of organization on four continents, I have found the absence of control theory to be of devastating consequences. In this original work (1991) I wrote:

Take Corporate America. Any large company today is 20 to 30 divisions in search of a corporation. The pendulum of centralization-decentralization is more a yo-yo contest with no clear winners, only painfully confused losers. Trauma is written on the face of American enterprise. Meanwhile, this once powerful and energetic nation doesn't seem to know what is happening.

I wish it were possible to declare that Corporate America has changed, but as you read this book, you will see it has changed little. While work has evolved from brawn power to brainpower, from blue to white collar, from managers to professionals, from assembly lines to software manufactured products, from brick, mortar and steel institutions to online universities at a fraction of the cost of higher education, from distinctive technological disciplines to complex hybrids, and from hierarchies and position power to Skunk Works and knowledge power, managerial approaches have not changed.

The failure to embrace *System Theory* continues to throw Corporate America off its stride, and thus every worker. Think of how you can apply the lessons learned here to your job, and by extension to operations in general. The first step is to take charge of your work, which is the best way to take charge of your life. Damn the torpedoes. We don't need managers. They need us.

James R. Fisher, Jr., Ph.D.

The American Dilemma and the Phantom Challenge --
Amerikas Krankheit: The Trauma of the Modern Corporate Organization

This new century, which began with such paternal control and obedience for America, has run amuck. Now, nothing (and no one) is in control.

Take Corporate America. Any large company today is 20 to 30 divisions in search of a corporation. The pendulum of centralization decentralization is more a yo-yo contest with no clear winners — only painfully confused losers. Trauma is written on the face of American enterprise. Meanwhile, this once powerful and energetic nation doesn't seem to know what is happening.

An *undeclared psychological war is* being waged within most major enterprises today, with bodies falling on all sides, and nobody's paying attention. The principle players are worrying about *what's* 'in,' *what's* 'out'; *who's* 'in,' *who's* 'out'; *who's* making points, *who* isn't . . . while the marketplace is disappearing into the sunset. [1]

Chaos masquerades as *business as usual* Friedrich Nietzsche (1844 -1900) asserted chaos is the ultimate route to discovery — but what we are experiencing in America is absurd.

As wont is our American Way, the *paralysis of analysis is* substituted for a quiet appraisal of what is happening. A new frame of reference appeals little to the American *mind of the time.* The American appetite is for the quick-and-dirty solution, with the stamp of *corpocracy.*

Amerikas Krankheit ("The American Disease"), as the Germans put it, is running rampant, out of control. Formerly confined to government bureaucracies, it is now a rash affecting corporate American business, education, and industry. *The Corporate American Disease of Corpocracy* has these common characteristics:

- *Management is insensitive to its employees.*
- *Management supports company politics at the expense of productivity.*
- *Secretiveness is the measure of communication.*
- *The principal product is paperwork.*
- *Endless meetings are the 'way' (when in doubt, hold a meeting).*
- *An internal focus is maintained, so potential markets are ignored.*
- *Short-term planning and thinking is preferred to embracing challenges ("Plan, plan and then plan some more!").*
- *Individual initiative is never supported ("You never know where it might lead.").*
- *Management has isolated itself from employees by building mahogany towers between them.*
- *A 'covert' hostility to innovation is maintained while it is overtly praised.* [2]

No organization of any size is above suspicion of such a charade. Not long ago, I was part of a United States multinational corporation's European headquarters in Brussels, Belgium. In that cozy setting our Human Resources operation, alone, had a vice president, two directors and two managers, and a supporting staff of nine professionals. Productive work was as 'foreign' to us as catsup is to French cuisine. We were a corporate resource with symbiotic connection to the corporation's confederation of divisions. We operated with:

- *A perceptible lack of organizational control and focus;*
- *A cadre of non-thinking-thinkers organizing non-doing-doers around non-thing-things.*

Take a closer look at your own operation. Do you see any of these same distressing features? If you do, it's time to ask, "What shape are we in?"

I've watched this scenario for many years, even participated in it, but have always waited for someone to shout, "Enough already!" Instead, I've been treated to a confection of bromides, euphemisms, improvements, justifications, and outright con jobs . . . with the latter seemingly winning the day.

As the American *ship of state* sinks deeper into dead water, and my personal breathing room becomes increasingly limited, so departs my sense of humor. I've had it!

This is my *personal view* of what I see happening. In this book, I tell what I think needs to be done to get us out of this predicament. It is one man's view, not an antiseptic view from the *ivory tower of academia*, but a view from the trenches by a *practicing social scientist*. It is the view of a man who has attempted to cut through the special interests that hold most of us in *economic, social, and psychological bondage.*

Toward An Ecology of Mind

Quite frankly, I feel a kinship in this enterprise with Rachel Carson's *Silent Spring* (1962), which alerted the world to another kind of pollution, the use of synthetic chemicals as insecticides. Scientists of the day rebuked her for lack of cool scientific objectivity, her anecdotal evidence, her passages of purple prose laced with innuendoes of doom. She was stepping on an industry's pocketbook, and it felt the pinch.

In Ms. Carson's book, the chemical insecticide *DDT* was king, and empires were built on the spine of this complex, synthetic chemical's success. Much as microelectronics and cybernetics are the gods of today, *chemistry*, some years ago, held the world in its sway. After all, *DDT* had saved millions from the suffering of such insect-borne diseases as malaria. Small wonder it was elevated to public idolatry, for it carried the promise of an insect-free age.

This spirited woman's mission was not that of the iconoclast. On the contrary, she readily admitted the benefits of chemical pesticides. Nor did she advocate the complete end to their use. Her advocacy was for moderation and a more realistic appreciation of the limitations of these chemicals.

Similarly, my advocacy is for moderation in the use of hyperbole in the world of organization, and realistic appreciation of the work force in the world of work. Simultaneously, I condemn the *free lunch* brigade and the soft-bellied optimists who seek 'gain without pain,' and 'having it both ways.'

Rachel Carson's aim was condemnation of the trigger-happy, indiscriminate use of insecticides of which science knew so little in terms of ultimate ecological effect versus possible benefits. She warned that tragedy may await *over the horizon* if we continued our cavalier disregard for our planet's *ecology.* Melodramatic? Perhaps. But she, in an almost mystical presage, envisioned the shrinking of our Earth's bounty. Her work was a biological warning, a social commentary, a moral reminder of our finitude. I consider my message in that same vein.

Our lagging response to this type of foreboding is painfully remembered with the Three Mile Island fiasco and the Chernobyl tragedy. In the wake of these events, I wonder if Ms. Carson's message was forceful enough.

Pollution continues as our planet's most pervasive problem. But pollution has taken on a more ominous, personal dimension — psychological pollution; what I call *mind pollution,* or the *'free lunch'* mentality.

Rachel Carson was given to such provocative, emotive phrases as *elixirs of death* and *irreversible chains of reactions.* Her obvious aim was to penetrate a complacent public conscience. So is mine. She saw public ignorance as a communicable disease. So do I. She foresaw an impending biological time bomb. I foresee an impending psychological time bomb.

Ms. Carson observed her planet and was horrified by the terrible waste; by the public's flagrant disregard for ecological prudence and economy. My concern is focused on our *internal environment;* on our flagrant disregard for the *ecology of mind.* She envisioned a threat to our well-being from 'outside,' while I see a psychological bomb ticking away within us that threatens our *collective will to survive.*

The *pollution of mind* rides on the *free lunch* mentality; the mentality that believes there are acts without consequences, growth without pain, something for nothing, television as reality. . . luck.

It is the world of the *spoiled-brat generation* and the *Jacuzzi economy*, where what you have is more important than what you are. . . where becoming has more attraction than being. . . where personality and performance are used as synonyms. . . where the artificial is more splendid than the real. . . and where *real work* has been given a bad name.

The American Dream — and all that it entails — is an illusion. Yet, the *free lunch* mentality persists as if this dream were real.

My hypothesis is that the *free lunch* mentality increasingly pollutes our very will and challenges our ability to see, much less deal with the real problems of our diminishing capacity to perform productive work. It's the reason this book was written.

Rather than deal with these hard questions, it would seem we prefer to be entertained with palatable solutions. Give us dessert with our *free lunch*.

So, we move into the 21st Century no longer innocent, but not yet worldly. . . and neither especially cruel nor corrupt. We leave the 20th Century no longer youthfully ignorant, but not yet wise and civilized. We are a *nation* that aspires to greatness while forever celebrating mediocrity. Illusion and self-destruction have shielded us from the reality of our actions because *we are Americans,* and, so are not expected to act otherwise. No longer. Excess has caught up with us.

References

(1) Such books as Lisa Birnbach's *Going to Work* (New York: Villard Books, 1988) provide a complete guide to the *best* neighborhoods in which to live, which schools to attend, stores to shop; and where to get *power* haircuts, *power* shirts, *power* watches, etc. It is 'bonding and belonging' brought to the point of hedonistic excess.

(2) *Wirtschaft Woche,* January 16, 1987.

The American Mind of the Time

American workers, over the course of this century, have become self-critical to a fault. Self-contempt more than selfishness would appear to rule the mind of many contemporary workers. From the *Tyranny of Technology*, to the abandonment of the sacred, from the *Culture of Narcissism* to the banal greed of the YUPPIES (or whatever they currently call themselves), there seems a pervasive cynicism clinging to the American conscience. Still, cut through the facade of Ivan F. Boesky and Boyd L. Jeffries, who led a gang of Wall Street traders with inside information, and you are likely to discover this naked cynicism . . . riding on a free lunch mentality. [1]

If these characters were really bad, it would be easier to accept. But they appear too much like ourselves. Regrettably, we live in a time when most of our sins are venial sins and most of our sinners lack imagination and daring. This is the most grievous of indictments. No prior age had giant saints without giant sinners. We have neither.

So, this book is also about the *Outsider*. Since the first human beings took it upon themselves to step out of the cold and into the warmth of mystic fire, life has been guided by leaders who were *Outsiders*. The tribal side of mankind has always responded to the *Outsider* who understood the insider; to the person who could step back and outside the warmth of limited reason to embrace the coldness of the arational [2]; who could construct and rearrange but not judge; who could escape the rigid patterns of experience and belief and not be afraid to lead.

Finally, this book is about *you* and *me*. The paradox of our time is that we say all the right words but seldom live them. Words have become surrogates for thinking, feeling and behaving. We have become a passive people with a horrible waste of energy and light. So, it is written to feel the *discomfort* of that fact. The future is not out there. It is here. It begins and ends. . . with you and me.

We no longer have the luxury of externalizing our pain or projecting our guilt. We cannot wait for a miracle. We cannot wait for someone else to 'harness our fire.' Time has run out. It is the fourth quarter of the ultimate game. . . which is our American destiny.

References

(1) Lasch, Christopher, *The Culture of Narcissism: American Life in an Age of Diminishing Expectations* (New York: W. W. Norton & Company, Inc., 1978).

(2) Edward De bono introduced this term with his concept of *Lateral Thinking* (1970). De Bono sees three fallacies to our conventional method of thinking: (1) that the established way of looking at a situation is the 'only way, because it is

right'; (2) that through logic, alone, you can arrive at the 'best' perception; and (3) that no matter where you start with your inquiry, if your logic is correct, then you will eventually reach the 'right' answer. Of course, this is the rational approach, which De bono sees as horribly in error and, therefore, why he admits to the prominence of the arational.

Need For
A New Organizational Paradigm

"It was the best of times, it was the worst of times, it was the age of wisdom, it was the age of foolishness, it was the epoch of belief, it was the epoch of incredulity, it was the season of Light, it was the season of Darkness, it was the spring of hope, it was the winter of despair, we had everything before us, we had nothing before us, we were all going direct to Heaven, we were all going direct the other way — in short, the period was so far like the present period . . ."

Charles Dickens, British novelist

So begins Charles Dickens in *A Tale of Two Cities* (1859), writing about the French Revolution and its impact on society — especially the societies of London and Paris. Dickens goes far beyond this and suggests the basic difference between changing society and changing oneself. All change starts with the individual, he said. The most dramatic change occurs when the individual voluntarily chooses to act differently.

In every period of history there has been a gulf between revolutionary ideas and traditional values. This is embodied in the conflict between personal honesty and expediency, rational calm and panic. It characterizes the American character and culture in today's troubled times.

Dickens could have been writing about late 20th century America and the persistent struggle between workers and managers, over organizational control and worker involvement. And the organization's attempts to mask this struggle tend only to intensify it.

Make no mistake. We're in the middle of a revolution. Ironically, the focus continues to be on management. Workers remain outside the equation, due largely to the determined, albeit faulty belief that if you fix management, everything else falls into place. The focus must be shifted to workers, or continuous change will cause an eruption into discontinuity and catastrophe.

Real power has shifted dramatically from management's domain to the dominion of workers, but workers behave as if management still possesses the power. The organization waffles like a rag doll in the wind, struggling against this reality. Uncertainty reigns supreme and power is falling between the chairs.

Several factors have contributed to this dilemma:

- *America's values have changed.*
- *The changes have affected the way Americans relate to one another, both in the workplace and the home.*
- *The knowledge explosion has produced a very distinct type of worker, with a perspective and style different than we have known in the past.*
- *Moreover, the critical mass of the organization has shifted from activity to information; from doing to thinking; from producing to serving; from working to symbolic interaction.*
- *The information edge no longer resides with management, but is well distributed throughout the work force. Consequently, management is not only at the mercy of expert systems, but of experts who design and control those systems.*

Finally, as a result of the shift from 'doing' to 'thinking,' there is a veritable struggle to determine what constitutes *real work.* With the product as likely to be 'software' as 'hardware,' there is mass confusion as to what to do, let alone who is in charge.

Because vested management is *results oriented,* and real work has shifted to being primarily *process driven,* there is a strong need to re-examine work in terms of process and outcome:

- *When work is measured in terms of 'results,' management perceives workers as costs. This is reflected by cost cutting practices aimed solely at reducing headcount.*
- *Making an impression and keeping one's job thus become more important than making a difference.*

Conversely, when work is viewed as a 'process,' attention focuses on doing the right things, rather than doing things right. Doing the right things fosters teamwork, whereas doing things right promotes finger pointing and results in dissension in the ranks.

Where the focus resides is more a matter of *personal values* than of management style. Yet, most discussion in past years has centered on management style. Today, quality is the focus of discussion, and the same absurdity that possessed those bent on the *right style* has American organizations scrambling to do things right. Because the current focus on quality tends to be a *stylistic overlay,* superimposed on workers by management, it will fail. It will fail because the organization has not thought through the quality problem with the people who cause it — American workers and their management — and the crippling impact of their *cultural biases.*

The quick, cosmetic fix will no longer do. If this continues to be the only approach acceptable to American organizations, then America will not survive the 21st century as a first-rate nation.

America is not Europe, nor is it Japan. What works in Europe and Japan fits neither the American culture nor the American value system. America's essence is unique to America. This is where the problem lies, and where the answer will be found.

Meanwhile, America's dilemma is that it perceives this challenge as a phantom. When America's physical survival was threatened with the Japanese bombing of Pearl Harbor, we mobilized our resources quickly and won World War II.

December 7, 1941   December 7, 1989

The American Dilemma and the Phantom Challenge, or 'When you don't feel it, you don't react to it.'

When Russia launched Sputnik in 1957, our pride was on the line, and we consolidated our technology and put a man on the moon in another decade. But with our economic survival threatened, most of us — financially comfortable look beyond the 31 million homeless and starving and say, "pass the sugar."

World War III has, in reality, been raging for more than 30 years, as an economic war. And most of us remain unconcerned, because it has not touched us. The landscape in our mind remains the same, despite the pending earthquake of changing values reverberating beneath our troubled surface.

A New Look At Old Values

Not unlike Dickens' *A Tale of Two Cities,* subtle but massive changes in American society and the individual have led to a cultural breakdown. The main cause of this breakdown is denial. A secondary cause is attempting to make traditional approaches work in the face of these cultural changes.

The established culture of American society, the *common good,* has failed to support the society that it would define. Yet, many of its advocates, often located in American think tanks, stubbornly insist it is the only way. Against this reality, the culture of *personhood* now struggles to establish itself.

Americans of World War II vintage generally think in terms of "what is good for the country, state, church, school, family, and company is good enough for me!" But Americans of the post-Vietnam War era think more in terms of "the right to know, the right to an opinion, the right to be wrong, the right to fail, the right to work, civil rights, and civil disobedience." In a word, they think in terms of controlling their own destiny, rather than having it dictated to them.

Traditional American workers continue to value the *common good,* while modern professional workers increasingly value *personhood.* This is becoming a distinct difference.

	Common Good	Personhood
Authority	Position Power	Popularity/knowledge
Loyalty	To the organization	To self/peers
Discipline	Reward/punishment	Caring/respect
Motivation	Fear	Challenge/contribution

Shifting American Values

This difference has already had pivotal ramifications across America, from the home to the workplace. Adversaries have been made of parents and children, teachers and students, the clergy and laity, managers and workers. . . leaders and followers in all walks of life. It has also produced a perceptible gap between expectations and achievements in the organization.

So traumatic has the situation become that many parents, educators, executives, clergy and leaders are abandoning the conflict. They have abdicated in frustration, proclaiming that they are 'powerless.'

Meanwhile, the few who are still hopeful remain convinced that the answer lies in the *common good*. They invariably turn to quick-fix fads and techniques involving 'change' in the way we train, work, and manage. What is missing is looking at the person differently.

In the organization, the myth persists that if workers are managed and trained differently, and if work is defined differently, problems will dissolve and workers will automatically change. But the myth proves to be a lie. Results of these efforts have demonstrated little or no significant change.

In the Defense Industry, billions of dollars are being spent in the name of *Total Quality Management (TQM)* to redefine work and train managers and workers in the workplace. This represents a panic attempt at appearing to be in control, when everything is running out of control. It has the illusion of dealing with the problem, without embracing it (which has become an American pastime).

This approach is consistent with our American history: "It hasn't been fatal in the past, so it won't be fatal in the future." Consequently, there seems little inclination to understand and respect the changing values, beliefs, and expectations of the dominant new breed of American workers.

From a cultural perspective, management is no closer to understanding modern professionals than modern professionals are to submitting to the edicts of management.

This failure in understanding is the reason nonfunctional or reactive thinking dominates the organization's every activity. This is painfully displayed in the dominance of the 'rumor mill,' where backstabbing, duplicity, chicanery, Cover Your Ass (CYA) and Show Your Ass (SYA) games are part of 'standard operating procedure.' It is also where *six silent killers* of the organization feast on the organization's preoccupation with the negative. . . and with itself.

These crippling propensities are discussed later as the *Six Mad Monarchs of the Madhouse*: passive aggressive, passive responsive, passive defensive, malicious obedience, approach avoidance, and obsessive compulsive behaviors. These behaviors epitomize the effect (not the cause) of organizational instability and fatigue precipitated by management's failure first to acknowledge, and then to deal with, the cultural shift from *common good* to *personhood*.

Workers of a Different Mind

Average American workers who were formerly tied to their jobs by fear, lack of skill, and ignorance have become educated and mobile, discovering new horizons

53

of opportunity. Reared largely in latchkey or single-parent homes, these workers were left mainly to their own devices while growing up and, by default, became essentially their own parents.

In the absence of external control and paternal regulation, they developed their own internal self-monitoring systems. Parental absenteeism denied them the security of traditional values, leaving many of them bruised or scarred by life experiences for which they were not adequately prepared. But it also produced individuals who, in an effort to survive, had to find their *own centers*; had to think for themselves. [1]

These individuals respond quite differently than their parents to external control; to conventional motivation and wisdom. They are more inclined to intrinsic interests (what they want to do) than extrinsic interests (what they have to do); more stimulated by challenge than external manipulation.

These new American workers learned to make choices. Attempts to manage, manipulate, and motivate them with traditional reward and punishment fail miserably. They actually find these attempts amusing.

Giving professional workers time off as a punishment and more money as a reward, consequently, hasn't been successful in changing their behavior. Work is not the center of their lives, so time off is neither an embarrassment nor a concern. As for money, they will take it, "thank you very much," and go on behaving as before. Indeed, attempts to preserve the 'traditional' American value system with them have only quickened its demise.

Control, known in the organization as power and influence, now belongs to them. And, because it emanates from within, if they don't know this, they certainly sense it. Even if not consciously aware of it, by refusing to submit to management's dominance they demonstrate their sense of power in their behavior. Questioning the system, the role of management, and the requirements of work itself are manifestations, as is a failure to respond to conventional management practices. Professional workers are gradually discovering that they are both the controller and the controlled.

Empowerment — a word that has become associated with all workers — first gained legitimacy with *Women's Rights*. When women started to insist on being treated as persons and not merely as chattel, they made a break through. Now, empowerment is a gift that workers give to the organization only when it meets their professional, emotional, and psychological needs.

Ironically, these needs are well known to the organization, but rarely understood. The sheer dint of publicity and executive 'psychobabble' makes them well known (thanks largely to the 'script' written by Human Resources).

Human Resources is a profession that has grown out of what I call *The Prison of Panic Called NOW!* Or 'Why Johnny Won't Work,' which is covered in some detail later. Paradoxically, Human Resources has grown exponentially with the decline in the health and stability of our American economy. Rather than examining American workers and developing a strategy to take full advantage of their potential, Human Resources has elected to deny the essence of the problem (the changing values of American workers), and to deal with its symptoms (declining productivity).

Human Resources has created processes and programs that deal with this decline by rewarding conforming behavior. This conforming behavior develops a 'machine mind' that is unresponsive to innovative activity or sudden change — both 'givens' in the modern organization. It creates a reactionary constituency, with the machine mind distorting the reality of its experience. More energy is spent, as a consequence, in dysfunctional behavior than is devoted to actual work.

Alan Valentine puts it succinctly, "Whatever else may be made mechanical, human values cannot." [2]

Yet, safely ensconced in executive intrigue, far removed from the trenches, Human Resources has had a splendid opportunity to make a difference, and has elected instead to 'make an impression.' It has become more enamored of presenting, packaging, and promoting illusive ideas, than spearheading breakthrough actions.

With CEOs of most American Fortune 500 companies educated in science and engineering, Human Resources has promoted what will sell, not what is needed. It has appealed to the rationally ordering, mechanistic minds of these executives with *Quality of Work, Quality of Work Life, Quality of Management, Total Quality Management, Total Employee Involvement,* and *Participative Management,* so that their respective acronyms have become burned into their psyches.

With so much time, energy, and expense spent on this attractive packaging, little remains for implementation. So, each of the initiatives listed above, with few exceptions, has sputtered to death — only to be replaced by yet another. And so it goes.

These imperfect attempts have come to be far better known than understood; more a conversation piece than a better way of doing business. There isn't a CEO in American industry, commerce, education, religion, government, or the military whose staff cannot produce an impressive slide presentation to document their organization's commitment to these initiatives. Yet, American management and Human Resources are grasping at straws, and building cathedrals out of them.

Unfortunately, the only employees who respond consistently to these initiatives are from the disappearing rank-and-file of blue-collar workers. They have been led and conditioned regimentally and take these types of exhortations in stride. Still, there is nothing more damning to society than conforming children who become uninspired, unimaginative, conforming adults. More than that — reminiscent of the *Hawthorne Effect* — these workers are as much motivated by the attention given as by the consideration received. [3] Accustomed to being treated primarily as machines in the workplace, the slightest display of humanity evokes positive response from these workers.

Meanwhile, professionals, who are much less responsive to such manipulation, play their sly game of 'smoke and mirrors' (or, what you see is not necessarily what you get). They are 'on' to the game, and want no part of it.

In essence the dichotomy between professionals and blue-collar workers is as sharply defined as that between the *common good* and *personhood*. But the nuances of these differences are neither acknowledged nor understood by management, let alone the workers. For convenience, and consistent with a rationally ordering, mechanistic mind-set, management stubbornly insists on interpreting motivation as if all workers respond to the same values and beliefs. This, of course, is far from the case.

Not surprising, given this propensity, management seeks to magnify its effectiveness by saluting the achievements of blue-collar workers, while remaining self-blinded to the almost total apathy, on the part of professionals, to its leadership. Blue-collar workers may be the last bastion of the *common good*, but they are also a shrinking minority.

In any case, blue-collar workers are not the problem. On the contrary, thanks to a good assist from automation, hands-on labor costs are dropping precipitously, making American blue-collar workers among the most productive workers in the world. But hands-on labor represents only 10 to 15 percent of the cost of a product or service. True cost savings and operating efficiency are found in indirect labor costs — the costs of services of professionals.

In the face of this, what does management do when it feels the crunch? It initiates cost cutting redundancy exercises by laying off those who have the least political leverage in the organization — blue-collar workers, janitors, secretaries, technicians and yes, professionals who don't conform. It is incredible when you think about it. To wit:

Management prunes the organizational tree by cutting at the roots. Meanwhile, those who have spent much of their time managing their careers and little of their time doing real work keep their jobs, thus precariously weakening the organization.

Is it any wonder we're in trouble? Each time management engages in such activity, it makes the organization less resilient. Like a rubber band that can be stretched only so many times before it loses its elasticity, the organization ultimately experiences a nervous collapse, a cultural breakdown. It no longer can respond to accelerating demands.

Judicious pruning of the management pyramid is a noble mission. Speaking conservatively, top management can be cut by 10 percent, middle management by 25 percent, and first-line supervision by 15 percent without cutting a single blue-collar worker, janitor, secretary, technician, or professional, and most organizations would almost immediately become twice as effective. This represents true tree pruning. Like the trees of nature, it will stimulate growth, and give a new zest and color to the organization's foliage.

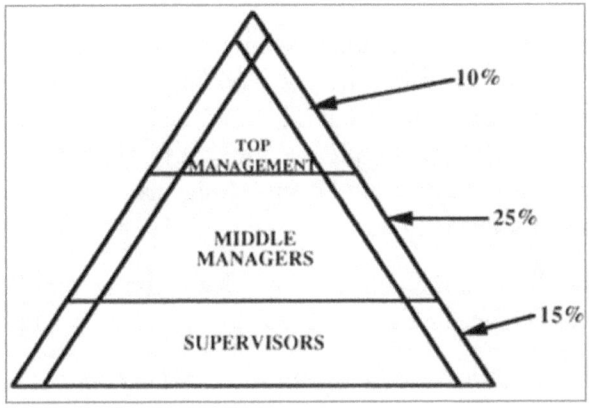

Pruning the Management Pyramid for Organizational Effectiveness.

Enter Management's Union

But instead of confronting this problem *(management creep).* Human Resources has concentrated on using acronyms to play 'Quality Monopoly.' Ironically, the game of quality, which has been so effective with blue-collar workers, actually arises out of the value system of *personhood.*

While organizations are reducing their raw numbers of people, there is a deceptive *management creep.* Staff engineers and other designated specialists are sharing in the executive bounty as the ratio between managers and workers grows perilously narrow. Soon it will be a one-to-one ratio, with as many managers as workers. Who, then, will delegate to whom?

In 1980, a high-tech division of one Fortune 100 company, with 4200 employees, had 250 managers, supervisors, and staff engineers. In 1989, several iterative reductions found the same division with 3200 employees, and 400 managers, supervisors, and staff engineers. Over the same period, the operation had doubled its sales. In 1980, for example, the Human Resources Department had 65 employees and seven managers. In 1989, the staff had been reduced to 34 employees, but there were still seven managers. Meanwhile, most professionals had to do the work of two or more people.

Human Resources professionals — supposedly the employee's advocate — have had the opportunity to educate management to the cultural shadings of *personhood* and the relationship of those shadings to professionals. They have also been in a position to create a psychological climate to facilitate this educational process. But, due to a lack of comprehension or courage, they have contributed instead to organizational strife and dysfunction.

Is it any wonder, then, that nonfunctional behavior dominates the organization, and that those so disposed rule with a contemptuous disregard for the organization's mission? Professionals have learned how to appear busy without being gainfully employed; how to please the boss without doing anything productive. This behavior clearly results from telling management what it wants to hear, rather than what it needs to do.

Human Resources has been at the center of this deception and in the process has become, by default, *management's union.* It has lost its identity and its role.

Human Resources has become more inclined to be management's advocate than *to serve* employees; more comfortable playing management's tune than discovering its own music. It has had the responsibility of the 'inside outsider' from the start, but has elected to play the role of the sycophant. Consequently, it has declined the function of the provocateur — the role of the consultant — choosing instead that of the consoler; the role of the 'yes man.' And so Human Resources has gravitated to being what the organization didn't need — a union for management. As a result, it has put the organization in jeopardy; perhaps not by design, but certainly by dereliction of duty. And this at a time when the organization urgently needed a leader and a healer. With the organization in such infirmity, a tremendous opportunity was lost.

By being in a reactive, obsequious mode, Human Resources has denied the reality of the situation — the need for radical restructuring to serve the organization's *first customer,* its people.

Individual Success and Organization Values

The structure of the American organization is at war with what is going on inside the American worker. The structure does not fit the behavior required.

Why? If you treat people with respect and dignity, accepting their values and beliefs, you get one type of worker. If you take people for granted, imposing your values and expectations on them, you get another. They imply different structures. And the American organization is imposing the latter.

Consequently, an amazing amount of energy and individual/organizational health are put at risk daily. And because work does not take place in a vacuum, inappropriate or irrelevant activity will fill the void if the climate is not right for productive effort.

The *collision of values* can easily be illustrated by what success means to today's professional and to the traditional manager. You may well discover from the following actual case study on which side your personal values lie.

Dirk Edwards, a corporate director of international operations for an American multinational corporation, lived in Brussels, Belgium. He had accepted the assignment because he wanted to learn why the *European Economic Community* was so successful against American companies. He also felt he could make a contribution, given his specialty in organizational development. Neither money nor career enhancement entered into his decision to accept this assignment.

The entire thrust of Dirk's discipline was *enabling*, not manipulation. He was trained to help people do what they wanted to do, not what he thought they should do. But, because organizational structure seldom permitted this, he was well acquainted with irrational behavior.

Recognizing that behavior follows structure, Dirk created self-management work teams, and watched 'irresponsible' workers become responsible and productive. To him, success meant contributing to the success of others. "If we serve well our first customers — our peers and the users of our services," he would say, "we will be successful, and so will our customers." This belief found him more inclined to pay attention to what those below him thought than what those above him demanded.

He was not into 'correct behavior'; nor was he into making workers perform to someone else's standards. Everyone likes to be measured, he believed, but only if they can have input into the design of the standards by which they are to be measured. Dirk schooled his people in processes that permitted them to make such determinations.

Dirk also fulfilled his role as servant to his people by providing them with the tools, resources, training, and conditions they felt would allow them to do their best work. Once they had a clear view of what needed to be done, he stayed out of their way.

This supportive behavior made Dirk popular with his people. His people got results. Within the company, he gained a reputation for effectiveness. Management saw the results, but demonstrated little curiosity as to how they were obtained, assuming Dirk managed much as they did. In any case, he was seen as perfect for the European assignment.

Given these circumstances, perhaps naively, he moved to Europe, and continued his quest to serve.

And then, about six months into his European assignment, the following conversation took place between Dirk and his boss during a three-hour train trip from Brussels to Amsterdam:

Boss: *"I get the feeling I want you to be more successful than you want to be."*

Dirk: *"Define success for me."*

Boss: *"Well, making an impression on the (European) affiliate general managers, keeping our corporate fathers happy in the United States, keeping me out of trouble."*

Dirk: *"What about the operations?"* Boss: *"What about them?"* Dirk: *"What if doing something significant requires making some people uncomfortable, making you unhappy? What then?"*

Boss: *"You don't do it. You're only over here a few years. Don't try to be a hero. Remember, all I want is to make you successful. That's my point."*

Dirk: *"What do you think motivates me?"*

Boss: *"What motivates you? What motivates us all: pleasing the boss, promotions, belonging to the club, making the bucks, getting the perks, being able to provide comfort for the family? Right?"*

Dirk: *"What motivates me is challenging work, the freedom and control to do it in my way, and your trust, respect, and support when I fall short of the mark. Money has little to do with my motivation; nor do promotions, perks or status."*

Boss: *"Bullshit!"*

This exchange illustrates both a strained relationship and a deep breach in values between the two men. They clearly operated in 'separate realities,' and neither understood the other. There was little trust; little feeling that they were on the same team. Dirk had no sense that his boss was on his side, let alone that he would be there for him if he was in trouble. The boss failed to realize that true leadership calls for his people to respect him; to believe in him. Only then will they follow him.

Curiously, because he did not respond to the expected motivators, Dirk intimidated his boss. The fact that Dirk's authority came from within was incomprehensible to his manager. Meanwhile, Dirk sought his manager's trust in order to enhance his own *self-trust* — so that he could act more responsibly. Ironically, this is what his boss desired as well. But the boss believed he could best accomplish this by weakening Dirk's will to be his own person; by making Dirk more dependent on him for success. Not surprisingly, this growing gap in value orientation ultimately ended in Dirk's being sent home early.

Need to Please Others

To the traditional manager, success is commonly measured in terms of status, money, promotions, and perks. These are external factors that affect a person who is motivated by a 'High Need to Please Others.' They also arise out of the culture of the *common good*.

A Need to Please Others should not be confused with the need to *serve others*. On the contrary, the *Need to Please Others* is actually self-serving and reactive. It promotes the inclination to be tentative. Such a person doesn't cast a single corporate vote until they are sure which side will prevail. It is the abode of indecisiveness.

Paradoxically, a Need to Please Others is likely to exhibit a preoccupation with *position power* at the expense of *purposeful performance.* Purposeful performance is chiefly driven by accurate, relevant information. Timely and appropriate information, not frenetic activity, is the basis of organizational success. Unfortunately, given the current bias toward appearance (style) rather than substance, the person with position power is often the last to know. Why? Because information must pass through layer upon layer of managers who all have a *High Need to Please* with each tailoring their information accordingly.

Consequently, relevant information seldom gets beyond the functional group or operating floor. And, because relevant information represents the 'candle power' necessary to see through the fog, this has critical repercussions in the modern organization. The bureaucratic lens of formal authority can then be likened to an organizational cataract adding to the murky condition, rather than improving the vision.

Organizational climbers are much more adept at serving those above them than serving the organization. To the climbers, those above them *are* the organization. Not surprisingly, they display an uncanny ability to anticipate their superior's needs and react to them. Doubtlessly, this skill is of some merit in the traditional organization, but it represents a colossal handicap to today's mainstream organization.

This handicap goes beyond the problem of the promotion of disinformation, debilitating as that is, to a dearth of leadership. Because their chief talent is bureaucratic tact, rather than strategic engagement, *organizational climbers* are incapable of leading. They have been schooled to react to situations, not to create them.

One of the most mundane indicators of this behavior is paper. Organizational climbers show an amazing facility for reacting to paper generated by others, red penciling it and making astute comments. But give them a blank sheet of paper and ask them to create, and they go blank. Panic sets in.

Speaking parenthetically, this is one reason for the advent of consultants and the promulgation of fads. The organizational climbers are the buyers of these services and techniques. They don't know what they want because they have never thought through their problems to an original need basis. What is worse, they don't even know what they don't want.

Given this — the present state of most American organizations — obsequious behavior has served the organization poorly. Still, the value system of the *common good,* which such behavior identifies, resolutely holds on. It is not that the 'common good' is an undesirable ideal. It is simply that the organization is not served well by those who now practice it.

In Choosing a Different Path — Need to Please Self

Question: In an age of mediocrity, where are the great minds of today?

Answer: They are everywhere, fighting a debilitating existence in stultifying organizations, rather than focusing on their greatness.

To the new breed of professional workers, success is measured in terms of challenging work. . . in doing something significant, in having freedom and control of what they do, in being trusted and treated with respect and dignity. Regrettably, most organizations are not structured to abide, much less promote, this climate. Meanwhile, professionals grow tired of bureaucratic constraints that sponsor *non-thinking thinking and non-doing doing of non-thing things.*

Make no mistake, the society of the *common good* was, and is, a different society than the society of today. What's more, we can't go back to the way it was. That is an illusion.

Yesterday, a family meant a man, woman, and child — not two or more members of the same sex in an intimate relationship. Religion meant 'faith,' not a Church of Scientology. School meant a building dedicated to education, not a satellite dish beaming a television lecture into a room with only one student. Government meant a national entity, not an international marketplace. And work meant making a product, not creating information. It meant a place away from home, whereas now more and more it means working at or near home.

Remember, the structure and infrastructure of the society of the *common good,* were designed by autocratic, authoritarian minds who envisioned a static bureaucratic world forever.

These designers, many of whom are still actively among us, hold nostalgically to divine rule, where control, order, place, and dependent obedience are manifestly the norm.

These values of the 18th century, and earlier, served American society well up to, and through, World War II. But with that war, *the entire world changed.* One of the most remarkable changes was the arrival of American professionals — a post WWII phenomenon. These workers have evolved over the past 50 years to differ radically from other American workers in terms of education and experience, attitude and disposition, motivation and perspective, discipline and outlook.

Spiritually and materially, they are more authentic because they blatantly reflect the conflict in our society.

Of every five American workers today, three belong to this category. The number will increase to four out of five by the turn of the century. Yet, the organization behaves as if its people are sealed in a 1950s time capsule.

Regardless, today's professionals are set on choosing a different path, even though the organization gives them little room in which to maneuver. These professionals see the organization as manipulative, using people to get results rather than developing their skills to enhance organizational success. They see information being managed, telling workers 'only what they need to know.' They see 'shading the truth' to be a common practice; the avoiding of sensitive issues an accepted routine.

Wherever they look, *comfort* is embraced; there is a preoccupation with safety. Caution is sponsored at the expense of courage; dependency at the expense of initiative; maintaining the status quo at the expense of greatness.

Greatness, which Walt Whitman celebrated without embarrassment, is throbbing in every professional's heart. But to reach for it remains threatening to the status quo of a maintenance-driven culture.

Perhaps the best index of today's aversion to greatness is the venality of our times. It is reflected in the quality of our sinners. Periods of historical significance are punctuated by extremes in human behavior. To wit, to have great saints, you need great sinners. Neither are to be found in the American firmament today. Our sinners are wimpishly venial. There's not a mortal sinner in sight.

Contemplative professionals are motivated mainly by internal factors, or what they think; they have a *High Need to Please Themselves*. Pleasure comes from being committed to, and involved in, something of consequence. They are appalled by 'busy work,' by people without opinions, by people who have a high need 'to be liked,' by people who are secretive, by people who are terrified of somebody 'losing control' or 'showing their ass,' by people who are afraid to disobey, by people who are afraid to fail, by people who avoid those who tell them what they think.

In the traditional sense, this motivation could easily be read as selfish and calloused. Nothing could be further from the truth. On the contrary, what motivates professionals with h this mind-set is *enlightened self-interest,* with the principle drive being *to serve.* Robert Greenleaf captures this essence in his description of the *servant as leader.*

"A new moral principle is emerging which holds that the only authority deserving one's allegiance is that which is freely and knowingly granted by the led to the leader in response to, and in proportion to, the clearly evident servant stature of the leader." [4]

Greenleaf goes on to say that those who choose to follow this principle will not casually accept the authority of existing organizations. On the contrary, professionals will only respond to those chosen as leaders who are proven and trusted as servants to the organization. Greenleaf concludes that, in the future, the only viable organizations will be those that are predominantly servant-led.

Be aware that this is consistent with the common drive of professionals. They desire to be useful, to do something worthwhile, and to make a significant contribution to the wellbeing of others. This also epitomizes the expression of greatness.

Further, as opposed to the impotency of bureaucracy, professionals thrive in a chaotic atmosphere, where diverse control emanates, and surprise is routine fare. *Role identity* is important, but responsibility and authority are blurred:

With *role identity,* you know your capabilities and limitations, and the contributions you are expected to make. In other words, *role identity* is skill or performance-based.

Responsibility and authority, on the other hand, are derived from the formal organization, which is expressed in rather meaningless job descriptions and formal organizational charts.

As quickly as these descriptions and charts are made, they become obsolete. Consequently, anyone who wants to get something done pays scant attention to them. Actually, because they discourage cooperation and teamwork, they are a hindrance to performance and contribution. Therefore, when *role identity* is well understood, responsibility and authority move necessarily with the dynamics of routine — from interdependence to autonomy, and back again.

On balance, work brings professionals pleasure when it is focused on their customers, on the people with whom they work (their peers), and on the people in the organization they support (the user community). It is this propensity to serve that drives them toward greatness. With it, they have a *sense of role;* a sense that greatness involves the *courage to serve,* to take risks, to sometimes embrace failure in that service. Unfortunately, the soul of the organization, at this time, is fixed on maintenance, caution, and success.

What is perhaps surprising about professionals is that, no matter their discipline, they have more the *mind of the artist* than the analyst. They appreciate the limits of technology, and the greater possibilities in serving humanity through expressions of humility and love. They see society's dependence on hard science becoming a veritable entrapment. And, like Alice in Lewis Carroll's *Through the Looking Glass* (1946), they have looked deeply into the mirror and seen how we have become nearly helpless to extricate ourselves from it.

- *Question: Are these professionals different from the rest of us?*
- *Answer: No. They only accept what we have refused to see — 'ourselves as we are.'*

Boldly confronting their limitations and their mortality, they see the world as it is. Beyond that, they embrace the challenge to create dangerously; to surpass the limits of 'pleasing others' to the pleasure in 'pleasing self,' by embracing the greatness that resides beyond the horizon of self in the land of serving and leading others. Here, greatness demands supreme risk and possible failure in the belief that there is an organizational will to create a more relevant organizational culture.

With so much mind power, professionals are choosing a different path. They prefer an atmosphere of chaos, diverse control, collegiality, surprise, and autonomy to the culture of bureaucratic certitude. The latter drives them toward maintenance and mediocrity in a culture preoccupied with safety, fostering the belief that progress means 'not making mistakes.' Caution, rather than courage, is the byword, for mistakes are punished more vigorously than achievements are rewarded.

But the most punishing indictment is that confidence decreases, as does risk taking, as one moves up the hierarchy. This creates an imprisoning climate for professionals, and makes the organization tantamount to a madhouse.

This is atavistic management. Professionals suffer vainly in this managed world, which is mismanaged to the extreme. They are managed as if they are *things* doing things, the way blue-collar workers have always been managed. But professionals have been trained to think, not to 'do' in the sense of things. And management continues to force the issue by driving them, at the expense of their capabilities and the needs of the organization, to be activity minded, fawning, and reactive.

Because management can do only what it knows, however, *learned helplessness* is nurtured and promoted. This is destroying the American organization's will to survive, much less prevail.

When management forces these thinkers to become routine doers, it denies the psychological shift from external to internal motivational control; from the *management-centered* to the *worker-centered* organization. Moreover, by this denial management makes the organization ripe for rebellion or suicide. Peter Drucker is correct when he warns, "For the rest of this century and far into the next, the competitive battle will be won or lost by white-collar productivity." [5]

We are losing the battle. And we are heading for catastrophe by our refusal to acknowledge the shift in power, and to embrace a new organizational paradigm.

References

(1) Karl Zinsmeister of *American Enterprise Institute* puts this in perspective: *"While only five percent of the children in Japan live in something other than an intact two-parent home, in the U.S. the figure is currently 27 percent and rising. . . about two-thirds of all American children will spend some time in a single-parent household"* before they leave their teens (*The Tampa Tribune*, April 10, 1990).

(2) Valentine, Alan, *The Age of Conformity* (Chicago: Henry Regnery Company, 1954) p. 81.

(3) In the famous *Hawthorne Study at Western Electric* in 1927-1932, no matter how the conditions were altered, the workers responded positively. It was the attention and desire to please that was uncovered as the motivator. See *The Human Group* by George C. Homans (New York Harcourt, Brace & World, Inc., 1959) Chapters 3-6.

(4) Greenleaf, Robert K., *Servant Leadership: A Journey into the Nature of Legitimate Power and Greatness* (New York: Paulist Press, 1977) p. 10.

(5) Elizabeth Whitney, "The Real Laggards: White-Collar Workers," *St. Petersburg Times*, January 17, 1988.

Echoing Footsteps

"In modern-day business versions of Greek tragedy, executives are leading the charge on their own companies. They carry out Wall Street's orders to restructure, often before learning that their company is a target.

"The increase in self-restructuring is an important ripple effect of hostile takeovers. Most restructurings occur not because the firm lost a takeover battle. They occur because top executives pull the trigger on their own companies. A defensive strategy of Downsize, Dismantle and Debt, of 'raid yourself first and be safe,' has taken hold. When top executives put their own restructuring into motion to 'save' the company . . . they usually bring on the same terror they hoped to prevent . . . Although the recent wave of corporate streamlining has greatly improved profit margins, it has so decimated executive ranks that America may never recover . . . By the end of 1990 a million managers will have lost their jobs."

Paul Hirsch, Professor of Business, *Northwestern University*

"Whatever folly their kings commit, it is the Greeks themselves that suffer. Let Kings go mad and blunder as they may, the people in the end are sure to pay."

— Horace (65 B.C.-8 B.C.), Roman poet

The corporate boardroom is under siege. Panic is in the air. The organization is going through a transforming, exchanging, and discarding phase as it focuses on 'cipher management' and other panic strategies. Although unrecognized, this is the precise *discontinuity* that is moving the organization from a *management power center* to a *worker power center*. The imminent catastrophe will come without warning, taking a 'quantum leap' from the stable state of management to a worker power base.

Because nobody is paying attention, an enormous amount of energy and destructive capacity is being expended in this transition. Although the current discontinuity forewarns of this happening, it continues to be denied. Meanwhile, it appears the organization could, literally, go quite mad before a sense of sanity and stability is reestablished.

Conventional tools for tracking and predicting these developments have proven inadequate. Because they fail to capture the social morphology of organization, demographic and psychometric/cultural (attitude) surveys cannot identify this type of discontinuity, nor can sophisticated statistical trend analyses. Quite the contrary! These 'exercises,' instead, conceal the situation, misleading the organization into either a more optimistic or pessimistic perspective — seldom a realistic one. Consequently, this finds some executives believing cosmetic changes will suffice, while others see precipitous action as the only recourse. Everything — even market standing, technology, and basic wealth-producing capacity — may be sacrificed in order to offset the immediate crisis, or to 'keep the stock price up.'

At any other time in our history, to behave in this manner would have been perceived as certifiable lunacy. Today, it is accepted as *SOP* (Standard Operating Procedure).

To an organization under siege, just a slight stimulus can produce a shattering response. Forget the continuity the organization is struggling to maintain. *Discontinuity*, when it flexes its psychic energy (which is surely gaining momentum), will not be denied. Given this situation, an organization under siege can be suddenly demoralized or toppled by a single rumor, or in a single moment — by mass hysteria generated by corporate paranoia. Thus, the goodwill built over a hundred years can be destroyed with an irresponsible act. Many American corporations fit this description too well, yet they would be the first to deny it.

Organizational stability is controlled by *awareness* and *acceptance*. Awareness (i.e., conscious competence) compels the organization to be fully conscious of what it is (and is not), where it is, and how it got there, where it wants to go, and what it must do to get there. It sounds simple. Under siege, however, where the organization wants to go gets short shrift, overwhelmed by the flood of impulses to act compulsively. This is unfortunate, but almost inevitable. The *mind of the organization*, which is not quiet, cannot think clearly. It is caught up in the madness that it would attempt to avoid.

The problem is a simple one. These corporations are trying to solve *the problem* with the same kind of thinking that got them into it in the first place. All solutions are dominated by left-brain linear logic and labeling. *The left brain is the seat of logic, analysis, and rational problem solving. It is also the seat of language.* And, my, how language is used against itself to explain away the essence of the dilemma. In order to soften crushing reality, euphemisms become the order of the day; *fads* and *'quick and dirty'* solutions become life buoys in an

LEFT HEMISPHERE	RIGHT HEMISPHERE
Verbal	Nonverbal, visuo-spatial
Sequential, temporal, digital	Simultaneous, spatial, analogic
Logical, analytical	Gestalt, synthetic
Rational	Intuitive
WESTERN THOUGHT	EASTERN THOUGHT

economic maelstrom.

The Bicameral Mind: Two Cognitive Styles.

Meanwhile, a corps of 80,000 new *MBAs,* epitomizing the quintessence of the verbal, analytical, and rational mode of 'left-brain thinking,' annually march out of American universities to exacerbate the problem rather than resolve it. [1] Remarkably, because we have turned to MBAs for salvation, we have fallen further into our own inferno.

MBAs appear to have developed no real, discernible skills to help them understand the problem, much less deal with it. The basic problem, you see, is not primarily economic — although there *are* economic implications. The basic problem is the utilization of American manpower, which is psychosocial in origin. The key issue is the American people, and how they deal with the reality they refuse to face.

This takes 'right-brain thinking,' integrated into the rationale of 'left-brain analysis.' In other words a holistic perspective. It is a combination of visual, perceptual, and intuitive thought, centered in the right hemisphere of the brain, acting in consort with the rational mode of the left hemisphere. Because it sees a problem in its smallest parts and as a whole, the right brain serves this thinking. Conversely, when the left brain takes exclusive charge of a problem, it moves hastily over *defining the problem,* placing most of its energies in the nightmarish labyrinth of *problem solving.*

Having said that, American corporations are throwing *Hail Mary passes* everywhere, hoping against hope that someone 'on our side' will catch them. Yet, at a time when the industrial world's economic forecasts for the 1990s are bright, the long business expansion generated in the United States during the 1980s appears to have ended. A deep economic slump looms on the horizon. Many American corporations that acquired large amounts of debt from leveraged buyouts and junk bonds are struggling. A period of slow growth could result in a wave of panic, followed by a large wave of bankruptcies that might very well thwart the American spirit to survive as a first rate international competitor.

In the face of these portentous possibilities, Americans continue to demonstrate irrefutable contempt for this reality. Take education, for example. Against Germany and Japan, its prime competitors, America is falling behind educationally. During the last decade of this century, one million American youth will drop out of school annually. The estimated cost of this dropout is $240 billion in lost earnings and unearned taxes over their lifetime.

In America, learning is primarily viewed as a necessity — like taking medicine when you are sick. Ironically, this medicine is most frequently confined to the classroom, not considered a lifelong experience. Many, once they are out of school, put learning on the back burner. The joy of learning and the privilege of a public school education are taken for granted — or not taken at all. Meanwhile, the quest for success, and the drive to attain it through education, finds German students going to school six days each week, and the Japanese more than a month longer than American students.

Likewise, Americans have a contempt for saving. We are the poorest savers in the industrial West! This thinking contaminates *both* the American government *and* the American corporate world. As U.S. trade deficits spiral, the Germans and Japanese are creating huge surpluses. Put more graphically, the average Japanese worker earned half the income of the average American in 1973. Today, he earns 20 percent more. German workers, who in 1973 were making two-thirds of our average income, are now a third ahead. If this trend continues, Americans will awaken one day to the lowest standard of living in the free world.

Before you consider this an exaggeration — if U.S. trade deficits continue at their present level, major borrowing from abroad will be required. This, in turn, will result in more buildup of foreign debt. The United States already has foreign obligations of over *$500 billion.* By the early 1990s, that figure could reach *$1* *trillion*, requiring debt service of some $8 billion to $10 billion per month. [2] This is money that would otherwise be available to invest in such areas critical to American life as schools, police forces, anti-drug campaigns, medical research, environmental cleanup, and repairing of the infrastructure of American society.

But an even more debilitating barrier — after taking into account quality, marketing savvy, and exchange rates — involves the social and cultural implications of plummeting personal performance on the job. The decline of the work ethic and productivity is especially apparent among American professionals. This predicament is discounted by optimists who point out the $210 billion spent annually by employers on *training*. And, they remind us of our habitual technological leadership and economic clout (saying, for example, "The Gross National Product is double that of Japan, and four times that of Germany").

For one thing, we don't need to intensify our efforts in training. The whole rationale of training is wrong for these times and this work force. Training is what blue-collar workers have always been given, which remains essentially an indoctrination into the 'how,' but not 'why' of things. The 'how of things' is simply not enough to keep professionals interested, much less involved. This mechanistic formula is a legacy of the turn-of-the-century *cultural bias* towards workers, epitomized by Frederick Winslow Taylor, the father of 'scientific management,' who declared:

". . . *One of the very first requirements for man who is fit to handle pig iron as a regular occupation is that he shall be so stupid and so phlegmatic that he more nearly resembles an ox than any other type.*"[3]

This powerful bias towards workers is still extant today reflected in the fact that most training is confined primarily to instruction, not enlightenment; to the 'nitty-gritty' operant conditioning advocated by such lights as B. F. Skinner, et al. The focus of such training is on behavior modification, or of 'doing something' differently, not thinking differently; on behavior, not commonly held values, beliefs and expectations.

But we don't need more instruction. We need greater enlightenment; clearer insight into the futility of our present efforts. Obviously, we are working hard, but on the wrong things. *Training,* as pointed out elsewhere, fails to deal with the *cultural biases* of the organization, which are directly responsible for poor performance. Before we can change behavior, we must first attempt to change these biases. The capacity to change depends heavily on previous learning and the biases stored in the brain of each individual worker. Giving individuals

72

uniform instruction without regard to the biases they bring to the learning effort virtually guarantees failure. Education, on the other hand, meets such biases head on.

When the *One Minute Manager* (1982) created such excitement, Catherine Tritsch observed, "Shamu the Whale may be better trained than most U.S. workers." [4] True, this book developed a precise formula for training. Apparently killer whales at Sea World's aquatic show respond positively to this mechanistic formula. Actually, this is not too surprising, for animals can be trained, but people must be educated. This has never been truer than today since the biases of the organization's culture have had such a powerful influence on performance. Consequently, conventional training, even with all the impressive devices of modern technology, has little capacity to change behavior or staying effect as performance everywhere indicates.

More importantly, however, training has little impact on *cultural biases*. Therefore, for all intent and purpose, these billions of dollars are being poured into a bottomless pit. This is because training is not designed to deal with cultural change. Only education can deal with the organization's cultural resistance to change because it uses previous learning as a basis for building a bridge to new learning experiences.

Education does this by assisting the individual worker in exploring their cultural basis of operation and how it meets, or fails to meet their performance needs. Such engagement, over time, generally finds them discarding the old and making way for the new. It is a slow and patient process that is generated by the momentum established by the will of the worker. Once this momentum takes hold, however, there is breakthrough to incredible achievement. Meanwhile, training is too frequently a panic response to an ill-defined problem. Regrettably, when this occurs, training comes to be known as an activity for its own sake and little more.

As for technical leadership and economic clout, these are evanescent when it comes to individual will and creative spirit. *Will and spirit* are intangibles that personify the thrust of a national psyche. Here reside the sense and will to survive, founded in common values and beliefs. These abstractions are energized by the pain of history and the challenge of reality. But when the twin cultural narcotics — *comfort and complacency* — invade the American psyche (as they surely have), then there is little sense of the danger ahead, for few can hear 'the echoing footsteps.'

Ironically, it is the gift of technology that has deadened the senses. There is only one reason man has survived on this planet: the *human brain*. The brain is a necessary apparatus for human survival, with the human mind the software recording of that struggle. What is imprinted upon the mind dictates the way human beings behave. Paradoxically, as technology has pushed back the veil of ignorance, it has lost the coordinates of wisdom and humor.

Whether science or religion, whenever either becomes dogma or ritualistic consensus, civilization takes a step back into the *Dark Ages. Awareness and acceptance* have become buried in these times, yet the situation *mandates* that the American people disavow their resistance to reality and embrace what reality demands. Our inclination, however, is denial. Today, defensiveness, excuses, justifications, and denials combine with *comfort and complacency* to depict the *landscape of catastrophe.*

Unfortunately, these are words. Only words. If they are not felt, not valued, not believed, not understood, the echoing footsteps of catastrophe will not be heard. What is so disconcerting is that this seems to be the case.

Organizations. . . because they refuse to deal with workers differently than in the past. . . appear helpless in the face of mounting challenges. Despite expending enormous amounts of energy, time, and money, it seems impossible for them to see the situation clearly.

American organizations are currently throwing prodigious amounts of resources at their *cant nemesis* — poor quality. Quality has become the New Messiah, with 'salvation through quality' the new litany. "It will save us from ourselves, and win our redemption." This is a panic response to the strategic issue of "how do we get back on track?"

Global issues require global strategies. But we are not comfortable thinking in such terms. Global strategies require a conceptual framework and theoretical speculation. But thinking conceptually gives us a headache, and we have little time for theories (or, for that matter, for theoreticians). Such a framework entails qualitative analysis, or subjective thinking. But we are extremely skeptical of this type of analysis, finding it too abstract and fuzzy-headed.

We prefer quantitative analysis, with concrete references. This we see as objective and 'value free.' No matter how often this disappoints or fails us, we invariably return to the 'quick and dirty' solution, the newest fad, or the 'miraculous.' We live in the *Prison of Panic Called 'Now,'* and have little desire to escape its punishing comfort. This, then, explains the popularity of Harris

74

Polls, questionnaires, statistical analysis, and astrology. It is reduced to quantitative mathematics, neat and tidy summaries — not messy, inconclusive speculation.

We want something that deludes us into thinking, "If we do this (reduce cost) and this (improve quality), the problem will automatically solve itself."

This implies that our problems are more quantitative than qualitative; more operational than psychological. Therefore, cost-cutting and continuous quality improvement necessarily will improve the health and stability of the organization.

None of this is true, of course. On the contrary, it is a cultural issue. If you design a bad system, and the people believe in it, it will work. If you design a 'perfect' system, and the people do not believe in it, it will invariably fail. It is true that Western Europe and Japan are setting the economic pace in the world market. But to focus on their quality and productivity as an exclusive algorithm would be unwise!

Western Europe, in particular — because the culture is so richly nurtured and maintained — has been responsive to almost any economic system. Max Weber's *authoritarian bureaucracy* is firmly in place. The Germans, especially, are a resourceful people and respectful of their authoritarian tradition. This resourcefulness is not to be confused with being industrious, which they are not. Certainly, they are not nearly as industrious as Americans. But when they work, they work. They find little solace in 'working for work's sake.' Moreover, with an average annual vacation of five weeks, and an additional nine to 14 paid holidays, they make the average American's two-week vacation look anemic.

Ironically, Europeans seldom carry vacation over to the next year, whereas this is common with American workers. There is a saying, "When Europeans are working, they are thinking about their holiday. When Americans are on holiday, they are thinking about their work."

References

(1) For comparison, Western Europe, which represents a population of approximately 100 million more citizens than the United States, produces only 4,000 MBAs per year.

(2) Garten, Jeffrey E., "Japan and Germany: American Concerns," *Foreign Affairs*, Winter, 1989/1990; p. 91.

(3) Taylor, Frederick Winslow, *The Principles of Scientific Management* (New York: W. W. Norton & Co., Inc., 1911), p. 59.

(4) Tritsch, Catherine, "How To Be A One-Minute Trainer," *Successful Meetings*, August, 1983.

The Merry Monarchs of
The Corporate Madhouse

"Whatever liberates our spirit without giving us mastery over ourselves is destructive."

Johann Wolfgang von Goethe (1749-1832) German poet, novelist and philosopher

"When people are free to do as they please, they usually imitate each other. Originality is deliberate and forced, and partakers of the nature of a protest. A society which gives unlimited freedom to the individual, more often than not attains a disconcerting sameness. On the other hand, where communal discipline is strict but not ruthless — an annoyance which irritates, but not a heavy yoke which crushes — originality is likely to thrive. It is true that, when imitation runs its course in a wholly free society, it results in a uniformity which is not unlike a mild tyranny. Thus the fully standardized free society has perhaps enough compulsion to challenge originality."

Eric Hoffer (1902-1983), Longshoreman philosopher

The *crippled genius* of the American worker contains many paradoxes. Take the way Americans behave when they are *full of themselves,* contrasted with when they are not. In case of the former, they are obsessed with *self,* spending an inordinate amount of time preoccupied with *things.* American workers have an essential drive *to acquire,* but an equal need *to give.* Yes, the paradoxical nature of the American character takes on many forms.

A few years ago, after a winter thaw, the Mississippi River at Waterloo, Iowa, threatened to flood the city. Faced with this crisis, the city mobilized its resources, and people of all age's filled sand bags, mounted them on trucks, and distributed them throughout the city to form man-made dikes.

Hundreds of citizens worked 'round the clock — beside neighbors and friends and, yes, beside strangers as well. The separate identities of age, race, religion, values, and profession dissolved into a faceless common challenge. For a brief moment, a *sense of community* possessed their consciousness.

After the crisis had passed, several participants were asked why they did it. The consensus was "because it had to be done; the city had to be saved!" Would they do it again? "Yes, of course," they replied in unison. They would submit themselves to the demands of *crisis management*. Waterloo, that moment, had no *insiders* or *outsiders*. . . it was a community with a *common mission*.

This is but one event in the kaleidoscopic spectrum of American *self-forgetfulness* in times of 'perceived crisis.' As previously mentioned, whenever *physical survival* is at stake (e.g., WWII), or *psychological survival* is an issue (e.g., launching of Sputnik) — whenever the threat comes from *outside,* the sense of belonging to a communal tribe is apparent. But the key words are *perceived crisis.*

Throughout American history, tension invariably produces *music,* while relaxation typically generates *noise.* If we don't feel it, as with the current economic crisis, it doesn't exist. Yet, tension is as natural to the American spirit as joy is unnatural. We are tense and intense, and find difficulty in dealing with things that are going well. We are always waiting — even anxiously — for the other shoe to fall. For some reason, we have to work very hard at enjoyment. Leisure is, in fact, intimidating.

The odyssey of American workers and their quest for satisfaction has not been a particularly joyous one. When you see joy on their faces, it is likely a mask concealing the tension of struggle and fear within — struggle to become what they are not; fear of being found out for what they are.

Pretend and *pretension* – both derivatives of tension – are prominent features of the American character. Show me a youngster smiling easily in play. Instead, we have seven-year-olds playing football as if they were in the NFL. Their parents-as-coaches can be heard yelling at these prepubescent youngsters, whose bones have not yet matured to take such punishment. "Put your head down and take him out," they cry. "Hey! Hey! What's your problem, fellah, where's your toughness?" Would that such energy and enthusiasm were directed at their education and enlightenment. Their minds are quite nimble for such challenge, if their bodies are not.

On the distaff side, watch six-year-old baton twirlers, toothy grins barely covering actual grimaces, displaying little joy in the exercise. How many chose such activities? How many more are playing out someone else's fantasy?

There is a much greater pull in the American culture to *please others* than to *please self-*. . . justified by "it is good for you." More often than not, it is *parental authority* over adolescent powerlessness and its *need to please*. What this creates in a developing youngster is *self-doubt* and internal conflict.

Translated, this is *tension*. It is an American disease, orchestrated on the young by well-meaning parents. "Doing what is right" is inadvertently interpreted as "doing what is expected." Disquieting at best, the whole process turns to viciousness when the aspect of *competition* is added.

American workers assume that competition is as inherent to their nature as breathing. They wear it as a badge and swagger with a sense of what they think it means. Author W. W. Rostow sees it otherwise. He believes that before America can *compete,* it must first learn how to *cooperate.* It must first discover its tribal capacity for communal action. Rostow fears America may go the way of Great Britain which, between 1870 and 1971, went from 32 percent of the world's industrial production to generating only four percent. He suggests the only way out is to develop an organizational infrastructure of cooperation. [1]

Toward the Fully Developed Human Being

Competition imitates initiative in a deceptive manner, obfuscating understanding. The competitive person trains to 'outperform' the competition. Providing they are successful, we imagine they enjoy a sense of initiative. Not so. They are in a reactionary mode. They are becoming the other person. . . only better. The standard is not what they are capable of doing, but what the other person can do. This develops the veneer of skill and the appearance of competence. Taken to the extreme, it can actually reflect what is hated.

Roger Bannister, on the other hand, typifies the innovative person with initiative. A British medical doctor, Dr. Bannister was the first person to break the legendary barrier of the *four-minute mile.* He did this, not by being more competitive or imitative of the training of past great middle distance runners, but by studying his own physiology. He then trained against this standard, expunging from his mind the psychological limitations imposed by competitive zeal since the age of the Ancient Greek Olympiad, more than 2,000 years ago. Thanks to Dr. Bannister, today well over a hundred individual runners have broken the four-minute mile in little over a thirty-year span.

Compare this to the *organizational climber*. Competitive? Yes. Competent? Probably not. With success comes the almost certain requirement of initiating policy and dealing with situational ambiguities demanding original thinking. But this person is groomed to think imitatively — to adopt the 'party line' (otherwise known as getting promoted) — so functional imagination is out of the question.

Resourcefulness has been trained-out of the individual, who only knows how to imitate existing patterns and thinking. Besides, the individual is 'safe!' Given a challenge, such a person is in 'uncharted territory,' with neither the freedom of mind nor the passion of heart to create new forms. When old forms fail, it is an invitation to become ruthless to survive. . . typical behavior under duress.

True organizational leadership requires the capacity to see and the ability to serve. The organizational climber is devoid of both. In fact, there is a lack of vision in most American corporations today, and little sense of service to the organization. Service is either self-aggrandizing or beholden to the traditional power structure. The organization is myopic; structured to encourage relentless campaigning for promotion. It has not always been so.

Henry Ford is credited with mass producing automobiles, and Thomas Edison with inventing the incandescent light bulb. Neither of these achievements compares with their visionary leadership, however:

In 1914, when most industrial workers were earning less than a dollar a day, Ford created the $5 work day. This created a guaranteed market for Ford automobiles. Beyond that, he created a $30 million profit-sharing plan and other incentives, which helped to establish the working middle class.

Edison, on the other hand, envisioned the city being eternally illuminated. To accomplish this he invented the Pearl Street Municipal Utility in New York City, the first central electric-light power plant in the world. . . in 1881.

Think of it. Ford never got beyond grammar school, and Edison was essentially self-taught, dropping out of school at an early age due to a hearing disability.

This is the rich stuff of our American heritage, but it has been replaced by 'hype' and 'pedigree.' Most of the men who built America couldn't get an interview today, much less a job in their own companies. They were *doers*, not takers; *performers,* not personalities.

Erich Fromm wrote, *"Man himself, in each period of history, is formed in terms of the prevailing practice of life which in turn is determined by his mode of production."*[2] Man's primary motivation is to contribute, not to consume. Capitalism makes the wish *to have and to use* the most dominant of human desires. A man so dominated, Karl Marx reasoned, is a 'crippled genius' with the ambition to *acquire* overpowering his desire to *accomplish.* Yet, neither private property nor profit is man's mission, but the free unfolding of his human powers. Fromm captures the essence of this:

"Not the man who has much, but the man who is much is the fully developed, truly human being." [3]

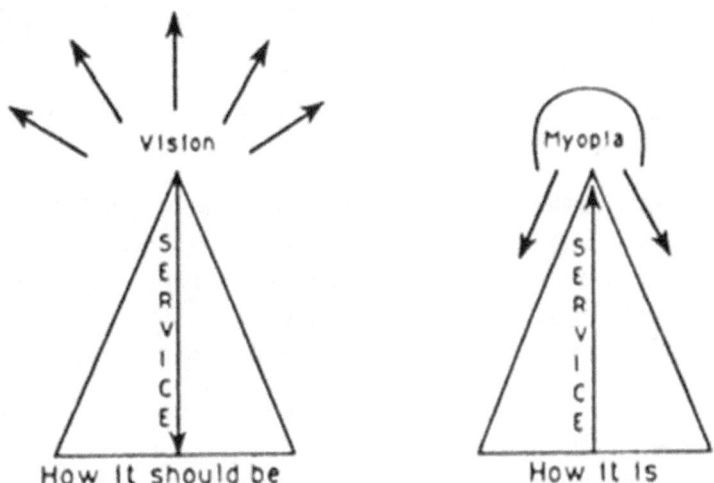

The leadership requirements of the organization are the *capacity to see* and the *ability to serve.*

This is the crux of our problem today. Materialism is out of control in the American culture, and spiritualism has taken a holiday.

Why Johnny Won't Work

A better question than "Why won't Johnny work?" is "Why should he?" *New York Times* Journalist Daniel Rodgers writes, "We have exaggerated the death of the work ethic largely because its converts have so greatly exaggerated its existence." The work ethic has always been a minority phenomenon in American life. The idea that hard work is the greatest good in life never cut deeply into the South. It was violated in scores of 18th century frontier settlements, in rich men's ballrooms, and in most of the nation's workshops and factories. From the beginning, it belonged to a fraction of the population, primarily the Northern Protestant propertied classes (White Anglo-Saxon Protestants, or WASPs).

WASPs were an immensely influential minority, who did their best to nationalize their intense faith in hard work. They drummed it into school children, poor recipients of relief, freed slaves, immigrants, and industrial workers of all sorts. The lessons never fully took, however, so the story of the 'work ethic' is one of conflict and commitment.

Yet, the dreams of self-made success continued to win converts to the work ethic through the 19th, and well into the 20th century, as thousands of Europeans and Asians sought the 'American promise.' Once immigration was restricted, the ranks of the believers diminished dramatically. Hard times took up the slack, as did economic relocation, and with them a renewed respect for work arose temporarily. In the 1930s — the years of the *Great Depression*, when work was hard to find — respect for work grew appreciably.

But since the late 1940s, the workplace has become a veritable war zone. The struggle for the eight-hour day, resistance to job changes and increased production quotas, broke repeatedly into public view. Despite this, American factories a century ago were much more turbulent, with employee turnover double what it is today, and absenteeism better than ten percent.

The dramatic change was primarily caused by *leisure*, not work. There was little leisure for most Americans a century ago, so it wasn't threatening, as it is today. In fact, many Americans today refuse to take their accrued vacation, some being proud of their disdain for it. They would rather be paid for this benefit than face the break in their routine.

Indeed, the conflict between work and leisure is a real one. Seeing *work and leisure* as part of the same whole is seemingly incomprehensible to the majority. So, leisure is grudgingly compartmentalized. Like a giant cavity to be filled, leisure time is crammed with frivolous goods and entertainment, the opium of an impatient people.

This was illustrated dramatically by the 1960s 'furlough experiment' at Bethlehem Steel and Aluminum Company of America (Alcoa). In *Crisis in Bethlehem* (1986), John Strohmeyer explains how such steel industry excesses actually crippled 'the goose that laid the golden egg.' Steel workers in the 1960s, when the 13-week 'furlough' program was inaugurated, already had practically every benefit and financial concession imaginable. This program allowed the senior half of the work force to be given an additional 13 weeks of paid vacation every five years. This was also true of Alcoa, among others.

The furlough experiment was designed to manage manpower requirements more effectively, to give the work force the incentive to pursue self-enhancement interests (including educational pursuits), and to improve productivity. What it did, instead, was produce a nightmare. Most furloughed workers acquired second jobs. When the time came for them to go back to work, because they needed the additional income to maintain their 'new' standard of living, many continued their second jobs. Attempting to manage two jobs soon resulted in poor performance on both. So, for many, instead of a broadening experience, it was compressed into anger and resentment. . . directed at its benefactor, the company. Work was what they knew, and work was what filled the 13-week void.

What's The Point of Working?

Despite this ambivalence, the price of freedom is still 'work.' When Adam and Eve exercised their freedom by disobeying God, they were driven from the womb of nature and into the real world of work. A prejudice against work has prevailed ever since. But late 20th century life has played a trick on this cultural bias. Most work is more playful, weightless, and more spiritual than leisure, no matter how much we try to see it otherwise. In the words of poet Kahlil Gibran, it is *"love made visible."* We have been driven back into the *Garden of Eden.*

Meanwhile, 'work' continues to be treated as punishment. Work is made into what it is not. Studs Terkel commits this error in his book *Working* (1974) with the opening: "This book, being about work, is, by its nature, about violence. . . to the spirit as well as the body." That was obviously true at one time. The historic horrors of child labor and Dickensian squalor now translate into robotic busy work on the production line, and the pretense of work in the office.

For many of us, struggle has gone out of work, pain has taken leave, and the motivation to work has become confused. Work has gone from the toil of moving the great stone of mortality. . . to moving the weightlessness of the human spirit. It is hard to measure 'work' when you are mainly spectator to it.

Guilt holds closest to Terkel's dictum. As is man's inclination, work is avoided whenever possible. Now, when it is not necessary to avoid it — when work is not threatening — Americans appear obsessed with it. Their priorities are out of control. Madness has taken center stage.

The modern American is ill-prepared for this development. Work for economic survival is fading. It is primarily sustained by spending money before it is earned, or being forever a loaner rather than an owner. Clearly, self-management is at issue.

Actually, when work as struggle abates, the *motive* to work changes. Traditionally, American parents worked to provide a better life for their children. Hut this, too, is fading. Disillusioned by the insolence of their spoiled brats, parents are retreating from this noble objective. Many, after surrendering their homes and possessions to their children's avarice, are too tired or burned-out to complain.

The *spoiled brat generation* feeds on itself (the more it gets, the more it wants), and everybody else. It has no sense of purpose; no vision of its reason for being. And, therefore, this generation marches to middle age suspended in extended adolescence.

Work has been distracted by leisure — doubly so because work and leisure have become interchangeable. Given this predicament, there is an insane effort to make the simple, difficult; and the banal, profound. It is the cultural bias of 'non-thinking thinking,' generating 'non-doing doing' of 'non-thing things.' Work, too, is feeding on itself. The principal product of work today is the generation of more work. . . with no discernible outcome, other than more work. Therefore, work has become essentially counterfeit.

With the *Great Depression,* the *Dust Bowl,* and the *Bank Holiday* [5], now mainly forgotten, there is little sense of pain for these events of the 1930s. Even recession and inflation are hardly felt experiences. Today, elaborate financial cushions, including unemployment insurance, pension funds, union benefits, welfare payments, and food stamps have taken much of the catastrophe out of unemployment or economic downturn. It would take total economic collapse to get most people's attention. We are prisoners of the organization — going from a sense of individualism and independence to a sense of organizational counter dependence. From the *Culture of Contribution,* through the *Culture of Comfort,* to where we are now — the *Culture of Complacency.*

Work today — being geared more toward impressions than outcomes — is respected for the identity it provides more than the satisfaction it gives. So, what is the point of working?

Think about it. What gives us the greatest satisfaction? It is being useful in the service of others. Now! It is no longer a vague ideal, but a real possibility. Work has gone from punishment to pleasure; from something we *have to do,* to something we *want to do;* from a vocation to an avocation; from *work* to *play;* from extrinsic interests *(outside demands)* to intrinsic interests *(inside commands).* We have choices we've never had before.

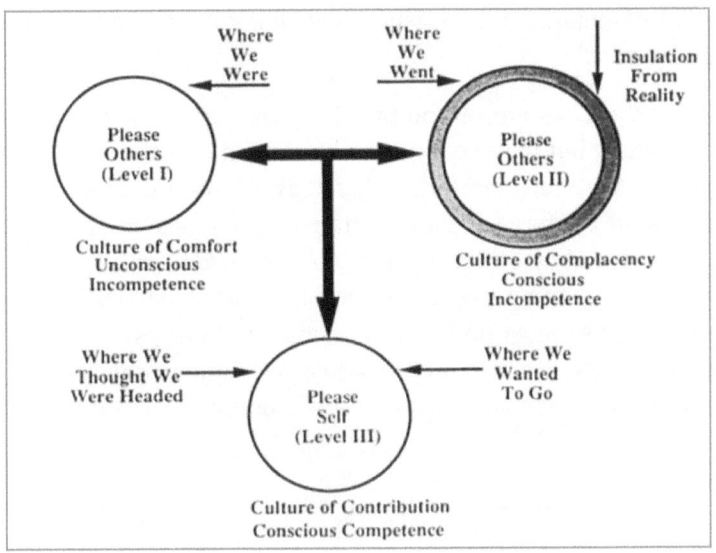

The Present Dilemma Illustrated.

Almost imperceptibly, the spiritual component of *giving* is competing with the conscious pursuit of *getting*. For the first time in man's history, masses of people across advanced societies no longer must focus on work as the central concern of their existence. They have the luxury of harboring ideals and giving them life. They may choose to work or ignore it in pursuit of other interests. Unfortunately, when it comes to such choices, most Americans are essentially primitives – with little appreciation of things other than work. To them work remains defined in terms of *struggle*.

Work, so defined, is the only thing they understand. And now that work is more ambiguous, they are confused. Americans have reached the age when rote learning and robotic behavior, which has hitherto dominated the requirements of most work, is not enough to keep body and soul together. . . something ignored without penalty by most Americans, until now. Suddenly, work has become manifestly spiritual and self-directed, which is beyond the comprehension and experience of the majority.

While America's ancestors struggled for economic survival in the New World, most Americans today have little sense of economic deprivation. Consequently, turning from the *concrete world of getting* to the *abstract world of serving* is baffling. *Service to others* is more subjective and qualitative, whereas the objective world of quantitative measurement, the cynical world of greed, is the world they know best.

Paradoxically, Americans are on the threshold of having enough leisure time to create a better world, but they continue to be trained and conditioned for a world that no longer exists and, therefore, what they are doing appears to be *out of control.* In a time of conference calling and Fax machines, microwave ovens and home computers, a study, entitled *Agenda for the 1990s,* finds time pressures and resulting stress levels getting worse. The result is that American professionals are finding it impossible to meet both their personal and professional demands. This study, examining lifestyles of 1000 businessmen and women in 14 industries, discovered that time savers and efficiency-enhancing technology, oddly enough,

---

Working More and Enjoying It Less

- *85 percent said they work more than 45 hours per week*
- *48 percent feel stressed every day 65 percent work more than one weekend a month*
- *89 percent take work home with them*
- *53 percent spend less than two hours a week looking after their children*
- *4 percent said child-care facilities were available at their workplace*

Agenda for the 1990s survey of 650 men and
350 women professionals.

---

contributed to the dilemma.

These Americans are working for technology, rather than technology working for them. With so much information available, and so little time to deal with it, they have become *proactive* (a buzz word of these times) in producing even more technology. The increasing volume of information has become a demon — demanding more hours and causing more stress, creating a *decision-making dilemma.* More and more decisions must be made in a finite period of time. Thus, qualitative decision making is subjugated to the quantitative demands of 'non-doing doing' of 'non-thing things,' which, increasingly, is the basis of most work today.

Panic is in the air. When genuine leisure is a distinct possibility, the leisure society in America is a myth. In 1989, for example, the sales of the Filofax Company, whose elaborate notebooks help people navigate through the clutter of their lives, hit $4.2 million, double its sales in 1987. Meanwhile, more executives, professionals, self-employed people, journalists and bureaucrats confess to thriving on 60-70-hour work weeks and the fast pace of the electronic workplace. Yet, economists trained to study the impact of this frenetic activity fail to discern any appreciable benefit to the American economy. One explanation might be that many of these people are just 'spinning their wheels;' that working longer and harder is a subconscious way of avoiding the pain of working smarter. . . a repressed way of avoiding the discomfort of changing their behavior patterns. Consequently, the average professional is destined to spend at least three years of their life in desultory meetings and more than two years playing telephone tag.

This preoccupation with vacuous *doing* deprives professionals of the time to embrace their transcendental heritage. In the early 19th century, Ralph Waldo Emerson expressed this uniquely American spiritualism with his celebration of experience. Emerson's famous essay, *Self-Reliance* (1844), emphasizes the wisdom of self-trust and perspective:

"To believe your own thought, to believe that what is true for you in your private heart is true for all men. . . that is genius."

Where is our genius today? Why do we embrace madness when our transcendent al past — the world of Emerson, Thoreau, Melville, Poe and Hawthorne — provides a more relevant education?

Emerson had a different vision of the educated American than the *professional-technical elite* we have produced. He envisioned a person with a strong bent for experience, supported by a spiritual insight into being; a person with a sense of balance.

Emerson believed education should promote the ability of the common man as much through experience as from books. For him, the basis of a democratic education was the cultivation of ordinary experience to its spiritual essence. From this faith in the sovereignty of the individual sprang his vision of the unity of self, nature, and society. Emerson could see experience melting into the essence of the national character, producing a model of the possibilities of a democratic culture for the world. Repeatedly, he expressed the sanctity of *individualism,* combined with the responsibilities of *self-reliance.* Late 20th century America has drifted far from this transcendental course.

Consider the arrogance of individualism today and the conspicuous lack of self-reliance. Where is the sense of place and space; the sense of experience or self-determinism? American workers, by their own admission, find little joy in work, less joy at school, and still less joy in their private lives. They are being 'taken care of,' and they resent their *organizational counter dependence.* They lash out silently at phantom obstacles, failing to realize they are both the enemy and ally of the organization — the silent killers of lost momentum, as well as the secret weapon to newfound hope. They live the remorse of Eugene O'Neill:

"We talk about the American Dream, and want to tell the world about the American Dream, but what is that dream, in most cases, but the dream of material things? I sometimes think that the United States, for this reason, is the greatest failure the world has ever seen."

But if this is so, who can change it if not American workers!

References

(1) Rostow, W. W., "To Compete, Americans Must First Cooperate," *International Herald Tribune,* March 16, 1987.

(2) Fromm, Erich, *Beyond the Chains of Illusions* (New York: Simon and Schuster, 1962) p. 41.

(3) Ibid. p. 41.

Why We Can't Get from Here to There

"The brain uses the principle of 'the match' by which incoming information matches, more or less exactly, the patterns stored in the brain, or else it is not recognized . . . Biasing involves all that is stored in the brain, relevant to a program decision, from experience, from plans, aims, fears, and from the current situational input. To effect change of behavior, or 'open a new door' to learning, we must try to change biases, not behavior directly . . . Present learning depends heavily on previous learning and biases stored in the brain of each individual.

Giving individuals uniform instruction without regard to what they bring to the learning effort virtually guarantees a high incidence of failure."

— Leslie A. Hart, Educational psychologist

Sisyphus Alone!

Imagine a small high tech operation in which 400 employees conscientiously come to work. This operation — once a highly competitive leader in its specialized field — suddenly finds itself in a desperate survival mode with executives working seven days a week (some ten to 12 hours a day), vainly struggling to keep the operation afloat.

In this situation, *work* means executives cordoning themselves off from other employees, frantically running from meeting to meeting — from marketing to sales; from engineering to production; from crisis to crisis. The operation is under siege, and no one has time to think, much less smile, as morbid activity fills a humorless void.

Meetings provide the *worry beads* for this anxious group with preparation for meetings leaving little time for calm reflection. *Work*, albeit undeniably laborious, finds no one with either the inclination or courage to call 'time out' for a sanity check.

Yet, at this most critical moment, the focus is shifted suddenly from 'the problem' and refocused on the demands of the corporate fathers for a *management review*. All energy is now rededicated to an elaborate presentation of the 'State of the Business,' combining *CYA* and *SYA* 'show and tell' documentation. A veritable *magnum opus* of 1300 pages is generated, with copies, of course, for all corporate fathers. The text is then featured in a four-hour, 400-viewgraph presentation *in living color*.

Someone from another planet watching this spectacle might conclude "there is no intelligent life on the planet earth."

The corporate fathers, numbed to the bone at the conclusion of this exercise, reciprocate by directing the staff to return to the drawing board and "simplify, codify and verify your findings."

After weeks of Herculean effort, you would think the profound shock of this would break staff members' composure — if not their decorum (Figure 5-1). Instead, you see faces filled with weary resignation (except the secretarial pool — their marriages are on hold, and to them, it is "enough already!"). As one secretary put it, "It's as if all my energies were poured down a black hole, without the slightest hint of light."

Sisyphus in Hades - condemned to roll a stone up a hill, only to have it roll down again as it nears the top for eternity.

This epitomizes *corpocracy* at its most debilitating stage. *'Non-thinking thinking'* to do *'non-doing doing'* of *'non-thing things'* becomes a matter of routine — or "if you can't dazzle 'em with brilliance, baffle 'em with bullshit." This was the effort of 80 men and women against an organization of 400.

Stated otherwise, 80 *self-appointed saviors* operated without the support, input, or involvement of the other 320. Yes — 80 people were observed pushing the great stone of Sisyphus up the slope, while four times that number stood by and watched (laughing through their teeth).

"It's not our problem," the multitude sings in chorus. *"Management got its tit in the ringer! Let management get it out!"* These workers are 'having none of it.' So glib. So righteous. So comfortable in their ignorance. They are not irresponsible; they are not responsible.

Not one person interviewed stopped to think it was their job, not management's that was on the line. Management takes care of its own. Shake the tree and it lands on different branches; or at the very least is given a *golden parachute* to break its fall. Not so for the workers. Poverty faces them. *Outplacement counseling,* two-week' severance pay, and encouraging words don't feed a family.

When Getting Fired Looks Pretty Good

The *golden parachute,* at least in theory, was originally 'divined' to keep management honest with its focus primarily on the interest of business rather than self-aggrandizement. But that has not materialized in practice. In fact, with these golden parachutes, getting fired looks pretty good. For example, should Sidney Jay Sheinberg, the CEO of MCA, Inc., lose his job within a year of the company going through a 'change in control,' he would take home $16.8 million in cash, or roughly 23 times his normal annual salary. But it doesn't stop with him, for the severance package for MCA's top five executives would cost a minimum of $33.45 million. Add to this another 364 MCA employees guaranteed lump sum parachutes of three times their normal annual salaries, plus benefit packages and stock options. These additional parachutes approximate another $82 million.

Not to single out MCA, CEO John W. Amerman of Mattel (the toy manufacturer), faced with a similar firing, would get $5.5 million; Irvine-based FLUOR Corporation guarantees its top executives two to three times their annual pay plus cash payment to compensate for lost benefits; Los Angeles-based National Medical Enterprises would give its top three people a total of more than $11 million plus stock and incentive items; Apple Computer would give its chief financial officer, Joseph A. Graziano, $2.4 million if he were fired, and senior vice president Delbert W. Yocam $1.6 million; and Carlsbad-based Decom Systems, Inc. guarantees its top officer four times his base salary if he is fired, twice his salary if he is unable to return to work because of a disability and a year's salary if he just decides to quit.

But possibly the most lucrative severance package is that of 92-year-old Armand Hammer of Occidental Petroleum. The value of his package exceeds $16 million. And if the IRS deems this excessive payment and imposes a 20-percent excise tax on it, Occidental agrees to pay that tax bill. Hammer is guaranteed his salary, bonus (adjusted for cost of living increases), perquisites, and employee benefits until the end of his employment agreement, which runs until 1998 when he will be 100 years old. [1]

An Economic Holocaust?

When a plant closes, it is an inconvenience to the management team and a veritable disaster to the rank and file. Yet, this response is typical of American workers outside the decision-making process.

There are many horror stories which illustrate the devastating impact of 'plant closings,' but none more graphically than that of the grocery chain, Safeway

Stores, Inc. The Leverage Buy Out (LBO) of Safeway Stores epitomizes a new level of employee insensitivity. Working in a food chain used to give one a sense of security, "Everyone has to eat, right?" In fact, the longtime motto of Safeway was:

"Safeway Offers Security."

After the LBO, it was changed to the *cipher management* lingo of:

"Targeted Returns on Current Investment."

Suddenly, employees went from being persons to being things.

More than 63,000 managers and workers were cut loose from Safeway through store closings, sales or layoffs. Many, when they finally found work in the grocery industry, went from an average of $12 to $4 per hour; many lost their homes; many went through divorce, serious illness or bankruptcy; a few even attempted or succeeded in committing suicide. The majority, however, took it on the chin without complaint as they watched the three investment banks that worked on the LBO receive a total of $65 million with law and accounting firms sharing in another $25 million. CEO Peter Magowan of Safeway and other directors and top executives received another $28 million for their shares in the company, with $5.7 million alone going to Magowan. He and 60 other top Safeway executives also got options to buy a total of ten percent of the new Safeway stock at $2 (in 1986) per share. Today those options, four years later, are worth more than $100 million or $12.125 per share.

Meanwhile corporate raiders, Herbert and Robert Haft, who orchestrated the unsuccessful hostile takeover, still managed to make $100 million by selling their Safeway shares they had accumulated to Kohlberg Kravis Roberts & Co. (KKR), the LBO specialists who managed the reorganization. Incidentally, KKR charged Safeway $60 million in fees just to put the deal together. In a word, everybody made money (and continues to make money as the buyout group aggressively sells assets and consolidates profits). . . at the expense of long-term, loyal and dedicated employees. Safeway was an economic pogrom for these employees no less psychologically damaging than the survivors of the *Holocaust.* [2]

Workers' perception of their role is to dutifully put in eight hours and 'the company be damned.' Let management worry about the health of the company. No one ever told them, and meant it, *'YOU ARE THE COMPANY!'* But they *are*!

Without workers, there is no company — only buildings. Management is not. . . nor has it ever been. . . *'The company.'* In the past 50 years, however, management's function has gravitated increasingly to custodial powers without portfolio; which, even then, it treats shabbily.

Management's role, especially with the advent of the professional worker, is *to lead* and *to serve* its first customer, the organization's workers:

- *Lead the organization, and it will realize its opportunities and adjust to its challenges.*
- *Serve the workers, and they will serve the organization. . . and, in turn, serve everyone.*

But that's not what happens. There is a *cultural bias* that promotes *style* over *substance, conformity* over *contribution, loyalty* over *leadership.* This thwarts workers from doing real work, fostering instead the preposterous nightmare described above. Counterfeit work has become, as a result, an American institution.

The Law of Entropy

Something is terribly wrong with the American organization. The organization has become *The Prison of Panic Called NOW!* Draining and depleting America's most critical resource — its people. Attempts to manage American enterprise out of this insane economic hell have driven it only deeper into the Divine Inferno of Sisyphus.

Workers and managers, rather than joining forces to attack the problem, too frequently have chosen instead to declare war on each other. . . with no one seeming to understand what is happening or why. Meanwhile, Europe and Japan 'run away with the store.'

What is wrong is that *entropy* has set in. Entropy, the Second Law of Thermodynamics, is what Einstein called "the premier law of science." *The Law of Entropy* states that energy can be changed in only one direction, from available to unavailable, from usable to unusable, from order to chaos. Entropy, then, is the *Law of Limits* (i.e., everything created eventually dies).

Paradoxically, out of chaos comes order, creativity, growth and development. . . a new level of consciousness. As Ernest Becker reminds us in *The Birth and Death of Meaning* (1971), when what we think no longer serves us, meaning must die to give birth to new meaning and a more valid culture.

You can liken the conscious/unconscious model to an iceberg.

To experience breakthrough or to surface some of these true motivators the worker must experience pain (discomfort). Also, management must decode what people say to what they mean. For example, "pay" is at issue when the person's self-esteem, sense of worth is on the line.

Despite this, man tends to create, out of freedom, *The Prison of Panic Called NOW!* The *Pathology of Normalcy* stubbornly maintains the status quo. . . when it is clearly destroying us. This is demonstrated each time management imposes its fiction on a problem, and thereby over-controls it.

Such behavior plunges us deeper into a 'hell' for which the 'only way out' is to deal with the pain and risk of *new experience.* Being aware and understanding of reality demands 'growing up' — demands reaching a higher level of consciousness. This once moved me to write:

"America is dead! Long live America! . . .

On the eve of our 200th birthday, we have been shocked awake from our illusory dream. We have discovered belatedly that success is in the mind and not the body politic; that being Numero Uno is reaching after a child's fantasy; that progress carries the seeds of its own destruction. . . America remains like a child. And like a child, the focus of America's existence has always been on becoming, rather than on being; on the competitive drive, rather than on cooperation; on the illusion of progress, rather than on reality . . . But alas! Thanks to a decade of corrupt and incompetent leadership, the wasting of our natural resources, the impatience of youth and discriminated minorities, the dream has died. . . . And in doing so . . . we have embraced despair . . . despair is the only cure for illusion. Without despair. . . we will not grow up. Thus, on the eve of our 200th birthday, we are in a mourning period for our cherished illusions and protected fantasies. . . In the end, time runs out on a nation's adolescence. The youth must die to give birth to the man. That is why I proclaim, America is dead! Long live America!" [3]

The *American Century* is over, and the culture that made it so is dying. The sooner it is replaced, the better.

Cultures, be they societal or organizational, begin with the confidence of shared values and the infrastructures that support them. But once established, cultures irrevocably move in the direction of random chaos and waste. Waste can be defined as dissipated energy. Cultures inevitably die, but out of their ashes comes new life, as surely as the seed must 'die' to give birth to the flower's bloom. America is in the throes of this imprisoning dilemma:

- *While most Americans appear economically well off, their standard of living is declining rapidly.*
- *There is little sense of this, however, because economic survival remains a phantom that is not felt.*
- *Therefore, the dying status quo is resolutely maintained.*

Put tersely, America's prosperity is false, and the bills are coming due. The citadel of 'the illusion of normalcy' is the organization, which is decaying from the inside out.

Economist Robert Heilbronn finds America not only losing ground to Europe and Japan economically, but losing ground with respect to America's capacities as a society. What he sees as impoverishing America is "the inadequacy of our infrastructure, the public underpinnings without which a society cannot be healthy or an economy prosperous." [4]

Following WWII, spending on the infrastructure absorbed 6.9 percent of the nonmilitary federal budget. This share has declined ever since, plummeting to about one percent today. For this neglect, it will now cost (1985 dollars):

$50 billion to repair the nation's 240,000 bridges

$315 billion to repair our highways

$25 billion to modernize air traffic control

$20 billion for public housing

Inestimable billions for water supply and waste treatment facilities. These totals include only hard investments.

The 'soft' portion of our infrastructure — especially public education — is also badly neglected. Spending on elementary and secondary education reached 4.4 percent of G.N.P. in the 1970s and fell by ten percent during the past decade. This is import ant because the quality of our labor force is deteriorating rapidly, both at the bottom and at the top. . . and thus is a major reason we are falling behind.

This has happened, Heilbroner insists, because we have been unwilling to impose taxes on income, consumption, or even sin to pay for public improvements. Consider this against the fact that Sweden's 1985 tax structure was 51 percent of its Gross National Product (GNP), Germany's and Great Britain's were both 38 percent, while ours was only 29 percent. Among advanced industrial societies, only Japan's was lower at 28 percent. [5]

Additionally, *fear* of deficits — and the Russians — has immobilized us. While military spending more than doubled between 1980 and 1989 ($ 143 to $300 billion), and the deficit continued to climb, Heilbroner argues that the public has been misinformed. Without new taxes, we could pay for improvements to the infrastructure by doing what Corporate America does for plants and equipment — borrow. Corporations finance by writing checks against earnings. Precisely the same avenue of finance is open to the government because investing in the infrastructure now contributes to economic growth later.

Still, the fear that deficits will bankrupt us is a built-in *state-of-mind cultural bias*, which is unlikely to change soon. And now, with 'peace breaking out all over,' much of the military budget can be redirected for infrastructure repairs. Applied to the improvement of our infrastructure, we can see a change in the quality of life, as the number of school dropout's declines, the air gets cleaner, the economy becomes more productive, and our society grows more decent. But none of this is likely if our *cultural bias* for maintaining the *Pathology of Normalcy* is not seen for what it is and dealt with accordingly.

Many organizations are obsessed with the need for *Tradition-Structure-Order-Control*. They fail to see that these obsessions keep them from responding to changing cultural and environmental demands. Likewise, they are intimidated by the ambiguous, the ambivalent, and the chaotic. They desire the madness of 'a place for everything, and everything in its place.'

The *Law of Entropy* implies that the best way to restore order is to accept the lack of it — even to embrace disorder and our resistance to it. Paradoxically, when an organization initiates a campaign to tighten control, it invariably loses it; creating, instead, islands of dissension, disorder, confusion, and mounting chaos. Such organizations are condemned to the fate of the legendary King of Corinth, Sisyphus, who rolled a heavy stone up a hill in Hades, only to have it roll back once it was near the top. . . for eternity.

An excellent illustration of this is the management of one organization of 4000 professional/technical employees where 'many things are changing, and nothing is changing at all':

The *Total Quality Management* (TQM) theme is promoted. . . but because the organization's cultural bias is being ignored — it's more a buzz word than a commitment to quality, and the operation is going pell-mell into the *Madhouse of the Mad Monarchs*. This is not at all where it intended to go — which was into continuous quality improvement.

Were this 1945 rather than the 1990s, what management decreed might have been achieved. . . but not today. Work must be conducted on terms that are responsive to the needs and requirements of professionals, or it becomes counterfeit.

Actually, *TQM* fits the requirements of professionals when it is implemented appropriately.

- *TQM requires a process orientation, which means shifting the focus from an obsession with results to a concentration on processes — — Results orientation reflects a commitment to linear objectives and standards, quantitative measurements, Management by Objectives (MBOs) through operational Goals and Objectives (G&Os), close attention to the pecking order, with tight tops-down controls. . . all of this captured in explicit action items and neat, clean schematic flow charts. Clearly, it is management's game plan. . . and so nothing happens as charted.*
- *Process orientation depends on subjective analysis of processes, which represents a consensus on what constitutes qualitative standards. The integrity of the operation is also an indication of mutual respect, trust, competence, and shared values and attitudes about work. . . a common culture in a teaming environment. As self-management work teams, workers respond quickly to process change requirements because their*

focus is on the process, not on reports; on making timely decisions, not on waiting for approval.

- *Result orientation demands a lot of checking and waiting; process orientation requires trust and some risk taking.*
- *Structure is endemic to results orientation; adhocracy is standard operating procedure for processes.*
- *Order, control, conformity, and discipline are orchestrated to realize results; creative exchange and natural enthusiasm promote processes.*

Not surprising, given this disparity in orientation, tradition won out, and TQM was established 'like any other program.' When it failed to take hold, management looked for a reason for the failure, and found it in an old reliable, performance appraisal. So, a new comprehensive *Performance Appraisal System* was inaugurated in which 350 managers and supervisors spent literally tens of thousands of hours on the effort. Of course, this took managers and their people away from productive work.

As mentioned earlier, a typical work force finds 15 percent each of high and low performers, with the remaining 70 percent falling in the middle zone. Of the 4000 employees, then, roughly 600 (15 percent) should be having some performance problems. But in this case, only six employees were declining in rating, and four were designated as 'needing improvement.'

This was clearly an exercise, not a viable process; an end in itself, not a means to an end. Supervisors and workers participated in the charade because they were told to, not because they were convinced it was a vehicle for establishing improved performance. Getting workers and managers to talk to each other is worthwhile, but when that discourse becomes one-directional, it is a mocking expression of organizational ineptitude.

With three-fifths of the work force currently 'professional,' and moving rapidly to 90 percent by the end of this century, the autocratic *'Parent/Child'* management/worker relationship is no longer appropriate. The interdependent *'Adult/Adult'* relationship is obviously more suitable.

Workers are no longer expendable, interchangeable parts. Indeed, by the year 2000, it is estimated that the critical shortage of knowledge workers will number as high as 16 million. These highly skilled professionals are indispensable to organizational success. The organization cannot survive without them. They have the power. They are in control. But, considering how they have been, and are, treated, the question is: *Do they have the will to work?* It's a matter of entropy.

Author Jeremy Rifkin insists that entropy must be felt as well as understood. This is especially true considering its apparent paradoxes:

- *The more we attempt to improve order, the more chaos we create. Conversely, the more we accept chaos, and the creative verve flowing from it, the more quickly order is established.*
- *The more rigidly formal the structure of an organization, the less efficient; the more flexible the design, the more efficient it is. Informal processes, which dominate organizational culture, thrive in a flexible climate.*

The most dangerous course is the safest course. A situation that does not permit risk and failure is a setup for contrived success. [6]

The *Law of Entropy* implies that the organization cannot survive if it continues to ignore the reality of its situation. Yet, as most organizations decline and slip into chaos, denial becomes a pressing factor. Many prefer to cling to the fiction of their situation than to deal with its reality. Ironically, this fiction can be promoted by resorting to *technological overkill. . .* that is, an inordinate dependence on robotics/computers, or creative finance, such as (but not limited to) capital manipulation, mergers, acquisitions, and leveraged buy-outs.

These 'solutions' actually accelerate an organization's mad dash to social disruption, discontinuity and, finally, maximum entropy, which is *organizational death*. This is when *incipient catastrophe* occurs.

The Changing Cultural Landscape of Work

For the past quarter century, the word, productivity, has been etched into the American psyche, reminding us of our decline. Since 1962, when the Japanese launched their full scale assault on American markets, three American citizens born in the first decade of this century have managed to change the world: W. Edwards Deming, J. M. Juran, and Peter F. Drucker. Largely due to their synergistic efforts, war has changed from military to economic confrontation.

Dr. Juran came to America from Rumania as a small boy, and Drucker from Austria. Only Deming was American born. To put their contributions in perspective, Juran and Deming worked at Western Electric's Hawthorne Works in Chicago, when the famous *Hawthorne Study* was conducted. Moreover, they worked with Frederick Winslow Taylor, author of *Scientific Management* (1911), and inventor of the assembly line and mass production.

Meanwhile, Drucker — the youngster of the trio — became an early student of management and the organization. He is, perhaps, the premier social thinker of our times. What is most remarkable about these men is that, as I write these words, they are still publishing books, consulting, giving lectures, and feeding their ideas to this, *The Age of Octogenarians*.

The problem is, America was late in 'hearing' the message of these distinguished Americans, who have had more impact on the rest of the world than on their own country. The Asian societies — particularly Japan, Singapore, and Korea — offered these men a cultural climate conducive to their ideas. Why? Because these societies create institutions to perform basic cultural tasks, including ensuring that nearly all their children are well educated; keeping most families intact, systematically diverting money from consumption to investment, and attracting high talent into government service — all of the things we have failed to do and which are critical to organizational success.

In *The End of the American Century* (1990), Steven Schlossstein finds that, compared to most East Asian societies, the United States has a disproportionate number of children who never learn the basic skills of modern life. Schlossstein considers these children as America's greatest competitive weakness.

On the other hand, academic standards in the best American colleges, and the schools that feed them, are above those of their Japanese, Korean, and Singapore counterparts. But putting pressure on these schools won't reverse the trend. It is the pervasive culture which makes the difference.

Most scholars of Asian education emphasize that their elementary and high schools succeed precisely because the worst graduates are so well educated. Applying that lesson to the ghetto schools in America doesn't work because, as professional-class consciousness has risen, the sense of the public good has declined. Once again the values of the *common good* have been superseded by *personhood*.

REFERENCES

(1) Source: Kathy M. Kristof, *The Los Angeles Times* reported in *The Tampa Tribune-Times*, May 27, 1990.

(2) Susan C. Faludi, *The Wall Street Journal* as reported in the *St. Petersburg Times*, May 27, 1990.

(3) Fisher, James R., Jr., "America Is Dead: A Time To Begin," *St. Petersburg Evening Independent*, January 1, 1976.

(4) Heilbroner, Robert, "Seize the Day," *The New York Review*, February 15, 1990, pp. 30-31.

(5) 1988 U.S. Statistical Abstract Table No. 1397, 1985.

(6) Rifkin, Jeremy, *Entropy: A New World View* (New York: Bantam Books, 1981).

So What!

"Transformation of American style of management is not a job of reconstruction, nor revision. It requires a whole new structure, from foundation, upward. . . Transformation must take place with directed effort . . . Failure of management to plan for the future and to foresee problems has brought waste of manpower, of materials, and of machine-time, all of which raises the manufacturer's cost and that the purchaser must pay . . . The inevitable result is loss of market, loss of market begets unemployment. Performance of management should be measured by potential to stay in business. . . not by the quarterly dividend.

"It is no longer socially acceptable to dump employees onto the heap of unemployed. Loss of market, and resulting unemployment, are not foreordained. They are not inevitable. They are man-made.

"The basic cause of sickness in American industry and resulting unemployment is failure of top management to manage."

W. Edwards Deming (1900-1993), American statistician

It is tasteless, colorless, and odorless, and neither felt nor feared. But it is poison nevertheless. It has been attacking the vital organs of the American organization and making it quite ill. While the poison's cumulative effects have not yet killed the organization, it has severely limited the organization's ability to see itself clearly — much less deal with the challenges ahead. And the cause?

The American organization can be observed to be 'sucking up its own exhaust fumes.' Were it more a conscious act, it undoubtedly would be considered an attempt at suicide. In any case, should the toxicity persist and the will to survive as a first-rate nation continue to fade, the point is moot. A more pressing concern is this:

Does the American organization, as is, have the capacity to survive if it rediscovers its will?

Although this book is a diagnosis of the disease rather that a prognosis of the cure, an analysis rather than a solution, its theme has a bearing on our course of action. Organizations differ little one from the other. Here is my analysis of this cultural landscape:

The need for a new organizational paradigm

The failure to make this shift produces anxiety, frustration, and anger among professional workers especially, who have little sense of the shift in power within the organization. . . from management to them.

The current situation suggests that organizational control may collapse at any moment and give rise to dramatic changes. When, or in what form, that may occur is impossible to predict. The most optimistic possibility is an integration of management and working professionals into a common leadership guild.

What is forcing this 'final solution' on the American organization are the echoing footsteps of economic competition largely from Europe and the Far East, but also from the waning markets in North and South America. As America's market share shrinks and many leading American industries are threatened with extinction, there is disheartening evidence that, while competition is 'eating our lunch,' many Americans continue to presume it is free.

The combination of a 'free lunch' mentality that rides on repressed management 'panic' has resulted in the American organization more resembling a madhouse than anything else. Six silent organization killers are considered in depth, noting that the organization, oblivious to these threats, continues to operate essentially as it has since WWII, with, at best, only cosmetic changes. You would think, from this madcap behavior, that America's WWII victories were only yesterday and that the world was still 'America's oyster.' Clearly, due to the persistent poison of euphoria, there is little sense of impending danger. . . The war changed our values and relationships to each other, as well as to the rest of the world. We had markets, products and profits we never dreamed of — a standard of living beyond our most optimistic desires. We went off to college, got good jobs, and became owners (not loaners). We lived well, and all was right, for 'God was on our side.' We helped rebuild Europe and Japan, and felt good about ourselves. When those we benefited started to pressure our markets, to become self-sufficient, and to resent our intrusion, we smiled at their resurgence and continued to feel good about ourselves. After all, America made it happen! We even bought their quality products, while reflecting that the price was right 'because they work cheap; Americans don't.

Not to worry — we went off to war in Korea to police the world and to Vietnam to show we were still made of the 'right stuff.' We put a man on the moon, took most of the Nobel Prizes in Science and Technology, and continued to feel good about ourselves.

So the balance of trade was in bad shape, so the national debt was 'out of control'; so our basic industries in steel, coal, paper, petroleum, and textiles were in trouble; so hundreds of thousands of workers in key industries would never get their jobs back; so our streams were becoming increasingly polluted, and our air threatened to be unbreathable; so our bridges, highways and railroads were crumbling; so our kids went to school, got their diplomas, and still couldn't read or write; so the rate of productivity per worker was falling precipitously; so American manufacturing was being called a 'hollow industry,' with more and more manufacturing done for American producers abroad; so what!

We were Americans, and everybody wants to be an American — the envy of the world — and that is that!

There is no sense of urgency, only panic. Panic denotes hysteria: urgency denotes seriousness. Panic finds the organization pressing and management fresh out of ideas. The workers — now, for the most part, college-trained thinkers, no longer factory fodder — aren't buying into the panic. Worse yet, they aren't buying into the urgency nor into anything else. They are off playing *Corporate Mad Monarch games* with reckless abandon, deriving their satisfaction mainly outside of work. They go to work to support their lifestyle, to complain, and to socialize; too busy themselves, with non-thinking, to do non-doing of non-things. . . not to make a contribution.

Meanwhile, productivity rates continue to fall through the floor, with the situation growing more and more precarious by the moment. It's time for action — a time to deal with the *American Dilemma* differently.

Enter Human Resources with its "gosh-do-we-care-about-our-employees" hyperbole — from employee benefits to executive bonuses — which has little relationship to purposeful performance. Deja vu. The workers (now mostly professionals) retreat into a modern form of post-World War I isolationism, cut off from the world and the reality of their own experiences by a potpourri of ill-conceived humanistic interventions.

So what has happened to the *Culture of Contribution* and purposeful performance? They have been displaced by the cultures of *Comfort* and *Complacency*, where work is either an accidental or counterfeit activity.

Yes, the American organization is 'sucking up its own exhaust' and getting sicker by the minute. At a time when it should be thinking most clearly, it can hardly think at all. About the best it can manage is to go through the motions, and slowly, at that. That is the very reason it is imperative to know where it is, how it got there, and what it needs to do to get out of the crippling zones of comfort and complacency.

When the Simple is made to be Complex

There is a difficult, protracted struggle ahead for the American organization. The process of purposeful performance is a simple one, but the requirements to 'make it happen,' unfortunately, are not equally simple.

Mere reform, as W. Edwards Deming reminds us in *Out of the Crisis* (1986), will not be enough; nor will 'aspirin management.' The American organization must be rebuilt from scratch, with different thinking and values, a more appropriate infrastructure, new leadership, and a new sense of what constitutes purposeful performance.

The organization must change the way it sees reality, it must also abandon the way it thinks and processes information for the way it thinks and what it sees are a significant part of the problem.

The organization must recognize and accept the significant change in American values. Nobody ever did anything just because they knew. Knowledge must he operationalized. To operationalize knowledge it must be felt. Values are 'felt knowledge,' which shape the cultural bias of organization. Cultural bias is the mechanism of organization that governs behavior. The organization tends to resist change, preferring to sustain the values that it knows and understands — that it feels. To ignore this fact spells doom for organizational change. The sooner this is understood the sooner the change process can begin. Value change is a slow, painful process for everyone, and there are no short cuts or negotiable detours. Cosmetic changes — saying 'change has occurred' — do not make it so. Time, patience, and experience are its only determiners.

The structure of organization is pathetically out-of-date with the relationship of managers to workers, and to all work itself, structured for another time and place. The organization must be formatted to reflect changing values, the changing skill mix of employees, the changing technologies of organization and — most directly of all — the changing requirements of work. As matters now stand, the organization is lethargic and unresponsive to ever changing and accelerating demands. . . precisely because it stubbornly insists on substituting activity for action, deliberation for decision-making, comfort for contribution, quantity for quality, and panic for patience.

Leadership of the organization is wrong — all wrong for the requirements of the organization and its people. Real leadership is essentially the 'seeing where the organization is and where it is going,' and the 'serving of all of its people,' starting with its first customers — the employees below it in the hierarchy. Not only is the professional work force a hedge against the pusillanimity of leadership — it appears the only source of light in this otherwise bleak picture. . . yet, it continues to be ignored. On the other hand, the professional work force is lost in its own confusion — wailing at the system for not showing it 'the way,' while continuing to 'suck up' its own exhaust fumes.

The nature of what constitutes 'real work,' and how it is to be conducted, has all been changed — but has been essentially ignored. Real work is much less manual, much more mental; much less tied to activities and contributions of the individual, more to synergistic processes that involve teaming or group contributions; much more self-actualizing than conforming to arbitrary standards. [1]

In the absence of a foundation-in-understanding of these implications, workers and managers reared on precise worker/manager roles do not appreciate the shift in emphasis and power.

Even the teaming concept is confusing. The fluid dynamics of operations in the current climate call for behavior more akin to that of a basketball team than of a baseball team:

A baseball team is nine individual contributors who happen to be on the same team. Baseball is called 'the Great American Pastime' because it is obsessively and statistically driven by individual effort, with little interdependent behavior required. Cricket is a similar game for the British, and we know where they stand in the world of commerce. [2]

A basketball team, on the other hand, is five interdependent players irrevocably involved in the fluid dynamics of a process in which success depends on them working together. Moreover, basketball is intuitively and situational driven, while baseball is cognitively and strategically driven. Notice, too, that the leader in basketball is called a 'coach,' a facilitator of the action; while in baseball, he is called a 'manager,' or a 'caller of the shots.' Now let's examine these points in more detail.

Thinking Differently On Purpose

Perhaps the only way to realize purposeful performance is not to seek it but to create it.

The rationally trained mind might have trouble with that statement. "Give me the facts," it would demand, "and leave out the B.S." After nearly a century of 'facts' cascading into the fathomless void of American enterprise, you would think Americans would challenge this philosophy.

But the American culture is deeply impaled in a deterministic approach, or the *'Blitzkrieg School of Problem Solving'* (i.e., exercise an all-out assault on 'it,' and spare no money or resource to claim a victorious solution). Being only comfortable with nitty-gritty deductive reasoning, we expect the effect to follow the cause:

- *"Find the cause for AIDS,"* so the logic goes, *"and we will eliminate the effect."*
- *"Find the cause for America's industrial collapse, and we will once again regain world dominance of the marketplace."*

Rest assured, medical science will spend most of its resources on trying to isolate the AIDS virus through research, and then develop a miraculous vaccine to prevent it. Yet, the cause does not lie exclusively in the subatomic world of microbiology, but also in the social psychology of human relationships. The disease lies as much in the mind as it does the body (the two are part of the same whole, but we treat them as strangers to each other).

Ironically, once the AIDS virus is identified, and the miraculous vaccine applied, the virus is likely to mutate to a new, more impervious strain. . . and thus the vicious cycle continues. Only the medicine of behavioral change will complete the miracle.

Analytical thinking is the religion of the modern mind. It is the wholehearted push in the direction of 'Artificial Intelligence.' 'AI' enthusiasts hold that all human thinking, whether conscious or unconscious, is merely the enacting of some complicated computation. There is no room for the mystical or the spiritual. Indeed, the theology of that religion is *logical positivism*, the dominant philosophy of the 20th Century American mind. [3]

106

There is a dogmatic belief that logical positivism (also known as *scientific empiricism*), can solve anything. This fuels the belief, "Don't worry about pollution — science will come up with the answer one day."

Medical science, for instance, has created the most sophisticated toys to reinforce this belief of infallibility, including 'CAT scanners that direct X-ray beams through the skull from multiple directions; computerized blood analyzers with impressive printouts; cardiac pacemakers; renal dialysis machines; and on and on.

It is clear that 'Nuclear Man' has gambled almost everything on a mechanistic, quantitative, mathematical approach to his dilemma. This has been done in the belief that the 'Heart of God' resides in science; that man can ravage his environment in wanton glee, or abandon his mind, body and spirit to senseless pleasure, and 'Science as Superman' will be there at the most critical moment to rescue his mortal body (if not his immortal soul) from his reckless behavior.

What is paradoxical about science is that the cleaner the methodology, the more abstruse the ramifications. Take nuclear power plants. How dangerous is the waste that's being created by this so-called 'cheap' energy source? We haven't the foggiest notion! Barges of nuclear waste roam the American continent in the night like 'vessels without a country,' looking for a haven in which to dump their dubious product. Scientific reassurances notwithstanding, each reactor annually produces tons of radioactive waste that remains toxic for thousands of years. With no truly safe way to dispose of this waste, it represents a horror story beyond comprehension.

Then, does 'logical positivism' suggest possibly abandoning this approach in favor of another energy source? Of course not. It concentrates instead on solving an unsolvable problem, doing what we all do in our rational approach to problem solving — ignoring the real problem (i.e., safe disposal of radioactive waste), and concentrating on a solution to a problem it believes can he solved (e.g., more efficient production of nuclear energy).

What we need is an energy source that is renewable, economical, efficient, and safe. Eureka. . . we have it! Solar energy meets all these criteria. The main obstacle is not technical, but political. [4] The shift from nonrenewable to renewable resources involves dealing with a stubborn *cultural bias* (i.e., of compelling oil companies to give up their dominant role in the world economy and to change their function). So, it is not a rational, but an irrational dilemma related to anachronistic power; and the biases of that power.

Obviously, logical positivism would hold no store with this assessment. It would produce the litany of technical and scientific achievements over the last century, failing to mention that science created most of the problems it ultimately solved.

Scientific empiricism arrogantly denies the spiritual component of man. It holds the view that generalizations can be held valid only when tested by objective techniques, and verified by sense experience. Empiricism is based on the belief that only that which can be experienced by the senses is real, and that the final test of scientific truth is the experience of the senses. It is a logical progression from the works of three men, René Descartes (1596-1650), Isaac Newton (1642-1727), and Ludwig Wittgenstein (1889-1951):

- *René Descartes' Cartesian Philosophy formed the basis for the division between the mind and the body; between the spiritual and material worlds of man.*
- *Isaac Newton, better known for Newtonian physics, also formed Newtonian psychology, which described man as essentially a machine personified by a well-made clock.*
- *Ludwig Wittgenstein, and his dedication to empirical observation, believed man could maintain a value-free and scientific perspective.*

Each man contributed to building a more persuasive argument for the division of man:

- *Descartes between behaving (material world) and believing (spiritual world);*
- *Newton between thinking and feeling;*
- *Wittgenstein between subjective and objective points of view.*

What is fundamental to purposeful performance in the workplace is the recognition that:

- *We are both subject and object;*
- *We are never 'value free';*
- *Thinking and feeling are part of the same process;*
- *We live in a world that is both abstract and concrete. Both are parts of the same essential whole. To deny the one is to deny the other.*

Difficult as it might be to grasp, purposeful performance grew out of chaos and confusion — not out of order and consistency. To strain for order, then, is to embrace disorder.

Purposeful performance is a dynamic process that may reflect chaos from a segmental view, but order from a holistic one. That is because we are an integration of these diverse parts:

- *Mind-body-spirit;*
- *Subject-observer-object;*
- *Thinking feeling-behaving.*

So, to deny one part at the expense of another is to intensify the conflict within us and between us. Conversely, to accept this diversity, and to work toward full integration, is to establish wholeness, which is identity.

Identity is the beginning of understanding and accepting ourselves as we are. And, therefore, making us ready to accept and understand others as we find them. This — looking at the individual as a system — is what J. Krishnamurti meant when he wrote in *You Are the World* (1972):

"In oneself lies the whole world, and if you know how to look and learn, then the door is there and the key is in your hand. Nobody on earth can give you either that key or the door to open, except you."

The current popular jargon — especially in the business and professional world — is 'the systems approach.' This holistic view is consistent with identity and purposeful performance. Systems researcher Russell Ackoff puts it poetically:

"If you take a system apart to identify its components, and then operate those components in such a way that every component behaves as well as it possibly can, there is one thing of which you can be sure. The system as a whole will not behave as well as it can. Now that is counter-intuitive to Machine Age thinking, but it is absolutely essential to 'systems thinking.' The corollary to this is that if you have a system that is behaving as well as it can, none of its parts will be."

These new ways of thinking have tremendous implications for the organization. When a department is trying to outperform all others, it means it is not supporting other departments as well as it might. Or, it is doing well at the expense of other departments. Likewise, when an individual is not accepted on the basis of his or her peculiar characteristics, attributes, and talents — instead is force-fitted into a job — the results will surely be discouraging for all.

A systems perspective requires recognition and acceptance of differences — different skills, different attitudes, different dispositions, and different personalities. The current climate in the American culture, however, has room for words that denote 'differences,' but little room for the requisite behaviors.

109

The organization continues to 'kill' itself trying to make workers fit the job and its preordained expectations. The more the organization fails in this obstinate effort, the harder it tries to make it so. Linear logic is its guide, and no one seems to notice that, like a horse with blinders, it plows directly ahead — missing opportunity after opportunity with employees who have a range far beyond its expectations. And, once again, everybody loses.

Putting Our Macho Complex to Rest

We must rethink much of what we have been taught to think and blend the possibilities of the Western mind with Eastern maturity. This involves marrying the left brain with the right brain and uniting our ability to think rationally with our ability to think intuitively. The left brain is the home of technology; of science and industry. The right brain is the home of art, music, and religion — where the symphony of the human intellect paints the landscape of life.

The left brain resists the intuitive hunch because it is not founded on facts. The right brain resists the left brain because there is little display of sensitivity. It is a war, more damaging and ubiquitously threatening than the destructive power of thermonuclear weapons. It is a war that's been waged since the dawn of man, continuing now in the afternoon of his experience.

We know so much about so many things, and so little about ourselves. We establish societies and nationalities; create languages and cultures to support them; and then we maintain our splendid isolation from ourselves and our reality.

What is germane to this discussion is that the *Religion of Technology* has created a new dogma that forms a *cultural* barrier between the left and right brain, the worker and work, the worker and manager, and the Western and Eastern world of thinking.

Workers and managers are struggling with each other. The results today are lower productivity and less purposeful performance in America; tomorrow, in the world. Now, with the globalization of economic interdependence, it has grave con sequences. Find the answer to individuals and their relationships with themselves, with each other, and with their respective organizations, and you are well on your way to finding the answer the whole world is seeking.

The left brain is associated with the male; the right brain with the female. In human biology, of course, masculine and feminine characteristics exist in everyone. Sex roles are learned, not genetic behavior. Nobody has a predisposition to act 'male' or 'female.' Yet, all men are supposed to be

110

masculine, and all women, feminine. This has meant giving men leading roles and most of society's privileges.

The rational mind is linear, focused, and analytical. It belongs to the realm of the intellect, whose function is to discriminate, measure, and categorize. Thus, rational knowledge tends to be fragmented.

The intuitive mind is based on direct, nonintellectual experience of reality arising out of a state of expanding awareness. Intuitive knowledge tends to be synthesizing, holistic, and nonlinear. Holistic, incidentally, is from the Greek 'holos,' whole, and refers to an understanding of reality in terms of integrated wholes whose properties cannot be reduced to those of smaller units.

America's traditional expectations of men and women

EXPECTATIONS OF MEN	EXPECTATIONS OF WOMEN
Active and Productive	Passive and Receptive
Rational and Cognitive	Irrational and Intuitive
Aggressive, Competitive, even Ruthless	Responsive, Cooperative, and Consolidating
Conscious of Themselves	Conscious of Environment
'Thinkers'	'Feelers'
Inclined toward Science	Inclined toward Mysticism

Looking at the list of opposites, it is easy to see that American society consistently favors the 'masculine brain' over the 'feminine brain,' rational knowledge over intuitive wisdom, science over religion, competition over cooperation, exploitation of natural resources over conservation, etc. This emphasis, well-supported by our paternalistic system of management, has led to a profound cultural imbalance. This imbalance lies at the root of our current crisis — an imbalance in thoughts and feelings, values and attitudes, and our social and political structures.

In the Eastern view, there appears two kinds of activity:

- *Activity in harmony with nature;*
- *Activity against the natural flow of things.*

111

The Eastern mind prefers the former to the latter. The Western mind, on the other hand, has been determined to conquer and exploit nature; to make nature conform to the requirements of man. A recurring misconception is that the Eastern viewpoint is, therefore, passive, while the Western view is active. This is misleading.

LEFT BRAIN	RIGHT BRAIN
Masculine	Feminine
Demanding	Contracting
Aggressive	Responsive
Competitive	Cooperative
Rational and Cognitive	Intuitive and Affective
Analytical	Synthesizing
Concrete Orientation	Conceptual Orientation

A Framework of Reference

Exploring American Cultural Values and Attitudes

The Eastern view seeks a balance between man's needs and the requirements of nature. Conversely, the Western view sees us retreating from polar opposites, rather than integrating them into a cohesive strategy. For example, the American culture takes pride in being scientific. Our time is referred to as the 'Scientific Age.' Science is used to making nature submit to its will. Clearly, nature has been seen as the enemy, and all the guns of science have been trained on this adversary.

Consequently, the natural has all but disappeared in our foods, with chemical additives and preservatives robbing us of Nature's natural flavors. There is no telling how much damage science has done to ecosystems and their ecological balance. Incidentally, in Europe they still use natural fertilizers and refrain from adding chemical preservatives to milk and bread. This means the shelf life of these products is nil. And you must shop daily for these staples. The taste, of course, is well worth the inconvenience.

Unquestionably, America is dominated by rational thinking and scientific knowledge (which is frequently considered the only acceptable knowledge). This 'Macho Complex' finds little room for intuitive knowledge, or awareness, which is just as valid and reliable. Generally speaking, intuitive knowledge is not recognized at all. We are mesmerized by the near magic powers of science, unwilling or unable to consider the costs of this adulation. This attitude is widespread, pervading our educational system as well as our commercial, social, religious, and political institutions.

Since the celebrated statement of Descartes, "I think, therefore, I am," we have, as Fritjof Capra puts it, "retreated into our minds, forgotten how to think with our bodies, how to use them as agents of knowing." [5] In so retreating, we have cut ourselves off from the natural environment; have forgotten how to commune with nature and cooperate with man.

What left-brain 'Macho' dominance has meant is that virtually everything gets thrown out of proportion. A simple example is the idea that 'more is better,' or if something is good, more of the same will be even better.

As another example, we have expected intellectual power, scientific knowledge, and technological skill to go hand-in-hand with wisdom, ethics, and spiritual well-being. But you can see from this discussion that there is great disparity between wisdom and knowledge. As noted here, the vast majority of our leaders — whatever their profession or discipline — are close to bankrupt when it comes to wisdom and ethics. And this has nothing to do with how knowledgeable they might be.

From yet another perspective, it is unfortunate so much emphasis is placed upon sexual preference. When you think of how little of our actual life is sexual, and how much more our preoccupation with it dominates our thinking, one can puzzle at this misdirected energy.

This obsessive compulsive behavior has made a major industry of a fantasy product, sex. As the preeminent sociologist, Pitirim Sorokin, has written, it is when we are least sexual that we are the most preoccupied with sex. [6]

People of a particularly gentle persuasion, for example, are frequently well acquainted with 'right brain' thinking. They have a different perspective (and perception) than their 'Macho Male' brothers. They have made meaningful contact with their feminine nature, which we all possess, and have learned from it. They often demonstrate a subtle awareness of things cultural, showing a natural affinity for the aesthetic, from poetry to painting, from drama to didactics. And we desperately need minds of this kind in the boardrooms across America, as well as in every other walk of professional life. We need poetry in commerce, government, and industry. Engineers, economists, and political scientists have done about all the damage we can stand. . . perhaps more than we can absorb. [7]

America's one-sided, one-dimensional progress has reached the alarming stage. This situation is so contradictory that it borders on insanity:

- *We can control a soft landing of a space craft on distant planets, but we cannot control the polluting fumes emanating from our automobiles and factories.*
- *We propose Utopian communities in gigantic space colonies, but we cannot manage crime in our cities.*
- *The business community salutes the terrific growth of the pet food and cosmetic industries as signs of progress, but we cannot afford to feed the homeless or to provide health care for the needy.*
- *We are among the 'best educated' of Western nations in terms of per capita high school and college graduates — with arguably the best university system in the West —but fewer Americans read books, are multilingual, or are familiar with the culture or geography of other nations, much less their own. In fact, some see the American educational system as 'killing the spirit' of the American student to learn.*

Regarding the latter, noted historian Page Smith in *Killing The Spirit* (1990) leaves no doubt on the failure of America's great universities to educate. He sees these universities divided into departments which compete against each other for funds and students and speak in jargon comprehensible only within themselves, forming a modern Tower of Babel. Indeed, the problem is pervasive throughout the American culture.

Recognizing and Dealing with the Ambivalence of American Values

Some 300 years ago, America broke away from the confining shackles of European society to establish its own identity. Some 200 years ago, America produced an incredible body of men who were multidimensional and dedicated to the expression of the individual American spirit. They were not afraid to be different, not afraid to be *Outsiders*, not afraid to cultivate the inner world of expression as they sensed it.

Walt Whitman captured this spirit when he proclaimed with innocence and exuberance:

"I am larger and better than I thought. I did not know that I held so much greatness."

Yet, we bristle when someone makes such a proclamation. We think greatness is rare, whereas Whitman knew that the seeds of greatness are in all. Where are the Walt Whitmans of today? Where are the voices of *The Outsider* who march to their own drummer as did Henry David Thoreau?

Many of the giants of our republic lived in the late 18th and early 19th centuries, including John Adams, John Quincy Adams, William Cullen Bryant, Aaron Burr, John Calhoun, James Fenimore Cooper, Ralph Waldo Emerson, Benjamin Franklin, Horace Greeley, Nathanael Greene, Alexander Hamilton, Nathaniel Hawthorne, Oliver Wendell Holmes, Andrew Jackson, John Jay, Thomas Jefferson, Abraham Lincoln, James Madison, Herman Melville, James Monroe, Henry David Thoreau, George Washington, and Daniel Webster.

These men were essentially aristocrats in temperament and democrats in spirit. They had a quiet reverence for things mystical, but a consuming passion for living life to the fullest. America was young and had not yet succumbed to debilitating mediocrity. Nor had it been consumed with self-conscious self-approval. To Henry David Thoreau's *Walden* (1854) from Ralph Waldo Emerson's *Self Reliance & Other Essays* (1844), there was a spiritual comfort with nature and man in *'Transcendentalism.'*

Transcendentalism flourished briefly in New England during the first half of the 19th Century. Never a systematic philosophy, it held the romantic view that individual intuition was the highest form of knowledge and that God was immanent in nature. Much influenced by Eastern religious teachings, many of these early American thinkers and doers held a mystical belief in individualism and in harmony of all things in the life of nature. In a word, the greatness that these early Americans displayed was that of 'balance.'

It was during this same period that Alexis de Tocqueville captured this rich nuance in his perceptive study *Democracy in America* (1835). He outlined in this classic of political literature the advantages and shortcomings of democratic political and social systems. Tocqueville saw values and hazards of the democratic way of life that are still pertinent today.

This found journalist Richard Reeves reliving Tocqueville's journey in his book, *American Journey: Traveling with Tocqueville in Search of America* (1982). Reeves reaffirmed how right Tocqueville was when he could see the nation moving away from greatness toward comfortable indifference. Put otherwise, a case can be made that America has been trading off its early greatness for the past 150 years. [8]

Look at any organization in America, and you will find the same arid landscapes Tocqueville warned could develop due to laxity under an indifferent democracy. Education is an excellent example:

Even at our most prestigious (and expensive) universities, Page Smith proclaims in *Killing the Spirit* (1990), there is not an opportunity for a decent education because teachers are not personally involved with their students. Students get instruction, not education, in the form of 'information transfers', 'communication techniques,' or some other impersonal and antiseptic phrases to cover 'non-teaching teaching' to facilitate 'non-learning learning.'

Interaction between professors and students is minimal or non-existent because professors are preoccupied with scholarly research and publication. Career minded faculty, Smith notes, cannot afford to spend time with students. They must 'publish or perish' by having their 'scholarly' tomes appear in the 'right' journals. This helps them win promotion and tenure, which means they stay employed.

The results are what Smith calls a 'cult of dullness,' in which clear writing and inspired lecturing are deviant and suspicious behaviors. Nothing is done to challenge the system — the prevailing mode of thinking or 'doing.' This, incidentally, fits nicely into the industrial model of 'non-thinking to do non-doing of non-thing things,' because what these professors have to say, according to Smith, amounts to practically nothing at all.

This has been the curse of such acclaimed American writers as John Updike. Granville Hick's *Saturday Review of Literature* critiques of Updike's early books were laced with the constant lament, "he writes like an angel, if only he had something to say."

'Style has come to eclipse substance; impression to take precedence over making a difference.' Smith calls this 'scientism,' a devotion to the scientific approach to all fields of study, including the humanities. This has driven the spiritual values out of our universities, leaving an arid climate like the desert.

This dedication to research would be defensible, Smith admits, if it involved purposeful performance in the sense that the product of the research had some value to the classroom or to the greater society. "The vast majority," he writes, "is mediocre, expensive and unnecessary."

And who pays for all this 'non-teaching teaching and non-learning learning'?

At first blush, you might say it is borne by the parents who make the sacrifices for their sons and daughters — now as high as $100,000 for a four-year degree. However, it is our American heritage that ultimately pays for this 'busy-work,' as will the future generations of American society.

What Tocqueville predicted about America 150 years ago has largely come to pass. What will it be like 150 years hence?

Cut across American society, from the academic community to the government, from industry to commerce, from religious institutions to charitable organizations, and without exception, you will find there is no place for greatness to exist, or to be cultivated. These organizations appear instead to be obsessed with internal politics, which often are so vicious there is little energy left for coping, much less for excellence.

The paradox is that the only hope for America is with the rising aristocracy of professional/technical workers. The burgeoning professional class must take hold of its power and celebrate differences and diversity as 'aristocrats in temperament and democrats in spirit.' Obviously, the traditional formula for organizational continuity and succession planning will never get us there. Indeed, it has succeeded magnificently in giving relevance to the Baron Macaulay refrain:

> *Was none who would be foremost*
> *To lead such dire attack;*
> *But those behind cried "Forward!"*
> *And those before cried "Back!"*

We need leadership as we have never needed it before. We need greatness as it once existed when we were relatively new as a nation. We need changes; real changes. We need balance and humor and love and industry. We need thinking that is inter disciplinarian and holistic.

What we don't need is an organization of 'like-thinkers and-doers' who have rarely experienced an original thought, but know how to get promoted. You know the type:

- *They buy the 'company line' lock, stock, and barrel.*
- *They research the company etiquette and then teach the course.*
- *They 'get results,' and the results they get are the results expected.*
- *They epitomize the corporate value system, from the way they dress, to how they walk and talk and carry the company torch.*

- *They have the kind of family they are expected to have (preferably two-children, a boy and a girl, who are bright, good looking, and a credit to the family and company).*
- *They belong to the right religion, and they go to the right church in the right congregation, on a regular basis.*
- *They volunteer for the appropriate causes and become involved at the level expected.*
- *They live in the right neighborhood, with the right type and style of house, which has appropriate architecture and landscaping.*
- *They shop at the right stores, buying the appropriate brands of merchandise, supporting the products of customers and vendors alike.*
- *They prepare the right kinds of meals, entertain at the appropriate time excepted of them for their function and level in the organization, and with the right kind of decorum.*
- *They spend the expected number of hours at work and at home with their family. Outside of work, they pursue familiar pursuits of someone like them in their station and career.*
- *They vacation in a manner appropriate to their level of compensation and consistent with what others like them have done in the past.*
- *They are friends with their colleagues on the basis of invitation and approval.*

Men and women of this description are running America into the ground.

On the other hand, Americans of a 'different persuasion' — who live, breathe, and understand what is actually going on in the organization, and who have all the appropriate skills to do the job — would have little chance to be candidates for promotion, much less accepted members of this group if they were any of the following:

- *A 40+ year-old bachelor or spinster*
- *A confessed lesbian or homosexual*
- *Openly promiscuous*
- *Suspected to be chemically dependent*
- *An AIDS patient*
- *Too short, too fat, too tall, too thin, too old, too young, too experienced, too inexperienced, too stupid, too bright, too obsequious, too independent, too secretive, too candid, too gregarious, too reclusive, too aggressive, too passive . . . too extreme*

118

- *Openly disenchanted with company policy*
- *Openly opposed to the bureaucratic 'games'*
- *Bored with 'motherhood' pontifications of the CEO and openly expressive of that fact*
- *Too self-righteous and individualistic; 'not a team player'*
- *Too theoretical, conceptual, abstract — too literate*
- *Too prone to 'tell it like it is'*
- *'Not for sale!' 'Can't be bought!' 'Nobody has a line on them.'*

Many young men and women enter the organization with their idealism and values clearly on display. From that point forward, they give in or give out, because most American organizations have a low tolerance for diversity of opinion and behavior. . . and, again, everybody loses.

Throughout our history, greatness has come in strange packages. Walt Whitman, an acknowledged homosexual, would tail President Lincoln as if obsessed with capturing a glimpse of him. A strange, wonderful man, today many critics consider him America's greatest poet. Whitman proclaimed the freedom and dignity of the common man, and he sang the praises of democracy. He had an incalculable effect on later poets, inspiring them to experiment in prosody as well as subject matter. Indeed, he celebrated himself: "I did not know that I held so much greatness." But could he function in today's American society? Would his genius shine?

Dealing with a One-Dimensional Society

To discover the source of this aversion to greatness, you need look no further than our educational system. Romantic formalism and the quest for egalitarianism have placed 'skills training' above 'knowledge building' or content learning. And so, instrumental education has taken precedence over terminal classical education, or knowing over thinking.

Consequently, the managers of most American corporations and government bodies have received vocational training at the expense of the classics. Page Smith sees Ivy League education being reduced from thinking to technique, and from teaching to instructing. And, because you deal with what you know, that is what the organization and its people get — vocational leadership and vocational training.

This represents a problem for the organization. If its management thinks mainly in terms of utility (e.g., from a vocational education perspective), or what it can get out of the individual, the individual will logically think in like terms — or what can be gotten out of the organization. This equation contains no interest in 'giving,' 'sharing,' or, for that matter, in 'purposeful performance.'

At another level — similar to what we learned about the behavior of professors at our great universities — vocational education puts the emphasis on doing only what makes people successful in their careers. "That is what America values," they say to themselves, and they gravitate toward an America that is increasingly becoming a *One Dimensional Society.'*

In this context, a MBA degree is merely a vocational degree. It is as vocational as learning a trade in trade school. Essentially ignorant of their world, many MBAs scoff at the mere mention of the cultural implications of their work. Moreover, being trained in a set of skills (finance, management, information systems, etc.), they are unlikely to be acculturated to the background reading listed below. This reading, incidentally, might prove useful to them for a truly multidimensional, international perspective of the competitive world they have joined:

> *Homer's The Iliad: The Odyssey*
>
> *The Bible*
>
> *The Trojan Wars*
>
> *The Torah*
>
> *Aristophanes (The Birds)*
>
> *The Koran*
>
> *Euripides (Cyclops)*
>
> *The Bhagavad Gita*
>
> *Sophocles (Oedipus Rex)*
>
> *The Holy Crusades*
>
> *Plato (The Republic)*
>
> *Alexander the Great*
>
> *Julius Caesar (The Gallic Wars)*
>
> *The Epistles of St. Paul*
>
> *Mediations of Marcus Aurelius*
>
> *Edward Gibbon's Decline and Fall of the Roman Empire*

As the French say, "The more things change, the more they remain the same." This tip of the cultural iceberg would probably surprise novice readers, reflecting as did Solomon, "There is nothing new under the sun." After all, we are the product of thousands of years of acculturating experience, which makes knowing something about our cultural heritage a good deal more consequential than being obsessed with our family genealogy. The 'family of man' is technically and culturally a family, making us all brothers and sisters. The better we understand this, and the more we know about how to use it the greater the possibility we can live and work together in harmony throughout the world.

Chances are this discussion of the 'one dimensional' character of American society has made you anxious, perhaps angry, or even bored. . . all indicators of the deterministic bent of our American minds. Most of this type of reading has been excised from high school and college curricula, being placed under the heading of not applicable information.'

Look at the leaders of our government and the major corporations of American business and industry. Most of them have little time for reading and less inclination to this type of acculturating experience. Rest assured, if you read books written by these 'no nonsense' government and corporate leaders, you will find few references to their ancient counterparts. They are essentially uneducated men and women, with a vocational mind-set and perspective, playing 'quick and easy' games with America's future. If that seems harsh, it is meant to, for there is little evidence that we can be reassured otherwise.

The Hunt for the American Character

Given this 'one dimensional' mentality, it should come as no surprise that we have sought the answers to the American Dilemma with a one-dimensional approach to the problem. We have placed all our trust in the 'rational solution' to purposeful performance by using half our brain and, as a result, have come up 'half empty.' We have attempted to solve the problem with the same type of thinking that caused the problem in the first place.

Over the years, the deficiency of this approach has been acknowledged with *'Reader's Digest*/McCult-type' systems for closing the cultural gap between the left and right brain:

- *There is the 'Aspen Institute,' catering to executives in a rather picturesque distracting clime.*
- *The Great Books Club, which caters more to professionals who feel they have been educationally 'short changed.'*

- *Then there are such corporate-sponsored Learning Centers as those exemplified by Xerox and General Electric, which are sometimes 'on' again and 'off' again.*
- *And, across the continental United States, we have 'not for profit' and 'for profit' satellite cultural-fix operations, such as The Center For Creative Leadership (Greensboro, NC.) and The Tom Peters Group (Silicon Valley, CA.), which genuinely attempt to make a difference, but mainly make an impression.*

All of these efforts are 'instant pudding' attempts at developing more integrative thinking in promoting cultural awareness, leadership and value change, which, given the most generous of resources and the time allotted to attack the problem, should take at least 50 years. You cannot overcome a century of progressive neglect by the miracle of laudatory enterprise.

Only time and attention will overcome the *cultural bias* of the American character. It will be decades before the American psyche will routinely:

- *Reestablish the sanctity and stability of the American family;*
- *Advocate creativity over conformity;*
- *Champion cooperation over competition;*
- *Celebrate greatness over mediocrity;*
- *Honor students with original ideas over students with good grades;*
- *Award high school diplomas only to students who are minimally bilingual and pass a comprehensive basic skills examination;*
- *Prize making a difference over making an impression;*
- *Mobilize and utilize diversity and difference in organizational effectiveness;*
- *Sponsor, recognize and reward teamwork over individual performance;*
- *Encourage a cosmopolitan perspective over a parochial point of view;*
- *Find parents willing to support their offspring's school debate or piano recital over their athletic achievements;*
- *Support the arts equivalent to that of professional sports today, including comparable compensation for artists to that of athletes;*
- *Support making teachers the highest paid of all professions, rather than, now, being nearly the lowest paid.*

If this sounds ambitious, compare it to what our main competitors are doing right now and then give pause.

Changing the Organization Structure from a Physical to a Psychological Climate

If the organization knows what it wants to accomplish and is structured to accomplish it, it will succeed because it will experience purposeful performance. On the other hand, if the organization knows what it wants to accomplish, but is not structured to accomplish it, it will fail because it will experience dysfunctional performance.

Structure should be designed to facilitate the organization's strategy. Likewise, structure should facilitate three-way communications, vertically and horizontally — up and down and across functional lines. It is imperative everyone who needs to know, does, preferably before, not after, changes are made.

In any case, the information explosion has made quality communication more important than ever. 'Quantity' communication, which is somewhat in vogue, springs from the belief that employees should know about everything that is happening. This is not only impossible; it can be highly counterproductive.

- *The actual Information Requirements of Employees follow the rules of common sense:*
- *Employees want information to do a good job.*
- *They want to make the right decisions in their work.*
- *They want to have the information that affects them personally.*
- *And they want information that ensures their personal growth and development.*

The four common-sense Principles of Communication are:

- *How does the information affect me personally?*
- *How does the information affect me professionally?*
- *How does the information impact on what I am now doing?*
- *How does it 'sound' (i.e., is it believable; does it make sense)?*

The organization's structure should facilitate decision-making at its lowest levels in order to expedite real-time response to changing work demands. The criteria for truly effective decision-making are that it:

- *Occurs at the right level;*

123

- *Involves the right people;*
- *Takes place at the right time.*

Structure must clarify *roles* and *resources* available for carrying out the intended strategy. In the same sense that job descriptions have become meaningless, concerns about responsibility and authority are passé' in this context. It is *role identity* that is critical to organizational success — *role identity and the relationship of roles*. Once these are understood, authority and responsibility flow naturally to the requirements of the situation.

Using our basketball analogy, one player's role may be 'to penetrate the defense as point guard and create the offense,' while another's role may be 'to screen the weak side guard to set up the small forward in three-point range,' etc.

Pat Riley, the successful former coach of the Los Angeles Lakers, tells a story on himself as a player, which illustrates the importance of knowing your role and the relationship of roles.

The Lakers were playing in the championship game, and only seconds remained on the clock. The ball came to Riley at the top of the key. He was wide open and took the shot. He missed. The Lakers lost. In the dressing room after the game, trying to console himself on the missed shot, he said, "I was wide open," to nobody in particular. "You were wide open," Wilt Chamberlain, the great center declared, "Because nobody was guarding you."

It was sharpshooter Jerry West's role to take the shot. Riley's role was to get the ball to West. But he didn't because — momentarily — he forgot his role and tried to assume the role of another. This happens every day in the organization and with similar consequences.

Role identity should be based on special skills and the knowledge to do a particular job. Each person contributes to the process on the basis of well-defined, complementary roles — not on position power. A particular role, however, may find an individual 'taking charge' when his expertise is demanded. On another occasion, his role may be that of supportive player.

Many organizations are exploring 'self-management work teams.' Understandably, these are experimental pilot programs, and they must create *the psychological climate* necessary for the role identity to work as it does on athletic teams.

As purposeful performance eludes it, the organization continues to play one of its favorite games — *reorganization*. Since reorganization is recurrently an act of frustration, devoid of patient deliberation, this seldom works and more restructuring follows. Constant restructuring is a good sign the organization is *'out of control.'* Missing in this understanding is that structure today is:

Far less a mechanistic or physical activity and

Far more a psychological climatic condition.

Such activities, as relocating personnel; moving offices and furniture; redefining functional responsibilities; and feverishly updating organizational charts, actually have little positive impact on the life and effectiveness of the organization — perhaps no more than 20 percent.

Meanwhile, in direct contrast to this inconsequential activity, the appropriate *psychological climate* can produce an improvement in organizational effectiveness as great as 80 percent.

Management — playing its 'worry beads' of reorganization — may placate itself temporarily, but such activity has little permanent impact on the organization as a whole. On the other hand, cumbersome as an organization might be (even with too many levels of nonfunctional management), if the organization's psychological climate:

- *Advances an easily, identifiable mission statement, which all employees can understand and buy into, along with a set of guiding principles supporting that statement;*
- *Cultivates a common language reflecting the shared values, which all workers support and believe to be true;*
- *Presents a consistent message in all its communiques that is in tune with this mission, these principles and values; and*
- *Walks its talk in virtually everything it does, recognizing that symbolic interaction and man aging perceptions are critical to the success of its leadership; then,*
- *Because its people have the will to do so, the organization can overcome insurmountable deficiencies.*

Remember, it is not 'the perfect' organization that succeeds, but the happy and healthy one. Such an organization has a sense of humor about itself, along with the wisdom to balance risk and opportunity with prudence.

This is not to suggest that 'tree trimming' is not advisable, but simply to point out how powerful the *psychological climate* can be in creating purposeful performance. Far too frequently, it is ignored as more of that soft stuff when it produces nothing but consistently hard data.

By the same token, once the 'psychological climate' is established, managers who are dysfunctional will wither-away like Nature's dead branches on a tree, eventually falling off on their own accord, thus strengthening the organization. Once again, a reminder that purposeful performance is realized largely by not seeking it.

The Structure of a Psychological Organization

One American automotive company has made a major turnaround in a ten-year period. So remarkable was this resurrection that an acquaintance, in a consultant's role, called on this company to learn more about this success. The morning of the visit, when he tried to start his rental car, it wouldn't start. Thirty minutes late for his appointment, he expressed his trust rat ion and embarrassment to the security guard at the information desk upon arriving at the company's international headquarters.

Looking the consultant in the eye, the guard asked, "What kind of car are you driving, sir?" — And breathed a sigh of relief when told. "I would have been very surprised if it were one of ours," he said. "You see, our mission is to make the best automobiles in the world. We are all dedicated to that purpose."

The consultant smiled, put on his visitor's badge, and proceeded to the elevator. There, while waiting, he engaged in conversation with two engineers, bringing up his recent car problem. Their response was quite similar to that expressed by the security guard. Intrigued with this coincidence, when the consultant reached the appointed office, he checked to see what the secretary's response might be. Again, it was the same. Without fanfare, each person clearly and simply repeated *Ford Motor Company's* 'mission statement.'

This was not an accident. Nor was it coincidental to learn that everyone spoke the same language or that considerable effort had gone into circulating a consistent message. Clearly, the psychological climate here made a deep impression on the consultant. As one United Auto Workers union official put it, "We've always had these banners around 'Treat People with Respect.' Now, it is clear that we mean it."

Mixed Messages

This caused the consultant to look more closely at some 'mixed messages' that had been advanced in other organizations — organizations that were finding it difficult to even decide what business they were in, to the confusion of many employees. In conversations with these employees, here are some typical responses:

"We are told, on the one hand, that we want to grow the business and, on the other hand that we need to cut costs."

"We are encouraged to be innovators — even entrepreneurs — and then they define our jobs, responsibilities, and activities so absolutely that we have no room to move, much less think."

"We are advised of the importance of performance, and then the emphasis is put on conformity."

"We play psychological games with each other — nothing gets spelled out in behavior."

"We verbalize about building trust and use the words like empty calories out of the vending machines."

"We speak constantly about 'team work' as if you can get anywhere if you are a team player. Come on!"

"We talk about 'planning our work' and 'working our plan.' In 30 years here, I've seen only one kind of management rewarded — crisis management."

There is a perverted consistency here as well, for these remarks came from a diverse group, including senior managers, engineers, administrators, and custodial workers.

The 'psychological climate' is pervasive in any organization, driven by its 'cultural bias,' and can be either positive or negative, managed or out-of-control. People are not bricks, mortar and cement. They need special cultivation and attention, but the payback is many times greater than any other physical asset.

Psychological Forces within the Organizational Structure

Getting a grasp of the situation starts with recognizing that employees are organizations within themselves. They are the nucleus from which the organization builds itself to purposeful performance — or to relative dysfunction:

- *You can't treat some employees with respect and not others.*
- *You can't favor some employees and expect other employees to applaud your efforts.*

- *You can't share 'company secrets' with some employees and put other employees in the category of 'not needing to know.'*
- *You can't make demands on some employees and treat others with 'kid gloves.'*

An Aerospace Proposal Team Mission, Values and Guiding Principles

It doesn't work. All employees must feel that they are special; that they are important; and that they are making meaningful contributions to the success of the organization. Three basic psychological forces within the infrastructure of peoples' make-up determine whether they are in control of their lives and in a 'readiness' mood to make a meaningful contribution:

The Forces within the *Self* — between the 'Ideal Self' and the 'Real Self';

The Forces within the *Situation*, which determine how the situation will be defined;

The Forces within *Others* — between 'Self-Demands' and 'Role Demands.'

If the organization fails to communicate a *clear mission,* to develop a *common language*, and to resonate a *consistent message*, there is likely to be a constant battle of individual employees with themselves (between 'the *Ideal Self* and the *Real Self*'). We are not very accepting of ourselves as we are and look for reasons to justify this conflict. On the smallest pretense, we can move away from seeing things clearly, to reading all kinds of negative implications into organizational communiques, or the behavior of others towards us.

Self-deception plays an important part in poorly *defining the situation,* whereas self-acceptance plays an equally important part in seeing things 'as they are.' When things are seen clearly, *The Corporate Mad Monarchs* have no place in the equation. When the organization and the individual are in tune with each other, these six silent killers vanish and purposeful performance takes their place.

Paul Hersey likes to use 'maturity' or 'readiness' to describe purposeful behavior in his *Situational Leadership Model*. Maturity is a useful term for this discussion. When the organization treats its employees with maturity (i.e., as adults), their *readiness* to act responsibly improves significantly. They are more apt to respond positively to otherwise negative situations, including occasional ambiguities, chaotic developments, or even sporadic crises. The key here is:

How the organization views them in terms of maturity and the type of climate it creates for them.

They are more prone to be flexible and able to meet unforeseen challenges, if their minds and bodies are healthy.

If the forces within the 'situation' and the individual's 'self 'are in a healthy state, then the individual should have little problem balancing *self-demands* and *role-demands*. If not, the individual's behavior may be erratic to the extreme of paranoia. Once again, there is a natural conflict between these two demands, which depends largely on the maturity of the individual. The more mature ('ready') the individual, the more appropriate their actions will fit the situation.

What a difference people make when their personal systems (i.e., their values, beliefs, expectations and perceptions), are working toward the same purposeful performance. Likewise, when the forces within the organization are in balance:

- *The structure facilitates carrying out the organization's mission.*
- *Everyone knows what is expected of them and why.*
- *Work is congruent (it is organized to meet a common goal, not structured to create conflict and confusion among functional disciplines).*
- *The structure supports teamwork.*
- *The structure fosters cooperation, collaboration, and open communication.*
- *Work is fun, and everyone enjoys what they are doing.*
- *The structure supports a creative climate of purposeful enterprise.*
- *The structure supports individual growth and development.*

Thus, the problem with structure is less a physical phenomenon than a psychological one. It should not start with 'flattening the pyramid.' That will come in due course, as role identity, role relationships, and teamwork evolve, thus fragmenting and eventually dissolving inappropriate *cultural biases*.

Even 'management creep,' which is certainly a concern, will first stagnate and then drop off precipitously, as the psychological climate is created and sustained. . . for professionals 'to show their stuff.' As this climate pulls the organization in the direction of contribution, purposeful performance will eventually eclipse dysfunction, driving out many of the dreaded symptomatic organizational problems of today. Again, it is indirection that is the answer. The best way to realize purposeful performance is not to seek it.

The Cry of the Future! [9]

Ford Motor Company has shown what a giant can do. But even Ford admits it is involved in a revolution that will take at least a generation or more to reach its appointed objective.

Coping with Corporate Leaderless Leadership

The 'paradoxical dilemma' of our times is that we cannot lead and we do not want to follow. Do you want to lead? Probably not. Does that mean most of us want to lead? Again, probably not. Now, here comes the rub. Why is it most people don't like to be led? They want to believe they are in charge. Then, why don't most people lead? *Because they simply don't know how to lead.* And so, most American organizations have a management system and call it *leadership*.

The central issue of leadership is understanding what is meant. Does it mean 'strutting your stuff '— does it mean compliance, coordination — does it mean management?

Compliance suggests some arbitrary constraints to affect behavior, such as coercion and manipulation, neither of which connote leadership. People follow leaders, not because they have to, but because they want to. When there is *coercion,* it is 'leadership' of a most finite duration. People will only take so much coercion and then they rebel by resisting. Before they rebel overtly, however, they'll sabotage operations via the *six silent killers.*

Obviously, there has to be some *coordination* in order for the followers to effectively follow. But when 'coordination' is the central thrust of 'leadership,' it becomes simply management. Management is a mechanistic, maintenance function which secures and perpetuates the *status quo*. It is the comfortable home of *logical positivism* and *scientific empiricism*. Management was invented to sustain the 'secular religion' of technocracy. When the German philosopher Nietzsche proclaimed, *"God is dead,"* the religion of materialistic scientism was born, and nascent management, in all its bureaucratic splendor, followed soon after.

We, as followers, want an opportunity to express our ideas, to be appreciated for our contributions, to give vent to our aspirations, and to demonstrate our unique individualism. We yearn to display our talents, to show our form. In brief, we want to manage ourselves with an acceptable level of freedom, control and trust:

- *Freedom to give individual expression to our work;*
- *Control of the work we do;*

Trust that we will be successful, but empathetic support if we should fail.

Given a supportive work climate, we will follow with exuberance as long as the leadership leads us to improvement on the job and in our capacity to control our lives. But this is also where it becomes a somewhat 'sticky wicket':

If we follow at the expense of *Pleasing Self,* deluding ourselves that we are happy and fulfilled, or that we have 'no choice,' we are moving toward *management dependence* and the *Culture of Comfort.*

If we get caught up in "what a great job I have — benefits and all," or "what a great place it is to work here — all the people are so wonderful," forgetting about improving our skills, growing our talent and making a significant contribution, being as "snug as a bug in a rug," chances are we have stopped challenging ourselves altogether and are securely ensconced in *arrested development* in the *Culture of Complacency.*

A Difference of Perspective

There is a certain amount of *moral courage* to followership which somehow gets displaced as we move up the organization. Take the case of the woman who was working at her station when the CEO of a major multinational corporation, and his executive entourage, stopped at her work station to chat during a ceremonial plant tour.

"And how are you feeling today, young lady," the smiling CEO asked. She turned, looked him full in the face, hands planted firmly on hips and said, "Horseshit!" And turned back to her station resuming her work. The stunned CEO, with caring in his voice, said almost in a whisper, "I'm sorry," and moved on.

Fortunately, one of the executives broke rank and talked to this woman for a few minutes. It turned out she was a single parent with two preschool children; that her set-up man didn't show, which meant she would have to work at least two hours overtime to meet the shipping schedule. She had no idea who could pick up her children at Day-care, and so she was at her wits end to know what to do.

Now, this blue-collar worker had 'had it!' She wasn't fearful of her job, nor much impressed with the 'big shots' who were in the plant that day. She was full of her problem and when asked, unloaded. To the manager who stayed behind, she admitted no sense of courage or regret, nor did she feel anything but anger for her situation. It was an honest emotion, honestly wrought without malicious intent or dubious motivation. And it was accepted in that same sense by the CEO. You could even go so far as to say there was genuine compassion and concern in the CEO's voice as he expressed his regrets.

Change the scenario to an executive the CEO might encounter on a similar tour. Imagine one of them reacting in like fashion on a particular bad day saying, "Horseshit!" when asked how they were. Imagine, if you will, the inevitable consequences.

The psychodrama which would surely unfold would find 'self-demands' and 'role demands' amalgamated into mortal conflict. Not so for the hourly worker. The frustrated or angered executive is not expected to have, much less show, feelings; certainly, not to 'lose control.' Only hourly employees have that privilege.

The CEO knows their power is largely symbolic with the work force; that the influence of leadership falls more on their ability to symbolically meet the humanistic needs of the majority than those of their top executive staff. You could even say the CEO feels a sense of 'ownership' of this staff, having purchased the 'rights of servitude' through executive compensation, bonuses, perks and privileges given. Hence, the executive staff is available largely at the CEO's convenience.

So, the higher one climbs the hierarchy, the more courage it takes to be oneself. Consequently, few muster such courage, succumbing instead to the seductive powers of comfort and conformity. Undoubtedly, they reason they have 'too much to lose.' And so they are bullied into obedience if not obsequious subservience and call it 'loyalty.'

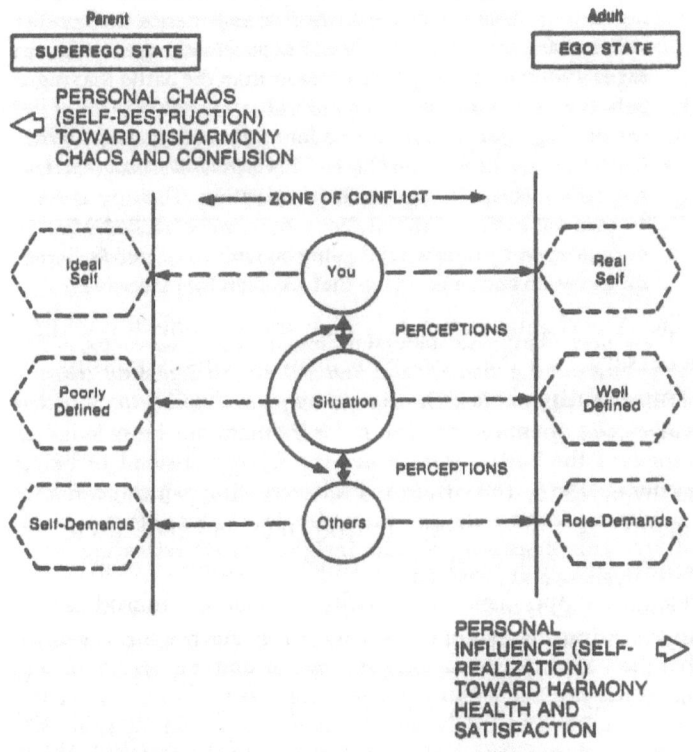

Fisher Model of Conflict and Stress Resolution

• Cooperation is voluntary and given freely. • Compliance is involuntary and coercive.

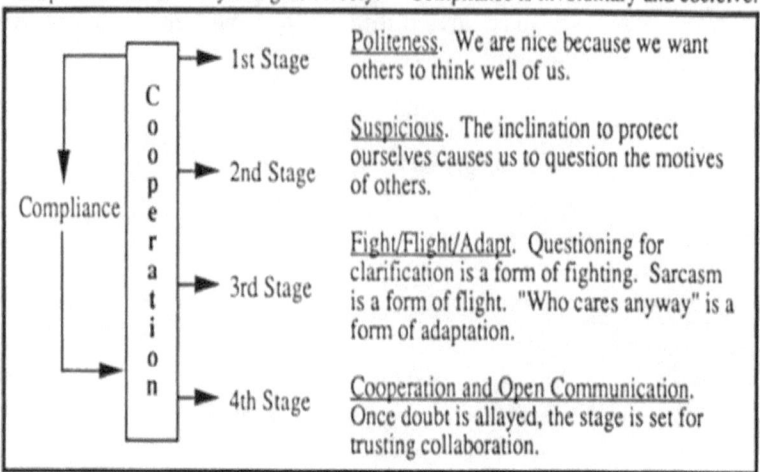

Fisher Sequential Chronology of Interpersonal Relations.

Indigenous to the American character is also an aptitude for taking risks and enduring the necessary pain that goes with growth. This is missing in these two cultures. More importantly, *there is no leadership in the Cultures of Comfort and Complacency, only management.*

Where there is true leadership, there is always a dynamic-tension and pull between leadership and followership. Indeed, they enhance each other. At the same time, leaders and followers are intimately connected in *interdependent* action. Surprise, disappointment, conflict, chaos, incredible levels of achievement, and continuous growth are part of the vigorous process. There is no comfort, little safety, no room for complacency, and no living off yesterday's achievements. Every day is a challenge and an embrace of the unexpected. Here the *Culture of Contribution* resides and the *Please Self* disposition flourishes.

"Leaders," suggests James MacGregor Burns, *"represent the complete follower."* This is true. To lead you must first learn how to follow. Leaders learn how to lead by being ardent, passionate followers. Leaders and followers are indissolubly connected, but followership precedes leadership.

Peter the Great, who singlehandedly brought 18th century Russia into the modern Western world, would wander amongst his people in disguise to learn what they were thinking and feeling. In this manner he checked the pulse of his leadership, not through sycophants, but through direct contact. He loved his people and he wanted desperately to understand them so that he could more ably become their servant.

- *Leaders are not concerned about leadership qualities or even charisma, but with purposeful performance.*
- *Leaders think in terms of their followers. Followers are the best guide to how leaders lead.*
- *Understand the work climate and know the degree to which they can be open and trusting, or guarded and suspicious; know that the organizational culture must be prepared for an open and trusting climate before any attempt is made to operate in this fashion, or trouble is around the corner.*
- *Use the human resources they have; invest in their development because they know that 99 percent of their people are capable. But, perhaps as much as 90 percent are either not challenged, or lack opportunity. Paradoxically, the more outstanding the employees, the greater the problem. Employees must be guided by their own light. Better that leaders get rid of good people than have them go sour, or become guilt ridden for having to move on to greater challenges. The job of leadership is always development. Therefore, leaders should not punish themselves for doing a good job.*
- *The subtle difference between leadership and management is in the psychology, not the functionality. If leadership and management were performed by a machine, they would be interchangeable. But they are not. Management does mechanical things well — planning, budgeting, organizing, controlling through formal authority. Leadership, while doing these same things, educates its people to think differently about work through inspiration and visioning.*
- *Leadership is committed to Growth and Development*

Something is wrong in the American organization today. Leadership covets leading but is disinclined to serve. Instead, it aspires to be served. Worse yet, having little knowledge of its followers, its perceptions are too frequently based on anachronistic stereotypes etched in 1945 nostalgia.

What's more, such leaders see themselves 'as the organization,' managing it thusly as if they in fact owned it. Likewise, they take it upon themselves to 'own' most of the organization's problems, sharing with their followers only what they deem necessary to execute 'the correct strategy.' Too frequently, this is done with limited information and knowledge. And so, not only are such problems insufficiently resolved, but they often exacerbate into major snafus.

More incredible still, these 'leaders' often think they are leaders because they are treated preferentially; that is, they have their own private bathrooms, executive dining privileges, special parking with free car maintenance and care, private club memberships, access to the company's private plane, interest-free loans, and so on.

Many managers would sell their most prized possessions to belong to such an exclusive club. Seldom do such incentives, of course, lead to the service of others. The message these perks generate is 'to be served,' not to serve. And so, today that is the 'leadership' the representative American organization too often begets.

The Triangle of Growth

The remarkable feature of humanity is that everything begins with 'man' in the singular, progressing to 'collective man' in the plural, or in the sense of this discussion, the organization. With regard to growth, there is no static or safe period for either the individual or the organization. Once the individual or the organization attempts to play it 'safe,' it loses. Things start to fall apart. Likewise, when we, or the organization, stop growing, atrophy sets in; plants, animals, man, organizations... all the same. Eternal struggle is indigenous to all life without exception.

Struggle starts when we learn to talk, continues as we strive to walk, attempt to master a three-wheeler, try to roller skate. . . and beyond. Ever know anyone to look graceful the first, second, third or fourth time they put on a pair of roller skates?

Roller skating is embarrassingly difficult. The reason is, the 'center of gravity' changes as we negotiate the corners by a 'cross-over' of our legs, leaving us precariously off balance. If we avoid the 'cross-over' maneuver, of course, we never actually learn how to skate gracefully. To become a graceful skater requires enduring the *pain* of embarrassment and the near constant *risk* of falling on our tush, because we will fall many times before we perfect the maneuver.

If unwilling or unable to endure this pain, or to take the risk, we will never learn to skate. This could be one of our first encounters with 'embracing resistance.' It requires us to 'let go' of ourselves, trusting that our intrinsic psycho-motor skills will suffice to give us control of our balance.

And, of course, that is precisely what happens. Those who have mastered this maneuver have embraced their resistance to self-consciousness. They have given themselves a psycho logical edge for when the next challenge comes along.

But, alas, we tend to forget these successes. 'Embarrassing skills' are most successfully learned, as a consequence, when we are quite young; when we are not afraid to make a 'fool of ourselves'; when we are not intimidated by failure. Failure is not even relevant. Indeed, the young are open to diverse new experiences, taking risks, and possibly getting hurt.

Incidentally, our aversion to physical pain seems to 'level off' at an early age, whereas our aversion to *psychological pain* never seems to crest. Since the pain we experience as we get older becomes more associated with 'psychological pain,' we tend to go to great extremes to avoid it. Because of past 'hurts,' we avoid certain relationships, economic opportunities and life experiences. . . such as the awkwardness of learning a foreign language in our mature years.

Young organizations differ little with this. Take the early days of *Apple, Inc.* *Apple* demonstrated an incredible capacity to take risks and court embarrassment. Now, regrettably, *Apple* has become as cautious as *IBM*. Once organizations get 'a little long in the tooth,' they tend toward conservatism. Likewise, if they have a traumatic experience, they tend to shy away from similar opportunities.

'Success,' however you define it, is the outcome of careful attention to the *process,* nothing more. We learn precious little from success, the *outcome* itself. We experience it, may trade on it, and sometimes become consumed with it, but we seldom grow from success.

The essential component of growth is the part the American mind prefers to ignore, the inevitable 'plateau.' Every individual and organization experiences plateaus several times in their existence. . . if they are truly in a growth mode. If they play it safe, however, they can remain on a plateau for an eternity, the plateau of arrested development.

Ideally, the period of static development might be called the *Plateau of Failure* in an effort to dramatize how important 'failure' is to our success and that of our organization. [10] Plateauing is a period when we finally confront ourselves and that reality. The processing of the knowledge gained during this period can then become useful in the form of invaluable insights. An added advantage to this phase is that we are likely to be given more 'room,' or avoided, as if 'failure' were a communicable disease.

Make no mistake, this is a remarkably meaningful stage of development. It is here the 'chemistry of being' in all its naked splendor reveals itself. . . if only we allow it to happen. All growth has an appropriate gestation period. This is ours.

It is the *place* and *space* where wonders can break through to our consciousness, putting us into a different strata of knowing, feeling and being. On the other hand, *we don't have to worry about letting the group down* because it is not likely to be around. And like an unassuming child, *we don't have to be smart,* being totally in a learning configuration.

We often think of individuals who have 'plateaued' as going nowhere. This is not true. Or if it is, it is because those individuals have misinterpreted their own experiences. The *plateau* is a period of incubation. Pregnant with past experiences — both successes and failures, we are inclined toward introspection, taking inventory of ourselves. It could be called a 'time out' period, much as athletic team's take 'time outs' in tense moments of competition to regroup and reassess their situation.

Attention is focused on *being,* not becoming. 'Being' involves us with ourselves, of finding out how to *Please Self,* as well as to discover what 'makes us tick.' This is a healthy form of self-involvement. *Becoming,* on the other hand, involves us with others, and our frantic efforts to meet their needs and live up to their expectations. . . in short, to find ways to *Please Others.* This is an unhealthy form of self-involvement.

Corporations, through their lack of leadership, can attempt to be all things to all people — employees, stockholders and customers, ending up being nothing to everyone. Instead of using a period of leveling off in the business as an opportunity to look at things differently, the organization, like the individual, can go through a period of denial, depression, projection (e.g., finger pointing), stress and strain, and ultimately, panic. It is moved by *forward inertia,* which displays its limited vision and contains its corporate self-doubt.

Real Road to Growth and Development

Unfortunately, there is little learning in this process because the organization is attempting to 'appear smart,' or to look like it has its act together when clearly it doesn't.

Since plateaus are an inevitable phenomenon, no individual or organization escapes them, but everyone can contribute to using them as launching pads for 'blasting off' to new experiences. The American mania of 'action for action's sake,' however, is not the way. In other words, "He who hesitates is lost," or "When in doubt, it's better to do something, even if it is wrong," is not good

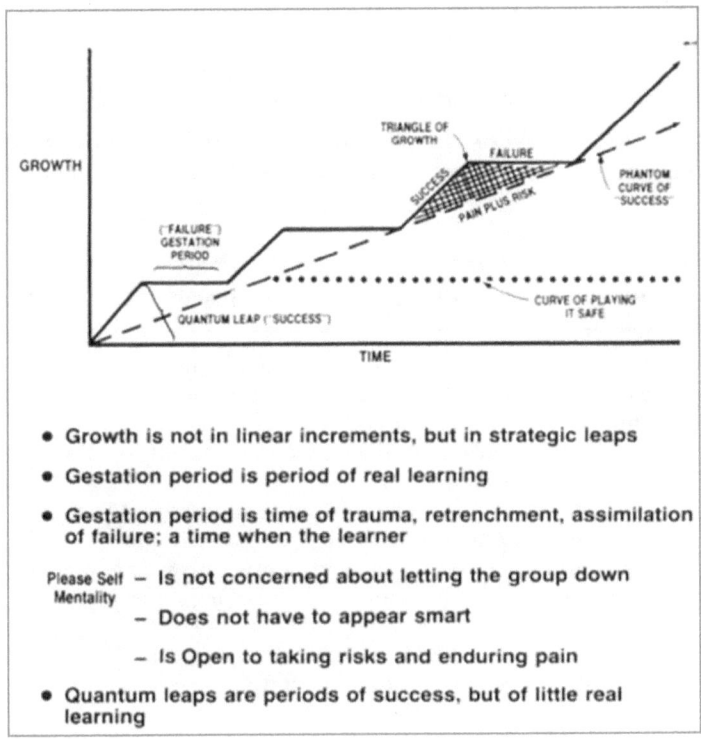

- Growth is not in linear increments, but in strategic leaps
- Gestation period is period of real learning
- Gestation period is time of trauma, retrenchment, assimilation of failure; a time when the learner

Please Self — Is not concerned about letting the group down
Mentality
     — Does not have to appear smart
     — Is Open to taking risks and enduring pain

- Quantum leaps are periods of success, but of little real learning

executive action planning.

Acting now can actually exacerbate the situation and extend the time on the plateau.

This impulsive, impatient behavior describes a common American management practice. It is the inertial isolationism expected of someone in a state of panic, unaware or incapable of dealing with corporate reality.

Breaking the Loop

While our international competitors begin to live their economic dreams, America itself is stranded on a plateau, the nightmare of *comfort* and *complacency*. What got us there will not get us off. We must first encounter and admit to our doubts and inadequacies. This is not a time to complain, justify or rationalize. It is a time to learn. The internal dialogue of the American organization is a vicious cycle of delays and denials. This dialogue has become a closed-loop circuit which finds the American organizational psyche going *'round and 'round,* producing little movement or progress because it is fixed on fantasy.

To break the loop, we must find our 'roller skating legs' and embrace our resistance to *right brain* thinking, for only our right brain recognizes and accepts a warped vision without defensiveness. It is our *left brain* that defends the circuit

---

Survey of 900 United States Executives

- 93 percent said managers were not rewarded for developing subordinates for leadership. On the contrary, managers are often rewarded for killing off talented managers who are threatening their own jobs.
- 87 percent said it was impossible to make lateral moves in their companies, an essential for developing leaders who will know how the whole company operates, not just a portion of it.
- 80 percent said they had inadequate programs to identify what people needed in order to develop leadership skills.

---

of cyclic thinking.

A Call for Leadership: Managers Need Not Apply

Ironically, the increasing importance of 'breaking the loop' places the *Outsider* in the mainstream. The *Outsider*, having no vested interest in the outcome, can be instrumental in convincing us to focus on the process. More significantly, the *Outsider* can surface our most painfully embarrassing concerns, issues the *leaderless leadership* would prefer to avoid. Leaderless leadership fancies itself riding the crest of economic advantage secure in the safety that "It didn't happen on *my* watch!"

The *Outsider,* lacking personal involvement, being neither a 'bleeding heart' nor a 'crusader,' has no investment in either anger or cause. More importantly, the *Outsider* is not interested in the concern 'to be free,' but is passionately committed to the ideal of 'to become free.' And herein lies an important difference.

Rejection of the *status* quo is the first step toward freedom, but this is 'negative freedom.' This only produces 'to be free.' Most criticism and rebellion today ends in 'negative freedom.' With the *Outsider,* it is not enough to repudiate what is now not acceptable. While this is the first step to be taken, the resulting 'negative freedom' will not put America back on track. We have been pushing 'negative freedom' for all its worth for the past thirty years. . . and you can see what it has accomplished, *forward inertia.*

To become free ('positive freedom'), on the other hand, helps put America back on track because it involves recognizing the natural interdependence of the organization and dealing with situational forces as they develop. It involves doing something positive (or what is possible) not being preoccupied with the negative, (or what isn't). This means everyone accepts themselves as part of the problem and, therefore, as part of the solution. The problem is not outside anyone, but permeates all interests. To solve it together, as a single entity, is *to become free. . .* to become 'one organization.'[12] It over comes *inertial isolation ism,* which is endemic to the American character.

The bearing of 'to be free' and 'to become free' on this discussion is that the American organization is admittedly struggling against itself for survival. The best medicine it could possibly take, given this predicament, might be to embrace struggle as a way out of its misery and not to seek purposeful performance directly. True, there is risk involved in entertaining such an idea, an idea which at first may not be an improvement over the old approach. Change cannot be expected to occur without difficulty and inevitable setbacks.

To change, in any event, requires the positive force of the faculty called 'imagination' to be brought into play. Colin Wilson in *Access To Inner Worlds* (1983) points out 'imagination' is actually "the ability to re-create experience, in all its complexity and richness. And the *right brain* is able to do precisely that." [13]

Meanwhile, the ranks of the disgruntled and disenchanted grow — that is, those who want 'to be free.' Well-intentioned professionals of all ages placed their confidence in a *system* that they now feel has betrayed them by imprisoning them or stultifying their development. Obviously, they are still not looking to themselves for the solution, but to 'management,' whatever management may mean to them. This has buried the dilemma only deeper in their subconscious and made challenge a greater phantom.

Gregory Bateson in *Steps to an Ecology of Mind* (1972), describes this as a *double bind* which causes these professionals "to feel lost in the labyrinth of roadblocks, detours, and new construction across the main thoroughfares of their minds." [14] Their perceptions have not held up well to reality testing. They are beginning to understand they cannot maintain their present high standard of living (S.O.L.), for exam pie, without eventually paying. As matters now stand, the American government is borrowing money to maintain the *S.O.L.*, while it watches our per capita rate of productivity continue to fall.

Professionals are finding it increasingly difficult to separate themselves from the corporate problem of American society. The nice home, good pay, and comfort are all threatened. . . with the ominous signs over the horizon which they would like to ignore, if they could. But the evidence they see proves we cannot have it both ways:

We can no longer pretend we are the 'best and the brightest' when our performance deteriorates against world competition.

No matter what our association, chances are the organization is shrinking, and with it, our confidence.

Consequently, lost or alienated from what we thought we were, many of us have decided that if reality doesn't mean what we thought it meant, then there is no meaning at all; that we might as well 'pack it in.'[15] But America's decline is clearly a choice. It is not inevitable.

Consider this absurdity. What would we think of a man who lived out on the lawn in a tent, while he built himself a magnificent home, and then absent-mindedly went on living in the tent and left the house empty? Colin Wilson sees that as precisely what we have done. [16] Perhaps we are trying too hard to solve our dilemma, and not taking the time to appreciate the vast richness of our magnificent country. With a predominant 'sense of panic,' we have slipped deeply into an insidious habit of anxiety, tension, and over-alertness. This is not to be confused with awareness. 'Over-alertness' is a legacy of the past. We need crises to keep us alert. The management of crises fuels 'over-alertness.' It leaves the house empty.

When we consider this absurdity more closely, we realize we already know the answer. We have chosen to retreat into *comfort* and the *status quo* at the expense of our *identity* and *reality*. Now, we may choose to move 'out of this tent' and into our magnificent home. *We may choose to be purposeful with intentionality. We may choose to put our lives in focus.*

Finding Our Way Back To Purposeful Performance

"We have designed organizations which ignored individual potential for competence, responsibility, constructive intent and productivity," wrote Chris Argyris two decades ago. [17] Regrettably, it still holds true today. The organization pays close attention to every detail that enhances individual potential for *purposeful performance* except the workers themselves. They are left out of the equation.

The *psychological infrastructure of the organization* has not changed at all, permanently secured in the 1945 model. At a time when we need to think and behave differently in the workplace, we *reorganize* or move the furniture and call it 'change.' This only masks the problem.

Work as *purposeful performance* is both a structural/ functional and psychological problem. The difficulty with performance relates to the *structure of work* and the *function of work* as they both relate to the *organization,* on the one hand, *and the psychological perception of the structure of work* and *the function of work* as they relate to the *worker,* on the other. The organization has paid conscientious attention to the structure and function of work as it relates to itself, hut has ignored the psychological perception of these components of work, as they relate to the worker, with near disastrous consequences.

Conventional wisdom of the organization equates *structure* and *function* with *control* and *results.*

Professional workers equate *structure and function* with *self-control* and *process.* And this equates to their level of satisfaction.

Conventional wisdom can boast that work has been designed with the latest scientific ergonomics to enhance productivity and worker satisfaction. It can proclaim the structure of the organization is streamlined to pose minimal barriers to productive work. It can even refine the selection process to attract the most able, yet all is for naught, if it does not satisfy the workers' psychological needs. And what are these needs?

Professional workers today are not impressed with what management can do *for* them, or even *to* them if it does not include:

- *Freedom to express themselves in work,*

- *Control of how work is accomplished,*
- *Trust that the work will be done correctly.*

This is the *symbolic currency* that makes a difference — currency, to date, conventional wisdom shows little inclination to advance. It sees such currency as surrendering traditional power. Management is willing to spend enormous amounts of money to 'window dress' the problem, than accede to these implicit demands. Management neither trusts workers to be more productive for this concession, nor does it feel a pressing *need to share power*.

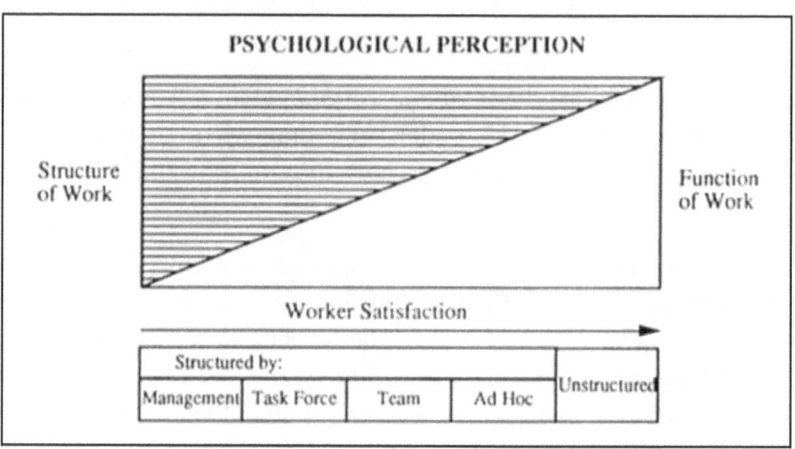

Control as Satisfaction as a Function of Satisfaction

Now, there are genuine exceptions to this with phenomenal results. Some organizations have, in fact, created this type of climate by allowing work to define itself. H. Ross Perot, founder of Electronic Data Systems Corporation (EDS), has been attempting for years to *wake up America* to the needs of workers and their potential for contribution. Incidentally, he sees *all* workers as professionals, establishing the following credo at EDS with great success:

First feed the troops, then the officers. (Not only does he see the bonus system as ludicrous, but self-serving.)

The running of the corporation belongs to the workers. (He does not see it belonging to 'custodial power,' or management.)

144

If there is to be a bonus rule, the same rule should apply to the workers and managers alike when it comes to special compensation. (EDS has had gain-sharing for years.)

Management, believing it holds the 'Keys to the Kingdom,' gives itself 'Nobel Prize-like' awards, while giving the troops 'baubles and beads.' (Perot considers this not only senseless, but poor business.)

Management, as a word, should be eliminated: inventories can be managed. . . people led. [18]

This is an important statement from one of our few corporate statesmen. It is the basis of *Work Without Managers*. We need leaders, not managers; and we need professional workers to become self-managers in the full sense of the word. And we need to 'live' the words by rewarding those that do.

Ever combatant and irascible, Perot took on General Motors as a project worthy of rehabilitation. This premier American firm commits most of the sins of this discussion, and in mega-numbers, while operating, according to Perot, "in a blanket of fog." For his trouble, General Motors dumped him off its Board of Directors with a payoff of $700 million for his stock and resignation.

So, generally speaking, management has not been willing to 'step up to the bar' and face reality. It has not been willing to cross a new frontier. Naively, it clings to the *psychology of inertia* as we sink deeper into this incomprehensible abyss.

References

(1) See Buchholz, Steve, and Thomas Roth, *Creating the High Performance Team*, ed. Karen Hess (New York: John Wiley & Sons, Inc., 1987).

(2) No accident, there has been a plethora of 'baseball books' in this period of uncertainty, from the crafted prose of George F. Will's *Men At Work: The Craft of Baseball* (New York: Macmillan, 1990) to the scientism of Robert K. Adair's *The Physics of Baseball* (New York: Harper & Row, 1990). Baseball is architecture of the 'frozen music' of the atavistic American spirit.

(3) *Logical positivism* is a philosophical position holding that truth of any statement lies in its verification through sensory experience (i.e., based upon experience, observation, and/or experimentation). Any statement that cannot be verified through sensory experience, such as metaphysical statements, is held meaningless.

(4) Capra, Fritjof, *The Turning Point: Science, Society & The Rising Culture* (New York: Simon and Schuster, 1982), p. 453.

(5) Capra, op. cit. p. 23.

(6) Sorokin. Pitirim. *The American Sex Revolution* (Boston: Porter Sargent, 1956).

(7) Economists, for one, readily admit they are operating in a fog. From former Chairman of the Federal Reserve, *Arthur Burns* ("The rules of economics are not working quite the way they used to.") to *Milton Friedman* ("I believe that we economists in recent years have done vast harm by claiming more than we can deliver."); from former Secretary of Treasury, *Michael Blumenthal* ("I really think the economic profession is close to bankruptcy in understanding the situation, before or after the fact.") to *Juanita Kreps*, former Secretary of Commerce, when asked if she would go back to *Duke University* upon leaving government ("I wouldn't know what to teach."). Source: Interview: *Washington Post*. November 5, 1979).

(8) Robert M. Tucker and David C. Hendrickson offer a nostalgic piece which gives substance to this argument in "Thomas Jefferson and American Foreign Policy." *Foreign Affairs*, Spring 1990.

(9) Cartoon by Bill Day originally appeared in *Detroit Free Press* and in the *International Herald Tribune*. February 24, 1988.

(10) Judith Bardwick in *The Plateauing Trap* (New York: Chandler Publishing Company, 1986) does a superb job in showing how plateauing can be the beginning, not the end of things.

(11) Kotter, John P., *The Leadership Factor* (New York: Free Press, 1988). Kotter insists leaders are made, not born. His survey of 900 U.S. executives indicates 'corpocracy,' the American bureaucratic disease, stifles people from becoming effective leaders.

(12) See *The Outsider* by Colin Wilson, (Dell Publishing Company, New York, 1956). Wilson was in his twenties when he wrote this explosively popular international "bestseller." He attacked the problem of man's increasing retreat into comfort and the status quo at the expense of his identity and reality.

(13) Wilson, Colin, *Access to Inner Worlds* (London: Rider & Company, Ltd., 1983), p. 125.

(14) A *double bind*, as defined by Gregory Bateson, is a situation in which an individual feels he is receiving contradictory messages from a highly significant other person. This happened in one organization when all professionals were asked to take a voluntary *pay cut* across the board, while the CEO and his direct reports were given a 20 percent bonus.

(15) Hayes, Robert H., and William, J. Abernathy, "Managing Our Way to Decline," *Harvard Business Review*, July-August, 1980. This hard hitting article profiling American management's obsession with short term results as a major factor in our economic decline was not disputed. It was almost as if American management was resigned to the fall. A decade later (1990), it is even worse.

(16) Wilson, op. cit. pp. 128-129.

(17) Argyris, Chris, "A Few Words In Advance," *The Failure of Success*, ed. A. J. Marrow (New York: *American Management Association*, 1972).

(18) Perot, Ross H., in a manifesto article titled, "How I Would Turn Around GM," *Fortune Magazine*, February 15, 1988.

The Worker, Alone!
Going Against the Grain

"For the past quarter century, we have had a bombardment of ideas on how to manage change. Actually, change in the workplace is of only secondary importance. Change will come about naturally, over time, once workers and managers bring about change in themselves. Order comes from within. To establish order takes more than good intentions, more than a change of attitude. Order requires a radical change in mentality, a structural change in how workers and managers view the world. Such radicalism requires the individual going against the grain."

Foreword

The Worker, Alone! Going Against The Grain is about working stiffs, wherever they are. The world is changing around workers, and they are expected to "go with the flow," maintain the status quo without misgiving. Half of all workplaces in industry and commerce have no collective bargaining. Unions are the dinosaurs of the times. While the rhetoric of empowerment rises to a crescendo, the workforce itself is more powerless in the workplace than ever before. Some actually think that a powerless workforce is the only way to have economic growth, while others feel it is the condition which will lead back to trade unionism. Neither outcome seems

realistic. The disempowerment of the workforce will certainly not lead to higher economic growth, nor is it likely to lead to a rebirth of trade unionism. On the contrary; what impresses Dr. Fisher about the present climate is the unimaginativeness and inertia of management on the one hand, and the passivity with which the workforce as a whole accepts its disenfranchisement on the other.

The evidence suggests workers everywhere see themselves at the mercy of employers, bosses, "the system," and yet they do nothing. Oh, they may feign concern, but the proof is in that nothing changes. Workers deny reality, go along with things as they are, ventilate frustration on a need basis, but always at the expense of colleagues or loved ones, never at their true adversary, themselves!

The price workers' pay for disenfranchisement at work and indifference as citizens is an inflationary housing market, unsustainable consumption booms, mountains of accumulated debt and constant flirtation with economic recession. Despite miraculous maneuvering of the government, led by the Federal Reserve, this will always be the case, so long as disenfranchisement of the workforce remains "what is."

Workers don't get it. They are in charge of their destiny, and don't know or want to know it. They are waiting for the "company store" to provide their staples. No matter how many times they are sideswiped by reality, no matter how often their social, economic, spiritual and emotional status rides the roller coaster, they dream of calm waters, flat playing fields and Nirvana!

Dr. Fisher punctures this dream in this brilliant essay. It is designed to show workers everywhere what is happening and why. More importantly, he brings the reader to the full realization that virtually everyone is alone; that putting their house in order is entirely up to them. Fisher insists, being alone is okay! Once aloneness is accepted, true togetherness is possible, but not before. What often masquerades as togetherness is collective indifference. Chaos, he asserts, gives way to order one person at a time. Once the choice is made workers can build towards a more rational ordering society.

Dr. Fisher's books probe the effect of big passions on small people, for he considers himself one of the small people. Born on the proverbial "wrong side of the tracks," this Phi Beta Kappa graduate of the University of Iowa, argues that he has seen "the haves" take his world, turn it upside down and make a shambles of it. He has no intention of mouthing pleasantries over this fact, not with management as he demonstrated in *Work Without Managers: A View From The Trenches* (1991), nor with the working man or woman as he proves in this spellbinding book, *The Worker, Alone! Going Against the Grain.*

Dr. Fisher has worked for, observed, and been consultant to American and international concerns for the past thirty years. He is a former international corporate executive of Nalco Chemical Company and Honeywell, Inc., working in North and South America, Europe and South Africa. Fisher holds a doctorate in organizational and industrial psychology, and resides in Tampa, Florida with his wife, Betty, where he continues to write and consult.

Dr. Billy G. Gunter

Professor of Sociology, University of South Florida

21st Century Reality Check — The New Old Plague

This is the era of the professional worker. And, paradoxically, it's an era in which the workforce is regimented for jobs and workplaces more often than not, which no longer exist.

While literally everything has changed, conditions for the working professional, that vaunted knowledge worker, have not. In shameful fashion, workplace professionals are assigned, evaluated, categorized and promoted by means of criteria intended for a time long past with protocols that have little to do with their professional potential, ethics or, incredibly, actual job requirements.

Inexplicably, "modern" workplace professionals are managed, motivated, mobilized and manipulated in conformance with a long-outdated model, a model characterized by *position power* hierarchies, ritualistic routines and restrictive practices that contribute little to the bottom line; to the contrary actually.

In part, we can blame this on the unrelenting explosion in technology, which has accelerated since *The Worker, Alone!* Was first published in 1995. This tsunami of technology resulted in spiraling costs to employers and constant coping by workers. Call it an enormous distraction. If the obvious purpose of a company is "what it does," and "what it does" is simply cosmetic housekeeping, not aligned change with corporate objectives, then it becomes a serious problem, and it has.

Meanwhile, against this backdrop of coping with new technology, the corporate "system" engages tenaciously in *business as usual* practices with implacable authority, despite setback after setback. It operates as *knowing* rather than *learning* institutions, disregarding valuable lessons.

150

Rx For a Healthier Workplace

How then do we reawaken and revitalize a profoundly unconscious workplace? It's easy to point fingers at management, but that does not adequately address the issue. Nor does it deal with the larger problem of a devotion to the *status quo*; workers are content to wait for someone to take charge and lift them out of their malaise while managers reprove workers for their reluctance to exercise initiative. Ironically, professional workers wait and hope for someone to lead, when it is they, alone, who possess the necessary tools and acumen. They wait, timidly, for the vested powers to finally come to their senses, when those interests have far too much invested in the current reality to gamble on change.

Meaningful change will come about only when workers, aided by managers, summon the courage to bring about change from within. There is neither an upside to hope nor a downside to courage. But make no mistake; courage is both the engine of survival and the means to prevail.

Change as a natural occurrence has its own impetus, but lacks conscious direction. It is aimless and unreliable. Change is a random variable in the work environment and thus of secondary concern. Change of the deliberate sort, needed change, comes from having a center, a central governor, and manifests as a behavioral construct.

There are pitfalls to avoid, however. Needed change takes more than a change in attitude, more than good intentions, more than catchy slogans, more than a positive work climate, or a generous confection of incentives. Necessary change requires a radical change of mindset accompanied by a structural change in the way workers and managers execute their roles and conduct their relationship vis-à-vis each other. Simply, it takes hard work. Favorable impressions may result, but they are not the goal.

Essential change now calls for professional workers to go against the grain, to oppose the status quo. Plainly stated, it is time for professional workers to take charge!

How We Got Here

The corporate luxury of passively believing that "doing everything one can for workers, and in return expecting workers to be motivated to do everything they can for the company," is an extravagance companies can no longer afford. It's a strategy that has proven counterproductive to the extreme.

Entitlements and perks were expected to increase worker creativity and productivity. Instead, these confections have resulted in counter dependence and learned helplessness. When the connection between contribution and compensation was lost, workers became isolated from the reality of company dynamics, from the imperatives of daily operations in meeting the relentless demands of the marketplace.

Replacing this essential linkage was worker reliance on the comforts delivered by management. It led to professional complacency and counter dependence on the company for their total well-being. These workers brought their bodies to work and left their minds at home. Captive to this chronic disorder, many companies now struggle to remain solvent and to compete in the global economy.

Contrary to what orthodoxy insists, harmony is not the glue that holds a company on task. Managed conflict is. But employees have been conditioned to shy away from confrontation, to avoid conflict, to be safe hires, to shun risk taking of any sort, the opposite of being self-directed.

More than a half-century of this programming has resulted in the workforce that we have today; one largely reactive at the expense of taking the initiative. Now, when creativity is required, workers are unable and unwilling to respond. It's simply not part of their makeup. For too long, companies promoted security, and were willing to give workers everything except control of work. Lethargy, and passivity is the bitter product of this oversight.

When workers operate as renters instead of owner-stakeholders, contribution consists of safely following protocols, not productive, purposeful collaboration between workers and managers.

Dumping the Trash

Envisioning a new reality, workers and managers can be equal partners, but not until we see the following changes:

Performance Appraisal Systems (PAS) phased out. Perfunctory PAS is an elitist management practice that does nothing except reinforce *position power*. The new relationship between workers and managers is organic, fluid and interdependent. Workers pursue goals entirely consistent with overall company direction, while management provides clarity and context.

Personal reward and recognition programs for professionals (i.e., cash and prizes) eliminated. Incentives have proven to encourage bad behavior and to demotivate and divide knowledge workers, inhibiting cooperation and fostering wasteful internal competition. Workers prefer ownership of what they do provided they are given the tools to do the job, and the liberty (control) to perform the task in their own inimitable style, measured against parameters understood and agreed upon. The work is the reward for professionals.

Business unit internal and external competition suspended as overall organizational performance is emphasized. Creating discrete business units or departmental functions to compete against each other stymies creativity and leads to imitation at the expense of the overarching mission of the corporate entity. Although counterintuitive, it is nonetheless factual that when each function or department in a complex system is performing as well as it can, the overall system is not. Conversely, when these departments or functions focus on one shared objective, the organization succeeds beyond expectations. It is the nature of synergy.

Cease and desist with micromanagement. Over control creates reactionary workers. When failures occur, it is "not my problem!" They wait for management to solve the problem, when only they have the moxie and facilities to do so. Micromanagement weakens workers resolve creating a vacuum in which chaos thrives. Crisis management follows, a perpetual cycle in which management solves problems it creates, while workers take pleasure in the charade, failing to see they are also its victims. On the other hand, when workers are given ownership of what they do, they quickly resolve each issue as it arises, not waiting for management to intervene. In this work climate, chronic problems are addressed at the source.

Cease to see management as distinct from professional workers. Managers are atavistic and management, as we know it, is anachronistic, an outmoded technology. No longer are eighty (80) percent of the workforce unskilled blue-collar workers, and twenty (20) percent management and administrative support. Now, less than twenty percent of workers are unskilled while eighty percent are professionally trained. Management today is essentially everybody. Therefore, workers need to have a sense of this new role and accountability. Stated another way, this new work climate cannot be partitioned. Quality, for example, is not only a quality department function, separate from human resources, engineering, production, administration, and sales and marketing. Quality is a matter of concern for everyone, as all functions are interdependent, part of one organic whole.

Refrain from faddism. There was a time when companies were "searching" for excellence, imitating successful companies to the nth detail. Many of these companies in the end failed. Emulation was often at the expense of a regard for their immutable uniqueness. Each company is as unique from other companies as individuals are unique from other individuals. Each company has a distinctive history, value and belief system, infrastructure and relational heritage, along with proprietary highs and lows, and matchless secrets.

Corporate essence stokes (internal) aspirations, manifested in its (external) propensities. As fixated as people may be, this is more the case with companies. They run on the momentum that has brought them to this time, place and space. Mergers often end poorly because this intangible cohesiveness is not considered.

The seeds for rejuvenation are never "out there!" The better wisdom for an enterprise is to create the new out of the ashes of the old. This exploits the collective mind. The reticent majority often reveals answers concerning survival. Too frequently in panic mode, these voices are dismissed as unimportant and therefore ignored. Instead, grandiose schemes and quick fixes are entertained. They range from "hot house" training programs to cutting edge technologies to tantalizing shortcuts supposed to ensure instantaneous course corrections and cures for decade's old faux pas. Stopgap measures usually carry the seductive scent of cosmetic change, while merely postponing the inevitable. Change for change's sake is no change at all.

Finally, Professional Workers Taking Charge

Twenty years ago it was "crunch time" for workers as professionals. This was essentially ignored, as they were too busy complaining to seize the initiative. Now they inhabit a dysfunctional system that they inherited, but did not improve.

A new crop of professionals is coming into the system with their heads down as well. They have invested heavily in education so far with a disappointing return on that investment, as good paying jobs prove difficult to find.

Once these professionals have a job, there is little sense of security as the train wrecks of conglomerates are heard in the distance. They are as angry at "the system" as were their elders, failing to realize they are the system.

The Worker, Alone! Is a book predicated on the principal that nothing changes at work until working professionals' change. Games of trendy themes like empowerment continue, because they're acceptable and safe, risking nothing to those in power. It is now urgently up to workers to put this house in order. Neither house cleaning nor finger pointing will do. Professionals must get off the dime and boldly take charge of work, their work, which is the path to taking charge in life.

James R. Fisher, Jr., Ph.D.

An Upside-Down World!

"Two extravagances: to exclude Reason, to admit only Reason."

Blaise Pascal, French mathematician

The English poet, John Donne (1572-1631), was wrong. He once wrote "No man is an island unto himself." Every man today is an island unto himself, and his only redemption is in the full knowledge and acceptance of this fact. The answers are not in government, nor industry and commerce, no longer in religion, and certainly not in science. So, you ask, "Where does that leave the worker?" I reply, "Very much alone!"

The expedience of naiveté does not improve the worker's longed for identity and recognition, nor does naiveté ensure the continuance of freedom, which is virtually taken for granted. The worker is on his own nickel, and there is no savior, no god, and no protector to shield him from the crush of history, from the inevitable force of reality, other than himself.[1]

What is missing is a lack of attention to fear. Workers are afraid to lead fuller lives, not because they embrace fear, but because they deny it by preoccupation with distractions. I understand fear. Fear runs through my body the way sap runs through a tree. I am attentive to fear each day of my life, for that day may be my last. Were I not so attentive I might be distracted and go to my grave without expressing these sentiments. Fear is a powerful positive in my life. It keeps me attentive. It finds me taking life seriously, but not myself.

The working world is upside down. This world today demands workers go against the grain to put it back on its foundation. What is killing this country in particular and the working world in general is too much HYPE, too much Harvard, Yale and Princeton Elitism in law, politics, government, commerce, religion and industry. These institutions of inflated grading and solipsistic egos, would in government restore order from chaos by cosmetic surgery (Crime Bill), revitalize trust by the appearance of propriety (New Declaration of Ethics), establish economic stability by treaty (NAFTA and GATT) and rejuvenate accountability by modification to the rites of passage (Term Limits in Congress). None of this touches society's sick soul.

The societal portrait of Dorian Gray withers grotesque, but remains undiscovered, hidden in the attic of denial. Meanwhile, society, as collective individualism, stubbornly refuses to grow up, determined to remain indulgently suspended in adolescence. There are few mature adults in charge, only patriarchal parents. Society goes from child to parent, parent to child, only to skip the adult phase. Society is waiting for someone to "take charge," but no one is conditioned for such responsibility, especially the rank and file worker.

A patriarchal driven society pushes for morality, which is only a mindset of the time, not a definitive proposition. While parents push for "what should be," children escape into impulsive pleasure. Parents, mystified by their collective ineptitude, abandon their values and join their children in "joy-living" distracting aberrations. It is the world of everything, anything, now! In contrast mature adults display the patience and grit to deal with "what is," holding firmly to their beliefs, values and expectations.

With a disturbing absence of mature adults, polite chicanery is the order of the day, especially in the workplace. Appearances justify everything. Looking good eclipses doing good. This is very Socratic, for Socrates reduces philosophy essentially to a matter of manners, or refinement. He argues that the greatest wisdom, and best differentiation between good and evil is displayed in appearances. Well, HYPE exudes good manners. They hold their fork correctly, use four-letter words only in private, or with their own kind, and find their vocation as courtiers to power. For the past half-century, they have been busy promulgating Teflon means to justify synthetic ends, and workers everywhere have said nothing. Yet the fault lies not with HYPE, but with the workers, workers who sought sanctuary as children from cradle to grave.

Whatever the enticement, the response of workers-as-children is always the same. Take the newest craze, information technology. The panacea of the atomic age, with its promise of cheap energy, now gives way to the information age. Workers have been persuaded that the logic of science translates into ever-expanding economic opportunity. Conveniently forgotten is the fact that nuclear power creates a waste that is impossible to destroy; that nuclear power has already upset the ecological balance of our planet, due in no small measure to society's collective ignorance of nuclear fallout.

Now, the blitzkrieg of information technology invades the defenseless mind and social fabric, encountering little skepticism. With modems and Internet software, the virtual community is a reality. Workers no longer have to sit in front of television screens and watch program patterns as they did in the 1950s. They can sit in front of their television screens now and talk dirty to the world. The virtual community, which Internet provides, replaces physical and psychological intimacy with confinement to a monitor screen, or the equivalent of self-imposed solitary confinement. Progress, isn't it wonderful?

Pop artist, Andy Warhol: "When I got my first television set, I stopped caring so much about having close relationships."

Now, children as young as two or three have their own electronic pads to play games from sun up to sun down, only to look up to eat when they are hungry. Warhol didn't live to see this implausible perversion of human relations. In a world of some seven billion souls, more than half of whom lack this luxury, they remain invisible to people in advanced industrial societies. These people fail to see them or each other as they, too, have their heads down texting, tweeting or exploring apps on laptops or handheld electronic devices. No one seems to appreciate the absurdity.

Incredibly, information technology displaces many workers from jobs and turns potentially skilled workers into low-level computer technicians. Computers may facilitate the work of scholars, scientists, engineers and writers, but computers also turn them into essentially typists. Yet from this most articulate, gifted and intellectually elite community, one hears nary a complaint.

Silent Invasions!

"A man of clear ideas errs grievously if he imagines that whatever is seen confusedly does not exist; it belongs to him, when he meets with such a thing, to dispel the mist, and fix the outlines of the vague form which is looming through it."

John Stuart Mill, English philosopher

We live in a world of invasions. Countries invade other countries without provocation, governments invade our bedrooms as they attempt to legislate morality, men invade women as if it is their right, television invades our homes and minds to create a wasteland of purpose, obscenity as art invades our culture forsaking its role of promoting the nobility of man, and information technology invades all aspects of our private lives so that everything once sacred is now profane. Conceivably, to invade each other's privacy is the basic way perhaps the only way workers can relate to each other. There is little intimacy. The void created by its lack is now replaced by licentious gossip.

Supportive of this is daytime television, which thrives on invasion. It celebrates the most bizarre deviancies as common fare, while workers take "time out" from their banal lives to devour barbarism without a whimper of protest. It is apparent by the ratings these programs generate that the audience delights in self-negation, self-degradation, for every person so exposed, violates everyone. What redeeming value does such exposure have for the human soul?

Moreover, as a society, workers tolerate an extraordinary amount of intrusive noise. They accept Muzak in shopping malls and airports, boom boxes on the street, television surveillance in banks and department stores. The electronic eye follows them everywhere, or subliminal aural stimulation attacks their subconscious. To an incredible degree, workers relish intrusion, especially media intrusion. They live vicariously through the personal lives and foibles of celebrities. Their own lives are so dull and boring to them that they may spend hours, which can literally grow into days, glued to their television screens following the lurid carnival of sex, crime and mayhem of a certain celebrity personality. Gossip is more grist for the mill than personal intimacy, while noise is a welcomed relief from intimidating silence.

Clearly, intimacy is taboo. It is too personal. Preferred is the scandalous, like sleeping around, or playing with that fantasy. This represents the reduction of behavior to instinct in order to fill a painful void. This is far less sinful than simply a waste.

Humans think and dream. They love. Love requires intimacy. Without love, there is no intimacy. Intimacy is quite possible without being sexual, but intimacy is absolutely a disaster when sexual without being intimate. Intimacy is synergistic. Its total emotional effect is greater than the sum of its parts. Conversely, promiscuity is consuming. Its emotional impact is to leave both parties exhausted, empty and despairing.

Despite this, workers hold to taboos against intimacy, the same way they cower from fear. Love is a four letter word with which most workers are uncomfortable. Yet love is the sinew missing from the muscle of today's organization: love of work, life, friendship, and being useful. Lust, greed and pleasure are the void fillers for those afraid of love.

Young people don't buy into this mind set. When young people suffer life a little, they crave intimacy. They move toward, not away from doubt. Being good lovers is not a primary quest. That is what their parents think and fear. Why? Because parents attempt to save their loveless marriages with sex.

Young people are driven by a need for identity and recognition. This is the motor of existence. They don't feel a need to rush nature. They can afford to let nature take its course. On the other hand, a common invention of parents is "perversion by example." Parental sexual conduct contaminates and invades the sanctuary of their youngsters. Were parents to behave differently, the behavior of their children would follow.

To take nature in stride is discarded by workers. Think of this a moment. Clocks are speeded up. Everyone is in a mad rush to go nowhere, with no idea why. Workers are so busy getting nowhere that they have no time to take inventory of their personal lives. As a result, what should be important is mainly relegated to an afterthought. Life experience is an atavistic gesture which requires toys of distraction to fill the punishing void.

Dr. Larry Kubiak, psychologist: "Parents of teenagers spend an average of only 14 minutes each day communicating with their children. Only one minute is positive communication, and one minute is neutral. A whopping 12 minutes are negative."

Many need to cry out in the void of their emptiness to authenticate themselves. The more embarrassing the circumstances the more they feel validated. This finds many compelled to "go public" with the most intimate details of their personal lives. Daytime television was made for them. Here talk show hosts raise humanity from the barbaric to the banal. Viewers privately scoff at this public display of disgrace. But who is the greater philistine — the exhibitionist or the voyeur? The more graphic and blatant the confessions the better. Such programming defines a society which has lost its center and moral compass.

Exhibitionism as therapy has become legitimate business. It is the main doctrine of Alcoholics Anonymous (AA). Alcoholics, who leave this high church and attempt to maintain their sobriety on their own, are called "dry drunks." Disclosure (and attendance at meetings), AA insists, is key to rehabilitation. Many other addiction centers say, "Amen!" Disclosure as therapy is used for smokers, gamblers, overeaters, spouse abusers, and the list goes on. Invasion of the personal domain is axiomatic as ends justify means. Privacy is suspended for cathartic relief as the cry reverberates, "Let it all hang out!"

What seems implicit in this expression is that workers don't know who or what they are. They need someone to tell them. They are desperate for approval from others so they may approve of themselves. Workers are in a virtual struggle for identity and recognition, for being reborn with a fresh sense of self.

Their historic dependency on management, or people in authority has eroded. Their counter dependency on the workplace has been torn asunder as many find themselves displaced persons, forced out of their jobs . . . ten, fifteen or twenty years before retirement age . . . and like Joseph K in Franz Kafka's compelling novel, *The Trial*, "without having done anything wrong."

Before, they took the boss's word as gospel, and the job as a certain thing. Now, that is all gone. They are alone, on their own, and they have never been taught to think and behave as mature adults. So, many escape into vices, vices which drive them to despair, with despair driving them to disclosure. . . "And the beat goes on."

As children, the focus of existence was on becoming somebody, not on being involved and committed to something now; on the competitive drive, not the spirit of cooperation; on the illusion of progress, not on the reality of experience.

But alas, thanks to decades of corrupt and incompetent leadership in all institutions, the squandering of natural resources, the impatience of youth and discriminated minorities, the persistence of psychological and physiological abuse, burgeoning chaos and violence, the dream has died. In so doing workers are now forced to embrace despair. Despair is the only cure for illusion. Without the penetrating pain of despair, workers fail to grow up. In the end time runs out on suspended adolescence, the dominant state of workers in the past century and now as well in the 21st century. The youth must die to give birth to the mature adult. It is a painfully slow and agonizing process, but inevitable.

The pain of reality drives workers now to an ever-expanding consciousness. This goes beyond seeking rational economic parity. Workers demand more, not less, control of their lives at all levels: spiritual, intellectual, emotional, economic and political. They have had it. They find they can trust no one but themselves. This new found sense of self can only lead to the collapse of tyranny in the workplace — the tyranny generated by comfort, by the patronizing paternalism of omniscient and benevolent management. A pat on the head will no longer suffice. Workers want their power back. But before this will occur, human nature will take a circuitous route to this objective, a senseless but inevitable escape into regression.

This is where we find workers today. "Want" has become need; legitimate tools, toys. Computers, iPads, laptops, cell phones or the yet to be invented new widget will get their power back. Still, these distractions are embraced for they are marketed as essential to "empowerment and liberation." These are sophisticated tools which have become toys of distraction, toys which everyone must have. These legitimate tools have become gimmicks. Workers as buyers congratulate themselves for they see these devices as "expanding individual choice and demonstrating freedom." What these workers fail to understand is that what they are doing is escaping into Toyland. At this writing, many middle class workers are slaves to call waiting, e-mail, text messages, tweets, the Internet or their video cell phones—acting out their roles as historical caricatures of the times.

The history of workers is not revealed in causes, nor silent invasions. History presents only a blank succession of unexplained events. Society's *historical persona*, as it is normally written, usually represents public events which hyphenate technical achievements. Meanwhile, spiritual or inner events, which are most real, and what life is all about, are largely ignored or forgotten.

Life is meant to be lived, moment to moment, not explained or justified. Only unconscious activity bears fruit. Workers, who play a part in their times, never understand their true significance. Should they attempt to understand them, as the politically correct would have them act, they are struck with sterility.

The bleak truth is the more workers condone silent invasion the less authentic they become to themselves. Invasion has come to represent the social machinery for concealing the spectacle of human impotence and irrelevance and blindness— the ordinary details of daily existence.

Most observers mistake the outer accidents of existence, events which lie outside the worker's soul—social, economic, and political realities—for that which alone is genuine, the reality of experience.

Isaiah Berlin: ". . . the individual experience, the specific relation of individuals to one another, the colors, smells, tastes, sounds and movements, the jealousies, loves, hatreds, passions, the rare flashes of insight, the transforming moments, the ordinary day-to-day success of private data . . . constitute all there is."

Technology as gimmick is widespread, exposing joyless materialism, lonely crowds, complacent consumerism, an anthill culture and the homogenized food of the meatloaf era. Everything is meant to be gulped down, not tasted. Culture is inauthentic; too many paperbacks, too little creativity. Ubiquitous technology narrows and isolates consumers into more minuscule pigeonholes of tastes to be targeted for exploitation. This is another silent invasion of privacy. Yet, the invasion is not simply forgiven, but applauded. Workers celebrate the compelling distraction of technology from reality. What feeds the mind is not necessarily food for the soul.

The Price of Innocence!

"In our time, what is at issue is the very nature of man, the image we have of his limits and possibilities as man. History is not yet done with its explanation of the limits and meaning of human nature."

C. Wright Mills, American sociologist

Technology is a whirling dervish. No one has any idea where it will lead. Obviously it tampers with the mind, and creates bizarre confusion in the heart. This is observable every day and everywhere. Take the housewife I observed standing in line at the supermarket, as I waited to pay for my purchases. With cell phone in hand, she talked to herself leaving a telephone message on her recorder at home, then turned to me and laughed in my ear, "Isn't this crazy, but I'd forget otherwise." Little did I know that day that this peculiar behavior would represent only the tip of the iceberg of what has become the norm.

The blurring of the real and the imagined finds workers electronic junkies oblivious to their surroundings. Listening to this housewife put me in mind of a television production. I fully expected someone behind me to yell, "Cut, print and wrap," as if this were a film clip to spoof art imitating life as excess.

The world today is not a new-found absurdity as it was for Jean-Paul Sartre and Albert Camus. It is a place where absurdity is the plausible norm and manages to sound, to all but the most satirical minds, like truth and reason. Indeed, today absurdity sounds like honor and service and sacrifice and virtue, a monument of logic. Even using a cell phone or iPad like a toy is normal behavior, a triumph of technology. You don't have to ask your lymph glands about it or become embarrassed at passing wind.

Meanwhile, entire communities have become sink holes of despair, rife with crime, violence, illegitimacy, illiteracy, poverty, homelessness, disease and chaos. Ambushed by free floating anxiety, workers have lost touch with touch. They are clowns in everyday dress. Hostile, perhaps even hateful for losing a job or being taken for granted, they strike out blindly at shadows. They adopt the tactics of their enemies — paranoia, gossip, innuendo, and blackballing. Whatever their inclination — homophobic, militant or racist — they become essentially their own worst enemy.

The obliging media unwittingly contributes to this deception as they position mirrors to capture "the best" glimpse of workers — strong, fearless, purposeful, alert, skillful, responsible, industrious. What these mirrors fail to capture is the real self, which is far less pretty, closer to the opposite — weak, fearful, ambivalent, lethargic, inept, irresponsible, and indolent. To no one's surprise workers insist on the image of themselves as hero to that of wimp.

Still, these mirrors reflect only the outer self, the guile of invention, not the inner self, the engine of the soul, which lies beyond the depth of mirrors. To wit:

Workers believe this the land of unlimited opportunity, even as opportunity disappears. When failures occur, blame is the game. At one level, failure is the nervous tic of the worker's lack of skill, initiative, greed or indifference. At another level, failure plays against the inept elements of society, which are judged to be distortions in "the system." Fix these aberrations and all will fall into place. Politicians happily play these nonsense strings and point their finger in every direction but at the problem. No one talks about a finite world, an increasingly crowded world, or a shrinking economic pie with limited opportunity. Instead, godlike, workers have been persuaded by these demigods of the *Establishment* that it is their destiny to remake the world into their "own image and likeness." Workers embrace the warped vision of a "New Golden Age." They tie their hopes and aspirations to a scientifically managed society which cures all social ills. All signs to the contrary are ignored. Optimism governs the rank and file worker, but she never governs wisely.

Workers see economic parity as their birthright. They see themselves with an ever-expanding share of the economic pie. It has never happened before, and it is unlikely to happen in the future. The proportionate distribution of resources has not changed dramatically since the 17th Century. During the American Revolution, 40 percent of the wealth was controlled by 10 percent of the population. On the eve of the Civil War, 70 percent of the nation's resources were still controlled by 10 percent of the people. Industrialization had an even more devastating effect on the distribution of resources. In the first decade of the 20th Century, 60 percent of the nation's wealth was controlled by 2 percent of the people, while the bottom 65 percent controlled but 5 percent of the wealth. Since World War II, the top 20 percent has controlled 40 percent, while the bottom 40 percent controlled less than 6 percent. Although workers admittedly benefitted with a generous slice of the economic pie immediately after WWII, between 1968 and 1981, real wages for the average worker declined 20 percent. The cushion of comfort, provided by post WWII demands, has disappeared. In 1947, United States workers produced 60 percent of the world's industrial goods. Today it is 30 percent. Manufactured goods, such as automobiles, agricultural machinery and telecommunications have declined as much as 30 to 50 percent.

Workers insist in the belief that they live in a classless society. Decreasing economic mobility, however, emphasizes class lines. Moreover, workers are tired; tired of social climbing; tired of explaining their individual failure, or the failure of their national leadership.

As tired as they are, they still cower from reality, seeking refuge under the canopy of denial. Workers cannot accept that the boom is over. Meanwhile, politicians exploit their ambivalence. Both political parties assure workers that the boom is not over. Both sound the same, the rhetoric is the same, the assumptions identical. The common good, upon which the Republic was founded, now a radical idea, is missing, replaced in both parties by majority interest. Polling controls the mind of government, and by extension, the minds of the governed. Workers fail to see how this sponsors and spawns leaderless leadership, or how it places their well-being in permanent jeopardy.

Badly misled, workers have been conditioned to see the whole in terms of the part — mesmerized by their own special needs and requirements. Maniacal ethnocentrism is the common addiction of workers and politicians alike. Such addiction brings out the Renaissance man in some, the corporate fascist in others. Workers are primed for fascism, for a quick fix to the overwhelming problems of crime, violence, economic turmoil and social unrest. Caught between two colossi, one of which has no heart and the other no head, they are primed for this as they gulp down tasteless food, sit indolently in freeze frame before their televisions or computers, as they listen to mechanical noise alluding to be music, or wax robotic discussing automobiles (made in Japan) or electronics (made in Taiwan).

Workers favor computers in the classroom, the earlier the better. First graders have laptops, many even cell phones. Yet eight, ten or twelve years later, these same students cannot do their multiplication tables, long or short division, fractions, cannot balance a check book; don't know how to diagram a sentence; don't know a gerund from a participle; or cannot spell 200 common words, while reading at the dull normal level. This is painfully illustrated as more than a million skilled workers are imported each year because students-as-workers are ill prepared.

Technology promises to make for a more educated society, a society which will lead to a more harmonious society. The exact opposite is occurring as we become more technology friendly. Eminent futurists such as Arthur C. Clarke, James Martin, and Loy Singleton declare that hand-held electronic pocket tutors will revolutionize education worldwide. It sounds good, but learning is more a social process than a mechanical function.

Even the notable psychologist, Carl Rogers, sees high-tech communications as the key to person-centered education. He hails it "the promise of a new dawn of enlightenment." Rogers predicts global competition will be replaced by cooperation, respect for others, and mutual helpfulness. History suggests otherwise. Human nature has changed little in recorded history. It is inclined to hoard, bully, exploit weakness, frustrate purpose, divide and conquer.

These prominent voices seem plagued with the same feeble myths workers crave to believe. Mythology as hope does not beget courage. It assumes a linear connection between the distribution of sophisticated technology and the manifestation of altered states of awareness, and more idyllic forms of human behavior. There is no substitute for love, and love is not likely to be found in printed   wire   circuit   memory   boards.

Workers confuse rights and privileges. For instance, a public school education is the privilege of citizenship. This gives the individual, whatever his circumstances, an opportunity to expand his consciousness and tap his inherent potential. Public school education is a remarkable privilege of modern society, which has little to do with rights. But treated as a right, however, it is sure to be abused. Students feel they are doing society a favor by becoming educated. So, they fight it. What we obtain too cheaply, we esteem too lightly. When students complete twelve years of public education, at virtually no cost to them, and are unable to read or comprehend these words here, they, not society, have failed themselves. Blame it on "the system," ethnicity, family, or poverty, the fact remains the individual is ultimately responsible in this world for himself. The sense of this has been lost as rights are flaunted and privileges forgotten.

Late Blooming Roses

"Men are grown mechanical in head and heart, as well as hand. Their whole effort, attachments, opinions turn on Mechanism, and are of a mechanical character."

Thomas Carlyle, Scottish philosopher

Workers are addicted to lingering dependence. Who is to blame? Is it culture? Can a capitalistic society of liberal democracy produce a stable work force in which workers are satisfied? Is satisfaction an essential to economic solidarity? Does a democratically driven culture raise humanity only from barbarism to banality? Does such banality breed instability and spiritual deprivation?

Weighty questions. Many prefer to contemplate such questions as philosophers did a thousand years ago as if attempting to determine the number of angels on the head of a pin. Many promote this preoccupation, because it is an idle and safe activity, and takes them off the hook. What workers of such a mind conveniently forget is that they are the culture. They are society. It is not something "out there," but in their sinews, bones and running through their blood.

Workers can no longer play dumb or wax innocent. They have no one to blame for the present societal malaise, but themselves. They have not been deprived of outlets to strive for mastery of themselves. The plunge into chaos has been a gratuitous retreat. Instead of changing their ways, instead of taking matters into their own hands and doing something about the situation, workers have allowed themselves to be treated as interchangeable parts, and to perfect the pathetic role of victim of circumstances. Massive redundancy exercises in which tens of thousands of highly skilled workers have lost their jobs, represents a single factor — a lack of attentiveness.

Since the days of Isaac Newton, heads and hearts have been like parts to a finely tuned watch, machine parts only. Workers since Newton have been conditioned to think of themselves as machines. Machines control them, not only in the material aspects of society, but through philosophy, art, literature, and music. Workers are consumed with their mechanistic obsessions. All efforts, all attachments, opinions, turn on mechanisms, even redemption (Deliverance) is of a mechanistic nature.

Souls of steel provide little solace to pristine innocence. Sinclair Lewis in his 1920 classic, *Main Street*, saw how oppressive standardization was killing the moral fiber of community, and by extension, its spirit:

"It is contentment. . . the contentment of the quiet dead. . . it is slavery self-sought and self-defended. It is dullness made God. . .A savorless people, gulping tasteless food, and sitting afterward, coatless and thoughtless, in rocking chairs prickly with inane decorations, listening to mechanical music, saying mechanical things about the excellence of Ford automobiles, and viewing themselves as the greatest race in the world."

The primacy of workers is to fulfill their needs through a rational economic process. This finds them selling themselves and their integrity to the highest bidder. The ethics of this proposition never comes to mind.

But alas, economics have not been enough. Being well-heeled financially has not brought workers physical health or spiritual happiness. It has led instead to a state of panic, *The Prison of Panic called "Now!"* Workers behave as if the boom will last forever, while fearing it won't.

A cursory review suggests that for the past half century comfort and entitlements have been exchanged for power and control. What was thrown in by the workers, "free of charge," was their identity and individual recognition. Workers couldn't or wouldn't see past their noses. Short-term gain was the focus at the expense of long-term consequences. Workers trusted their employers and management — nothing wrong with that! What workers didn't expect, or consider, because they didn't pay attention, is that what goes up must come down. Nor did they consider what is likely to happen to a society as it moves along the continuum from boom to bust. Now, workers are powerless, millions jobless and epitomize the status of "the victim."

Anything as important as work cuts to the core of the human soul. Without work, there is little sense of self. Without work, it is an embarrassment to breathe. Society is driven by the pervasive theme, "He who works has clout and rules the roost." Mere reflection on this reminds workers how inattentive they have been. How they have tricked themselves.

Like Faust, workers have sold their soul, and now wish to buy it back at bargain basement prices. The current obsession with identity and recognition is nothing less than a consuming drive to get a second chance. This is the engine of an eventual societal revolution.

Seduced by the dollar, workers participate in a painful irony. They are always paid a dollar more an hour than they can afford to quit. This keeps a lid on their lips, their obliging spirits in a cage, and them forever fearful of taking control of their lives.

Workers everywhere know it is dangerous to be right about work especially when the company is wrong. The company is often wrong and could profit much by listening to its workers. Failure of workers to have a distinct voice in operations penalizes the company and the workers alike. Everybody loses. All because the almighty dollar blinds passions into fainthearted submissiveness.

So what do workers do? If they don't challenge the boss when things are wrong, how is their anger and frustration expressed? It is expressed in a cornucopia of grief. Workers whine about their plight to each other, sabotage operations, take bogus sick leave, participate in work slowdowns, and become passive personalities, as if the job were a separate entity apart from themselves. Few, if any, consider going against the grain and launching a constructive counterattack.

Nearly a trillion dollars is lost each year from worker self-betrayal, which is still defended with the motto, "Get as much as you can, while the getting is good! Stick it to them before they stick it to you!" Lost in this incredible confusion is that the workers, themselves, are the company! They are robbing themselves, killing their own possibilities.

A conspiracy of silence denies this. Even the most dedicated workers refuse to worry about, much less snitch on laggards, pilferers and saboteurs, or to concern themselves about cash-flow problems, profit & loss statements, expanding or contracting markets, cost of materials, or the reliability of design, because "That is not my job!" This is outside the province of their concerns, as industries, plants, markets and jobs disappear, or collapse and die. Selective naiveté does not beget security for anyone.

Managers are employees, too, no more owners than any other workers. True, managers traditionally assume the role of surrogate owner, and comport themselves as if it is "their company." This is an accidental invention triggered by the abandonment of power and control by workers.

Management is a relatively new profession, which has grown out of two World Wars in the 20th Century. Workers, with little forethought, empowered management to be their conscience, caretaker, benefactor and protector. Workers, in a word, gave up control of their lives for comfort. For fifty years now, workers have luxuriated in a climate of sublime comfort and complaisant dependence.

Now, workers want their power back, but without risk, pain or consequence. They want their cake and eat it, too. But what is given away can seldom be returned. This is especially true of power. That is why there are all these "fun and games" about empowerment, when, in fact, no power is given back, not one iota of it.

If power is to be regained, there will be the spilling of real blood. There will be struggle and sacrifice. Major League baseball players (indeed, all professional athletes) have Curt Flood to thank for their collective bargaining power. It cost Flood his career. Now, no one remembers him. Many workers will have to pay a similar price.

The whole empowerment movement is counterfeit. The sooner workers realize this the sooner they can adopt a strategy to recover what has been lost. Management has no intentions of giving up its power. It is content to play MONOPOLY with workers' lives, a game played with funny money, which buys nothing but delay.

In any case the workers are not ready. Power demands attributes missing in most modern workers — such attributes as accountability, grace under pressure, inclination to take risks, accept blame, endure failure, believe in themselves when no one else will, do their best even when no credit comes their way, and be driven more by an ideal than money.

Power demands other things as well. There is a considerable difference between securing a paycheck every two weeks, and worrying 24 hours a day if the job gets done and within costs, on schedule, fully meeting all customer requirements.

If you say many managers don't pass this test, you would be right. Managers are power brokers, not power barons. They must, as with workers, be kept happy, fully employed, with staff and resources up to capacity. This is the burden of real power. Identity and recognition are related closely to where the buck stops, and is often far removed from where the work takes place.

To many workers, the future is an illusion with denial the hammer of indifference. They refuse to see the handwriting on the wall and so turn to consultants to read it to them. Consultants are problem simplifiers. That is their role. Anything that will suggest to workers that the situation is "not their fault," or can project blame elsewhere is destined to be a big seller. Blame the situation on inadequate tools, poor training, cheap foreign labor, gender and race discrimination, unfair labor practices, inequitable trade policies, poor management, the National Debt, anything but on workers, themselves, and you have a responsive audience and customer.

Consultants, specialists and writers attack the disorder from the outside, as they must. They suggest reinventing or re-engineering the corporation, anything but asking workers to radicalize their thinking, or to challenge their potential contribution.

By attacking the problem from the outside, these well-meaning experts inadvertently fabricate a new "we/they" polarity, and promote a new rendition of an old song, disenchantment. Cosmetic surgery, for that is what is proposed, fails to touch the worker's soul.

Take the current obsession with quality. At first cut, this looks commendable. Who can argue with the validity of quality or quality standards in the conduct of work? The problem is with the obsession with quality standards. This is where the fault lies. Lost in this pursuit is the need for increased production and greater product diversification, essential components to the creation of new jobs.

Quality and performance standards are mind sets, not specific ways of doing things — not the A,B,C's of this or that formula (W. Edwards Deming notwithstanding); this or that model or paradigm; this or that fad.

Obviously, a mindset is important. If workers don't believe in a good idea, it will fail. On the other hand, if they believe in a bad idea, it will succeed. With quality or performance standards, there is no attempt to radicalize the way workers think. The approach is totally mechanistic, simplistic and therefore ephemeral. Still, workers, like obedient children, go along with the drill, and play out the charade. Once again, expediency wins.

Workers as thinkers is a new idea, an idea left out of the equation, not only in the workplace but in all phases of society. Workers as thinkers are far removed from community involvement in the collapsing social order of crime, poverty, homelessness, homicide, suicide, genocide and moral decay. Nor are workers motivated to get involved. They prefer to sit in the bleachers of society and criticize it from afar. They love television's C-Span where they can ventilate their frustrations with anonymity and without consequences. Once again, "Not my problem!" But it is.

Order is first established inside the individual, one-person-at-a-time, before any behavioral change is manifested outside in society-at-large. Change the man from a passive person to an active personality with a social conscience, involved in the management and maintenance of society, and you change the world.

This demands more than simply the changing of the worker's mind. It requires the creation of a radically different mentality. Anything less is to fall victim to mechanistic pretense, or irritating aberrations which fail to touch anyone.

Workers are compliant, amorphous, and like silly putty, can be molded into many forms. They may build castles of sand on psychic islands, drifting through life lost in a sea of confusion, or be programmed to obsessional levels regarding their physical well-being. Trigger words, such as "social security" and "universal health coverage," or "lifetime employment" and "eternal youth" can make them forget the spiritual foundation of their common humanity. These trigger words spell "comfort" and "security." Workers are ready to barter their souls for such satisfaction. "Getting" blocks out their natural inclination to "giving."

But mankind is a single entity, with every worker an essential part of a common fabric. Worker power, identity and recognition are not national issues, but global themes. If workers continue to be preoccupied with nonsense, with self-indulgent concerns, while allowing others to solve their problems, to make choices for them, then most employment is bound to be purposeless; bound to lead to an eternity of lingering dependence. It is time for workers, like late blooming roses, to come to grips with their situation. Otherwise, those made redundant will forever echo the tired refrain, "How can this happen to me, when I have done nothing wrong?" It is not a question of wrong, but what have you done right?

Corporate Architects of a Failed System!

"The path to joy leads through despair."

Alexander Lowen, physician and psychotherapist

It is time we admit that all attempts to correct the cultural slide of society, especially as it relates to workers, has failed. It is time we get inside these failures and examine them for what they are. By doing so, most problems can be solved. Three crucial flaws contribute to the social psychological chaos of our times:

Workers fail to grow up and seize the moment as mature adults. Mature adults are workers who accept reality instead of being obsessed with "what should be," or "has been," or "what's going to be." What we have, in the main, are workers as dependent children in a world which stubbornly refuses to grow up. These workers have the disposition, inclination, collective identity and impulsive rashness of children. They don't want the facts, they want more, and they want it now! They fail to realize feelings are facts, and nothing changes until they change themselves.

Workers are predominantly knowers, not learners. Our entire educational system produces knowers, not learners; apologists, not thinkers. Most workers learn a skill, a craft or profession, and then coast for forty years, essentially inattentive to what is happening around them, and then call it a career. This necessitates the invention of media pundits, pseudo-specialists, armchair scholars, and high priests of science and religion to fill the void. These omniscient promulgators dictate to workers what to think, feel, value, believe and expect. Lost here is that "experts" wallow in the same confusion as workers. Few are learners, only knowers.

Workers are obsessed with control. Control is everything. Few realize the absurdity of this obsession. Yet, the evidence is emphatic. The more workers attempt to control their nature the more nature controls them. It is equally so in the general as in the particular. Man delights in the conquest of nature, and has for centuries, treating nature as if a separate entity. And so the planet is out-of-control.

173

The controller and the controlled are but one and the same. Everything is related to the same whole. Unfortunately, a wedge has been driven between the mind and the body; between the earth and man. Division is celebrated, not communion.

Viewed in the particular, the more workers attempt to control their passions, appetites and behaviors, the less they control them. Good intentions count for little. Deeds, not words, make the difference. How could it be otherwise? Control is a maddening societal pursuit, which fractures, segments and isolates. An obsession with control creates chaos, not order.

But mechanistic man cannot think otherwise. A mechanistic mentality thinks in terms of separation, not connection; of conflict, not harmony; of the parts, not the whole. Mechanistic man would find it strange for one to propose that he think with his whole body. Yet virtually everything is connected; everything is related — subject to object; object to subject; cause to effect; effect to cause. Resolving a problem in the context of the part always creates another problem, often worse than the problem resolved. Resolution can only be realized when control is suspended and order is embraced. But order requires "letting go," which is practically unfathomable for a mechanistic mind.

Subsequently, we will discuss these flaws in more detail. For now, consider the impact of these fixations on behavior. Obviously, these flaws derail a good number of workers from satisfying lives. What workers think, they become. If the work they do is mainly thought to be bogus, then it follows their lives can hardly be considered genuine. Consider this:

A gainfully employed worker, firmly ensconced in reality, is more likely to develop and use his skills in the service of others, and therefore experience happiness.

Happiness is not the absence of sorrow, but inseparable from joy. Pleasure is also married to pain; success to failure; certainty to doubt; clarity to confusion, and so on. Happiness has peaks and valleys, for good and bad days are part of the same experience. With this perspective, a happy worker is unlikely to beat his mate or commit suicide; is not likely to become a criminal or a child molester. A happy worker is humble in the sight of his Creator and a law abider; not one to covet either another's property or mate. A happy worker is the foundation of a rational ordering society.

Now that we have established this premise, the question must be asked, whose responsibility is it for the worker to be happy? The worker's of course. The crux of society's problem is that this is not clearly understood or accepted. Happiness is about being, about living moment to moment as best a person can. Happiness is not about becoming, or achieving, not about comparing, or competing, not about security, and certainly, not about control.

Not Happy Campers!

"Happiness is something to experience, not explain.
Once you attempt to explain it, you lose it."

Alan W. Watts, British born philosopher

Most workers within my experience are not happy. They live in quiet desperation. It matters little whether these workers are surviving on unemployment compensation or managing six figure incomes. The melancholy is similar. Sixty percent of high achievers, according to one study, felt they had sacrificed far too much in pursuit of material rewards. They sensed they had sacrificed their identity and wasted years of their lives, and for what? These successful workers, many senior level executives, admitted to putting on a front of being cool, rational thinkers, while three out of four confessed to depending mainly on feelings and intuitions for their decisions. Moreover, outwardly they appeared unperturbed to criticism and disapproval, whereas three out of five admitted to craving acceptance, recognition and approval. These workers, at opposite ends of the food chain, are tense, depressed, preoccupied and consumed with fear, as if the burden of the world rested on their shoulders. Senior level executives, unemployed or underemployed workers, they all share several disturbing attributes in common:

They are surprisingly dull witted, humorless, culturally impoverished, shamelessly self-indulgent and as interesting to talk to as hearing the want ads read aloud. They don't stretch their minds, but on rare occasion exercise their hamstrings. Conditioned to react, not act; to complain, not communicate, they are consummate spectators to life, while pretending to be "hard chargers" and to have "no time." Secretly, they want to be entertained, not challenged; to vegetate, not think. Such lethargy spawns a cadre of celebrities to fill their empty heads.

These workers work for money, not self-realization or self-fulfillment. It would be career limiting for anyone to come out of the closet and declare himself a *bona fide* intellectual. Oh! God forbid! — An elitist!

Democracy loves mediocrity, but abhors, in equal measure, brilliance, idiosyncrasy, genius, or curmudgeons of any kind. Film action heroes, professional athletes and celebrity murderers compete for this worker's limited attention span. The media give these "superstars" more exposure in twenty four hours than an iconoclastic Richard Feynman or a cerebral Isaiah Berlin receive in a lifetime.

It has been my experience that. . . .

College professors read little more than the general public. Check their class notes. Most are ancient. If class notes are less than ten years old, you're dealing with a neophyte. Tenure is a communicable disease supportive of academic indolence.

Medical doctors don't pursue their professions much beyond what is required. Quiz your personal physician sometime for confirmation. They coast with the same rhythm as the lathe operator.

Psychiatrists talk in meaningless psychobabble. The fact is we have made little progress in predicting human behavior. Moreover, research has shown psychiatrists know little more about the workings of the human mind than the average citizen on the street. Psychiatrists are essentially psycho-pharmacologists.

Most engineers in this mechanistically driven society would re-engineer our social systems without a modicum of understanding of the human soul, which they refuse to accept exists.

For every problem the scientific community solves, two new problems surface in the social system. Should this alarm you, ask yourself: Is this world actually a better, safer, healthier and more pleasant place in which to live than it was 200 years ago?

Anyone who has had the sad experience of being embroiled in litigation knows they could better represent themselves than most lawyers. Yet, we have a plethora of this breed. In most major cities, there is one attorney for every ten citizens; in Washington, D. C. this ratio balloons to one in four.

The book publishing business symbolizes a cultural paradox. More than 65,000 new books are published each year, yet 90 percent of the public never reads a book after high school, and even brags about that fact. Fifty percent of Americans have such poor reading skills that they cannot read the warning labels on food and drugs. Moreover, the quality of books published is open to suspicion.

Few Europeans, and even fewer Asians admit to reading American writers outside technology. They claim most American writers are intellectually vapid.

The majority of corporate enterprises, and this extends to the academic and health care field, are run by courtiers (ass-kissers extraordinaire), an occupation requirement essential to "making it." The main ingredient to a successful executive career is neither brains nor pluck, but connections. Being amenable to the C.E.O.'s pet suppositions makes executives light as air, assuring their rapid ascent to the top. Despite this fact, workers pay homage to executive mediocrity. This is because, when push comes to shove, workers need a "fall guy." Invariably, the collective "they" (corporate staff), never the whimpering "we" (the workers in the trenches), are the focus of blame. *They did it to us, we had nothing to do with the outcome!"*

Most workers within my experience see themselves as paid to do, not to think, create, change, or improve, not even to feedback to management system discrepancies. Most workers fail to see themselves as part of the problem, and therefore outside the solution. Whatever management's decision, appropriate or not, represents no risk to them, "No skin off our teeth."

Anything which cuts to the core of the problem should be an embarrassment to everyone, not just management. Yet workers maneuver themselves to be outside embarrassment. They stand on the sidelines and scoff at management's ineptitude, feeling little sense of the implied irony. Workers, in the main, are fatalists, "Do with me what you will!" — paid robots, not thinkers and managers of what they do, and of course always beyond Harm's Way. This is a shared indictment of the lily fingered professionals as much as it is to the grubby gloved blue collar workers.

Workers have adopted a passive posture for reason. When a worker thinks for himself, takes a stand, goes against the grain of the prevailing norm, or fails to go along with the silent majority, all hell is likely to break loose.

First, the worker in question is labeled anything from troublemaker, maverick, gadfly, exploiter, disrupter, provocateur, or upstart to a bad influence. Once the labeling is secured, and the meek join in the name bashing, the "upstart" is given either a humiliating assignment, demotion, delayed raise, deferred promotion, or is selectively ostracized from the group. No one wants to be caught dead talking to him.

At the same time, in not too subtle a way, the worker who thinks for himself is subjected to a campaign of psychic duress. This includes not being invited to lunch with peers, not being copied on departmental memos, nor notified of meeting changes, while being constantly harassed by kidding and put downs. If this is not effective, he is treated as if invisible. Ultimately, the tormentors get their wish. He quits.

On rare occasions, even this *persona non grata* treatment fails to move the "upstart." Should this be the case, he is the first casualty of downsizing. The majority observe this and adopt a subservient posture, the demeanor of "the victim." The best workers thereafter operate at about 40 percent efficiency, and frantically watch their backs. They never know when the other shoe will fall.

Cynicism is a function of lost hope. Cynics know little about workers. They actually consider workers different than managers, more or less as children. Obviously, managers are needed to control these children. Cynics' further hold workers have little sense of the common good, that they are dominated by self-interests; that their perspective is exclusively on short-term gains (raises), not long-term benefits (careers). Guess what? Workers don't disappoint. They behave as children, even as incorrigible children.

"Keep your nose clean! Don't get in the way of the boss!" This is workers' code of survival. If the boss is incompetent and the operation goes to seed, "Well, that is the way the ball bounces!" When the plant closes, the buildings turn to eye sores, the town dries up, and there is no work anymore, who is to blame? Never the workers. Self-determined *learned helplessness* and ignorance absolves them of any collusion in their self-tragedy.

Most workers within my experience take it on the chin as victims far more often than they fight for their jobs and rights as victors. They behave as dependent children to management, or as counter dependent adolescents to the company. Workers fail to fight for their jobs and rights **before** they are put in jeopardy, because behaving as children, they fail to pay attention.

This could not happen to mature adults for reason:

Mature adult workers question work related decisions initiated by top management, because it is far removed from "where the rubber hits the road," and therefore clearly ignorant of all the requirements of work. Mature adults workers put their special knowledge to work at the level of consequences in a timely fashion, or to where chronic problems occur. Mature adult workers find it easier to ask forgiveness than permission when something vital to operations must be done, now!

Mature adult workers question a company's aberrations, such as its obsession with productivity criteria, fastidious bureaucracy or specialization, when production levels lag and diversity is ignored. Mature adult workers question a company's philosophy which focuses on "not losing," rather than driving hard "to win." Lagging production and failure to cultivate new markets ultimately translate into lost jobs and reduced security. If the market is shrinking, mature adult workers want a voice in the why. Perhaps they have ideas that could make for a turnaround.

Mature adult workers question entitlement benefit packages. These are treated like Christmas candy, which implies undeserved generosity of the company, as they are not tied to results. Mature adult workers know there is no free lunch. They have seen their real wages decline precipitously, and their benefit packages, too. They want an end to the charade. Mature adult workers want the company to level with them, to treat them as full partners in enterprise, not just hired help. Executives are employees, too. Executives have no more stake in the company's future than they do — perhaps even less. Mature adult workers are committed to a long term commitment to the company, while many executives attempt to put the best face on their watch in the interest of long-term career mobility.

Mature adult workers don't need to be told their worth. They know their worth. They don't need to be romanced with "touchy-feely" human resources programs. These turn them off and tune them out. They want full accountancy of the company's health on a regular basis, not when the company is about to go belly up. They resent the patronizing twaddle that attempts to keep them in line. They desire a reasonable voice in the conduct of business and a fair portion of the economic pie.

Mature adult workers resent slogans, campaigns, fads and copy-cat programs. What worked elsewhere worked because it was well suited to unique conditions. A plethora of failures in copy-cat programs, however, still fail to push this fact home. Mature adult workers question the emphasis on "quality participation," when they see themselves herded into improvised meetings, where the level of discussion is restricted to what color Kool Aid to serve their children at the company picnic, while executives, "down the hall," vote themselves stock options for the next quarter. Selective differentiation hardly begets teamwork or quality performance. Nor does the frenzied pursuit of quality awards mean much to mature adult workers. They see such pursuits as little more than exercises in executive gamesmanship.

Proof is in operations, before and after the award. Little if any change is noted in the quality of the working culture, and therefore, in the quality of the business. Quality is not an exercise. Quality is a mindset.

Mature adult workers would forsake the exercise and focus on the "vital few" problems by addressing the "right things," or the critical 20 percent that make 80 percent of the difference in operations.

With "quality participation," however, management offers them a menu of "the trivial many" problems to solve, with the focus on "doing things right." If workers were 100 percent successful in this activity, since the "trivial many" make up only 20 percent of the difference in operations, 80 percent of the operational problems would remain untouched. Mature adult workers know this. Doing everything "right the first time" sounds good as a campaign, or makes for an impressive executive presentation, but it actually sponsors cheating.

Doing the "right things," on the other hand, encourages ingenuity, cooperation, teamwork and sponsors real achievement. Workers can get excited about this, for it moves the company off the dime, and gives them a sense of pride in their role. They know they make a difference. They don't have to be told. Knowing spurs them on to even higher performance.

Mature adult workers question the value of rhetoric, which advocates a culture of contribution, but supports the twin cultures of comfort and complacency. A culture of contribution is dynamic, rife with conflict and confrontation, a spirited exchange of ideas of equal partners.

Conflict, not harmony, is the glue which holds a company to its purpose. Mature adult workers recognize pain, risk, uncertainty, failure and limits as necessary components of real growth. An investment in failure is acknowledged as the price of success.

Mature adult workers question cosmetic organizational changes brought on by real or imagined crises. Mature adults workers abhor solution driven approaches to structural problems, which they see as, at best, naïve if not faddish appeasements to stockholders. They recognize that defining the problem is hard work, and nigh impossible if the working culture is driven by personality, not performance; by making an impression, not a difference.

Making an impression has no place in a climate of purposefulness. Where making a difference matters, there is no fear of failure, so success can take hold; no place for arrogance, so confidence can be expressed; no need for pretension, so happy debate can lead to consensus strategies.

Mature adult workers are threatening, not only to the company, but to the existing social fabric of society. From attending school to taking a job, from paying homage to the church to the state, from birth to death, citizens are expected to behave essentially as obedient, disciplined, punctual and not problem children. Schools teach students to conform to authority. Jobs are described and managed in the same vein. The tenets of religious faith are written as if to starry-eyed children, while the conduct of government could not demonstrate a lower opinion of the human species.

Society is afraid of mature adult workers, afraid of the madness that adulthood demands, for with such madness things are seen much more clearly than by those who claim to be sane. Ergo, they see society running from itself, cowering behind its authority and autocratic rule. The evidence is overwhelming. Self-hatred is manifested in society in the form of violence and crime. Love no longer recreates itself. Love has been replaced by pervasive hatred, which has become like the rich, aromatic stench of the garbage dump.

A paternalistic driven society prefers workers never to grow up, that they remain perpetually obedient, submissive, indulgent and manageable children. With mature adult workers, control no longer resides in the parent-figure as overlord. It is in the mind, heart and hands of workers, where it belongs. The agony of our times is that children become parents, but skip adulthood. Parent-figures, as an ideal-type, bully their children as they had been bullied. Bullying behavior is then repeated with family members, workers, worshippers, students and finally, with citizens. Failing to become mature adults, workers regress to learned helplessness and seek guidance, direction and control as if suspended in terminal adolescents as obedient twelve-year-olds in fifty-year-old bodies. Despite this characterization, the redemption of society still depends on the production of mature adult workers.

Even if the dedicated mission of society were to produce mature adult workers, it would most likely take the better part of a century to see it realized. Cultural conditioning of modern workers is that extensive. Most workers are programmed in self-negation, feeling a compelling need to conform to group norms, to avoid conflict and confrontation at any cost, to comply with arbitrary standards no matter how ridiculous, rather than to cooperate with a sense of commitment to something meaningful and to which they can believe.

Most workers value the thoughts of others over their own thoughts. They are isolated from a sense of their own worth. It is as impossible for them to think differently as the majority as it would be for them to defy gravity and fly.

The Challenge of Learning!

"We have designed organizations which ignored individual potential for competence, responsibility and constructive intent and productivity."

Chris Argyris, American business theorist

Learning requires discipline, but not the conformity most disciplines display. Conformity isolates workers. It places them in cages of fear. In the past half century this fear has manifested itself in a mad dash "to be educated" with little apparent interest in learning in the process. The acronyms B.A., B.S., M.A., M.S., Ph.D., M.D., and so on, connote little learning, only meaningless educational labels. Ironically, such labels can be acquired with practically no learning taking place. It does not necessarily follow that being "educated," that is, to have a degree or several degrees, that you are educable. Education has become an industry with a factory mentality. It produces a product that doesn't always have concomitant value for the expense it engendered. That said many graduates, once they run into that first career disappointment, return to university for yet another degree without sorting out why they have encountered this early impasse.

Where conformity, obedience and imitation are sponsored, there is competition but never the act of learning. This configuration sponsors the act of following, "Waiting for orders from headquarters!" Discipline implies that workers learn, not as it is interpreted for them by specialists, put out in neat little chewable morsels of instruction, but by applying their own complex minds to daily existence. Discipline chisels impressions on the worker's *tabula rasa*, and reflects his uniqueness as a human being.

With discipline, workers learn about each other in relationships, not in conjugal athletics, but in shared intimacies. Discipline breathes life into relationships and resonates with purposeful experience. Disciplined workers are learners, not knowers, flexible and active, not rigid and reactive.

Workers in my experience have inert minds, minds on automatic pilot. They learn by rote, or from a particular person, curriculum, or doctrine; from an exceptional teacher, coach or preacher, or from specific books. They fail, in the main, to learn from their own observations and actions; from their own unique set of life experiences.

The result is that many workers are not happy campers. They have lost their moral compass and are looking for it in others, and through the experience of others. They strive for identity and recognition through conformity, competition and imitation. They seem unwilling to struggle for identity. The only way true identity and recognition can be achieved is through self-discovery, by being the person you were meant to be, not an imitation, but the genuine article.

The tremendous burden of attempting to always please others, both personally and professionally, and then to live up to their expectations, has made many workers' minds extraordinarily dull. After decades of turbulent discord within themselves, festering conflict with others, tiring accommodation, punishing doubt, plus the constant agony of imitation, many workers feel cut off from life, adrift and without anchor.

Through this maddening process of attempting to be like everyone else, many have become second or third-hand persons to themselves. They are always quoting somebody else, never mustering the courage to consider or voice an original thought or opinion. They check pollsters, as if heuristic box scores, to see if they are "thinking right," terrified at the thought they might be outside the prevailing norm. Their consumer choices, dictated by a cadre of experts, compel them to support the "best" films, books, automobiles, neighborhoods, cities, diets, mates, exercises, stocks, ad infinitum. Taste is designed by a committee with the lowest common denominator in mind.

When workers are disappointed, they can blame the experts in which they placed their confidence, for the choices were never their own. This surfaces an elusive problem. If the choices made are not considered theirs, workers are not likely to learn from their mistakes. How can they be accountable for their behavior? Identity and recognition thus become disingenuous, while their actions become clones of someone else's agenda. Rented minds never act like home owners. They pervade the climate of the home, job, school and community. A poverty of will and a concession to helplessness defines the identity of many workers.

Life's hard rule is that everyone is responsible for their own actions, and to learn from the consequences of those actions. Everyone gets a report card on their performance every day of their life.

Workers can be male, female, dark or light, tall or short, fat or trim, young or old, American or Armenian, Indian or Indonesian, life's flow is the same. Movement is similar. Every worker's destiny, whatever it is, depends on their observations in school, work, and play and in daily pursuits.

Discipline is not conformity. Discipline involves a mind alert to its own actions — a living mind. Conformity implies conflict between "what is" and "what should be." Conforming to certain prevailing ideologies, social norms and societal "truths," truths to which everyone supposedly subscribes without reflection, seeds conflict. A discriminating mind cannot absorb what makes little sense. Such a mind must probe and weigh the merits of what is professed against what is experienced. With conflict, there is always friction and the dissipation of energy. The worker can be so absorbed in the conflict that he is not conscious of reality. The result is confusion.

Each worker must put his own house in order, because no one else is going to do it for him. A mind in disorder peers out at the world through opaque windows, unable to see the beauty and balance of nature. The windows hold confusion in and beauty and other people out.

Most workers within my experience are consumed with the distractions of either toys or careers. For them, life is without beauty or order. It is a constant grind, day in and day out. "I work hard and play hard," they proclaim, failing to realize the implicit absurdity in this boast. They have learned the art of moral evasion.

Yet beauty, not wealth or security, is a delight of truth. And it is free! The spirit withdrawn into itself and out of sight, may not be completely destroyed, but it could go blind in the internal darkness. What is valued is not always what is precious.

A paternalistic society knows the value of toys, but not necessarily the essence of beauty. Give a child having a tantrum a complicated toy, and the child is absorbed, distracted from its anguish, quiet. The child enjoys the mechanics of discovery and is focused and involved completely with the toy. All mischief dissolves.

Such a society gives workers the toys of technology, the toys of ideals and the toys of beliefs to absorb their discontent. Some toys are treated as sacred (religious rites and rituals), others as profane (pop culture), still others as precedence (national holidays). Tradition as toy assures the maintenance of the company pecking order. No one disputes the C.E.O.'s omnipotence. Other toys are status symbols: money, stately homes, expensive automobiles, socio-economic status, knowledge. . . . . . .

Workers come to venerate ideals, beliefs, policies, customs, norms and hierarchical relationships without reflection. "It is the way it has always been, so it must be right." These come to be accepted as "truths," to which the majority subscribe, when they are actually "toys of the mind."

They are all inventions of thought and therefore flawed. Even so, some treat them as absolute truths, when there are no such things. There are no absolute truths, only a welter of contradictory truths embodied in the worker's imaginary self. This imaginary self is likely to form his "character." And character is but a mixed bag of relative truths which each worker may call his own.

Psychic toys are proliferating at an alarming rate. Still, they are seldom essential, more apt to be vain accumulations of gibberish and nonsense, the potpourri of a society reluctant to let loose of its past and face its present.

These toys are made by man's mind, by man's thought. This doesn't make them any less real, but it does make them less sacrosanct. They are now increasingly in the way. But workers have yet to develop a sense of humor about their toys, especially when they are no longer appropriate.

Toys have their purpose, and that purpose is mostly as distraction. When workers are absorbed in toys, like a child, they are extraordinarily quiet and obedient to the demands of these toys.

The toys may be concepts, special interests, or "things." They could just as well be computers, technologies, automobiles, boats, houses, planes, athletics, hobbies, the worker's own persona or profession. Wealth or ambition are also but toys of the mind. The list is endless, but the results are always the same. The toys absorb and distract the worker from the chaos of "what is," to the appeasing pleasure of selective forgetting.

With effective distraction, there is the absence of self. There is no need to think, experience, problem solve or learn. For the moment, the worker is totally controllable. He differs little with the greyhound at the race track who chases the mechanical rabbit, or the rodent who wanders through the maze for the promised piece of cheese. The Holy Grail of this anxious age is the perfect toy to seduce the worker's restless spirit into compliant behavior.

A Question of Control!

*"A violent order is disorder,
and a great disorder is an order.
These two things are one."*

Wallace Stevens. American modernist poet

The very process of control breeds disorder, just as the opposite: the lack of control breeds disorder. The more the obsession with control the greater the chaos. Everyone is bound and shaped by control. Most workers attempt to control themselves — their tempers, desires, appetites — because it is safe. There is security in control. Control generates a certain sense of safety, a certain assurance that with control, they will not fail. But is this prudent behavior?

When there is a need for control, chaos is always around the corner. Control manifests a division between the controller and the thing controlled. Virtue does not lie in such separation. This is so because control implies effort, the demand for security, all in the name of what is good. But control is the very denial of goodness and is therefore disorder. Does a tree strive for control? Does the universe exert effort to maintain ecological balance? The observer who separates himself from the thing observed is the source of failure, not success.

A mind which sees directly without the paralysis of analysis is a mind without division. It is a whole mind, a sane mind, a mind one with itself. On the other hand, a neurotic mind is a divided mind, a mind at war with itself, a mind obsessed with control. When such a mind believes it has realized total control, the body cannot move. The person is utterly in the grips of its mania, its neurotic need for control. Such a person is not free, more likely paralyzed with fear, caged in his own obsession.

Control is the basic neurosis of the workplace. Management desires to control workers to ensure that they are productive; that time is not wasted; that the organization operates at maximum efficiency. But do these worthwhile desires materialize? No, because the greater the intensity of management's obsession with control the greater the chaos.

Control is a function of order, and order is an integral function. Each worker and manager must embody order through their own volition; their own action. Together, worker and manager are one function. What they hold in common is productive work.

The differentiation of managers from workers is an arbitrary one, a division which causes chaos in the world of work. Because of the cultural inclination to separate the controller from the controlled, the analyzer from the analyzed, there is corruption, disorder, distrust, violence and much ruthless manipulation in the workplace. Consequently, the more hysterical the quest for control the greater the workplace paralysis. This is willfully ignored throughout the working world, because control is at war with freedom, when control and freedom are but a single entity.

This is not so with young minds. Such minds are not afraid to learn. They are not yet deeply burdened with knowledge and experience. To learn means to observe oneself without division, without analysis, without denial or the censor of "what should be" and "what should not be." There is no question of control. There is only experience.

Cultural conditioning is anathema to learning, the curse to seeing things clearly, to seeing things as they are. What cultural conditioning promotes is the idea of self-control in the individual, and the appearance of harmony in the workplace, both bogus ideas. This conditioning is the reason there is such madness in society, for the idea of control is the very embodiment of emotional rupture and breakdown.

There is no wisdom to self-control. Control is paradoxical. Those consumed with a need for control, lose it; those not bothered with control, have it. What is more appropriate is self-organization, self-order. Workers and managers worry far too much about changing or controlling each other, or other things which disturb them. This is guaranteed to create frustration and conflict, because the only thing workers and managers can change or control is themselves. Order flows from this.

For the past quarter century we have had a bombardment of ideas on how to manage change. Actually, change in the workplace is of only secondary importance. Change will come about naturally, over time, once workers and managers bring about change in themselves. *Order comes from within.* To establish order takes more than good intentions, more than a change in attitude. Order requires a radical change in mentality, a structural change in the way workers and managers view the world. Such radicalism requires the individual *going against the grain.*

As long as there is the analyzer, the supervisor, the director, the administrator feverishly consumed with maintaining order, there will be the problem of chaos. It is such censors who create the problems by failing to understand the dynamics of control. Unfortunately, as matters now stand, from the moment of birth to the moment of death, workers and managers seem consumed with the need for control of each other. The "must" and "must not," the "should" and "should not" are stenciled on their brains.

This posed little problem when society was moving at a snail's pace. No longer. The world is exploding with people; exploding with technology. Flexibility, not rigidity; creativity, not conformity are now requirements. If anything, less control is called for, thus establishing a climate for the controller and the controlled to merge.

Control implies conformity, imitation, following a particular principle, set of rules, an ideal all the way to respectability. Respectability is a moral dimension which better fits another place and another time. Morality is in the mind of the time, and it changes, not because of some great evil conspiracy, but because the requirements of the times demand it. Respectability cultivates a reverence for "what should be," not "what is," or reality.

Therefore, the very process of control breeds disorder. Disorder is brought about by the censor, the analyzer, the do gooder, the "true believer," the one who tries to impose what he thinks is right, instead of trying to understand "what is" effective — the person with a cause!

The mind of the censor is never a clear mind, capable of candid observation, because such a mind must ferret through various forms of authoritarianism, through vertical hierarchical arrangements, or must gingerly follow some system, guidebook, principle, or form of belief to which it is helplessly tethered. Such a mind does not belong to itself. It is lost to itself, impossibly entangled in the maze of its own stultifying conditioning. Alas, it is the mind of the expert.

The conflict between the controller and the controlled is programmed into workers and managers alike. They are actors in a drama in which they have no creative involvement. Religious and social sanctions control, shape, direct and cement the societal will to its purposes. And so it has been throughout history. This makes most workers spectators to their own lives.

The controller, whomever he may be, proclaims, "I have the answer!" The answer invariably represents a proposed solution to a fragment of the problem, likely a new fad, gimmick or rhetoric which provides expedient relief, but seldom a cessation to the aggravation.

The proclaimed answer is tied to the past, to what is known, not to the present or the present situation. It is old knowledge in a new suit of clothes. But reality requires a mind fresh, clear and undivided, a naked mind. Such a mind has no answers, nor does it worry about being offensive, stepping on toes, causing embarrassment, being prohibitively expensive, or fomenting argument. Nor does it worry about acceptance or going against the grain.

On the other hand, most experts reflect minds cluttered with knowledge, with what worked before, or elsewhere. They are lazy minds, impatient minds, the minds of soldiers, enlisted men in officer country, who readily respond to the command, "Get on with it!"

A mind which is one with reality knows it has no answers, no solutions, that all solutions are buried in the problems themselves. But such a revelation does not sell. So, more than likely the solution proposed is a clever, generic idea, simple to understand, comfortable to accept, causing no shift in power, taking the solution sponsor off the hook, reasonable in cost, and easy to implement. Executives are easily intimidated by thought processes or jargon outside the familiar. Their motto, "When baffled, it is better to do something, than nothing, even if it is wrong!"

A legion of consultants is at the ready to deliver this prescription in canned form with labels still bleeding to meet the demand. The solution fails in the end, as it must, because each situation is unique and requires great care regarding this fact. The controller and the controlled are integral, inseparable. Still, the "me" and the "not me," the "we" and the "they" strive to divide and control, sustaining disorder. Chaos has a firm grip on enterprise.

Consultants are not the problem. They respond to a need with what will sell. What will sell is "want," not need. Consultants are far better at inventing solutions than perceiving problems. How could it be otherwise? They have limited knowledge of "what is." Moreover, they are outside the process. The solution is always concealed in the problem itself, as certainly as the controller and the controlled are one.

The fallacy of paradigms and success stories is that virtually none of them apply to all situations. Each situation is unique and demands a careful, even proprietary response, preceded of course, by a concise definition of the problem. Defining the problem requires a fresh mind. It takes time to render the mind fit to see clearly "what is" the situation.

Generic systems, which is the stock in trade of consultants, are mainly a waste of time, energy and money. They change nothing. The history of generic systems supports this view quite emphatically. What succeeds in one place, fails in another. *Ask Tom Peters.* The difficulty revolves around the neurotic need for the appearance of control, the obsession with focusing on the part at the expense of the whole, and the insistence in seeing workers and managers operating in different universes. But perhaps the fundamental failure is that top management is afraid to get its hands dirty.

In the recent past we have heard much about "re-inventing" and "re-engineering" the corporation, Total Quality Management, Performance Management Systems, and now the *Edenic expectations* of the "information highway." The idea is that the postmodern world is Eden, or paradise through man's ingenuity. English philosopher Thomas Carlyle (1795-1881) was weary of this pervasive optimism. He wrote:

"The machine has gained control not only over the material aspects of society, but also over its philosophy, art and literature. Men have grown mechanical in head and in heart, as well as in hand. Their whole attachments, opinions, turn on Mechanism, and are of a mechanical character."

These mechanistic propositions can easily become toys treated as tools, or little more than distractions, if a holistic approach is not adopted, where cause and effect, the controlled and controller are treated as one.

Control is not a matter of doing something "to the system." It is realized only by a radical change in the mentality of each member of the workforce, where self-order is the outcome. Once movement is made in this direction, it will have a ripple effect, ultimately resulting in a revolutionary restructuring of the culture of the workplace.

To put this in perspective, consider the celebrated notion of the social contract, which speaks of the "vesting" of the wills of workers, in other words their power, in an individual (C.E.O.) and a select group (management). What kind of act is this "vesting"?

As a practical matter, it is a process where few challenge, as power is accumulated like a commodity without opposition. The "conferring" of power makes for the powerful, but this is not illuminating. What is "power" and what is "conferring"? Who confers power and how is such conferring done?

Nobody knows. The conferring is an act, but an unintelligible one. Conferring power, acquiring power, using power, is not at all like eating or drinking or thinking or walking. Workers everywhere remain in the dark: *obscurum per obscurius*. All they know is that power is another word for control.

What currently frightens workers, and well that it might, is that events prove over and over again that those in charge—the C.E.O. and his key executives know little more than they do about unfolding events. It is not uncommon that the lowliest worker in the trenches has as good if not better feel for the "state of the company." It can even be argued that only those decisions issued at the front line are likely to seem crucial in retrospect. Perfectly sensible orders, which seem no less crucial to those issuing them, but who are far removed from the action, often prove embarrassments, foiled by an unfavorable turn of events. Power (control) exercised in the wrong place invariably leads to a corruption of effort and consequences.

Alexis de Tocqueville's 19th century, *Democracy in America*, expressed anxiety about the pervasiveness of "soft despotism" in the conduct of business. His insight turned prophetic in the 20th century as we saw management attempting, and largely succeeding, to kill trade unionism with kindness. Its success has contributed to an undesirable outcome, worker disenfranchisement.

Unwittingly, management's self-interest, good intentions, rustic obtrusiveness and artless arrogance has put workers and managers poles apart. Much energy is wasted at this interface. Managers become combatants, armed with position power and knowledge; workers, trench fighters, armed with knowhow and apathy. The more managers know about the circumstances of the situation, and all its possible implications, the farther removed they are from timely decision making.

Meanwhile, first causes are accessible to trench workers, the multiplicity of perturbations to the smallest disturbance all lie within their ability to see, hear, remember, record, coordinate and act upon. Omniscience is in principle possible to empirical beings.

But workers do not act. They wait for their leaders to act. Control of the situation, when it is controllable, slips through their fingers and dissipates into embarrassment for all. This alone, and nothing deeper or more interesting, is the source of executive megalomania, and the repository of all absurd delusions.

What are executives? They are ordinary human beings who are ignorant and vain enough to accept total responsibility for the vitality and survival of the organization. They are individuals who would rather take the blame for all the cruelties and disasters justified in their name than recognize their own insignificance and impotence in the cosmic flow which pursues its course irrespective of their wills and ideals. Such executive leadership is a luxury workers can no longer afford. They must take charge of their lives and destinies. For workers to share the fruits of their labors they must endure an equal share of the responsibilities. This requires positive conviction, passionate faith and resolute determinism. Simply put, it requires mature adult workers.

Once established, there will be a different working mentality and a radically different distribution of power. No grand design will produce this outcome. It will be a gradual process based upon the primal drive of workers, survival! The focus will shift from disorder to order. Power will begin to flow organically according to demands of the task; decisions will be made at the level of consequences; managers and workers will be treated as teammates; C.E.O.s will be part of the workforce, as their compensation and entitlements will be brought more in line. Mythic executive omniscience and omnipotence will vanish. Interdependency will be the key to order.

"The problem," whatever it may be, is always integral to everything and everybody in the organization, without exception. What worked elsewhere may provide clues to an approach to resolution, but the solution remains unique.

To grasp this concept, consider control on a personal basis. If a worker is "envious," he is told he must control his envy. This is wrong. This tends to separate envy from himself. He says, "I must control my envy, must suppress it." This never works. Instead, he becomes more obsessed with what others have and are than ever before.

The worker is not separate from envy. It is not something outside himself. He is envy! There is no way to change this fact. He may try to control envy as though separate from himself, but it cannot be done. He may even attempt to imitate someone else who has successfully dealt with envy, and this, too, will fail. Not until he embraces the fact that "he is envy," that envy is integral to his nature, can envy be understood, and therefore controlled.

The worker, who deals successfully with envy, moves toward envy, not away from it. He admits to himself that envy is "what is," that he is the cause and effect of his own condition. This allows him to deal with his envy by bringing all the pain to the surface. Envy no longer is buried in his mind where it intimidated him. Subject and object are one. Envy is controlled. He no longer feels a need to control envy, so he can. Without cause, there is no effect.

Look at the 1960s and the *Sexual Freedom Revolution*. More than five decades later, sex is more, not less a problem. Ask yourself, are we, as a society, more or less attuned to our sexual nature? Do we have more or fewer psycho-sexual hang-ups?

Human sexuality in the 1960s became a thing apart from the person. It became this terrible mystery which demanded to be solved. Sexuality was treated as a beast which needed to be released from its cage, or society would go mad (cause). The mystery was not solved, but the beast was released. Once out of its cage, it leaped into another, the cage of sexual aberration. The mind became the enemy of the body, the natural perverted. Society submersed itself in sexual frenzy (effect), chasing the ultimate orgasm. This frenzy invaded all aspects of life.

Hedonism as therapy became the laboratory of experience orchestrated by a playboy mentality at the controls. Erotic junkies sold lust as love, pleasure as purpose, and greed as good. Copulation became a form of competence, more esteemed than caring. Sexual parlor games became the new religion. No one confessed to continence for it was an embarrassment to be chaste. Four letter words became the code of belonging, and no one would be caught dead admitting to being totally straight.

In the wake of the sexual revolution we have an epidemic of A.I.D.S., a rampant problem of teenage suicides, a plague in substance abuse, a scandalous increase in physical and psychological abuse, an atrocious increase in teenage pregnancies, with an upsurge in both abortions and illegitimacy. So, the question to ask is, can workers live their lives without a single control? Can anyone live a life, which is at present so disastrous, so mechanical, so repetitive, so calloused and chaotic, without a single control? The answer is, not likely.

Freedom from attachment can only happen when the mind is free; when the mind is still; when the mind gives complete attention to thought and is quiet; when the mind learns to live within the bounds of its limits, without the conflict which arises from control; when the mind puts aside its conditioning and sees the world "as it is"; when the mind and body are a single whole; when the mind accepts that the controller and the controlled are one; when the mind embraces its problems rather than apologizes for them; when the mind prefers order to chaos.

On balance, however, problems seem to become progressively worse the more we consider them. Why? Workers confuse attention with concentration. Attention and concentration are qualitatively different.

Most of us know what *concentration* is. Societal conditioning grooves our minds to concentrate at school, in sport and throughout our professional life. Workers are constantly told that they need to concentrate more. Wrong.

To concentrate implies bringing all energy to a single focus. But thought invariably intervenes and the mind wanders away from the focus. A perpetual battle then ensues between the desire to concentrate and the restless mind's desire to wander, and resist control. The conflict is merciless.

Attention has no control, no concentration. It is complete attention. This means all energies and capacities — mind, heart and soul — are given to attention. Few ever experience complete attention. If they do, there is no record of the attending, no action from memory. The mind does not record. It observes only. Whereas when concentrating, when making an effort, one acts from memory. Memory plays back old mental tapes and films — horror tales of "what was," or "what should have been." These memories get in the way of attention, in the way of seeing things clearly. Since attention is difficult, the mind is more likely to take a bypass to the more accessible mechanism of concentration, and so the vicious cycle continues.

With the mind, there is no need to record, except that which is necessary to get through daily life. Yet our minds are occupied, never still, filled continuously with fragments of thought. A busy mind is not a thoughtful mind. It is a spastic mind.

To learn how to observe, to see "what is," requires the freedom to observe. Most workers are disinclined to embrace such a challenge. They fill their heads instead with nonsense. It is not necessary to be saturated with useless psychological recordings, either of insults or flatteries, compulsive worries or "might have beens."

When one sees the futility of recording nonsense, the mind is free from its conditioning. It has removed its rose colored glasses. Most workers, sad to say, appear slaves to memory, slaves to taking seriously what others think of them, what others say about them, slaves to their failures and embarrassments.

Workers are programmed to believe they are different from each other; that successful workers are different from failures, and both are different from themselves. They are not. Alas, the very highest and lowest are painfully similar.

Workers are conditioned to being threatened by diversity. Yet all workers are more alike than different, for they have the same kinds of minds, and go through the same miseries and joys, the same happiness and sorrow, shed the same kinds of tears, and experience the same euphoria and elation when they achieve success together.

To comprehend this, the mind must be free to consider data which may not necessarily fit with what is already there. This takes courage. It demonstrates the need for workers to stand alone, and accept their isolation, before they can stand together. Most workers are afraid of this detachment, so the herd mentality wins their minds.

Such workers cling to others just like themselves, eternally chattering without saying anything, preoccupied with something or other, without being in charge. It is only the silent mind, the mind that is free, the mind that is not afraid to stand alone, that can see into "what is" and exercise control without the need to be in control.

Going Against the Grain— Personal Pronouncement

"Time is painted with a lock before, and bald behind, signifying thereby that we must take time by the forelock, for when it is once passed there is no recalling it."

Jonathan Swift, Anglo-Irish satirist, essayist and poet

The expressed challenge in all these books is for the professional to creatively and assertively express his individualism. This author has attempted to do so in his many careers, and occasionally, somewhat dramatically. The first instance was after facilitating the creation of a new chemical conglomerate in South Africa during the Afrikaner reign of Apartheid, or separate development of the races. Upon completion of that assignment, in my mid-thirties with a wife and four young children to support, I resigned taking a two-year sabbatical (*Devlin* is a psychological novel of this South Africa experience).

At the end of the sabbatical, I did not return to industry, but to graduate school to go from the hard to the soft sciences, spending the next six years in pursuit of a Ph.D. in the social industrial psychology, consulting on the side. I would eventually join a client, Honeywell, Inc. as a management and organizational psychologist at its Avionics facility in Clearwater, Florida. It was the keynote speech I gave during that employment that represented another instance of individual self-assertion and "going against the grain."

A Keynote Speech

The speech was given on March 30, 1984 at the Clearwater Beach Hotel (Florida) to a *Department of Contract Administrative Services* (DCAS) *Colloquium*, which included an audience of some 100 government principles, that is, senior military officers of U.S. Army, Navy, Air Force and Marines, consultants and *US Department of Defense* (DOD) administrators. It was given while I was a management and organizational development (OD) psychologist for Honeywell Avionics, Inc., Clearwater, Florida.

197

This was during the collective hysteria of the time. Japan, Inc. and South East Asia were making inroads into pristine American markets such as automobiles, machine tools, electronics, home appliances, televisions, light fixtures and steel production. In January 1980, Tom Brokaw of NBC television asked a crushing question of American industry: *"Japan Can, Why Can't We?"*

Avionics Human Resources (HR) stepped into the breach with *Quality Control Circles* (QCC) in an attempt to replicate the Japanese miracle.

At the time, I was the director of the largest QCC Program in the country at this Avionics facility of some 4,000 workers of which only 20 percent were blue-collar, the rest either engineers or professionals in support of engineers. Blue-collar workers responded to quality circles; professionals did not. Little note was made of the fact that Japan was a group-oriented culture versus America's individual oriented society. Nor did anyone stop to consider that 80 percent of Japanese workers were blue-collar whereas only 20 percent of most hi-tech firms were. NBC pricked the nation's denial button flooding its consciousness with collective hysteria.

From my perspective in the trenches, this was a charade. Workers had little power and less participation beyond cosmetic change, which had little bearing on either performance or outcomes. The speech follows:

"Participative Management: An Adversarial Point of View"

Man is a pragmatic animal. He does what he does because he thinks it is the best way to do it. He may listen to a contrary way of doing something, but if his heart is not into that something, there is little chance he'll give it his best.

During the past several years, I have attempted to facilitate the shift from paternalistic to participative management, from centrally located decision-making to autonomous work groups. This work was conducted in an ideal environment here at Honeywell.

For one, the team concept had been employed among the hourly workforce since 1972. For another, all of the operations of this 4,000-employee facility were on one beautiful campus in the Florida Sunbelt. For yet another, management had been educated in the *Quality Control Circle* (QCC) concepts with countless organizational development (OD) interventions, resulting in a significant number of changes. These were however essentially cosmetic changes: e.g., changing the lighting in workstations, having more flexibility in dress code, providing longer breaks, changing work hours, and so on.

In any case, this facility has perhaps the longest sustained participative working climate in the continental United States. There are 110 *Quality Circle* teams with more than 1,000 members of the workforce participating in the process. Additionally, there is a pilot program of some 200 professional workers and their managers immersed in *"Shared Management,"* which is touted as a "step beyond Quality Circles."

Virtually everything management could reasonably be expected to do has been done for the workforce. Are workers happy? Reasonably so. Are they productive? Relatively speaking, yes. Are they doing as much as they are capable of doing? No. Do they have the entrepreneur spirit? Not on a bet.

Then are you saying all this has been for naught? Compliance is not cooperation, and this is compliance. Fear or coercion is the motivator. Workers are aware of the *Great Depression in the Steel and Automotive Industries*, and say, "There go I but for the grace of my employer."

Meanwhile, management has been in a long slump, thinking in terms of 1955 competition and been close to panic. It has resulted in turning OD from a hybrid of psychology and sociology into a burgeoning profession without portfolio. Undaunted by this fact, management has stopped everything to listen to what we have to say.

"Process" has become the magic word, along with "systemic problems," in other words, explanatory rather than operational approaches. Jargon gets the attention of most managers. The irony is that the shock wave that has gone through management has escaped the attention of the workforce. They are huddled in passivity and willingly conforming to do whatever without complaint.

Participative Management's Hidden Agendas

Paternalistic management was authoritative, task oriented and bottom line driven. Conversely, the workforce was management dependent, authoritatively compliant, selfishly motivated and bottom line indifferent.

Enter the sobriquet, "Participative Management"

This ploy of appearing people centered and process conscious was expected to generate cooperation and motivation. True, workers felt good about the attention and the happy climate of work, but still bottom line indifferent. The good intentions did not translate into an entrepreneur spirit or productive work.

A recent experience I had at this plant illustrates this. I was talking to a production line supervisor, who said he and his best friend think these changes are terrific.

"Have you seen him lately?" I asked. "Oh, yeah. Over the weekend."

"How are things going in his operation?" I continued. "I don't know. We didn't talk about the company business. We talked about the new businesses we've started."

After he told me about this, I offered, "I guess it's the American spirit to be in business for yourself." "Yeah," he smiled. "You want to be independent. Be your own boss. Have something of your own."

Here was a supervisor who could see through the cosmetic changes without knowing he was doing so, and was keeping his options open if things didn't work out. Imagine the mindset of the people working for him.

The Rise of the Non-Doer Doers

The organization is made up of those who manage and those who do. Those who manage have grown into a force unto themselves with layer on layer of middle management buried in paperwork while acting as a buttress between the feudal lords of industry and the masses.

Arising out of this malaise have been parallel organizations. They support and serve management, but who neither manage nor do (I belong to this exalted community). These non-doer doers have been called "professionals," the white-collar class and "staff" to "line" (i.e., to the doers). You find these workers in personnel, finance, security, maintenance, marketing, and even engineering. Once a need is created for their services, it is impossible to imagine being without them.

Since WWII, pyramid building and climbing has become something of a natural phenomenon in all professions. It translates into too many people doing too many non-thing things.

So, the first problem that should have been noted when our competitive edge was slipping was this excess baggage, that is, one manager to every ten to twelve workers (industrial average) and one staff employee per every four managers (industrial average). Scaling down this pyramid, alone, amounts to megabucks in savings not to mention a much leaner organization. So, what have we done? Where has the focus been? On the doers, of course. The powerful on the powerless. In transactional terms, the Parent on the Child.

Since the ownership spirit is precisely what we are trying to instill and since supervisors have been sent to a number of courses to develop consciousness concerning such ownership, I said, "How does this differ with what you are doing here?"

He looked at me in amazement. "I don't want to do this all my life." Sensing that I wanted to know more, he continued.

"My wife is my partner in this." He started to laugh. "She has a real problem paying the help $4.00 an hour."

"Joe, that's not even a living wage," I responded. His expression was defiant – "So?"

This intrigued me. "As you know," I continued, "workers want more money not because they have done more, but because they need more. It seems you are faced with the same problem in your private enterprise that we are facing here."

He scratched his head. "I never thought of it like that."

"No, possibly not," I offered. "Perhaps because it is coming out of your own pocket now and you can feel the pinch."

"Yeah. I see what you mean," he replied.

And this was an experienced supervisor who had been given all the training and tools, which were designed to create a feeling of ownership, but he, too, was bottom line indifferent.

International Association of Quality Circles (IAQC)

A whole organization has sprung into being, IAQC, with a strategy to get the "most out of the least" – and they have. Dr. J. M. Juran calls this problem-solving strategy dealing with the "trivial many." Juran insists if doers knock out all the fat and become lean as a tooth, they still have solved only 15 percent of the problems facing the organization. What about the other 85 percent? That's management's job!

But management, which has become too much and too many has difficulty turning the x-ray on itself for the fear that it will see the "big C" – Capital neglect.

Management has purposely established a caste and class system of non-doers who are confused. Just as doers are inclined to be bottom line disinterested, they are more inclined to mistake self-interest outcomes (department goals) as bottom line, which could be even worse.

The Answer to Bottom Line Apathy — Serial/Parallel Careers

Add to this the fact that in this changing work climate where all sorts of wonderful programs are being sponsored, the workforce sees its benefits shrinking, its pay frozen, its promotional opportunities disappearing and its job security eroding. Is it any wonder that workers and managers go out and start businesses on the side?

I was writing this in the cafeteria the other day and there in the booth next to me was a company staff engineer selling an insurance policy to an administrative worker – two non-doers doing personal business on company time without apology, guilt or concern. It was as if "I have the right. I get this opportunity in lieu of pay . . .," or whatever.

For comparative purposes, out of this population of 4,000, there are 800 production workers (20%), 1,000 engineers (25%), 400 managers (10%), and 1,800 other professionals (45%). No less than one quarter of these professional workers are believed to have serial or parallel careers, much of which is conducted on company time. From selling real estate to selling diamonds, from pet fish to insurance, from restaurant to management consulting, from private teaching to private investigating, from motel operations to hardware store managing.

What all this seems to indicate is that a great number of attractive solutions have been developed without a clear understanding of what the problem is. Meanwhile, the rank and file are oblivious to the anguish and pain common to the organization. They fail to care because they don't see it as their problem. Let "management" (i.e., the organization) solve it. They see the organization as distinct from them, as if it has a life without their blood in it. If the organization bleeds, they would be hard pressed to see themselves bleeding, that is, until the organization goes out of business or moves elsewhere.

To understand how this dilemma has evolved one must revisit the history of the complex organization.

The Seeds of the Problem

Two hundred years ago, when most of the business of business was conducted in small guilds, there was great informality. People did what they did best. Somebody was in charge but it was an additional role besides being a line contributor. There were no job descriptions, no performance appraisals, no reward and recognition programs, no staff support, nobody else to blame if a product did not sell because it was made poorly or overpriced.

Survival was predicated on doing the best you were able to do with the skills you had, the materials and mechanics you had to work with, and pride and sense of ownership you brought to the work. Work was love made visible.

People knew who they were by what they did. Often, the work was dirty, grimy, exhausting with little profit, hardly a living wage. We romanticize this period now, but in reality, it was a harsh, hard existence. The guild workers had to work long hours, seventy hours a week was not uncommon. There were few if any entitlements, only work.

Were they happy? Not particularly. Were they productive? Extremely so. Were they doing as much as they were capable? Generally speaking, yes. Did they have the entrepreneur spirit? In buckets! They had no choice. The wolf was always gaining ground on them.

Then the *Industrial Revolution* exploded into their midst. These self-directed, self-managed, self-motivated workers were forced by necessity into a strange environment of huge machines and masses of people.

There was no perfect model to fit the purposes of the complex organization. The closest models were the Roman Catholic Church and the National Army. The goal of the church was to save souls; the goal of the army was to save lives. No confusion there. Everyone knew, understood, and could relate to those common goals.

But the complex organization was an organization of sub-organizations and sub-sub-organizations, all with their own goals along with hidden agendas of individuals. Meanwhile, workers, who were never comfortable with all these goals, dreamed in terms of their own private agenda. They saw themselves as renting their bodies for a price, leaving their minds safely at home, which included their motivation. They saw the factory as a voluntary prison that they entered because they had no other choice. They couldn't compete with the factory from the guild, nor from the farm. They had given up their freedom out of economic fear, the fear of survival.

And so, from the opening chapters of the *Industrial Revolution* to the *Post-Industrial Age*, the worker has never identified with the factory as "his" factory, or as an extension of his will and dreams.

This has been the domain of only a precious few, the senior managers of the organization. This is where the power rests, not in the stockholders nor, indeed, in capitalistic society. Curiously, senior management operates very similarly to the management of the guilds. There is a common will dedicated to the same set of principles and a consensus bottom line. They are workers in the same sense as other workers, but they see the organization as belonging to them with their destiny tied to its.

More curious still, the doers and the senior managers are cut from the same atavistic cloth. They both speak the language of the guilds. What makes for the problem of the modern organization is that there are ten or twelve layers of bodies between senior management and these doers.

What these doers hear, then, is a language that is remote and beyond their comprehension. Instead, they hear demands, threats, and candy-coated enticements, or directives that a child hears from a concerned or frustrated parent. And appropriately, like a child, the expected behavior follows: testing the firmness of the demand; accepting punishment as justification for challenging the demands; learning to say the right words while continuing to misbehave; treating the machines (Toys of the Mind) with disdain, neglect and contempt; seeing the organization as blocking them from what they want to do; crying, whining and embarrassing the organization into submitting to their will; feeling angry and hostile and unfulfilled after getting their own way; telling the organization what it wants to hear rather than what it needs to know; behaving in a way that says, "I want more" – when more is given – "I still want more" – "I will always want more."

The workforce is frozen in the adolescent-infantile state notwithstanding all the programs and all the slogans, which would symbolize the contrary. Put another way, the modern organization gets very little real productivity out of its people – perhaps only about 30 percent of what they are capable of doing.

Does this mean most workers don't care? Of course not. It means that the structure of the organization does not fit the tasks – the structure should enhance such accomplishment but too often it does not.

More importantly, workers are not treated as adults, as full partners in the enterprise. Oh! The words are used, but management's behavior does not compute with the words.

Granted, a great deal of attention is being given the environment in terms of *Quality Circles, Quality of Work Life, Quality of Management,* and *Quality of Work.* There are also cross-cultural awareness programs designed to get this blueprint on to the factory floor. *Management styles* are being modified in quest of the magic formula that will make the organization more productive.

What have these activities achieved? At best, marginal if ephemeral results. Why? The majority still march to the programmed cadence of terminal adolescence that has been the organization's drumbeat for decades. Why should anyone be surprised when workers fail to respond with maturity?

Stuck in Machine Age Thinking— Erik Erikson's Model of Human Development

Labor unions are in sharp decline, while management's union, Human Resources (HR) is soaring with its cosmetic interventions. Workers felt betrayed by labor unions and now feel exploited by HR as management's advocate. The "best and brightest" have become cynical and turned to making money rather than making a difference. That legacy has contributed to the economic crisis. The uncoupling of workers from managers has widened as managers no longer lead and workers no longer follow. Surprisingly, we have survived despite management's insensitivity and workers' immaturity during the Machine Age.

To understand this, let us walk through a cultural no man's land guided by Erik Erikson's six styles of human personality development:

(1) *autonomy;*
(2) *trust;*

(3) initiative;

(4) accomplishment;

(5) identity; and

(6) intimacy.

Erikson's model supports the premise that management is dealing with a wrongly conditioned workforce for the times, a workforce that enjoys little autonomy, only contrived trust, little opportunity to take the initiative or to sense personal accomplishment, which leads to a crisis in identity and an inability to demonstrate intimacy.

The workforce experiences from the crib to the company a high need to please which marks its arrested development. When workers as adults are needed, they are nowhere to be found.

It was surreal but nonetheless true when management thought it could construct arbitrary systems, such as *Quality Circles* and *Empowerment Programs* such as *Participative Management* and workers would respond with maturity and satisfaction. Obviously, this has not been the case.

Instead, the new wave of challenges and opportunities have been met with confusion if not shame, mistrust, guilt, a sense of insecurity, and isolation. This has perplexed management as it failed to see how more than fifty years of co-dependency has resulted in a workforce essentially suspended in terminal adolescence.

What needs to be done, fortunately, is revealed in *Erikson's model*. Management needs to maintain patience with the process. It needs to cut back on its demands and look for ways to cultivate workers for the long haul. *This can be done by encouraging workers to do the right things rather than everything right.* Workers know what makes the difference. Management needs only to solicit their views on common problems, which will gradually turn workers around from passive to active responders.

If this sounds like making workers full partners in the process, we are on the same page. Reality, when it is positive and reinforcing, finds workers at the ready, but when reality is negative and demanding it is another story. It will not be easy for workers to become more responsive and responsible. If they do, the dividends are considerable:

- *A sense of autonomy will build self-control, which will lead to self-management demonstrating the willpower of disciplined behavior;*

- *A sense of trust will fuel the drive and motivation to have faith in the future;*
- *A sense of initiative will give self-direction and purpose to work;*
- *A sense of accomplishment will lead to competence;*
- *A sense of identity will lead to loyalty and fidelity;*
- *A sense of intimacy will promote affiliation and love*

Personality development involves the formation of trust. Obviously, the trust in the best of organizations is only slightly above the "dog eat dog" level.

A sense of autonomy is constantly denied until most adults are products of *learned helplessness* with a *high need to please others* without any idea how to please themselves.

The sense of accomplishment is also thwarted because expediency dictates there is a right way, which is translated the only way. This leaves little room for initiative or for failure, which is the learning phase. In the absence of initiative and accomplishment, there is little room for personal satisfaction.

Identity is a stage that most would admit not handling too well. Role confusion and role demands lead to identity crises. When so handicapped, we become *other directed* with little idea what makes us tick other than being dependent or counter dependent on what we do for a living.

The psychological shrinking of America has created an industry for mid-life identity crises. One in every three Americans seeks psychotherapy or counseling from a doctor, preacher, teacher, guru or friend.

Yet perhaps the hardest is to attain a *sense of intimacy.* Sex is not intimacy. Love is. Sex and love can merge into intimacy but the problem is not only intimacy with others but with ourselves.

We are interested in having good friends, but the most important friendship must be with ourselves. If we cannot be intimate with ourselves, then intimacy with others in a sham.

The Search for the Quick Cure

The modern worker is a new entity. He is more skilled, better educated and self-confident. He also has different values, beliefs and expectations as well as interests. He doesn't respond well to blarney. He has power in his knowledge and is self-motivated and the new kid on the block. When he comes into an organization, it is like hitting a wall as he is now expected to be management dependent or counter dependent on the company for his total well-being. While not being especially timid, insecure, unskilled, undereducated, or naïve, it is soon clear to him that he is expected to take orders, be polite, obedient, punctual, and passive and appreciate being taken care of by management.

When he is unresponsive to charismatic leadership, and doesn't see the company as "his family," and fails to follow company policies and procedures to the letter, he finds himself in the wrong place at the wrong time. The irony is that he may just be what the company needs.

This has been the dilemma. Professionally trained workers find themselves being treated as if blue-collar workers when they see themselves as decision-makers and not passive responders.

Rather than admit the workforce is dominated by this new worker with fully eight out of ten, and soon nine out of ten workers being of such a mindset and temperament, companies have attempted to make them fit. Many pundits and writers have been at the ready to oblige management.

Terrence Deal and Allan Kennedy in *"Corporate Culture"* see the problem in terms of knowing what the company stands for; Bob Waterman and Tom Peters in *"Search for Excellence"* claim the best bet is to copy successful companies; and John Naisbitt in *"Megatrends"* sees visions beyond the pale of the cockeyed optimist.

These prescriptions fail to deal with Erikson's six stages which can flourish only in a culture that supports them.

Eleven corporate habits that get in the way

(1) The problem with top down communications.
>   Operationally, strategic planning doesn't necessarily translate into tactical communications. What is proposed in the Boardroom is compromised with too many filters to pass through to the operations level. Consequently, internal stress and accelerating external demands mount to the point that problems go unreported or misconstrued with timely decisions not made.

(2) Management by Objectives (MBOs), in practice, has proven counterproductive, time consuming expensive and ineffective.

208

Compartmentalizing objectives, and then rewarding each department for accomplishing its objectives has proven illusory. As systems analyst Russell Ackoff has shown, *"If you take a system apart to identify its components, and then operate those components as well as possible, the system as a whole will not behave as well as it could. It is counterintuitive to Machine Age thinking, but nonetheless true, if you have a system that is behaving as well as it could, then none of its parts will be."*

(3) The problem with the non-confrontational style of management.

Tension and conflict are normal fare in an organization. Asking questions, or disputing the problem solving strategy are necessary to a vibrant, engaged and energetic work climate. Harmony is the antithesis of efficacy as *managed conflict* is the glue that holds an operation on task. Americans tend to protest infrequently but violently instead of frequently and politely. It is not necessary that everyone like each other for an operation to be successful, but it is important that everyone respect and esteem each other's contribution.

(4) Management manages the way it is paid.

When lip service is given to quality, it is understood that compensation and promotion depend upon *meeting schedule* at any cost. Corners are cut, and ethical standards compromised to meet the bottom line. Workers see this and become cynical.

(5) Management has outsourced personnel management to human resources with dire consequences.

Feeling international competition, decaying infrastructure of plants and equipment, and the creeping obsolescence of technical skills, leading to demotivated workers, management turned to human resources to solve its personnel problems, resulting in a series of cosmetic interventions that have made the workplace like a playground at the expense of performance.

(6) Management is preoccupied with order which, paradoxically, makes it the victim of chaos.

In the *Machine Age*, where everything has in its place and there was a place for everything, obsessive order made some sense. Work, workers and the workplace were like a well-oiled machine with predictable outcomes and little variance, as it was essentially a robotic environment

209

with workers behaving like interchangeable robotic parts. That has all changed in the era of the professional worker, except in the workplace.

(7) The company attempting to be all things to its people has ended in being a disappointment to everyone.

When things were going smoothly and profits were soaring, management flirted with *lifetime employment*, and *entitlement programs* that had little to do with actual performance. Now when markets are shrinking, and costs are soaring, management plays the heavy. *US Steel* and *Alcoa* learned this the hard way. A program was initiated in the 1960s in which every five years veteran employees would be given an additional 13-weeks paid furlough. The objective was to leverage employees to greater productivity. Instead of traveling or honing their skills, most workers got second jobs. When back to work at *US Steel* and *Alcoa*, now enjoying the income from two jobs, many attempted to work both jobs with diminished performance, which led to anger with management.

(8) The John Wayne "Lone Ranger" Mindset.

Some company brass take pride in going it alone, taking big risks, cutting out new territory with a flamboyance that nothing can touch them, until it does, sending the company into an economic tailspin with workers in the end to pay. These no nonsense cowboys of reckless enterprise led to the *Savings & Loan scandals* where the books were cooked and people went to prison.

(9) The problem of professionalism.

Professionalism has evolved as we have moved through the post-industrial to modernity and into postmodernity all within a generation or so. We have become an *acquisitive society* not only in material sense, but also in terms of credentials. We measure capability by those who have degrees, and give little consideration to those who do not, as if a degree holder has a right to a job simply for being credentialed. *Intelligence is what it does*, not a BS or BA designator. Nor are credentials a shorthand for competence. Typically, when a professional runs into career stagnation, he goes back to school to get an MBA or Ph.D.

(10) The confusion between tasks and structures

No one is likely to argue that the norms for one company would apply equally to another. They don't! There are discrete cultural differences to every company. When the lights are dimmed at 6 p.m., it tells workers it is time to go home. If there are staff meetings routinely every morning, it means work is secondary to your expected presence. If you want to stay after six, the dimming of the lights tells you it can wait until tomorrow. If you prefer to work alone but everything is done in teams, then it is in team meetings where you should be. If none of this appeals to you, then it is best that you move on, but most people don't. *The structure of work determines the task of work; those tasks create the workplace culture; that culture dictates organizational behavior; and that behavior if it is consistent with your drives will be enhancing; if it is not you are in the wrong place.* What does it mean for the company? It means some companies will soar, some will vegetate, and others will flounder and expire. It depends on how much the structure supports the tasks at hand.

(11) Human Resources has unwittingly become management's union.

Management is remarkably dependent on a buffer between it and its people. Be that buffer an adversary or advocate is immaterial; the function is basically the same. Moreover, just as the labor union movement grew out of an erosion of worker power in the industrial organization, the *Human Resources movement* has grown out of an erosion of management power in the complex organization. Labor unions and human resources have had a similar function: insuring worker survival (labor union); management survival (human resources). The reason for drawing special attention to this "new unionism" is that it reveals how precariously the organization is in transition. Also, it indicates the void growing wider between the workforce and management.

With the labor unions, you may recall, union leaders bought into management's emphasis on productivity. Their attention was diverted from the erosion of worker power or control of what they did to sacrificing this for entitlements, compensation and job security. Now that has also all eroded. Labor unions were willing to give management increasing control as long as management made pay and entitlement concessions. This has hurt workers and management alike. Management believed that paying workers more would motivate them to do more. One need look no further than the steel and automotive industries to see that this did not work.

Now, we have the "New Union," Human Resources, orchestrating interventions that have turned the workplace into a playground. Just as management gave the labor unions the money, they said they needed, management is now giving Human Resources the power to promote morale with cosmetic perks:

(1) From parking to work concessions;

(2) From touchy-feely supervision to extraordinary fringe benefits;

(3) From beautiful work areas to wonderful group programs.

Whereas the labor union got management and the worker to think in terms of money concessions, Human Resources has gotten management and the worker to think in terms of comfort and climatic luxury. The net result in both cases is a demotivated workforce vacillating between comfort and complacency. It is time management becomes less dependent on advocacy (Human Resources) or adversary (Labor Unions) relationships, and more on workers and management becoming partners in enterprise.

So Where Do We Go From Here?

What I have attempted to do here is admittedly a risky analysis of a complex problem. There is no way such an analysis can be made without stepping on some toes including the hand that feeds me. Be that as it may, I have been waiting for these realities to surface:

(1) The modern complex organization is out of balance and has got to regain that balance;

(2) That balance cannot be discovered by ignoring history or by embracing untested new ideas;

(3) That workers work the way they have been programmed to work, and that conditioning cannot be summarily rejected by instituting prosthetics corrections (re: *Quality Circles* and *Participative Management Programs*);

(4) That management has had a haughty dependence on technology (or things), and a horrifying disregard and ignorance of workers (as persons);

(5) That workers have a fundamental need to contribute and own what they do because work provides them with identity;

(6) That workers need to experience growth in order to feel worthwhile;

(7) That workers will behave as children when they are treated like children;

212

(8) That the organization in the modern era has become increasingly immature in the home, church, school, and community as well as the workplace;

(9) That immaturity is a product of believing what is best for the individual without knowing what the individual needs, values, believes or expects.

(10) That *Participative Management* hasn't a ghost of a chance until the gap is closed between an adolescent and an adult oriented organization;

(11) That *Participative Management* demonstrates we are basically ignorant in organizational terms of what motivates the individual worker.

Having said all this, I think a first step is to recognize that the "management of things" and the "management of people" are discretely different functions. That managers and consultants must realize that listening is more powerful than telling; that framing the problem is more important than generating solutions; that we are on the threshold of a wonderful tomorrow if we can "let go" of all our precious false assumptions of the past, and allow a little reality to guide our way.

Reference

Keynote speech, *"Participative Management: An Adversary Point of View,"* Honeywell Avionics Conference: Host, Department of Contract Administrative Services (DECAS), Clearwater Beach Hotel, Clearwater Beach, Florida, March 30, 1984.

Embracing a Paradigm Shift

"The man who embraces a new paradigm at an early stage must often do so in defiance of the evidence provided by the problem solving."

Thomas S. Kuhn, American physicist, historian and philosopher of science

There is a discernible contrast between the reality of the worker's life today and its historical antecedence. The worker is at once an atom living its own conscious life "for itself," and at the same time the unconscious agent of change. Since workers are not, in fact, free, but could not live without the conviction that they are, it is better that they understand what goes on as they do in fact understand it, than to seek to subvert such common sense beliefs. "Happy ignorance" rules the head if not the heart of most workers. Even so, there is movement against the grain, now a slight tremor but rapidly building. The focus of this natural fault is apparent — the worker, alone!

"Great men" do not move workers from their epicenter, but "important people" do appear when discontinuity leads ultimately to the shock waves of catastrophe. These people are less important than they themselves may suppose, but neither are they shadows. They embody the strengths and weaknesses, the passions and dreams, the nightmares and madness of their times. For only a moment, however, they step outside and display wisdom. They appear when rhetoric is reduced to rubble.

To put "the worker, alone" in perspective, permit this brief excursion. The working man's faith in ideas has controlled his lot far more than he might believe. Belief is by far the most powerful motivator known to man.

In the Western world, workers once had a deep commitment to an ancient faith, Roman Catholicism. That faith has eroded in the last 500 years, with some insisting workers everywhere have disintegrated morally and politically. Closer to the truth, workers have changed. They have responded and adapted to stress and accelerating demands. Change is never born in the void.

Religion for centuries played its part in the persistent pursuit of the "toy of truth." The natural enemies of the spiritual were then as now, cleverness and specialization — products of secular reasoning.

The Church argued it, alone, understood the "inner rhythms," the silent march of things. Only those who understood this "truth" knew what could or could not be achieved, what should or should not be attempted. The "Doctors of the Church" believed they alone held the key to secular success as well as spiritual salvation. Omniscience belonged to God alone, and they were His agents. Only by immersing ourselves in His Word dare we hope for wisdom.

Against this cultural inculcation, another truth emerged, empirical or practical wisdom. This is knowledge of the inevitable: of what, given our world of order, could not but happen; or conversely, of how things cannot be, or could not have been. The rare capacity for seeing this we call a "sense of reality." This has been the domain of science and the scientist.

These "twin toys of truth," heart and mind, spirit and reason, religion and science, have been warring with each other for centuries. Men of God insist the human intellect is but a feeble instrument when pitted against the power of divine forces; that rational explanations of human conduct seldom explain anything. They are inadequate if only because they ignore man's "inner" experience. A high value is set on family life and on the superiority of the heart over the head, the moral over the intellectual.

Men of science stand apart. They hold that only by patient empirical observation can reliable knowledge be obtained; that this knowledge, even then, is always inadequate and incomplete, but that it must be sought.

The solitary thinker draws a gloomy picture of the impotence of the human will against the rigid laws of the universe. Yet men of science display the same vanity of human passion as they attempt to uncover the absurdity of rational systems, while failing to understand the non-rational origins of action and feeling. They aspire to reduce man to a manageable lot, to a condition of predictability, where, now passionless, man can no longer be frustrated, humiliated or wounded. Men of science have a near metaphysical belief in logical positivism; their religious counterparts, an equal attachment to the mystical or supernatural.

Doctors of the church and men of science represent the spiritual and secular half of the same whole. Both are foolishly dogmatic; both long for a universal explanatory principle, composed of the bits and pieces of the furniture of the universe, which may be reduced to a single unifying design. From their respective vantage points, they dissect and pulverize in order to reach the indestructible core, which paradoxically remains eternally elusive to them.

They are men, like all working men, and therefore their personal and professional lives are an inescapable tangle of unresolved conflicts and savage battles between their gifts as thinkers and their passionate ideals; between what they are and what they purport to be.

At no time in history has there been such an excess of them, so many men with such powers of insight — with the uncanny ability to determine differences, contrasts, collisions of people, places and things — as now, and yet, on balance, never have so many displayed such colossal, monumental ignorance! Society is lost because these men choose to believe themselves lost.

Could it be men suffer because they seek too much, are foolishly ambitious and grotesquely overestimate their capacities? Modern man seems the central tragedy of his time, obsessed with himself and mystified by his carping complexity. If only men would learn how little the cleverest and most gifted among them can control anything, how little they can know the multitude of factors available, how meaningless harmony is when chaos is the protoplasm of life.

From the beginning of recorded history, workers have struggled to find truth, failing to realize truth is relative. What is truth to you may not be truth to me. Religion has been at the forefront to carry workers on this journey. Science and moralism have played their part to reduce Eros to sex. Individualism and egalitarianism have turned intimacy into contractual matters to be litigated.

Religion and science combine to be "apostles of despair." Both preserve the same cynical disbelief in the improvement of society by rational means, both speak with the same angry irony, both are deeply skeptical of their own powers. They have lost faith with faith.

Organized religions seem hardly religions at all. They have been smitten by modernity, and dress up as if to prove they are "with it." Religious leaders appear out of gas, pusillanimous warriors. They have a distaste for anyone who deals in ideas, who believes in abstract principles. They have adopted the high-minded objectivity of the secular faith of science. Religion itself seems no more certain of its role in modern society than the average worker of his.

Church has fallen back on being a form of personal entertainment without meaning. The rituals, the vain repetition of phrases, the mechanical prayers, the pontification's, and the castigations are all inventions of thought. What thought creates is not sacred. It is a product of man's mind.

Still, religion as distraction has continued to foster the "should be" qualities worshippers' desire. There is a certain irony in this, even a certain manifest dishonesty and deception. It is an expedient design. It has not always been so.

Religion had vitality in the 16th century when a single cleric, Martin Luther, went against the grain of the dominant figure of the culture of the time, The Holy See of Rome, His Holiness, Pope Leo X, to post his 95 theses on the door of the Wittenberg chapel. This was unprecedented. Here a young cleric was putting his career and comfort in jeopardy for what he believed. He had little support, and was immediately labeled a heretic. Some called him a madman, pointing out the emotional character to his temperament. He was all alone. He made no apology for his act as he believed his regeneration could only come from within, and that the source of that inner life was concealed in his immortal soul.

The enormity of this act is difficult to comprehend today. Clearly, it was not motivated by self-interest, or to justify disobedience to the Holy See. It was an act of conscience and conviction, not deviance, an act with a complete willingness to accept the consequences. As an individual, he stepped outside the obedient rank and file and declared himself one with his Creator.

Scripture revealed to Luther a loving God, not the God he was programmed to worship. This loving God bestowed on sinful man the free gift of salvation through faith alone. The church's liturgical dogma necessitating good works to attain salvation was thus blatantly revoked. Luther's theology went against the grain of accepted Roman Catholic teaching, and cut to the core the hypocritical practices associated with indulgences.

Earning indulgences was promulgated as a way to avoid Purgatory, and to go straight to heaven upon death. Indulgences were created to award believers for good works. But the affluent, who had little time or felt little inclination to do good works, bypassed the process by buying indulgences.

Indulgences were sold wholesale the way scalpers sell tickets to rock concerts today. The practice was ludicrous and appalling, but no one did anything.

The Roman Catholic Church was the most powerful force in Western Europe, indeed, in most of the civilized world. It condoned the practice of selling indulgences by presenting a blind eye to the activity until one man, Martin Luther, demonstrated the courage to take on the entire Roman Catholic establishment, by going against the grain.

With that heroic act, Luther set the chain reaction which would release the worker from "The Dark Ages" of corporate dependency on Holy Mother Church, and plant the seeds for a growing individualism. Western man's whole mentality and disposition was thus to undergo radical restructuring.

What is most remarkable about this is that Martin Luther was not a saint, not cast in the mold of the "great man," not even an especially "learned man," a man with many of the psycho-sexual flaws of modern man, a man who made the same foot prints as his contemporaries. He was neither a demigod nor a scoundrel, only a man of intense passion and focus. But he was a man of substance whereas shallowness ruled his day as it does ours.

Like workers today, Luther's contemporaries immersed and submerged themselves in the medium of the mundane. Life was taken for granted with normal events considered inseparable from the workers themselves.

With such a mindset, workers do not and cannot observe themselves as if from the outside. They cannot identify, measure and seek to change anything because it is too much a part of what they recognize as themselves. They cannot even be wholly aware of, inasmuch as it enters too intimately into all their experience, is itself too closely interwoven with all that they are and do, for them to be able to lift themselves out of "the flow of things," and be able to observe themselves with detachment, as is an object.

Yet workers are their essential frame of reference, and that frame is integral to the way they behave. Workers are caged in their standards of truth and falsehood, of reality and appearance, of the good and the bad, of the central and the peripheral, of the subjective and objective, of the beautiful and the ugly, of movement and rest, of past, present and future, of one and the many. These categories, these concepts represent the ultimate framework, the basic presuppositions wherewith workers function.

This is the context and paradoxical dilemma of the problem of dramatic change. Martin Luther could not analyze his predicament from a vantage-point outside it, for there is no "outside." Yet he was more aware of the texture and direction of the submerged (and troubling) portions of his own and everyone else's lives; better aware of this than others, who chose either to ignore the existence of scandalous selling of indulgences, or chose to rationalize the tyranny of church authority.

The superficial, cosmetic and frivolous dominate every age. They are objects above the surface, the relatively conscious acts, which mask the disturbing tremors below. The prominent are those who can manipulate them with instinctive ease.

Wisdom is another thing. Wisdom abhors the superficial. It burrows through the pomp and circumstance to discount the ballyhooed "inevitable trends," "the imponderables," "the way things are going." Wisdom is not scientific knowledge, but a special sensitivity to the contours of the circumstances in which the observer happens to be placed. Wisdom displays more the mind of the peasant than the aristocrat, a mind which looks for simple truths and is not blindsided by the profound. Neither the rules of science nor religion need necessarily apply, but rather the inexpressible sense of reality, of "what is" to an open mind. Martin Luther was in this sense, wise.

His protest led to the establishment of Protestantism and a new identity for the worker. The worker would come to see his relationship to himself, his Creator and to his world in more accountable terms. Holy Mother Church lost a dependent.

John Calvin, the French theologian, was even bolder. He established the Protestant Ethic, which drew a marked distinction between the saved and the damned. Personal salvation, he professed, is tied to energetic pursuit of health, wealth and happiness to the honor and glory of God. Accomplishment in this life is not only important, but an indicator of "The Elect," or "The Chosen."

Believers demonstrate the right to the enviable status of being in God's grace by their conduct. These disciplined believers are known by their vocation or "calling." Success is sought in these vocations as a measure of God's grace. The man of property, not poverty is thus the embodiment of the man of God.

The fatalism of Catholicism was set aside. There was no honor in playing the victim, or celebrating humility. Individualism displayed in public works enjoyed a new dignity, success a new prominence. The need for a priest as intercessor in Holy Confession became unnecessary. Calvinism, as with Lutheranism before, taught that salvation is a pure gift from God, and cannot be earned.

Out of this came the Protestant Work Ethic, which advocated self-discipline, self-reliance, self-examination, hard work and dedication to duty. Capitalism was secure.

In going against the grain Western man has set the pace for prosperity over the past 500 years. This tradition is now eroding. The religious motivation, which inspired this radical departure from conventional thinking, is all but gone. Modern religion goes with, not against the grain of the prevailing norm. Religion has lost its moral compass and calling. Roman Catholicism is no longer its curse, but science. Religion cowers before science and imitates its deficiencies. There appear no Martin Luther's or John Calvin's on the horizon.

Workers in my experience have scant acquaintance with the Protestant Work Ethic. Nor do these workers subscribe to the philosophy of systematic profits through hard work, thrift and the reinvestment of earnings — basic characteristics of early capitalism. They play the Lotto, are habitual river boat gamblers, frequent state sponsored casinos (which are springing up like convenient stores), or look to inherit.

Increasingly, conventional behavior is driven more by luck than pluck. Going against the grain is an anomaly. Mature adult workers are in short supply. Perhaps this is why. The mind of mature adult workers is:

A mind which is utterly free from vain attachments, from foolish conclusions and concepts. It deals only with what actually is, not with what should be, or might be "with a little luck." Such a mind is impatient with societal excess.

Not sympathetic to patronage, benign or otherwise. Its agenda is not limited to a rational economic process. The mind of a mature adult worker is interested in power, identity and recognition. The tyranny of "top-down authority" is no longer acceptable. But bottom-up control is still a fantasy, because no one has the gumption to go against the grain.

Involved in everyday life, and with what happens, both outwardly and inwardly, such a mind wants to understand the complex problems of life and to deal with them on the basis of reality, not on the basis of "what should be." With such a mind, there is little room for denial in its makeup.

Free of denominational, racial, national, ethnic and socioeconomic prejudices, it is a mind also beyond tradition, beyond cultural inculcation, and free from all sense of historical direction. Its redemption is to be found in seeing society clearly in holistic terms.

One comforting thought is that if Martin Luther had not come forward, someone else would have made the breakthrough. When society is ready, its conscience surfaces.

Luther was the least superficial of men. He could not swim with the current without being drawn irresistibly beneath the surface to investigate the darker depths below. He could not avoid seeing what he saw and doubting even that; nor could he close his eyes and forget he was doing so. His appalling, destructive sense of what was false, which found him torn between God and death, as one historian puts it, prevented him from depressive struggles with self-deception. Alas, Luther was neither more nor less human than any of his contemporaries.

Earlier (see Preface) mention was made that depressives seem more in touch with reality. We live in an age fearful of such depression. Luther was not afraid of depression, and because he was not, his truth touched the silent cords of the tacit majority, which previously was unable to find language to describe, much less face its reality.

Clarity of mind is a necessary component in the pursuit of one's relative truth, whatever that truth might be, for it concedes there is not a single absolute truth, but only truth as we are able to perceive it. Luther's truth touched the personal certainty of his generation, and therefore came to be treated as its "absolute truth." Had that not occurred, history would have ignored him.

Certainty is personal, not objective, and everyone has a right to their own certainty. The mind of mature adult workers knows and accepts this. Such minds, however, currently go quietly about their duties with little inclination to go against the grain. They lack the passion, perhaps even the delirious conviction of Martin Luther, and so we wait for the mature adult worker to show himself and to construct the outlines of a new, more appropriate mentality. Such a person will not go against the grain because he is certain his truth will win the day. He does so because he must. As Thomas Kuhn adds:

"He must have faith that the new paradigm will succeed with the many large problems that confront it knowing only that the older paradigm has failed with a few. A decision of that kind can only be made on faith."

Life Without Cause!

"Arthur Schopenhauer points out that when you reach an advanced age and look back over your lifetime, it can seem to have had a consistent order and plan, as though composed by some novelist. Events that when they occurred had seemed accidental and of little moment turn out to have been indispensable factors in the composition of a consistent plot. So who composed the plot? Schopenhauer suggests that just as your dreams are composed by an aspect of yourself of which your consciousness is unaware, so, too, your whole life is composed by the will within you."

Joseph Campbell, American writer and mythologist

The worker, alone, is "what is," or reality. Going against the grain is the persistent demand of that reality. Mature adult workers know the universe has no cause. It exists. Most workers, however, insist on being driven by causes. True believers cannot function unless embroiled in some cause. It is the way they authenticate themselves.

The idea that the universe has no cause is overwhelming. "Why are we here, then?" cries everyman. Reality replies, "We are here because we exist." We come out of nature and return to nature. But most workers must believe there is more. They refuse to deal with nature "as is," feeling compelled to control it, no, even to conquer and change nature.

Man demonstrates his superiority by subduing nature to his will. But, again and again, as so engaged, nature vanquishes him. For such blinding pride, workers are but strangers to themselves and occupants of a dying planet. The culprit is their obsession with control, the need to subdue what the mind encompasses. Thought creates a duality between "what is" and "what should be."

"What should be" moves the mind away from the problem of "what is" to a fixation with effects. This springs to life in a mishmash of causes. Man is forever terrified by contemplating his own nature. He is hypersensitive, even hypocritical to what is most natural. Sexual pleasure has become a god, a ghost and a ghoul, depending on the orientation. Desire has given birth to consuming as therapy, while the issue of political correctness demonstrates the absurdity of sophistic causes.

Workers are not happy campers. They have come to take themselves far too seriously, and life not seriously enough. A focus on effects cures nothing. It only invents causes and then gives birth to an army of experts and crusaders. In the past century, the popular mind, better known as the "crowd of discontent," created a new Tower of Babel in which language devolved to the litany of complaint.

Workers as "true believers" find a sense of belonging in a cause, a cause which is never their own. A mania for causes creates the world of the crazy, the confused and the moronic, the world of today. Ask yourself, "Who put workers in their cages?"

Reality can never be changed into morality, or "what is" into "what should be." Nor can anyone put order into someone else's life. To realize order, workers must do it themselves. This can be done by breaking free from the madness of the cage, and embracing the freedom of choosing one's destiny, not having it dictated.

So, what do most workers do? They ask for cages. They seek relief from the cage of workaholism, and the stress that it entails, for the cage of libidinous excess, or the cage of chemical dependency. Others not so inclined, seek relief from their anguish by having no life outside of work. The only uniform they wear is that of organizational counter dependency. The cage is their escape from freedom.

The workforce today is better educated than ever before. It accumulates special knowledge — information derived from what others think or say — always careful to express and behave within accepted norms. Nothing is original. The workforce is stuck on the dime and therefore society along with it.

Many workers repeat and repeat what others say and think. This finds them confused, uncertain, stressed, driven from one corner to the other, from one state of anxiety to another, until the point is reached where they cannot think, feel or act alone. They are terrified of a room without noise, a space without people, or a single moment when the mind is quiet. They are spastic.

A mind caught up in knowledge as a means to freedom does not become free. It becomes enslaved to knowing. The more information it has the more it must have. A worker in trouble feels he needs another degree, another seminar, another shot of inspiration from the master, the person with all the answers, who, like his religious predecessor, is unlikely to have spent much time doing in the real world.

Workers have created the mystique which suggests they are not capable of taking care of themselves. Thus is born the syndrome of dependency:

In the workplace: The syndrome manifests itself as either dependency on the manager for direction and control, or counter dependency on the organization for security, identity and recognition.

At home: It becomes dependency on elaborate social outreach programs of the government meant to compensate for the disappearance of a family centered culture. Ninety percent of all families seldom share a daily meal together, the round table of a family centered culture. The fact that these programs exist indicates government now owns the problem, a problem which it can never solve.

In school: The syndrome becomes dependency on teachers and school administrators to assume a responsibility which is more appropriately that of the student. Schools are expected to create purpose, order, motivation and a desire to learn when this is the student's domain.

On television: It becomes dependency on the talking heads to entertain, enlighten, shock, embarrass and excite in order to fill the menacing silence with distracting noise, to divert the mind from its function.

In the community: The syndrome becomes dependency on Law Enforcement and the Criminal Justice System to orchestrate morality, to be the community's conscience when it has abdicated that responsibility. A community gets the police and justice system it deserves. If the community is hypocritical, these extensions of itself can be no less so.

A vast majority of workers find themselves in a "catch 22." They feel helpless and isolated on the one hand, and slaves to the system, captives to a world they did not create, on the other. They feel little obligation to belong or preserve the system's integrity. "Not my problem!" the chorus sings.

Workers sense the disorder in their lives, so they read, they listen to pundits on television, they surf the Internet, they explore apps on their iPads, they text and tweet, they look everywhere but to themselves for order. They argue among themselves. In the end they do what "the experts" say. Nothing changes, because they look always for the change elsewhere, not in themselves. It has been my experience that most workers expect:

Management to be more responsive, more caring, more sensitive to their needs than they are.

Social services to be more accessible, more effective and more equitably distributed than are their own lives.

Teachers and administrators to be better trained, more service friendly, and better motivators and much more understanding than they are willing to reciprocate.

Police to be less forceful, intrusive and belligerent, and much more friendly and conscientious than they prove to be themselves.

Notice where the emphasis is placed? Always on others! It is always "somebody else's problem," not the workers'. You would think these service providers would challenge this absurdity. But rather than challenge these demands, these providers actually attempt to do the impossible.

Workers tend to identify their frustrations with specific causes. The causes are nearly always outside themselves. These causes are packaged and promoted by self-interested experts, who have a stake in fostering a self-pitying and self-indulgent workforce. As long as workers are immature, continuously on edge and self-ignorant, these promoters have a customer.

But it is all for naught. Outward order begins with inward order. There is no other way. A community, a company, a family gets better one person at a time. This is true in the case of economic parity, or matters of recognition, identity and social consciousness. It is equally true of government, science and religion. Government cannot do for the citizen what the citizen refuses to do for himself. Nor can science forgive the A.I.D.'s epidemic by promising a miraculous cure for a social tic. Nor can religion celebrate the nobility of man by denying or degrading man's nature.

It is not the lack of leadership, alone, which is at fault. It is also the failure of workers to pay attention. Their lack of vigilance has driven them into the arms of madness. Madness has become the norm. It is sanity that has become suspect. How do I prove this? I ask, "What has been your experience?"

Life is without cause. There is no direction, no captain to steer the ship in this ocean of life, no cause to defend. Everyone is on their own nickel, responsible and bound to what is noble, right and good. Everything starts and ends with the solitary worker, for each worker comes in alone and leaves alone. He comes out of nature and goes back into nature.

Man is still unfinished. He is only a recent inhabitant of earth, here no more than a few hundred thousand years. The purpose of his life is to live it, period. What he does is an expression of that purpose.

The problem with many workers is that they seem unable to see what is true from what is false. They want to be told. They wait. The wait freezes them in suspended adolescence, grown children who refuse to become adults, and fall back on being parents. How long will this be so? It is difficult to say. The prospects are not encouraging.

A Leadership Manifesto—
Typology of Leaderless Leadership

"The wise man has his follies no less than the fool; but herein lies the difference – the follies of the fool are known to the world but are hidden from himself; the follies of the wise man are known to himself but hidden from the world."

Caleb C. Colton (1780-1832), English clergyman

Leadership is in a state of retreat bordering on confusion. Not only is leadership out-of-date but out-of-touch with the reality of work and workers. Leadership models are now in jeopardy because they were designed for another time and another workforce. Institutions today go from crisis to crisis, scandal to scandal, outrage to outrage. We wait for the other shoe to drop and have become the United States of Anxiety.

Misdirected Leadership Ideals

Jack Welch, venerated former CEO of General Electric (GE) never realized how short he was until he saw a picture of his high school sports team. Welch became the ultimate workaholic to compensate for this shortcoming, and one day found himself "like a man standing 6 feet 4 with a full head of hair," the quintessential executive and corporate leader.[1] Welch had his GE management team and rank and file basking in his reflected glory with soaring accomplishments.

Academics, such as Rahesh Khurana of Harvard, are not so easily impressed. Dr. Khurana suggests that leadership at GE has been superb for the past 100 years and that Welch's contribution to that leadership is consistent with that reputation. The system, Khurana points out, created the climate for such leadership to evolve. The system created Jack Welch, he did not create the system.[2]

Being newsworthy these days is not a function of culture and system, but personality and charismatic appeal, where the mystique of the brash 14-year-old in the 60-year-old bodysuit becomes the prototype of what constitutes leadership.

Welch fits the mold and worked to create the impression he was a regular guy and working stiff – even if he made 700 times more than the typical worker. What role did the 300,000 GE employees play in this success? Apparently little.

227

Why should a single CEO at the top of an organization be treated like royalty? This makes no sense when we consider that thriving organizations assign decisions to workers who are close to the level of consequences and depend on timely feedback from those workers to generate strategies with positive outcomes.

Yet MBA students are taught to focus on the management of things with only passing attention to the leadership of people as persons. They learn that people are expendable and are necessary only to accomplish given goals; the less people the better the financial advantage. One executive took this philosophy to heart and instituted a 20-40-60 plan: *re-evaluate all employees who have had 20 years of service, who are more than 40 years of age, and/or earn $60,000 or more.*

He is no longer CEO of this company, but the damage is done with the company struggling for survival.3

These outrages are labeled as the arrogance of power, and they represent a corporate society adrift without a rudder. They show the love of total war. Competition must be obliterated not simply beaten. The enemy must be destroyed, no mercy granted. If these actions cause collateral damage, such as people losing their jobs, so be it. This is *leaderless leadership*, leadership without a rudder, the dilemma of leadership today.

Leadership discussions assume everyone is talking about the same thing. Leadership often is personified in a charismatic leader (President Kennedy), a central figure (Pope John Paul II), or a person in the organization (Jack Welch).

Leadership invariably is reduced to an individual at the helm. I find this too narrow a perspective. I don't think charisma is relevant, and I don't believe leadership is personified in a central figure. I believe leadership is organic, an all-encompassing phenomenon in which everyone is a leader or no one is!

Typology of Corporate Leadership Behavior

Our institutions are failing, and such failures are always human. The fact that scandals grow nastier is evidence only that we have a problem – not a morality issue but a contextual problem. Because the leadership culture programs the way workers behave, and corporations get the leadership and behavior they deserve. Crisis, scandal and outrage do not occur in a vacuum. They are unwitting products of corporate design, and when the design is wrong, the social termites or "six silent killers" produce their silent havoc.4

Circumstances are forcing a re-evaluation of leadership. I suggested more than a decade ago that work could be conducted more efficiently without managers, that performance appraisals were a costly and counterproductive sham, and that the total quality movement was an expediency driven by crisis management.5 Time has not changed my mind.

People are failing, and we need a typology to describe the humanness of this failure. After observing people for over four decades, I have gleaned the typology of leadership behaviors described in the following sections. If you notice that these types focus on failure, it is because I have encountered far more failures than successes.

Manipulators

Manipulators believe everyone has his or her price, and the leadership system was made for exploitation. The more able the exploiter, the faster this *leaderless leader* rises to a position of consequence. Manipulators conceal hidden agendas and naked ambition, deceptively promoting an image of being straight arrows. Their weapons are fear and intimidation; first they try and cajole others to accept their perspectives; if that doesn't work, they threaten.

Frustrated Participants

These *leaderless leaders* believe in the corporate system and see themselves as dedicated managers. They often are frustrated but are reluctant to complain. When they find inconsistencies in company policy, flagrant violations of fairness issues, etc., they feel their role is to protect the company's image without protest. After a particularly exasperating experience, one frustrated participants was asked what he would do. He replied, "What I always do. Suck it up and move on."

Inside Outsider

Some *leaderless leaders* possess critical specialist skills, often having professional credentials that rank with officers of the company. Although they arrive to enhance their status by impressing others with their unique skills, hey don't attain the authority exercised by generalists and are never considered key players. They experience the paradox of being needed but not wanted. To the old guard they are cowboys, to the new guard, necessary evils.

Winning Side Saddlers

This type of *leaderless leader* appears more frequently at higher levels of the organization. They are consummate pleasers, which endears them to their bosses. They focus on what is wanted, not what is needed. They are chameleons with the capacity to change camouflage at a moment's notice. Should a power shift be eminent, they are the first to leave the old saddle and climb into the stirrups of the new boss.

Nostalgic Elitists

Remnants of a less egalitarian past, these *leaderless leaders* long for the way it once was, when a clear demarcation existed between workers and managers. Today's less structured, open-systems approach causes them great pain. They cannot fathom why their authority is challenged, why the less gifted are treated as equals, or why their superiority is no longer self-evident. Nostalgic elitists see a more permissive culture emerging, where everybody does his or her own thing. They fail to recognize that creativity and chaos are related and that open systems spawn creativity. Their attitude alienates peers, frustrates subordinates, and agonizes superiors.

Waiters in the Wings

These pragmatic *leaderless leaders* marshal resources, plan strategies, and develop tactics. They periodically compare their careers to company progress, having no desire to tie their future to a sinking ship. Their ambition is not obvious because they feel no need to campaign openly. Although they seem relaxed, they usually are impatient and are not willing to wait very long for recognition and promotion. Operationally, they make themselves indispensable and are self-confident, but they are not cheerleaders. They are balanced and maintain perspectives without being easily ruffled. This makes them calming influences in crises, and inadvertently threatening to those who are less secure.

Happily in Harness

These contented *leaderless leaders* love what they do and are appreciative and generous, good co-workers and supervisors, competent without being arrogant. They create a climate for peers and subordinates to grow – even if they are not always effective coaches. They are trusted and fair, consistent and honest. They never think of countermanding an executive order or bad mouthing a superior. They take pride in their ability to do the job, but are surprisingly tolerant of those that don't. Although laziness is foreign to them, they remain philosophical about lazy people. They are unlikely to rock the boat.

Quiet Soldiers

Although these *leaderless leaders* may appear similar to those that are happily in harness, they differ in some striking ways. They are comfortable as followers and identify with subordinates but are not necessarily happing in their jobs. They do only what they are told and don't take risks. They have talent but little resolve. They are apt to accept untenable situations rather than complain. "Not my job," echoes in their silence. Simply put, they are passive passengers on their own ship of destiny. In the past, quiet soldiers were the impetus to paternalistic authority, but now they are more often part of the logjam. They are an atavistic holdover from an anachronistic system.

Victims

This martyr-like *leaderless leadership* pattern is displayed by managers who expect to be trusted without being trustworthy, given cherished assignments without being dependable, and taken at their word without being credible. They delight in the failures of others, but find no humor when others delight in theirs. When others fail, it is because they're incompetent, when victims fail, it's because others let them down. "If only" is their litany and mantra.

Unbending Idealists

Idealizing life and living in a dream world, these *leaderless leaders* see themselves as saviors of lost causes and lost souls, explaining away failures. "He didn't mean to steal the laptop. He just forgot to bring it back." As apologists, they envision a world where there is no conflict or contradiction, only utopian harmony. The problem is that managed conflict is the adhesive that holds workers to their tasks, and contradiction is the natural evolutionary spark of ideas.[6]

Adventurers

As the category name implies, these *leaderless leaders* are consumed with adventure; they are out to push the envelope. Being productive is not exciting enough for adventurers. They are geared for the sensational. When cornered, they come out swinging with an incomprehensible explanation. Nothing is impeded by its possible consequences, as it never occurs to adventurers that they might get caught. They are often brilliant and could succeed without all the artful dodging, but it wouldn't be nearly as much fun. Often the adventurer is the darling of the organization, the daredevil and nonconformist that is envied for monstrous accomplishments that often seem unbelievable (and may be based on cutting corners, slipshod work, or outright fabrication).

Spin Doctors

Spin doctors see themselves as the eyes, ears, and voice of authority and their role to put the best possible face on the worst situation. These *leaderless leaders* tend to reduce everything to digestible sound bites, which often leads to credibility issues. Assessing explosive issues and putting a positive spin on them is no small achievement. It requires the skill of the illusionist to change to change complexity into simplicity, give the chaotic situation an orderly context, and cloak crisis situations under the umbrella of calm. The danger is that spin doctors' short-term solutions often create long-term problems. Spin doctors are apt to be quick witted, congenial, decisive, and backstage performers.

Reluctant Soldiers

Everyone knows and tolerates reluctant soldiers without expecting anything from them. They are in the same job and at the same level where they started. They are *leaderless leaders* who wandered into a job and found a home. Long ago they retired on the job. They have received increased compensation and improve entitlements for doing less and less over the years. To call them lazy is an oversimplification. They are often crafty with an instinct for survival. When first employed, they were considered safe hires and then were forgotten. Statistically, they are part of the 15 percent foot draggers that plague most organizations.7

Overachievers

Overachievers equate working hard with working smart. They demonstrate surface acumen that garners the attention of superiors. It doesn't hurt that they are usually likeable, agreeable, and never seem to sleep. Their attractiveness blinds others from how little they achieve. No one seems to notice their obsessive attempt to cover all bases rather than to focus on the critical 10 percent causing the problem. These *leaderless leaders* are actually not achievers; they are well meaning but get lost in the detail. They equate accomplishment with time spent doing, and intensity of effort with competence. Others see their whirlwind process but not their marginal product.

Messiahs

Whereas unbending idealists dream of a utopian world where answers are not needed, *Messiahs* believe they have the answers. They provide corrective recipes to what ails the workforce, assuming motivation can be defined, packaged, and disseminated as a product – along with style of management – to rejuvenate a lethargic organization. The solutions presented by *Messiahs* don't succeed because the culture dictates behavior, and the culture is driven by the structure and function of work. This requires architectural insight, which is missing in their answers.

Professionals

Professionals are a breed apart. They think in a language unique to their technology. No entry level salary or job for them. They feel they have paid their dues in academia and now they are entitled. Somewhere lost in this scenario is the importance of experience, the benefit of failure in the learning process, and the realization that a career is a journey. *Professionals* want positions, not jobs; they desire authority without accountability. In an age when much work requires self-management, when maturity is essential to deal with ever changing and conflicting circumstances, these leaderless leaders epitomize the spoiled child that feeds on itself and the system. Campaigning for the next position is a full-time job.

Ten Guidelines for Successful Leadership

To move from *leaderless leadership* to *leadership*, workers and managers need to remember the following points:

1. *All contributions large and small are essential to an objective. All work is ennobling.*
2. *No worker, manager, group, or function is complete within itself. Pulling together towards a common objective creates organizational synergy.*
3. *Competitors are not the enemy. An obsession with killing the competitions saps the collective strength and derails effort from the objective. Much can be learned from competition because competitors are serving the same customer.*
4. *Technology should be user-friendly, available, and applicable as a tool to fit requirements, not as a toy to exaggerate differences.*
5. *The best organization is not harmonious. The best employee is not the safe hire. Nor is comfort the best design for success. A Culture of Contribution is the key where struggle, failure, pain, disappointment, chaos, conflict, and confrontation are managed, as opposed to being avoided. What is a Culture of Comfort? It is organized chaos, a challenge to the existing status quo and modus operandi, to misguided authority, and to the objectives that are inconsistent with the mission. It is also a challenge to do more than what is expected.8*
6. *All organizations are in a state of dying. To survive hey must constantly be reborn, retooled, and redirected. This requires a change in mindset and culture, which often results in a step backward before taking a step forward, a retrenchment to reassess the situation. In sports, we call it a time out, in life, we call it getting a second wind, in organization, we call it survival*

7. *Any organization is a human group. People are not things to manage but persons to lead. Leadership must encounter and deal with suspicion and questioning of authority in order to realize cooperation.*

8. *People tend to compare and compete, to look at the "in" group and the "out" group, at the pecking order, on who is getting the perks and keeping score, and who is working and who is not. Given this tendency, there will be lapses – times when people won't be on the same page and times when the organization isn't working anymore. When this happens, don't bring in consultants or implement cosmetic changes; let the dust settle, re-evaluating where the organization is and how it got there. Don't point fingers, but apply strategic interventions that focus on the 20 percent causing 80 percent of the problem.*

9. *The vertical structure of organizations isn't working. Nor is vertical thinking based on linear logic and critical thinking enough. Horizontal organizational structure is needed to complement vertical structure. Likewise, lateral thinking, based on intuition and creative thinking, is needed to complement vertical thinking.*

10. *Organizational culture follows this formula:*
    a. *Structure of work determines the function of work;*
    b. *Function of work creates the workplace culture;*
    c. *Workplace culture dictates organizational behavior;*

Organizational behavior establishes whether an organization is to vegetate, flounder, expire or survive.

Summary

Corporate leaders don't know how to lead and workers don't know how to follow. The workforce has changed in the past 50 years from 90 percent blue collar to 90 percent white collar, but the mindset of management has changed little. Some feel the problem is management style, but it is not. Management, as it was paternalistically designed isn't working. Leadership is needed where workers are treated as partnering adults, not as dependent and obedient children.

Leadership is the vision to see and the ability to serve. To serve, leaders must become followers. They must understand the needs, desires, motivations, interests, fears, and dreams of workers – not by giving workers everything they request but by challenging them.

Every organization has the workers it needs to be successful; the problem is workers are reluctant to add their voices to the dialogue. Workers have the answers because they experience the problems!

These inclusive factors determine in large measure whether an organization has true leadership or *leaderless leadership*. They revolve around three spheres of influence of the Fisher Paradigm™; workers and managers (personality), the organization (geographic), and the prevailing culture (demographic). Where does your organization fall in this continuum?

Resources

1. *Ellen Goodman, "A Downsized Jack Welch," The Tampa Tribune, September 20, 2002, p. 17.*

2. *The News Hour with Jim Lehrer, "Executive Perks," Ray Suarez talks about pay and perks given to corporate CEOs with Rakesh Khurana, professor at the Harvard School of Business and Robin Ferracone, partner with Mercer Human Resources, PBS television, September 16, 2002.*

3. *James R. Fisher, Jr., Six Silent Killers: Management's Greatest Challenge (St. Lucie Press 1998), pp. 7-21.*

4. *Fisher, op. cit. pp. 83-142.*

5. *James R. Fisher, Jr., Work Without Managers: A View from the Trenches (The Delta Group 1990).*

6. *Edward de Bono, Parallel Thinking (Penguin Books 1995).*

7. *Most organizations form a performance curve: 15 percent foot draggers, 70 percent followers, and 15 percent hard chargers.*

8. *Fisher, op. cit. pp. 197-220.*

Note: This typology appeared in The Journal for Quality & Participation, Winter 2002, pp. 20-24.

Six Silent Killers:
Management's Greatest Challenge

Preface

The microchip has extended the reach of the human brain the way machines, beginning nearly two centuries ago, extended the reach of human muscle.

Steve Forbes, Fortune Magazine in *Foreign Affairs* (July/August 1996)

Over the past 40 years, my laboratory has been the workplace. Here, I have witnessed everything changing and nothing changing. What we call work has changed. The majority of people we call workers have changed. Steve Forbes writes sagely when he traces this change to the microchip. Knowledge has replaced brute force, finesse, naked energy. Yet what we call the workplace remains essentially an anachronism—a formal, regulated, highly controlled environment where the few dominate the many. Stated otherwise, the workplace culture has changed little in my working life although the color of workers' collars have changed radically from blue to white. Meanwhile, there has been more technological change in that period than in the previous 300 years.

My first exposure to the industrial workplace was as a student laborer for five summers in a chemical plant while attending university. I did everything from unloading raw materials to stocking 100-pound bags of finished product in railroad box cars. Upon graduation, I first became a bench chemist in a food processing plant, working in research and development, then as a chemical sales engineer with a specialty chemical company. There I moved rapidly up the executive ladder from line management in the industrial division to corporate executive status in the international division. The range of this experience put me in touch with workers from the shop floor and mail room to the board room and to operations across four continents.

Then in 1969, in my thirties, I chose to take a time out to assess my life. My assignment in South Africa had been completed when the world seemed to be coming apart at the seams. In America, after *Martin Luther King, Jr.* and *Robert Kennedy* were assassinated, riots followed in cities across the country, while

Columbia University's administrative buildings in New York City were occupied by students protesting the *Vietnam War*. Nearly 550,000 troops were in Vietnam, only to be rendered impotent by the *Viet Cong Tet Offensive*. At the 1968 *Summer Olympic Games in Mexico City,* two African American medalists raised black-gloved fists defiantly above their heads as the American National Anthem was played, while riots broke out at the *Democratic Presidential Convention* in Chicago and the *Republican's* in Miami.

Elsewhere, Soviet troops and tanks invaded Czechoslovakia with Prague fermenting.   In Warsaw, students were rioting; 300 Mexican students were massacred by the *Mexican National Police Force*; half of the universities in Italy were occupied by hostile students; students marched defiantly in Paris; and violence broke out in the streets of West Berlin. In Johannesburg, one of our servants had been murdered on our property, which was handled by the Afrikaner police as though the death were that of a dog. My disenchantment was further advanced by having to travel to meaningless meetings back to the states and to London at the expense of my work in South Africa.

Much later it would occur to me why I left the corporation so young. Work was killing my spirit, destroying my creativity. More to the point, I was allowing what was called work to do a number on me. I was earning a good living—several times what my laboring father had earned—but with little satisfaction. Moreover, I was in a cage of my own making with a wife and four small children to support. Somehow this failed to hold my feet to the fire. I became a dropout, a novel idea in 1969.

Once separated from the corporation, I retired to the west coast of Florida to read, think, and write. Two years later, when I was broke, I went back to the university for six years as a full-time student, consulting on the side to support my family. My practical desire was to become credentialed, while my passion was to acquire some tools to better understand my life. The deck, I decided, was stacked against me, not by some mysterious sinister forces, but by the benevolence of my benign cultural conditioning. I was programmed to be passively responsive to my life, not to be the actively and creatively involved. Perhaps naively, I expected the university to free me from this impasse. Instead, I found the university possessed with the same factory line assembly mentality obsessively producing a product, in this case *programmed education.*

Most professors didn't teach while most students seemed disinclined to learn. Professors had discovered a way to avoid confrontation with the real world, while students sought to gain credentials as quickly and painlessly as possible. Thus, I found *non-teaching teachers* were complemented by *non-learning student.* Even so, professors complained that publish or perish was their scourge and prevented them from being student-centered. Students protested the cruel and inhuman demands of professors who required them to read more than ten pages of text or to complete a research paper of more than 500 words between class periods. Authentic teaching and genuine learning were preempted by *crucial contact* hours for professors and passing grade point credits for students, both quantitative, not qualitative standards.

Alas, I discovered it wasn't only the workplace *with such a restrictive agenda,* but the classroom as well. Society, I decided, expected to play *dominant parent* to its *submissive child.* This gave me pause. The more I thought about it, the more convinced I became that I was programmed to simulate a microchip, a thing. Students were as averse to challenging their unproductive curriculum as were workers their inept work schedules. The best way to get along was to go along.

After earning my Ph.D., consulting became my full-time job. *Consulting*! There is a word which describes our times! Consultants strive to exploit *non-thinking thinking* and *non-work work.* They aspire to fill the vacuum left by a society bent on form at the expense of substance. Consultants seek to sell a proactive strategy to a reactive client. Little if any attempt is made to disengage the client from its passive orientation. Not surprising, most consultants prefer to see their role as the quick fix embellisher, not the pesky disturber of the status quo. This reduces most interventions to "smoke and mirrors," or cosmetic effects, which provoke little change, however arcane or entertaining. It was for this reason that I re-entered the corporation, not in a line capacity as I had in the past, but as a staff person. I wanted to see if I could make a difference.

The year was 1980. I had been consulting for ten years and now joined the human resources department of a high-tech (NASA and a defense contractor) company. This was at the peak of the touchy-feely human growth movement, where the delicate psyches of employees were being massaged with high priest solemnity. The high-tech workplace was perfect for this set of circumstances. It formed a cozy liaison with sensitivity gurus and quick fix social engineers. Money was no problem, as President Reagan's supply-side economics poured billions of high-tech dollars into Star Wars, NASA space programs, and defense spending, exceeding the military budget of World War II by several billion dollars. Optimism, not patience, combined with paranoia to rule the day.

American industry and commerce were waking up to the economic reality of Japan, Europe, and the Pacific Rim countries. The essentially reactive mode of industry was now displayed in panic and crisis management. In this atmosphere, fads grew to epic proportions, while tactics were celebrated as strategies. Everything was done to and for workers to make them more productive without understanding them or bringing them on board. Seldom, if ever, were workers involved in the creation of workplace improvement designs. More importantly, little note was taken that workers had changed the color of their collars as they were managed much as they had been fifty years before.

Once back in the corporation, I used the workplace as a laboratory. I started by taking an inventory of the meetings, reports, presentations, performance criteria, job requirements, and impact of work on its stated function as an organizational development psychologist. It proved to be nil. I concluded that most of work amounted to *non-doing doing of non-thing things,* which were defined as work. I looked around and saw my colleagues were robotically employed seemingly without protest.

Why? Because that is the way it had always been done before. Most of the training workers required to take was mainly generic. Seldom did it challenge future requirements or improve upon present skills and performance. Training, paradoxically, made workers more complacent and performance more inert. Yet training was essential to fill the boxes to be eligible for promotion. Consequently, nobody objected, nor were they inclined to ask for more appropriate skill-building.

Granted, none of this would register as disturbing were the rate of productivity against the Gross Domestic Product what it had been in the past or from the Civil War period until 1973.

During the past 20 years, this rate has wavered around 2.3 percent versus 3.4 percent for the previous 100 years. This amounts to a loss in the production of goods and services of $12 trillion, or a personal loss to every man, woman, and child (over that 20-year period) of nearly $50,000 in income, enough for a down payment on a home or a college education.

Jeffrey Madrick writes in *The End of Affluence* (1995), "if this trend continues during the next 20 years, each American will lose $75,000 over that period, and the loss to the nation in production will be $25 trillion." He argued, at the time, that if we had sustained the previous rate of productivity (3.4 percent) until the present, the debate over the national debt, welfare benefits, and national healthcare coverage would all be academic. Madrick has not only proven to be prophetic given the 2008 Wall Street meltdown and Real Estate collapse, but productivity has, indeed, slipped below 2.3 percent as we continue at an anemic pace in this second decade of the 21st century.

Hypothesis: We don't know how to manage, motivate, or mobilize our brilliant workforce. Perhaps this is because we haven't taken the time to understand our workers, nor, indeed, ourselves in this new world of work. In frustration, atavistic management attempts to impose an anachronistic workplace culture on workers. This spawns and proliferates *"six silent killers,"* which are destroying our will not only to survive, but to prevail. These silent killers are social termites, which burrow into the inner recesses of our workplace infrastructure. They are essentially unconscious and, therefore, undetected by a spirit-killing culture.

This is management's greatest challenge, not only in the United States, but in every advanced society. The answers are unlikely to come from breakthrough paradigms, but rather through the willingness of management to be learners, not knowers, in the conduct of work and to recognize that change comes in dribbles, one person at a time, and requires overcoming the enormous psychological inertia of our reactive cultural programming.

Novelist George V. Higgins in his book *On Writing* (1990) has a simple formula to help people decide if they can write, and after writing, publish. If there's a lot of writing in your files, "then the chances are you have the talent to write more. If you haven't written anything, you do not have the talent because you don't want to write." Higgins published more than a dozen novels but spent many years in partial or full obscurity. I know the feeling. I have been writing since I was eight years old. "Six Silent Killers" was first published in 1998 as my sixth book, three followed. All nine books are in this publishing set of second editions. A tenth book, "Confident Thinking," is now in the process of being published.

As a writer, I reject the idea of a perfect society or perfect human existence. The very idea of perfection seems vacuous and incoherent. Our status quo and hierarchical tradition look for trade-offs between good and evil without getting inside their incoherence to understand why we keep repeating the same behaviors and experiencing the same problems. There is no good without evil, or no evil without good. They are conflicting, to be sure, but inseparable, just as there is no success without failure.

We are also obsessed with solving problems when problems are never actually solved but simply controlled. This is revealed by the emphasis placed on results or solutions instead of framing the problem correctly and judiciously and then focusing on chronic perturbations in the process. This preoccupation is an affliction as common to our personal as to our professional lives.

We are left with the radical dilemma of choice which reason leaves in the lurch. Radical choice may be an oxymoron, but it is apropos to any discussion of salient ideas relating to work, the workplace and workers. The diversity of human nature produced by choice-making has everything to do with why these six silent killers exist, for they plague an organization quietly and unobtrusively until once discovered it is too late for damage control.

"Six Silent Killers" is about choice-making and self-creation. Human beings constitute themselves not only as individual agents but as practitioners of diverse cultural traditions with distinctive collective identities. These individuals form divergent worlds of practice, distinctive forms of discourse and thought, and develop diverse networks that are supportive in these choices and self-creation. This work here endeavors to make this abundantly clear.

A company cannot effectively search for an answer to its problem by imitating other successful companies but must discover the answer to its dilemma in self-creation and choice-making collectively in enterprise. The same holds true for the individual.

In 1990, I left the corporate world to devote my full time to writing. It has been a difficult but rewarding experience. Struggle, as I address in this book, is an essential ingredient to growth. I thank God for giving me the health and energy to persevere. I thank my wife, Betty, for her love and support and for editing this book several times.

I would like to thank my friend Jorge Fernandez for his support and belief in the ideas expressed here. I would like to thank Carrie Livingston who read this work in its original form and made several useful suggestions. A special thanks goes to the State of Iowa, where I was born and grew up attending St. Patrick's Grammar School, Clinton High School, and the University of Iowa. I come from working-class parents—my father was an Irish Roman Catholic brakeman on the Chicago & Northwestern Railroad and my mother a homemaker of inestimable persuasion. They provided a home where Irish mirth, storytelling, mischief, and religion were a concoction only God could appreciate. I would also like to thank the late Dennis McClellan and St. Lucie Press for giving me this opportunity to address a larger audience. .

James R. Fisher, Jr., Ph.D.,

Tampa, Florida

Six Silent Killers

Social Termites of the Corporate Madhouse

It's here, sir, that one is oneself with a vengeance;
Oneself, and nothing whatever besides.
We go, full sail, as our very selves.
Each one shuts himself up in the barrel of self,
In the self-fermentation he dives to the bottom,
With the self-bung he seals it hermetically,
And seasons the staves in the well of self.
No one has tears for the other's woes;
No one has mind for the other's ideas.
We're our very selves, both in thought and tone,
Ourselves to the spring-board's uttermost verge
And so, if a Kaiser's to fill the throne,
It is clear that you are the very man.[1]

Henrik Ibsen, Norwegian dramatist and playwright

The crippled genius of American workers contains many paradoxes. Contrast when workers are full of themselves with when they are not. In the case of the former, they are obsessed with *self,* preoccupied with *things.* With the latter, they are concerned with others and their well-being. Workers have an essential drive *to acquire,* but an equal need *to serve.* Their paradoxical nature takes on many forms. A few years ago, after a winter thaw, the Mississippi River at Waterloo, Iowa, threatened to flood the city. Faced with this crisis, the city mobilized its resources, and people of all ages filled sand bags, mounted them on trucks, and distributed them

242

throughout the city to form man-made dikes. Hundreds of citizens worked around the clock beside neighbors and friends and, yes, beside strangers as well. The separate identities of age, race, religion, values, and profession dissolved into a faceless common challenge. For one brief moment, a *sense of community* possessed their consciousness.

After the crisis had passed, several volunteers were asked why they did it. The consensus was "because it had to be done. The city had to be saved!" Would they do it again? Without hesitation, they replied in unison, "Yes, of course." They would submit themselves to the demands of crisis management. Waterloo at that moment had no insiders or outsiders. It was a community with a common mission. This is but one event in the kaleidoscopic spectrum of self-forgetfulness in times of perceived crisis. As previously mentioned, whenever physical survival is at stake (World War II) or psychological survival is at issue (launching of Sputnik), whenever the threat comes from outside, the sense of belonging to a communal tribe is at its strongest. The key words are "perceived crisis." Throughout history, tension invariably produces tribal music, while relaxation typically generates tribal noise. If we don't feel it, can't see it, or it doesn't touch us, as with the current economic world instability, it doesn't exist. Yet tension is as natural to the spirit as joy is unnatural. We Americans are a tense and intense lot. We find it difficult dealing with ourselves when things are going well. We are always waiting, ever anxious, for the other shoe to fall. For some reason, we have to work very hard at not working at all. Leisure is intimidating. Work is our sanctuary.

The Odyssey of American workers and their quest for satisfaction has not been a particularly joyous one. When you see joy on the faces of workers, it is likely a mask concealing the tension of struggle and fear within—struggle to become what they are not and fear of being found out for what they are. *Pretend* and *pretension,* derivatives of tension, are prominent features of the American character. Show me a youngster smiling easily in play. Instead, America has seven-year-olds playing football as if they were in the NFL. Parents-as-coaches can be heard yelling at these prepubescent youngsters, whose bones are not yet mature enough for such punishment. "Put your head down and take him out," parents cry. "Hey! Hey! Hey! What's your problem, fellah, where's your toughness?" Would that such energy and enthusiasm were directed at education and enlightenment. Young minds are quite nimble for such challenge if their bodies are not ready for such abuse.

This mania of forcing maturity on youngsters is programmed at a very early age. My grandson, Ryan James Carr, is two. He is a big boy for his age, about the size of many four-year-olds, but his mother is 6'1", so that is not too much of a surprise. He is attending a religious-sponsored preschool for two-year-olds, which is run like an army boot camp. These two-year-olds are expected to go to the bathroom precisely at 10 A.M., to play prescribed games without stepping out of line, to neither cry nor fuss with their peers, and to clean up their play area or be given demerits. God forbid, one of these little tykes should have an accident and go in their pants. First, they are scolded in front of the group, then asked to sit outside the group and, worst of all, to manage in soiled drawers until a parent comes along. The teacher sees nothing wrong with this. Listening to her, you would think she was talking about teenagers. What she is doing could not be more wrong. If a child is not allowed to have fun and spontaneity when he is young, the child will likely be a problem for society when he is older.

It doesn't stop here. Watch six-year-old baton twirlers, toothy grins barely covering absent teeth, displaying little joy in the exercise. How many of these little girls chose to be so regimented? How many of them are playing out their parents' fantasies? There is a greater pull in the American culture to *please others* than to *please self*. This programming is justified by "it is good for you." More often than not, pleasing others is simply *parental authority* over adolescent powerlessness and its *need to be pleased*. What this creates in a developing youngster is *self-doubt*, bordering on *self-contempt*—internal conflict when the child is starting to learn to be a friend to himself. Translated, this manufactures tension to replace natural nurturing. It is an American disease, orchestrated by well-meaning parents on the young. "Doing what is good for you" is inadvertently interpreted as "doing what is expected." Disquieting at best, the whole process turns to viciousness when the aspect of *competition* is added. American workers assume that competition is as inherently good as breathing is natural. Competition is worn as though a badge, and workers swagger with a sense of what they think it means. Author W. W. Rostow believes that before Americans can compete, they must first learn how to cooperate.[2] Americans, he argues, must first discover their tribal capacity for communal action before they attempt, individually, to outdo each other. Rostow even goes further. He fears America might go the way of Great Britain which, between 1870 and 1971, went from 32 percent of the world's industrial production to generating only 4 percent. Rostow suggests that the only way to avoid this catastrophe is for the American workplace to develop an organizational infrastructure that champions cooperation over competition.[2]

Enter the Mad Monarchs of the Merry Corporate Madhouse!

Termites destroy a person's home with no one the wiser until irreparable damage is done. Termites are invisible to the naked eye working diligently and effectively beyond anyone's awareness. But what of social termites, otherwise known as the *six silent killers* of the organization's infrastructure? We note and are alarmed with the tens of billions of dollars lost to sick leave misuse due to substance abuse every year. We also note with concern the tens of billions of dollars lost due to stress and emotional-related problems, including accidents, heart attacks, strokes, seizures, and mental illness. Then we note with an astonishing amount of tolerance others who manage to make it to work every day with diminished capacity due to smoking, eating, or drinking too much. Their major achievement is showing up for work and precariously piloting their way through the day. Still, these problems are visible and definable.

No surprises. *Awareness* takes the form of *Employee Assistance Programs* (EAPs) and generous medical insurance benefit programs. But the infrastructure damage caused by the *six silent killers* is beyond the pale of anyone's imagination.

Social termites are unconscionable, mainly on automatic pilot, literally eating away the hand that feeds them.

Social termites choose to deny reality, to become inauthentic to themselves, and obsessively negative to others.

Social termites look for what is wrong, not right; for what they can get, not give; for what they don't have, not possess with the glass (for them) always near empty.

Social termites develop political cunning just this side of amazing, displaying an incredible facility to manage, influence, and manipulate colleagues and superiors indiscriminately.

Social termites conveniently choose to see themselves as victims of a system that fails to appreciate them or satisfy their needs. Without knowing it, they have been seduced by the *six silent killers,* behaviors that can kill a career before it is underway, undermine all they could become, and literally destroy the enterprise for which they work.

Organizations plagued with these social termites find management preoccupied with damage control without dealing with the source of the problem. Managers, as manic monarchs, take ownership of the wreckage, while the social termites treat the workplace as their merry madhouse. It is like the plague all over again, a disease that contaminates everyone and everything, but the source of which no one seems to recognize. It is too obvious.

Silent Killer No. 1: Passive Aggressive Behavior

Examples are coming in late, leaving early, doing as little as possible to get by, or not as much as one is capable of doing. This silent killer is invoked somewhere in the world at least ten million times every hour of every work day, at a cost in productivity loss in the trillions of dollars. Small wonder bankruptcy is such a booming business. Passive aggressive behavior has several interesting components.

Perceiving Oneself Being Wronged!

Passive aggression is a strategy, seldom conscious, of punishing someone for a real or imagined slight. Passive aggressive behavior is actually an oxymoron—"passive" and "aggressive." While in a passive mood, the mind is racing with some kind of hostile thought or punishing conduct meant to put a hurt on someone or something. The perception of being wronged totally justifies any amoral conduct. This perception builds to a defiance that is manifested in poor performance.

The Need to Challenge the Rules!

Authority is symbolized as the enemy. The mind nurses the idea of being powerless and lacking self-esteem. It is the fault of authority that one thinks so lowly of oneself, and it is the fault of authority that one has little power. How to get back at authority? Nip at the rules, not enough to break them and get into major trouble, but enough to cause havoc in the workplace—such as smoking in the rest rooms, not wearing safety goggles in designated areas, dumping hazardous wastes into the sewer system when no one is looking, or not maintaining proper hygiene. The point is to violate as many rules or policies as possible to cause extreme irritation, but not enough to be considered flagrant. One engineer of such a mind, who had a comfortable five-figure income, chose to live in his car on the company parking lot. It took security and management nine months to get him to cease and desist. After all sorts of touchy-feely approaches—he had recently been divorced—management gave him an ultimatum either to live elsewhere or to turn in his security badge. He found a place to stay that very day and never caused this kind of trouble again. His anger against his ex-wife was turned against the company's authority until the company lost its patience. In a strange abstruse way, the company took responsibility for this engineer's fouled-up personal life and played rag-tag with the problem for nine months.

Fixation!

Occasionally passive aggressive behavior takes a strange turn back on the person. These people become so fixated with being wronged that they take it out on themselves—by eating too much and becoming fat and disgusting (because thin is in); or by drinking too much and causing friends to avoid them (see what a waste I am?); by disregarding normal hygiene (the engineer who lived in his car quit bathing, yet no one in his lab, including his supervisor, could muster the courage to tell him how bad he smelled, because appearance is in and smelling refreshed is expected); by using uncouth language and telling coarse jokes to display self-contempt (professionalism demands a certain refinement); or by doing, saying, or behaving in any way to mount self-deprecation to the extreme. In the twisted logic against the self, the idea is to punish the system by making it apparent that it (system) made this behavior necessary. Self-humiliation in public epitomizes this fixation.

What triggers this behavior could be anything from a failure at home, work, or school or in a relationship to a death in the family (yes, being mad at God can trigger this behavior), failure to be appreciated or recognized for some act, failure to be included in a select group or event, or failure to earn an expected promotion. Even self-contempt for not being healthier, happier, more attractive, more intelligent, younger, or a better lover or athlete can produce such reactive behavior, along with being upset with a national or international event only remotely related to the person in question. It isn't what triggers the behavior which is important, but how the behavior, once revealed, is dealt with. Being contemptuous of healthy, happy, productive, important, and engaged people can take the form of being antagonistic to persons who display these attributes.

Passive aggressive behavior is often a failure to communicate with oneself, which precipitates this ambivalent and destructive behavior. It rises out of an imagined sense of being powerless and lacking self-esteem. It is a way of getting even without getting hurt too badly or being discovered too quickly. Passive aggression is devastatingly disruptive, and yet most organizations cultivate it by first choosing to ignore it and then, once noticed, to deal with it ambiguously.

Silent Killer No. 2: Passive Responsive Behavior

Examples are never doing anything until one is told, then doing only that and standing around waiting for further instructions before doing anything else or bringing one's body to work while leaving one's mind at home. One word describes how a manager or co-worker is likely to feel about this person—frustrated. No matter what you do to or for them, nothing happens:

- *You flatter them—nothing.*
- *You reprimand them—nothing.*
- *You give their pay a boost—nothing.*
- *You cut their pay—nothing.*
- *You praise them before their colleagues—nothing.*
- *You reprimand them before their colleagues—nothing.*
- *You give them a letter of commendation for their personnel file—nothing.*
- *You threaten to put a critical letter in their personnel file—nothing.*
- *You give them a vacation day with pay "to think it over"—nothing.*
- *You give them time off without pay—nothing.*
- *You promise them a promotion—nothing.*
- *You threaten them with a demotion—nothing.*
- *You threaten to fire them—nothing.*

Nothing, nothing—nothing!

Not a single thing management does, or colleagues attempt to do seems to get through to this person's passive responsive behavior. He appears inexplicably beyond the skills of comprehension and communication. Too frequently this person's manager becomes obsessed with him. The manager is convinced that he is going to *save* the person from himself! The rescuer's mentality is just what the passive responsive person thrives on. Paradoxically, the tough-minded mentality, who would bounce the person off the wall, falls equally into this person's grasp. The passive responsive person is circulated from one department to another, never staying long, always with approval of his worth to his next manager. He endures, leaving in his wake tired, beleaguered, victimized witnesses.

Ultimately, in total frustration, a manager documents his every action. The cost of this documentation in terms of time wasted, energy expended, and money lost is beyond calculation. The rationale, which usually justifies this obsession, is never candidly disclosed. When asked, a manager will say he is trying to save a lost employee. That, of course, is an impossibility. Only an employee can save himself. That happens when the employee chooses to act differently on purpose. Perhaps closer to the truth is that a manager devotes so much time to this person because of the principle of the thing. He deludes himself into believing his job is to motivate workers to become top performers when that, too, is an impossibility. A manager's job is to create a climate for productive effort, then to facilitate that process. The rest is up to the worker. If the worker does not respond, the worker should suffer the consequences, not the organization. That means nipping the passive responsive person in the bud, not when he is a thriving menace.

One manager documented a person who was tardy for work for the 167th time. This documentation, submitted to the Marginal Employee Program, ran to seven typewritten pages, single spaced. When asked what was so magical about the 167th time, the manager scratched his head and said, "I really don't know."

Characteristically, such a manager takes ownership of the passive responsive person's problem. As far back as anyone could check, this person had had a manager who served as a sympathetic surrogate parent. Over time, the passive responsive person's sensitivity erodes to the point that he becomes totally insensitive to everything and everybody. No matter what the stimuli, he is utterly beyond responsiveness. Every time the passive responsive person had an opportunity to fail, somebody broke his fall, rescued him from the incident, or saved him from a learning experience. Such protectionism may rise out of duty, love, guilt, a sick need to dominate, or many other shades of human conduct that prevent growth through self-knowledge and self-understanding. It is a diabolical deception to cut a person off from the struggle of his own experience and then have someone else carry him on their shoulders. Life is struggle, and without this essential component, there is no life, only vegetation, atrophy, and passivity.

How, then, do you turn a passive responsive person around? You don't! You cannot easily overcome the disadvantage of 20 to 30 years of mismanaged development. There are no miracles. You can neutralize the impact of such a person on operations by cutting him off from the mainstream and placing him in an inconsequential job. If there is any flicker of behavioral change, and there may be some, reward him immediately, not in a big way, but in a way which indicates progress is in the desired direction. If he completes an assignment before it is expected, give him slightly more responsible tasks and then monitor his activity. If he shows little or no improvement, it is not the organization's problem. It is his only. The organization's mission is to establish a productive work climate, not save workers from themselves.

Generally speaking, 'Time and Attendance' (T&A) is not a very meaningful performance gauge. Focusing exclusively on punctuality projects the implicit message that conformity and obedience count for more than contribution and that showing up on time fulfills the principal requirement of work. Western society is brimming with workers who have never missed a day or have seldom been late. Many of these same workers are great socializers, coffee break specialists, rumor mill facilitators, and unlikely to make a smidgen of difference to the bottom line. Showing up is their major contribution.

The passive responsive person is an emotional cripple who causes pain to everyone he touches. The irony is that he generates so much concern that people want to help him when only he has that capability. There are basically three types of workers in any organization at any one time:

There are those variously known as *hard-chargers, winners, curve-setters, leaders, or victors*. These workers represent about 15 percent of the workforce. No matter what management does, what state of stability or instability the organization is in, or what the majority of workers are doing, including their peers, they go forward successfully. They are usually well ahead of the learning curve, understand and accept the naked reality in which the organization finds itself, and deal with it accordingly. They use the organization to foster and promote their own personal and professional agenda without any compunction. There are obviously climbers amongst their ranks, but these hard-chargers are not exclusively climbers. They are doers and make up about 75 percent of the positive energy. Were it not for them, the organization would be dead in the water.

At the opposite end of the curve, there are those known as *feet-draggers, losers, lagers, or victims*. These workers also represent about 15 percent of the workforce. The *six silent killers* nest here but spread well beyond the bounds of this category. Not only are passive responsive persons card-carrying members of this distinction, they are perhaps the biggest losers of all because they not only visit this haven, but live here. Losers fail to understand the organization or their own motivation. They are the walking wounded, unable to see what the organization can do *for them*, choosing instead only to see what it does *to them*. The feet-draggers have a great deal to do with forward inertia because the organization is unable or refuses to cut them loose from the fold. The remarkable thing about this category is that many in it survive the most drastic cuts in downsizing and restructuring. Upwards of 90 percent of these losers manage to share equally in wage and entitlement benefits that accrue to the true contributors. Evidence? Consider performance appraisal results (discussed later).

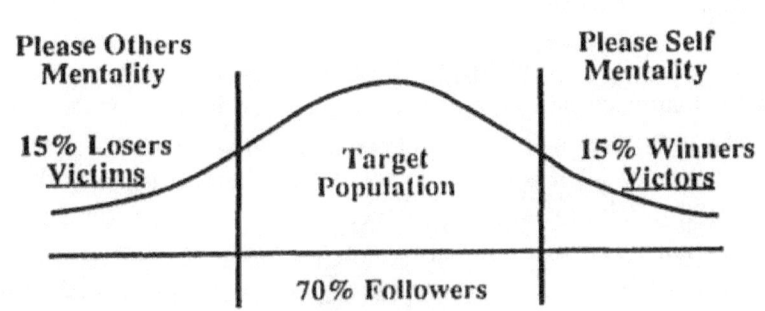

Please Others Mentality

Please Self Mentality

15% Losers Victims

Target Population

15% Winners Victors

70% Followers

- **Winners will contribute regardless of management style.**

- **Followers will move in the direction of the dominant culture.**

- **Losers will seldom contribute no matter what the style or culture.**

Normal distribution of a typical working population.

The balance of the organization, 70 percent, falls into the broad category of the *followers, soldiers,* or the *obedient many.* No organization can succeed without rallying this group to its cause. Followers move in the direction of the prevailing winds. If the wind is at management's back, it will be blowing followers in management's direction and on course to its goal. If it is not, followers will scatter, and management's ability to forge ahead is nigh impossible. Most of management's energy is devoted to sequestering this group to some semblance of order and purpose. The organization is a dynamic entity, so that means followers as members are likely to be moving in both directions of losers and winners. What direction (forward or backward) should display the greatest momentum is a factor of training and development, workplace culture, and the structure of the organization. Given the current dominant structure and workplace culture in most organizations, the chances of moving in the direction of winners are slim. If anything, most organizations neutralize the winner potential by imposing frustrating policies and procedures, ambivalent promotional schemes, and rigid rules for the conduct of business. The timid back away and play it safe, finding security well within the bounds of this category. Others who are just waiting for a chance to trash the organization retreat into the losers' category.

The winners, hard-chargers, leaders, or victors are winners usually despite rather than because of the organization. They are in your face, some with great subtlety and others with annoying style. Winners know their worth and use it to their advantage. What is desirable about these hard-chargers is that they get the organization to take risks it might otherwise not take. What is undesirable is that their personal victories are not always in the best interest of the organization. This implies that they, too, must be managed and supplied with limits in a conducive workplace culture and organizational structure. It is not prudent to allow them to play "lone ranger" in support of their personal agenda. Yet they are essential to organizational success. Too frequently management prefers followers to these winners because they are easier to handle. When management plays "cute" and ambivalent with winners and followers and fails to create a climate in which both can be productive, invisible behaviors take center stage, and the *six silent killers* raise their heads and play havoc with operations.

Passive responsive persons think several of the things actually said by passive defensive people. While passive responsive persons give the appearance that they could care less, the fact is they have been hardened to the vicissitudes of life. Robert Smith captures this in his book about children with the catchy title *Where Did You Go? Out. What Did You Do? Nothing* (1974). Passive responsive persons are suspended in adolescence. It is a safe place youngsters learn to go early in life, for it is easy to say, "I don't care," or "You don't understand." Most of us visit this place as a temporary haven when we are hurt and confused and have yet to develop the emotional maturity to deal with pain. We are in trouble, however, when it becomes home.

Silent Killer No. 3: Passive Defensive Behavior

Always having an excuse for why something isn't done ("Not my job!" "Nobody told me!" "How was I supposed to know?" "I never got that training!" "I didn't get that memo!" "I can't read your handwriting!" "I wasn't there when you gave the order!" "You must have told somebody else, thought it was me, and forgot!" "I can't read your mind!" "I'm waiting for somebody to tell us what to do. This is where they told us to go." "I'm new around here, okay?" "All I can say is I followed instructions!"), pointing fingers ("I did my job. Is it my fault that Sally didn't do her job?"), playing "show your ass" (SYA) or "cover your ass" (CYA) games by pointing out errors or having a memo to cover yours, and doing other people's assignments as an alibi for not doing your own ("I didn't have time. Sam asked me to give him a hand. What was I supposed to do, turn my back on a colleague?"). The passive defensive person is the passive responsive person with brains. They possess an interesting psychology. They appear to have their act together but have a faculty for getting into one unfortunate situation after another. As the conflict between what is valued in the organization and what is not grows more acute, distorted, and confused, persons of a passive defensive persuasion appear to flourish, taking these forms:

CYA games—Practitioners have an amazing faculty, no matter what they do or fail to do, to make everyone else feel responsible. The passive defensive person puts his adversary off balance and on the defensive by exploiting a known weakness of his accuser, which may or may not be relevant to the situation. The point is that the accuser has lost his advantage and the passive defensive person now rules the game.

SYA games—Practitioners go from self-love to self-hate to self-pity to the attack before the target of such attention can catch his breath. The practitioner sees himself as the hunted and immediately goes into a survivor's mode. He realizes that the only way to throw the hunter off his scent is to use "smoke and mirrors" by adopting the guise of the hunter rather than the hunted. Having painted himself into a corner, through some stupidity, he comes out with a "red pencil," caustic remark, or the phantom exception. His singular strategy is to throw his hunter off scent and off stride and on a wild goose chase. Once his adversary is off in the wrong direction, he plants innuendos, rumors, and "he said/she said" tales along the trail, which puts his hunter in the cage of his deception.

Reckless abandon games—Practitioners of this passive defensive behavior have used SYA games for all that they are worth, have come up short, and find themselves still under paralyzing scrutiny. They have reached the point of a zero-sum game as well as the point of no return. Psychologists call this person a Type "T" personality with a high risk-taking, thrill-seeking, rule-breaking, creative-abandon persona. Being primarily left-brain dominated, his reasoning easily gravitates to the bizarre. Paranoia, which is busily fermenting under a contrived calm surface, comes to dominate his mind. He is looking for trouble, for any justification to act as weirdly as possible, and invariably finds it. He finds that he is surrounded by enemies. He convinces himself that he is under siege and has no recourse but to act, if necessary, cruelly or absurdly, but, by all means, decisively.

The first two forms of passive defensive behavior are common. There are times when we all resort to CYA and SYA games. These brief lapses are part of our normal defense mechanism, a mechanism that many organizations unwittingly encourage by the way they are designed. Because most of us don't reach the limits of our emotional resources, we seldom encounter "reckless abandon" games. It is a stage where the person leaves the herd and the social barriers that restrain him and enters the wilderness of his primordial being where there is seldom any escape. It is a most dangerous place to be, yet an improbable number of talented people, as well as very disturbed types, are rushing into it in increasing numbers today.

We read about a "T" type personality who walks into a McDonald's and guns down an innocent lunch crowd, a disgruntled post office employee who blasts his way into his supervisor's office and kills her, the failed graduate student who kills his dissertation professor, or the unemployed handyman who throws gasoline on shoppers in a supermarket and then torches them. We seldom read about reckless abandon games where the scars are invisible and the victims carry them forever. Nor should we confine CYA/SYA and reckless abandon games exclusively to individual behavior. Many organizations are seduced by the same intoxicants of passive defensiveness. Intoxicants of money, power, status, glamour, immortality, fame, ambition, lust, or any number of variations of the seven deadly sins can play a role in this sinister silent killer.

Reckless Abandon Games — When the Scars Are Not Necessarily Visible!

What do Martin Siegel, Ivan Boesky, John DeLorean, Gary Hart, Dr. John Darsee, Jim Bakker, President Richard Nixon, John Dean, The Johns Manville Corporation, Continental Bank, E. F. Hutton, and Chrysler Corporation have in common? The answer is passive defensive behavior.

The Siegel/Boesky Connection

While still in his thirties, Martin Siegel had everything—a Harvard education, a prestigious position with Kidder, Peabody & Company, a $3.5 million home, a $4 million annual income—but it wasn't enough. Siegel had the whole world in his hands and dropped it! [3] He agreed to share privileged information (inside trading) for a price with Ivan Boesky, the legendary investment king. Why did young Siegel break the law and put his comfortable existence in jeopardy? Why did he turn his back on life's promise for a few silver coins? Why did he deceive himself that it was okay and, in so doing, cheat many? Only he knows. But the fact remains that he was enamored of power and flattered by the attention of heavy-hitter Boesky. "Imagine," he must have thought, "I am a confidant of the fabulous Boesky!" Siegel was heady, being important and successful and being professionally accepted by one of the pacesetters of the market.[4] With the cosmic soaring of his income, he spent with a compulsive fever to match it. He was hooked on the narcotic of money. If you have money, his behavior implied, people will love you, pay attention to you, and cannot hurt you. This passive defensiveness translates into a deep disabling spiritual want that no amount of money can satisfy. It is the domain of insecurity without wisdom.

John DeLorean

If ever there was an ideal type to depict the reckless abandon passive defensive personality, it was John DeLorean. This tall, handsome man with a coiffure helmet of steel gray, chiseled features, dark eyes, and ever-smiling lips resembled a swashbuckling hero from the Sunday comics more than a General Motors executive. Yet he took GM by storm with his creative flair, dress, and style. His more conservative, low-profile associates would cringe when he took over a room and accentuated the atmosphere with his latest story. He was a successful salesman through and through, a winner in a business where anything goes as long as you can sell automobiles.

When DeLorean left GM and formed DeLorean Motors in Northern Ireland, he was moving away from his strength into the no-man's land of his weakness. He was not a detail man, not interested in the labyrinth of minutiae that went into the bottom line. That was for others to handle. Just give him the facts! Soon, not long after this newest adventure was underway, problems started to mount. He found that there was much to the business that was foreign to him. He was impatient and found it necessary to cut corners with reckless abandon. Before, he had played the capitalistic game of business with panache and humor, mainly within the rules, because others were covering his ass with the boring details of the business. He couldn't be bothered. Once outside GM's broad protective umbrella and on his own nickel, DeLorean took on Nietzschean dimensions, personifying himself as the self-made, capitalistic superman. He believed the myth and then tried desperately to make it real.

DeLorean was always a self-promoting super salesman, never truly a businessman. He looked down on the species with minor contempt. Nevertheless, he convinced Northern Ireland to stake him with $100 million with the promise that he would bring hundreds, then thousands of jobs to the six counties of Northern Ireland, a region that hungered desperately for economic development. He betrayed that trust by going out of business not long after the paint dried on his first production run. Before the failure was finalized, however, he did a merry dance into the underworld of crime, attempting to rescue the misfired venture by being implicated in cocaine-trafficking charges.[5] This behavior demonstrates, as business writer Craig Waters so aptly points out, a profound naiveté about the nature of small business and the role of the entrepreneur: "He (DeLorean) had no appreciation of the role GM had played in his success during his 17 years there, no understanding of his limitations, and no comprehension of the finite nature of capital."[6] DeLorean got caught up in the high-risk, high-roller game of self-deception and fell like a stone to the bottom of his dreams.[7]

Gary Hart—The Inside Outsider

No political leader on the American scene was better prepared, harder working, or more focused on national issues than former U.S. senator and presidential candidate Gary Hart. His devotion to new ideas about American life brought depth and vigor to an otherwise lackluster 1988 presidential campaign. [8] Enter the femme fatale in the person of Donna Rice, and you have the beginning of Hart's demise. Who shot down Gary Hart? Was it Donna Rice? The press? Or was it the reckless abandon of Hart's passive defensiveness?

A half century ago, in the 1940 campaign for the presidency, Republican candidate Wendell Willkie openly campaigned with his mistress.[9] He had a good relationship with the press and refused to hide the complexity of his marriage. Even President Roosevelt had ceased to have an intimate relationship with his equally famous wife, Eleanor, and carried on a rather open relationship with Eleanor's secretary that was well known to the press, but not to the nation.[10] Hart's error was that it was a different time. His reckless abandon passive defensiveness was his refusal to acknowledge the morality of his time. For one thing, the press was much less inclined to practice journalistic voyeurism in 1940 than it was in 1988, and for another, the presidency had taken on the glamour of celebrity that did not exist in the earlier period. Willkie was soundly defeated in that 1940 election, but the war in Europe was already underway, and the United States has never shown an inclination to change leaders in a time of national crisis. So, Willkie's behavior had little to do with his defeat.

No, Ms. Rice did not shoot down Gary Hart.[11] His reckless abandon did the trick. He is an interesting study.[12] His fall from grace perhaps started with him changing his name, then progressed to being coy about his age, and moved on from there to finding it difficult to level with his friends.[13] Hart was an introvert who tried to wax the hearty fellow well meant, when his greater inclination was that of the scholar and idealistic thinker. He was an inside outsider who never joined the club but fought hard to acquire the credentials. He came to prominence when the world needed him, only to find he was playing on another circuit. In sharp contrast to Gary Hart, there is President Bill Clinton, who is the complete extrovert. President Clinton makes Hart's indiscretions look like child's play. Whereas Hart may have had too much soul for his own good, facile writer Garry Wills suggests Clinton "may not have any interior to withdraw to."[14] Martin Walker, author of *The President We Deserve* (1996), argues that Clinton survives brutal onslaught after onslaught because of his peculiar strengths of stamina, resilience, and unstoppable determination.[15] Wills adds that "Clinton looks like a person so external to himself as not to have met himself."[16] Hart, on the other hand, took himself far too seriously and became, in the words of a friend, "a time bomb waiting to explode." And of course, it did. Reckless abandon passive defensiveness is not only the act, but a perspective as well.

Dr. John Darsee—The Far Side of Paradise

Dr. John Darsee had a spectacular career from 1974 through 1979.[17] His research and hospital charts were written with bold, impeccable handwriting. One senior medical colleague described his writing as "meticulous, beautiful, almost like calligraphy." An envious peer went even further to suggest "you could almost photograph his notes and publish them in a text book" they were so complete. The clarity of Darsee's mind and the scope of his vision was legendary, and he was only 30. Dr. Darsee had it all, a quicksilver grasp of complex scientific concepts, high skill and compassion as a physician, the drive of a perfectionist, and the charisma and charm of a born teacher. He was popular among his younger colleagues and much respected by his influential seniors. Dr. Paul Walter, a prominent heart specialist whose name appeared as coauthor on 15 of Darsee's published scientific works, thought of him as "clearly one of the most remarkable young men in American medicine." Dr. Walter was right, but for the wrong reason. It appears that most of Darsee's convincingly presented data were, in fact, cunningly crafted lies. Walter, like dozens of other researchers, was dazzled by Darsee's talent, productivity, generosity (sharing credit), and skillful use of flattery. Consequently, they were remiss in closely scrutinizing the data he churned out.

Lengthy investigations at Harvard Medical School, where he graduated with honors, and at Emory University, where he did his residency, have uncovered a pattern of deception that is remarkable in the expanding annals of research fraud. Seventeen of his full-length scientific papers have had to be retracted from the scientific literature, as have 47 abstracts (short summaries of research results). But it goes beyond this. Many scientists have used Darsee's published works as reference to their own research, so more than 241 scientific reports have been compromised. Yet, the scientific community of medicine is asking, "How could it happen?" That is the wrong question. Why it happened is more appropriate.

This demonstrates the laxity and, indeed, the naiveté and preference of the medical profession to be more quantitatively than qualitatively driven. Because medical research, like research in so many other fields, is structured to be captivated by quantitative indices, the system is vulnerable to this type of deceptive manipulation. Making a clever impression with brightness and hard work, coupled with imposing credentials and a matching bibliography, is the passport to academic success. This gets closer to the why of Darsee. The drive to succeed at any price in the shortest span of years promotes cheating. There are no shortcuts. While these good doctors are lamenting how they have been deceived, it might be well for them to explore why they so readily accepted a byline to scientific work they did not conduct themselves. Even more to the point, they might wonder why the system encourages such behavior, and why the workplace culture and structure of the organization is not more diligent.

For every Dr. Darsee discovered there are literally scores preparing to take his place. Darsee represents a reactionary frame of reference that is the realm of reckless abandon passive defensiveness. How sad that Darsee didn't take his keen imagination and sculpt it into something authentic and meaningful, as have Michael Crichton and Somerset Maugham. Crichton, too, was a brilliant medical student at Harvard. He, too, had a flair for the written word. So much so that he wrote pulp fiction while he was a medical student to help defray the cost of his education. Upon graduation and the completion of his internship, Crichton wrote a most successful novel (*The Andromeda Strain*, 1969), as did Somerset Maugham (*Liza of Lambeth*, 1897), when he completed his medical studies. They both used their medical studies to breathe life into their literary careers, where fiction gives you the right to tell stories and to be lionized for the telling. This is the other side of paradise that beckoned Darsee but which he lacked eyes to see.

Jim Bakker's Ladder is Gone!

Irish poet William Butler Yeats writes, "Now that my ladder is gone, I must lie down where all ladders start, the fowl rag-and-bone shop of the heart."[18] Some of us scale to great heights, only to avoid ever running into ourselves. But, there is a time when crashing reality cuts through the fog, and we are face-to-face with our own humble selves as naked, exposed, and truly wretched beings. It is a wonder we don't have more compassion in our hearts for those that fall because everyone falls at some time in their lives, be it off a footstool or a mountain. Jim and Tammy Bakker were designed for falling off a footstool, but somehow found themselves falling off a mountain. How such totally ordinary people could rise so high and fall so far is a telling index of our times. Their "Praise the Lord" (PTL) television club was a resounding success, largely due to its commonplace familiarity and genius for understanding what may broadly be called the spiritual or emotional life of individuals as people.

Jim Bakker possessed something that intellectuals scorn as "common con," when it is actually an exceptional sensitivity to the heart of the lonely and lost, which includes most of us. He possessed antennae to troubled souls, something perfectly ordinary, empirical, and quasi-aesthetic. This gift entails the capacity for integrating a vast amalgam of constantly changing events—too many, too swift, and too intermingled to be caught and pinned down — as elements in a single pattern where simple prayer is the pragmatic answer. Denomination, dogma, liturgical scripture, and even the Bible were not the common focus.

Indeed, Bakker brought followers into his flock beyond Christianity. To be able to do this well seems to be a gift akin to that of the creative artist. He gave the impression that he was directly acquainted with his listeners' pain and texture of their lives, not just the sense of the chaotic flow of experience, but a highly developed discrimination of what matters most to the wounded.

Above all this, he had an actual sense of what fits with what, what springs from what, what leads to what, how things seem to vary to different people, what the effect of such experience upon them may be, and what the result is likely to be in a concrete situation of the interplay of human beings and impersonal forces. No, this was not the raving of a "common con."

Bakker demonstrated a sense for what is qualitative rather than quantitative, for what is specific rather than general in the lives of his listeners. He epitomized a direct acquaintance with pain, distinct from a capacity for description of pain or calculation of what the pain might mean to a Freudian psychoanalyst or a social engineer.

He presented no credentials as an expert. Nor did he attempt to present himself as beyond being flawed. He possessed what is sometimes called "natural wisdom" as opposed to scholarly erudition. What he possessed was an imaginative understanding, insight, perceptiveness, and intuition into the matter of ordinary lives of ordinary people. With this practical wisdom, he demonstrated a capacity for synthesis rather than analysis. His troubles began when he tried to analyze his own success and, with it, his audience's tolerance for his family's flaunted, blatant, and escalating eccentricities.

Somewhere between the Bakker home and the homes of millions of Americans, Tammy's mascara and war paint and Jim's cherubic grin became diabolical.[19] Essentially nice people in common with most, the Bakker's got caught in the war of ratings and the insatiable appetite for more glorious projects, which required more and more television dollars. Long before Jim's sex escapade and scandal surfaced, the PTL club had become "show biz," departing from its practical message and spiritual intent.

The PTL club became entertainment with a capital "E." There is no way to substitute the perceptual gift, the capacity for taking in the total pattern of the human condition, or an understanding of the way in which things hang together—a talent which Bakker possessed, then neglected—and expect to stay on course. When Bakker started listening to advisers with uncanny gifts for analysis and stopped using his natural wisdom, he embraced alien if not hostile forces. When that happened, the Bakkers commenced to behave like superstars with other people's money. The mansions, the Mercedes, the elaborate vacations, Tammy's shopping sprees—all became part of a growing scam that led to Jim's dalliance with Jessica Hahn.[20] Reckless abandon passive defensiveness—"you can't touch me!"—had come to dominate their lives and lifestyle. When that happened, the Bakker's became a "born-again disaster."[21]

Jim Bakker forgot that his rise had little to do with him personally and everything to do with his acquaintance with the ghosts that haunt us all. Failure came from his resistance to what worked best for him and from ignoring it in favor of systematic verification—polls and ratings—and then becoming enamored of and overwhelmed by his own genius. What happened to Jim Bakker could happen to anyone who climbs off the stool and starts trekking up the mountain.

President Richard M. Nixon's Weaknesses Undermine His Strengths

The thirty-seventh president of the United States was born in Yorba Linda, California, of a lower middle-class Quaker family of Irish descent. His father ran a combination small grocery store-filling station on land he was unable to develop. Dirt poor, his father had to sell, only to have the land turn out to be rich in oil. So, instead of the family becoming rich and prosperous, it struggled with dignity. Nothing came too easily to the Nixons, especially Richard. He

260

lacked athleticism and made up for this with brutal courage on the football field. He lacked social grace and made up for this with brilliance in the classroom. He carried the wounds of being "almost rich" and the death of his brother at an early age as the yoke of his life's responsibility—to live and perform always as two.

While a law student at Duke University, where his diligence as a student earned him the nickname "Iron Butt," Nixon's drive betrayed him, as it would several times throughout his remarkably long and successful career. One night, not able to handle the suspense of waiting until grades were posted, he broke into the dean's office to see his grades, only to be caught. He had top grades and was to finish third in his class, yet an anxiety at not knowing became a telling flaw that was to master his destiny.

His political career, much like his prowess on the football field and in the classroom, was marked by courage—fearless outspokenness and brilliant political tactics. Reckless abandon passive defensiveness marked every segment of his career—from his vicious campaign as successful candidate for the House of Representatives in 1946 to his crushing debacle with the Watergate Affair. Perhaps his finest hour was in 1960 when he lost the presidency to John F. Kennedy by the tiniest of margins, so tiny that there was broad suspicion that the election was stolen in the Chicago precincts of Mayor Richard Daley's machine. Nixon refused a recount and conceded gracefully.

Yet, the low state of his birth, the poor luck of his family, the anxiety over how he was being perceived, and his paranoia of Eastern seaboard money and its intellectual crowd haunted him. No matter how successful he was, this knowledge seemed never able to give him peace. Far ahead in the polls in the 1972 presidential campaign, he allowed his advisers to attempt (unsuccessfully) a break-in of the Democratic National Committee's headquarters located in the Watergate Hotel, Washington, D.C.

The purpose of the break-in was to place telephone bugs and acquire information damaging to the presidential campaign of Senator George McGovern. Countless Nixon biographers make much of this in terms of his legendary paranoia. By their own assessments, Nixon—known for his achievement in foreign policy (establishment of China–American accords)—is credited with making great strides in terms of civil rights and social welfare programs.

Still, he demonstrated a disconcerting capacity for senseless behavior.[22]Nixon lost credibility with the American people by claiming executive privilege for senior White House officials to prevent them from being questioned and by refusing to hand over tapes of relevant conversations. He resigned under the threat of impeachment after several leading members of his government had been found guilty of involvement in the Watergate scandal.

Obviously, there are many contradictions in President Nixon's character, from a Quaker upbringing to a tough-minded hawkishness, from an extreme discomfort around people to a public boldness bordering on bravado. It is within this veiled context that his reckless abandon passive aggressiveness resides. Columnist Tom Wicker captures the essence of Nixon and his time in his book *One of Us* (1992), which puts the American people on notice that he is much like the rest of us and that there is no way we can distance ourselves from what he was and came to be.

John Dean and Blind Ambition

John Dean was one of the actors on the Nixon stage. He was counsel to the president—the president's lawyer—and essentially young and untested in life. There is a tendency, like an invisible magnet in our makeup, which draws us to like-minded people, and which is sometimes a fatal flaw. When values and beliefs are poorly defined or essentially malleable to the situation, one is always on the threshold of the no-man's land of reckless abandon. Dean, in his autobiography *Blind Ambition* (1977), candidly admits that "making it" took precedence over everything.[23]

Cheating became not only the rule of convenience, but a necessity. Cutting corners became an art form of Machiavellian perfection, with the ends justifying any means. Dean was hooked on hoodwink. He operated quite successfully in this cynical world where cunning, duplicity, and bad faith were part of the arsenal of deception.

When he was made to take the fall for the entire Nixon administration, he reneged and sang like a songbird. Several White House officials of the Nixon administration who were indicted, charged, sentenced, and imprisoned have gotten "religion" as their way to expiate their fall and win back some social grace. Dean has chosen a quiet withdrawal from ambition, blind or otherwise.

Corporate Malfeasance — Johns Manville Corporation

It would be inappropriate to end this discussion on passive defensiveness without including its corporate character. The corporate landscape is as vulnerable to its seduction as is the individual to its appeal. The examples cited are not mutually exclusive but rather represent a disturbing trend that seems to grow with time. When a major company is under attack, as are tobacco companies at the moment, reckless abandon and CYA passive defensiveness appear to act like a hypnotic enchantment. The same might also prove true with regard to the recent White Water investigation in the House of Representatives. The cases referred to here, however, are now part of history and are presented for what might be learned from them.[24]

Johns Manville Corporation once enjoyed the status of a corporate giant. It has now disintegrated into a shadow of its original size, brought down by its principal product, asbestos. For many years, it seems the Johns Manville medical department took it upon itself to doctor data regarding the dangers associated with the inhalation of asbestos. This duplicity goes back at least to the end of World War II. Consequently, the sheer magnitude of the time span makes it impossible to estimate how many former employees suffering from debilitating diseases can be traced to their having worked for Johns Manville. The cover-up, in any case, falls into CYA passive defensiveness.

What is particularly disturbing about this case is the motivation behind it and the amorality displayed by those implicated. A lawyer recalls how, 50 years ago, he confronted Johns Manville's corporate council about the company's policy of concealing chest X-ray results from employees. He asked, "Do you mean to tell me you would let your people work until they dropped dead?" The corporate attorney replied without a quiver, "Yes, we save a lot of money that way."

Such reckless abandon and CYA passive defensiveness represent, to those who advocate this course, the least troublesome way to solve a punishing dilemma. The focus is on how much the company could lose if exposed, not how it could gain in goodwill if it came clean. Time is the enemy of such a policy, making it increasingly difficult to do the right thing.

By all standards of decency, a company is held to higher ethics than the individual. The pure absurdity of thinking that anything is justified as long as it saves the company apparently never occurred to anyone. Nor were human rights ever considered, only corporate survival. Concealing information, whatever its nature, is considered a way of protecting proprietary products and services and, therefore, the company. In the case of Johns Manville Corporation, this strategy became its death knell.

The Continental Illinois Bank

Before the savings and loan scandal, long before banks became ranking predators in their own right, the ninth largest bank in the United States was eclipsed into oblivion by its own chicanery. Similar to the gigantic fiasco of the thrifts and the multibillion-dollar "bail outs" of 1989–91, this bank now belongs to the Federal Deposit Insurance Corporation (FDIC) to the tune of more than 80 percent of its assets.

It was a different matter in 1976, when Continental Illinois had a dream that, through leveraged lending, it could become the seventh largest bank in America. To climb into the "top seven" was a heady goal. Corporate officers became recklessly aggressive in pursuit of borrowers everywhere with only one thing in mind—the realization of their dream. A banker's caution was deserted for the cocky flair of the salesman.

Their fearless diligence paid off.[25] Continental Illinois found a rich captive market in poorly capitalized areas, such as Oklahoma's oil producers. With this discovery, the corporate officers began to bet enormous sums on their dream. Eventually, a cool $1 billion worth of dreams found its way into Continental Illinois' portfolio, and another $1 billion of depositor's money flowed out to pay for the business. The trouble started when the price of oil collapsed. A combination of OPEC members cheating on each other, competition from non-OPEC nations, and conservation efforts of consuming nations, including the United States (introduction of compacts by American manufacturers), drove the price per barrel of oil down by nearly 50 percent. No one anticipated or prepared for this possibility.

Continental Illinois had become spellbound by lending and the growth it produced. It seemed disinclined to look too deeply into how that growth was achieved or how stable it was. When borrowers produced dry holes, which left their drilling equipment idle, the fat interest rates dried up, too.

Under the reckless abandon of passive defensiveness of growth—growth that was not subject to harsh scrutiny but which relied largely on luck—the sharp shrinkage of assets caught the attention of internal auditors. The dream died almost immediately. The auditors, without even trying, stumbled on the bottomless pit of deceit upon which the dream was built. One loan officer had purchased $800 million in gas loans from Penn Square Bank in Oklahoma City, where he had also borrowed $565,000 personally. He was issued a minor reprimand for this behavior. It wasn't until federal prosecutors entered the picture that such incidents of charity were called what they were—kickbacks.

As with Johns Manville Corporation, internal control mechanisms flashed danger signals, but they were either ignored or treated as routine. No one wanted to know. The bank was on a roll, and nothing was going to stop it. Once the word got out, however, the bank's instability nearly put it under, saved only by FDIC. The big losers in this, of course, were the bank's thousands of shareholders and more than 2,000 employees who lost their jobs. Continental Illinois is now a small bank made modest by a big appetite for delusions of grandeur and cover-up.

E. F. Hutton & Company

No fall from grace was more shocking to the national television audience than that of E. F. Hutton & Company.[26] The symbolic sense of this company was captured in a television commercial: "When E. F. Hutton speaks, everyone stops to listen." This was a financial institution to be trusted. E. F. Hutton, the nation's second largest independent broker, finally pleaded guilty to more than 2,000 counts of mail and wire fraud.

This brokerage firm systematically and with full awareness of its culpability bilked 400 of its own banks by drawing against uncollected funds or, in some cases, against non-existent funds. It would cover these funds after enjoying 24-hour interest-free use of the money. It was a scam treated as a normal conduct of business. Perfect. Who knew of the scam, how many knew, or when they knew nobody will ever know. Yet, it rivals Watergate and Whitewater in the sheer complexity of the cover-up. E. F. Hutton paid a modest fine of $2 million plus government investigative costs of $750,000. Additionally, $8 million has been placed in reserve for restitution to the banks in question. This is nothing but a pittance, a slap on the wrists. True, many officers lost their jobs. Several others are now or have been under indictment—the case is still not closed. Yet, it demonstrates that white-collar crime or crimes against property receive neither the attention nor the judicature that crimes against persons receive.

Meanwhile, investors' confidence level in E. F. Hutton is quite another matter. The corporation still suffers from the sting of this scandal. People don't forget something as spiritual as trust or as emotional as money. The irony is that most television viewers are not investors. They were offended, not because they lost money, but because their trust in an image was violated, and that's even worse. In that respect, then, not only E. F. Hutton was tarnished by this act, but an entire industry.

Chrysler Corporation

Thanks largely to Lee Iacocca, Chrysler Corporation had again become a household name, with automobile sales setting new records.[27] At the height of the recovery, when all the depressing struggle could be put to rest, a story of odometer tampering and damaged vehicles being sold as new automobiles shook this image.[28]

In one case, a 1987 Turismo driven by a Chrysler executive hit a pocket of water on a highway, flipped on its side, slid for several feet, and landed in a ditch, rolling over.[29] The executive luckily escaped serious injury, but the automobile was to have another fate. Instead of reporting the incident as it happened and then auctioning off the automobile as damaged goods, the executive and his co-conspirators decided to repair the car and to ship it off as a completely new vehicle.

No mention was made that it was shuttled between executives for their convenience. This was far from the exception. An investigation found that at least 40 Chrysler automobiles were shipped as new after being involved in collisions or accidents severe enough that frames were bent and doors damaged. Moreover, during an 18-month period (July 1985 through December 1986), this investigation uncovered that Chrysler sold more than 60,000 vehicles as new cars that had been driven routinely by company managers and executives with their odometers disconnected. The hidden odometer mileage often exceeded 400 miles, as these employees drove these automobiles to and from work and some even on personal trips.

When caught in this deception, the Chrysler chorus sang, "Everybody takes a free ride. What's the big deal?"[30] When there is a tendency to explain away clearly unacceptable behavior or when the attitude is to ignore what is happening that is unacceptable or in violation of corporate conduct, the behavior is in the realm of passive defensiveness. It matters not whether the behavior is intentional or accidental, corporate or individual; passive defensiveness is at work.

Silent Killer No. 4: Approach Avoidance Behavior

Examples are volunteering for assignments one doesn't intend to complete or to complete on time; proffering one's support for important initiatives and then withdrawing such support at the last moment; taking on special projects and then not showing up for the required work and necessary meetings; punishing others with one's knowledge to mask one's inability or unwillingness to learn new things; indicating a desire to be challenged but avoiding all the sacrifices and inconveniences required (such as working late, taking courses on one's own time, taking risks); appearing to be dedicated to doing something but, in actuality, refusing to do it; and displaying high RPMs for "whatever" but a low torque.

Approach avoidance behavior is much more common than one might suspect. It represents a flirtation with what is expected or required but with no real intention of performing at that level. A person inclined toward approach avoidance

266

behavior counts on obscure directions and forgotten orders. Work is a game to be avoided at any cost, only no one is intended to be able to either decipher the avoidance or make claim against the deadbeat for it. That is where the pleasure comes—in outfoxing the system!

This is the equivalent of the student who consents to do his homework but avoids it by going to his room and gabbing on the phone instead. The behavior involves *approaching* (agreeing to act), then *avoiding* (evading the necessary action) by whatever means come to mind. Telethon campaigners know the behavior well—a person feels obliged to make a generous pledge to say, public television, then ignores the frequent mailed reminders of this commitment. To the approach avoider, it is no big deal! It takes a special constitution to display this behavior.

The classic form of approach avoidance behavior in an organization is when a person committed to a project fails to contribute his part. Such failures mean others have to take up the slack, which lets the approach avoidance person off the hook. It might be a report not completed on time, an important reference not checked out, the right people not invited to a crucial meeting, failure of memos to be distributed, or any number of important "little things" that make for the successful completion of projects and thereby spell organizational success.

Most of us are guilty of approach avoidance on occasion, but the seasoned approach avoider consciously strives to find ways to dissemble his motivation. What may trigger this behavior is the conflict between the need to please others and the need to please self. The self-antagonism generated is demonstrated by keeping the organization and the people in it (especially those in authority) off stride and at bay. Irritation is the highest form of reward and is perfected to an art form.

Of all the "Manic Monarchs of the Corporate Merry Madhouse," this is the most ambiguous and most difficult to comprehend. A morality play is going on in the head of the individual. At once, he is driven by what he should do and should be (*ideal self*), only to be stopped short by what he is and feels inclined to do (*real self*).

This conflict between *self-demands* and *role demands* causes him to misconstrue the situation. He prefers to see things as he would like them to be, not as they are. This finds him accepting assignments (*role demands*), only to be stopped short by *self-demands*—"How could they ask me to do that? Don't they know that job is beneath me?" Self-demands take precedence over role demands when it is a case of approach avoidance. If this seems confusing, imagine the individual who experiences this ambivalence. If he can misinterpret the demands made on him, he will. When captive to such wrong-headedness, he is seldom apt to do what is expected or when it is expected. He is too busy massaging his delicate ego.

It is the old game of fight or flight—with one side of his mind wanting to fight *(approach)* and the other wanting to take flight *(avoidance)*. It is the problem Philip Slater illustrated in the last chapter—engagement versus non-involvement. Approach avoidance creates stress and anxiety. When a person is in the throes of approach avoidance conflict, the practitioner's pulse quickens and his temples throb, while he puts on a front that everything is under control. He feels the psychic need to avoid whatever is demanded of him, but cannot escape the fact that "it is his job"—thus the conflict and confusion.

"Anxiety is how the individual relates to stress, accepts it, interprets it," writes Rollo May in *The Meaning of Anxiety* (1977). "Stress is a halfway station on the way to anxiety. Anxiety is how we handle stress."[46] The problem with people subject to approach avoidance behavior is that their emotional circuits become flooded, and they are crippled by distress. This inability to deal with role demands, because of brutalizing self-demands, finds them getting less meaningful assignments. Because they cannot be depended upon or trusted to do the job, management unwittingly reinforces the behavior. At the extreme of approach avoidance behavior, the person is labeled and then treated as irresponsible and ultimately becomes non-responsible.

Silent Killer No. 5: Obsessive Compulsive Behavior

Examples are always wanting to be and have what someone else is and has, being obsessed with what one does not have and is not at the expense of what one does have and is, always seeing the grass greener on the other side of the fence, and being consumed with jealousy and envy. Obsessive compulsive behavior is characterized by obsessive ideas and compulsive actions.

It can be diagnosed as psychosis—a severe mental or personality disorder in which the person loses contact with reality and is unable to participate in ordinary social life. The cause may be either organic or functional. Obsessive compulsive behavior is, however, much more prevalent in the organization as a neurosis—a mild personality disorder or chronic emotional difficulty.

A neurosis is much less serious than a psychosis and is considered functional in character rather than organic. There are at least four ways to examine obsessive compulsive behavior as it affects organizational health: cultural, psychological, political, and economic. It has become the silent killer of choice, which appears to aggravate all the other silent killers.

Obsessive Compulsive Behavior—Cultural

Culture, as defined here, is the workplace climate and the shared values, beliefs, and expectations of workers. Culture is a recent managerial obsession, triggered by its emphasis by HRD. Over the past several years, HRD has attempted, unsuccessfully, to untangle the sins of organization with cultural manipulation. Senior management can now mouth the words, such as climate and culture, without understanding their meaning.

What is not communicated is that cultural bias dictates behavior. Unless the focus is on cultural bias, all cultural modification will be essentially cosmetic and ineffective. Established rites, rituals, and rhetoric dominate the will of the organization, with the informal group controlling the ebb and flow of how these established practices are working. Inherent in this informal structure is the current mind-set, not only toward these cultural biases but toward the organization as well. The combination of this mind-set and these biases dictates behavior—what is tolerated, expected, believed, valued, and experienced. There can be no discernible change without first understanding and then dealing with this reality. It is natural for the organization to resist change no matter how good the change might be—logic does not operate at this level—because it prefers to sustain its known value and belief system. To ignore this fact and to go plunging ahead without first dealing with it is to spell inevitable doom for the change process.

The formal organization is essential to generate an appropriate operating philosophy, consistent policy with a mission focus, and a fair-minded value system for growth and development. It creates the rites of passage, the rituals of operation, and the message of the mission. Once this is done, the informal group reacts to these directives and interprets them in its own best interest. The interpretation and reaction to this set of interventions determine the workplace culture.

It is this relationship between senior management and operating personnel that spells success or failure in any organization. Culture is always created from above and interpreted from below. If both are on the same page, everything runs as smooth as silk; if not, operations bound out of control. Management exerts little real influence on informal behavior once the cultural variables are defined and assimilated. Should they be changed, workers must be involved in the process for verification, acceptance, and support.

What we have seen in recent times is that circumstances have forced organizations to change quickly to stay afloat. Expediency became policy. Panic was reflected in a series of faddish activities—from "T" groups to QCC's, from team building to sensitivity training, from Muzak to ergonomic work centers, from worker-wellness programs to company-sponsored beer blasts on Friday night, from MBO to TQM, from 40-hour work weeks to flex time, from company day-care centers to EAPs, from shared management to symbolic management. . . and on it goes!

There is nothing wrong with any of these interventions except for one thing—they were done to the workers and for the workers with little or no input from the workers before the fact. They were gratuitous interventions—like giving candy to a baby not to cry—which made workers feel even less in charge of their destiny than ever before. Workers didn't show their resentment up front. They went underground and surfaced with the *six silent killers*.

These were tactics, not grand strategies. They demonstrated the panic of buying time. Work has changed. Workers have changed. Real work has gotten a bad name or gotten lost in the shuffle. *Value change*, which is essential to behavioral change, is served poorly by cosmetic changes. Fad merchants know their clients and their impatience. The quickest way for them to lose a sale is to tell senior management that it has to change first before anything else changes. Management, consequently, has gotten what it expected and wanted—quick fixes and non-involvement. Management remains obsessed with the idea of culture while becoming compulsive in its actions toward it.

There is no point in assessing blame. No one could have predicted the incredible changes or the demands of these changes in the workplace in so short a time. Management, in its naiveté, thought that whatever it did would get it to where it wanted to go. That has proven false. Preoccupation with fads has found the workplace going from the *Culture of Comfort* to the *Culture of Complacency*, at the expense of the *Culture of Contribution* (see schematic, page 78).

Obsessive Compulsive Behavior—Psychological

The psychological is defined in terms of relationships within the organization. Most executives are more adept at managing technology (things) than in managing, motivating, and mobilizing human resources (people). Management deals best with what it knows, which means people are often managed as things. People do not behave, react, or forgive the way things do, which is the basis of conflict.

Relationships imply conflict. As sociologist Georg Simmel observed, conflict can be the very glue which binds people to a task. Yet conflict is considered a pejorative. Disagreement is considered disruptive when it is a vital precursor to agreement. *Managed conflict* keeps the organization on course and is essential to its health. Where conflict is taboo, dissatisfied employees are ignored, not heard, and given a short tether, not access to the councils of power.

Too frequently, elitism sponsors favoring one group over another (engineers over administrators), while authority hides behind position power—a psychological climate ripe for backlash. The implication here is that loyalty to authority must take precedence over loyalty to self, that they cannot coexist. Human nature has trouble with this.

Perversity of relationships contributes to a psychologically sick organization. The more the organization resists the demands of human nature, forcing standards by which all must abide without recourse, the greater the intensity of internal stress and strain, and the less the organization (and its people) is able to respond to accelerating external demands. Given this predicament, the organization becomes easily polarized, traumatized, and dysfunctional. It becomes obsessed with its survival and compulsive in its actions to endure. Management may say the right words to defuse the situation, but its actions are likely to tell a different story.

Contribution is the key to organizational success. It is based on the authenticity of relationships. This means behavior must first pass through the filter of politeness, followed by the filters of suspicion and fight before arriving at cooperation. This is the route to communication and cooperation. There is no bypass route to this kind of consensus. Attempts to go from politeness to cooperation, avoiding suspicion and fight, achieve compliance instead of cooperation. Compliance is realized always through coercion or involuntary submission. Compliance propagates the *six silent killers*. Cooperation is given freely and voluntarily, and generates contribution.

The Personification of the Obsessive Compulsive

Going from politeness to cooperation requires work on the part of the person in question and the facilitator managing the process. It is not a neat, clean, and predictable relationship. Relationships are often messy, volatile, inconclusive, and troubling to those involved.

Consider this against the obsessive-compulsive individual who expects everything to fit. Imagine what drives this individual—avoidance of conflict, unpleasant or opinionated people, work that is inconclusive, and situations which are uncomfortable and unpredictable. There is a fatiguing preoccupation with the negative—what to avoid rather than what to embrace.

In contrast, this person may use lifestyle as a distraction from fatigue—spend as much as you make, live for Saturday night, and find an opiate in whatever. This includes being obsessed with losing weight, getting into shape, or becoming more cosmetically attractive. Diet books are bought and not read, exercise equipment is purchased and not used, and medical advice is sought but not followed.

Obsessively compulsive people keep psychotherapists, psychologists, dieticians, astrologers, and palm readers in business. Many are in love with their sickness and consumed with seeing it prosper. Others are awaiting a miracle pill, which will allow them to go on living self-abusive lives without consequence. *Redux Regimen,* the first diet pill approved by the FDA in 23 years, seems to be the answer to the fat world's prayer. Or is it? *Time* magazine (September 23, 1996) reports "Redux has side effects. Some are merely annoying: fatigue, diarrhea, vivid dreams, and dry mouth. But some are patently dangerous. The drug has caused significant, possibly permanent brain damage in lab animals. . . ."[32] This will hardly deter the obsessively compulsive.

The late Jackie Gleason bragged that his six-pack-a-day cigarette addiction and voracious capacity for booze and food were justified because "You only live once!" Such obsession is not living, but suicidal. Other celebrities equally compulsively addicted were John Wayne, Humphrey Bogart, Yul Brynner, Nat "King" Cole, Steve McQueen, Edward R. Murrow, Richard Burton, Desi Arnaz, Sammy Davis, Jr., Chet Huntley, Betty Davis, and Mickey Mantle. All died before their time.

Work continues to suffer due to obsessive compulsive behavior. Take AIDS. The current obsession with this disease has spawned a new disease, pseudo-AIDS. This disease is described as the anxiety that occurs when people experience recurrent fatigue, diarrhea, night sweats, and prolonged fevers, which are also early symptoms of AIDS. Given the sickness in society, this could one day blossom into hysteria.

Drug and alcohol abuse in the workplace is compulsively out of control. Research indicates that as many as one worker in four, at some time, uses dangerous drugs on the job. Seven young people out of ten join the workforce having used illegal drugs. In the United States in 1988 alone, alcohol and substance abuse cost the U.S. economy more than $100 billion in lost productivity.[33] In 1996 it was estimated to be approaching $150 billion. Even worse, 95 percent of business owners surveyed said they had direct experience with drug abuse among their workers.

Not only do these predilections translate into increasing operational costs, but they are serious contributors to "the enemy within" or liver, lung and colon cancer, strokes, heart disease, and heart attacks. Against this reality, does behavior change? Not necessarily. Many go for transplants. According to a 1996 study, transplant possibilities include cornea and sclera (coating around the eyeball), cartilage, lung, liver, pancreas, kidney, blood, artery and vein allografts, knees, pericardium (membrane sac that encloses the heart), heart, heart valves, hip, bone marrow, skin, muscles, and tendons. Medical science is capable of producing the bionic man but, alas, not the balanced man.

Obsessive Compulsive Behavior—Corporate

Corporations reflect similar inclinations. Obsessive compulsive behavior is common if not sometimes comical. Take the controversy over the Procter and Gamble trademark. For more than 140 years, P&G enjoyed the distinction of having a trademark that featured a man in the moon with 13 stars representing the 13 original American colonies. Anyone who saw this trademark immediately thought of P&G. It was that distinctive. Then one day this logo was condemned by certain accusers as being a symbol of Satanism and devil worship. These condemners urged a Christian boycott of all P&G products nationwide, including such popular brands as Pampers, Duncan Hines cake mixes, and Folgers's Coffee. This grew into a P&G litigious fixation of considerable cost and inconvenience.[34]

Accusers went so far as to point out that when a mirror was held up to the logo, the curlicues in the man's beard became "666"—the sign of the anti-Christ. To refute these claims, P&G filed a three-inch-thick brief that included a map of the United States showing the sweep of the rumors geographically; tallies of all the rumors, state by state; compilations of all the queries to consumer service departments; computer printouts of the day-to-day complaints and the precise nature of the complaints; and literally tens of thousands of follow-up tally sheets.

P&G's obsession was compulsively out of control. Rather than ride out the hysteria of its accusers and let nature take its course, for the problem was far bigger in P&G's eyes than in reality, expensive and compulsive denials and paranoid counterattacks were instigated. Less than one percent of P&G's

customer base was aware of this attack and were it not for P&G's own counterattack probably would never have known.

This seasoned organization allowed itself to become unglued by a psychological threat of little substance. In defeat, P&G modified its logo, although it is not known to this day who the accusers were. One lingering epitaph is this: "In the beginning God made the tree. Where does Satan get Charmin?" This demonstrates that any organization can be reduced to rubble if its collective psyche becomes obsessively compulsive.

Behavior is fatiguing when preoccupied with the negative.

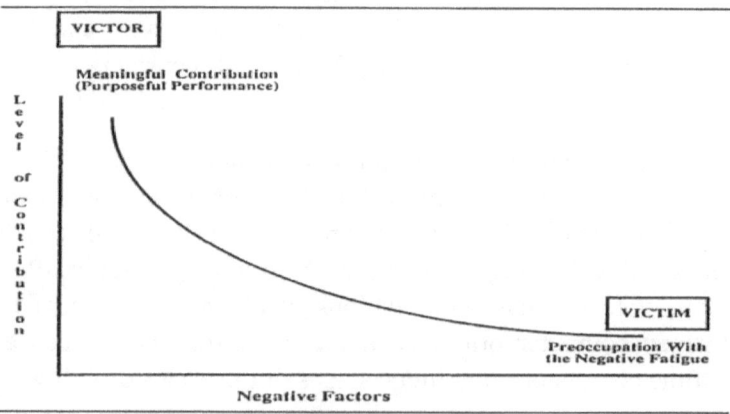

Obsessive Compulsive Behavior—Political

Lee Iacocca, perhaps unintentionally, reveals in his autobiography, *Iacocca* (1984), how obsessively self-absorbed we can become. The book, in places, reads like a television soap opera. Iacocca constantly talks about himself

274

in obsessional terms. In its conclusion, the following could have been lifted from "As the World Turns":

I never expected a showdown, but if it came to that, I was ready. I knew how valuable I was to the company. . . I was far more important than Henry (Ford). In my naiveté, I held out hope that because we were a publicly held company, the better man would win. I was also greedy. I enjoyed being president. I liked having the president's perks, the special parking place, the private bathroom, and the white-coated waiters. I was getting soft, seduced by the good life. And I found it almost impossible to walk away from an annual income of $970,000. . . I wanted that million dollars a year so much that I wouldn't face reality.[35]

It was this self-mocking candor that made the book a resounding best-seller. Yet, behind the candor was an obsessive compulsive man. Iacocca didn't invent the condition. He happens to be one of its more celebrated practitioners.

A less compulsive word than political is influence. As much as Iacocca made of his perks, his obsession was power, the more obvious form of influence. Dr. Lawrence Peter identified the cruel "pecking order" game in his book *The Peter Principle* (1969). Promotion, Peter found, is one of the more cynical ways of neutralizing an adversary, making it a common practice to promote people to their level of incompetence.[36] There they can do far less damage and are easier to control. Peter was looking at the organization in terms of competence, not influence. To an educator, competence is more meaningful than influence. Professors have little power and less influence, so they typically judge each other in terms of competence. Professional workers see themselves in a similar light—competence is everything! This sponsors a lot of nit-picking among the ranks, with mountains being made out of mole hills. Meanwhile, power, which they would have if only they exercised it, gets short shrift. The *six silent killers* first found life in academia and then spread from there into industry, government, and every other fissures of society.

Professors, forced to conform to the whims of unenlightened superiors, rebelled covertly so as to avoid losing tenure or their meager perks. This resulted in an obsessional and, ironically, incompetent educational system. Page Smith illustrates this in *Killing the Spirit* (1990)—professors focus on publishing indistinguishable scholarship at the price of educating students.[37]

Obsession with influence is well documented in John Kenneth Galbraith's *The Anatomy of Power* (1983). Galbraith devotes 90 percent of his narrative to the origins of power, much less to why it is amassed or even how it is used. Users of power, as a rule, don't write books. They are too obsessively involved in the power game. Galbraith, a distinguished economist and academic, is perhaps fascinated, like Peter, with how power players come to play the game. Galbraith, who was himself a U.S. ambassador to India, former dean of American economic liberalism, and adviser to several presidents, has had to use power. Both men agree, however, that corporate heads may be power-hungry if not power-mad.[38]

If power generates madness, it doesn't stop at the top. Nor is the obsession confined to results. The focus is far more entangled, convoluted, and fraternal, as the maddening web of intrigue and gamesmanship plays in the transfer of power. The *Divine Rights of Friendship* display the politics of obsessive compulsive behavior. When Lee Iacocca asked Henry Ford why he was being fired after leading Ford Motor Company to its two greatest years in history, Ford shrugged his shoulders and replied, "Well, sometimes you just don't like somebody." That was it! The rights of friendship are powerful and can exceed the transfer of power of royalty. And as with royalty, there are no guarantees that friendship will produce leadership. Like a toss of the dice, friendship is a risky business, but remains an important player in the power game.

Procter and Gamble's original trademark.

Obsessive Compulsive Behavior—Economic

There is a saying, *"The Japanese are obsessed with people and realize profits. Americans are obsessed with profits and realize people problems."*

This is not necessarily true, but it is commonly thought. It is reputed that the Japanese understand and play the business game far better than its inventor, the United States. History is kinder to these commonly accepted remarks than one might like to admit. Alfred Sloan, the legendary leader of General Motors, once boasted that GM, although forced to lay off tens of thousands of workers during *The Great Depression*, continued to pay stockholder dividends. A Japanese industrialist, even if circumstances dictated such action, would never think to say, much less boast of, such a deed. Openly valuing profits above people would destroy his relationship with his workers and produce chaos.

What is unremarkable about the Japanese executive's confession is that Sloan's boast has the same impact on American workers and with a similar long-range effect. It is not limited to a company or a country because it plays the same way worldwide:

- *Focus on workers, and they will focus on the needs of the company.*
- *Form a partnership with workers, and they will work to sustain that partnership.*
- *Practice what you preach, and workers will preach what you practice.*

There is no great mystery here. Workers can be channeled to do good or imploded to do great damage.

Managing things is easier than managing people. So people are often left to chance. The Japanese have divined that the only way they can keep up with a world favored over them is to tap into *people power* for the good that it can bring. Working with and through people is essential to organizational success. It is not so much that the Japanese do it especially well. It is the fact that they do it at all.

The perception persists that management thinks first of stockholders, then itself, next of the company's image, and finally of the customer. Workers are believed to be taken for granted.

Japanese management, in contrast, is perceived to think first of its country, then its company and its people, and lastly, of itself. Edward Wolff in *Top Heavy: The Increasing Inequality of Wealth in America and What Can Be Done About It* (1996) adds credence to this mixed perception. He does so by showing the salaries American management pays itself—CEOs make 225 times the compensation given to average employees under them. But it doesn't stop there! Add to it the trauma caused the average employee by executive perks; the panic with quality; the continuing restructuring, downsizing and streamlining; and the constant rumor of redundancy exercises, mergers, or leveraged buyouts, followed inevitably by forced bankruptcies and plant closings. If this were not enough, wealth is skewed so that the top 1 percent of the population owns 48 percent of the nation's wealth, while the bottom 80 percent is shown to own only 6 percent. Wolff suggests that a passive reactive workforce, like the American majority, fails to see itself as wealth creators and that reversing this psychological block could be a first step toward greater equity.[39]

When the organization is in trouble, as many are now, how often does management seek the advice and support of workers for ways to increase performance? It isn't that management is this great monster, and workers cower before it. The answer is simpler. Management has little confidence in its ability to communicate meaningfully with workers on crucial topics. It is even less confident in its ability to improve performance through people. It has more confidence in cost avoidance issues and cost reduction proposals or the world of things.

Being obsessively analytical and quantitatively compartmentalized, management is compulsively driven to redundancy exercises and resetting objectives. This is a way of dealing with workers without being involved with them. HRD, as the agent of such exercises, contributes to this folly by constant "worker satisfaction" assessments, which result in cosmetic changes and even greater dysfunction. There is no question that great energy is being put forth to make workers more productive. The only problem is that they need to be put in the equation, not forced to digest the prescribed medicine.

With management thinking of workers as "things" to be managed, its behavior suggests, "If we throw enough money at it, the problem will resolve itself." If this seems unfair, consider that more than $4 billion annually is spent on training and development alone by *Fortune* 500 companies—solutions looking for problems, as successes clearly show. Management's overriding flaw is its Presbyterian sense of being morally right, coupled with its need to be earthly right no matter what the cost. It could be argued that management is more interested in being right than being effective.

If workers are to make a difference, making a difference must be important. As argued elsewhere, there appears to be a cultural bias against making a difference, the emphasis instead being on making an impression. This is illustrated each time workers are trained with new tools.[40] With the shift toward TQM, workers are now trained in *Juran Methodology* (handling chronic problems), Deming's *14 points of Quality Management*, [41]Taguchi's *Design of Experiments* (focusing on the critical difference),[42] *Nominal Group Technique* (everyone involved), statistical process control, process flow analysis, teaming, listening, and coaching and counseling skills. These training modules represent splendid tools that are extremely useful in establishing quality if the workplace culture and the structure of the organization are supportive of such standards. But consider that Total Quality Management (TQM):

- *Represents a holistic approach, while most organizations insist on being operationally departmentalized and focused on MBO.*

- *Is a process of incremental, continuous improvement, while most organizations are programmed to hasty schedule changes.*

- *Is qualitative, force-fitted into quantitatively driven workplace cultures.*

- *Is subjective, while primarily measured in terms of objective standards.*

- *Is an attitude, a mind-set, a philosophy of doing business. It is not doctrinaire nor dogma. To enforce quality is to miss its point.*

- *Has a cultural bias for quality and a long-term commitment to quality standards. This conflicts with a bias for quantity and a short-term perspective.*

When this worker, trained in new quality skills, attempts to implement them in the old culture, he confronts dominant cultural biases. These biases prevent him from using his new tools. This puzzles the trainee as to why he was trained. It leads to an attitude of "Why bother? Nobody cares anyway. It's just a game. Go along with the game, and I'll be okay. Fight it, and I'll be out on the street." This trainee knows in his gut if it is a matter of quality and shipping on time, that schedule is going to win every time. Failure of training to make a difference is due largely to leaving out workplace cultural biases. It is culture that either supports or discourages workers from making a difference. This is the rule, not the exception. Cultural biases must be dealt with accordingly. Otherwise, no matter how sophisticated or how sincere management is in providing training, the results will be training for training's sake.

When Influence Falls Between the Chairs

The complex organization is a twentieth century phenomenon. If society doesn't have it quite right regarding the relationship between workers and managers, it is because the organization is still in a learning mode. Once management was tapped to be surrogate owner as operator, the relationship between workers and managers changed.

Managers took on the responsibility for the organization's success. From that sense of duty, it is easy to see how management might take advantage of workers or take them for granted. Management became the stick that stirred the drink. Wrong or right, that is what evolved. Workers went along with it, to a point.

Then the unions stepped in to complain that all wasn't quite kosher. The union movement was meant to look out for the interests of workers. It contributed instead to the current dilemma by surrendering to management the control of work in exchange for wage and benefit concessions. Unions are disintegrating at an alarming rate because that function is no longer necessary. Workers are adrift psychologically, however, and remain essentially reactive, hurting spiritually, if not economically. They hunger for the nostalgia of work when they controlled what they did.

To understand this shift, consider William H. Whyte's *The Organization Man* (1956).[43] Whyte profiled a new breed of elite managers dedicated to the goals of their leaders without question. These managers sacrificed family, personal comfort, and ego for the company. The *organization man* was loyal, obedient, conforming, hardworking, dutiful, and dedicated. He put the concerns of the company ahead of his own.

Over time, a peculiar thing happened. The *organization man* came to feel "he was the company!"—that the company belonged to him because he had more of a stake in it than anyone else. As *organization men* moved up the ladder, they perpetuated the myth, behaving as if they owned the company. Leaders, such as Iacocca, are custodians of the myth. With the shift in the knowledge base of the organization in the 1990s and with knowledge being much more critical to success, this arrogance has often found organization men running the company into the ground.

The *organization man* mentality persists in *Fortune* 500 companies. It is revealed every time a reporter asks a senior manager how he can justify an eight-figure income. A typical response: *"When I came into this company, the company had lost money for five years, the stock price and market share had been cut in half. We just had our second record year in a row, the stock price is at an all-time high and we have regained our position in the market. Considering that, I am underpaid."*

An *organization man* thinks he does it alone and feels little guilt for doing whatever to put the company back on its feet. Nor does he apologize for taking the compensation derived for his efforts. He sees his obligation to stockholders, not stakeholders—not the workers. Yet the role of the *organization man* has faded. His influence has shifted to institutions that manipulate the symbolic economy. Money, credit, and capital are no longer tightly bound to the real economy of produced goods, services, and trade.

We are seeing the collapse of traditional power and the introduction of synthetic power. Who would have thought that multibillion-dollar corporations could end up on the trading block or be driven to criminal activities for survival? *Archer-Daniels-Midland* was just fined $100 million for price fixing of lysine, a feed additive. Meanwhile, *Texaco* agreed to a record $176 million settlement for racial biases.

It is relevant to this discussion to mention how this came about. Richard Lundall, a senior personnel executive, lost his job in a *Texaco* cutback in 1994. In 1996, he released tape recordings of a *Texaco* senior management meeting, which took place in 1994. These recordings depicted him and other company officers belittling black employees and plotting to destroy evidence in a race discrimination suit. It became the basis of the nine-figure settlement. Now, it seems portions of these tape recordings were erased, reminiscent of the famous 18-minute gap in the Watergate tapes.

The plot thickens! Indeed, who would have thought the *Age of Capitalism* would descend to such vulgarity? But it may be happening in your own backyard. In the Tampa Bay area, *Publix Supermarkets, Inc.*, which dominates the food supermarket business in the Southeast and enjoys a reputation of being a first-class, first-rate employer, agreed to pay its 150,000 women employees $81.5 million to settle a sex and race discrimination lawsuit brought on by 12 former and current female store employees. What is reminiscent of the Texaco lawsuit is that senior management first took the class action suit as a joke and behaved badly. Senior management overrated its importance or imagined power, while it underrated, in both instances, the impact of modern workers once they get their dander up.

Profits have taken on the appearance of imagined power. Organizations are either more or less profitable, so traditional leaders are either enhancing or losing their imagined power base. The frantic search for profits finds many companies surviving on the basis of how well they play the money market.

John Kenneth Galbraith predicted this catastrophe many years ago, envisioning capitalism giving way to a mandarin like technocracy, where moving money would take precedence over making things.[44] *Sony Corporation* chairman Akio Morita, addressing the 1990 graduating class of the *Wharton School of Business* of the *University of Pennsylvania*, warned that America will never get back on course if its best continue to "chase the buck" instead of producing quality goods.[45] Only 50 out of an MBA graduating class of 840 planned to get into manufacturing, keeping Galbraith's prophecy extant.[46]

Peter Drucker, while more philosophical than Galbraith, sees the world economy in a state of flux, with classical economic theories no longer applying. *"The new symbolic economy of financial flow,"* he says, *"outweighs by a ratio of more than 35 to 1 the real economy of traded goods and services."*[47]

What is causing the demise of the real world economy is the uncoupling of the primary products economy from the industrial economy and of the industrial economy from employment. The result is that capital movement rather than trade is driving the economy. Moreover, information technology and services are taking precedence over traditional labor.

In light of these shifts, we are seeing a steady shedding of blue-collar jobs, with more than 5 million such jobs disappearing in the United States since 1975. America is experiencing what the world economy will eventually experience, and that is an accelerating substitution of knowledge and capital for manual labor. *"Without such a substitution,"* Drucker argues, *"no modern nation can remain competitive."*[48] Yet, the obsessive attempt to first preserve blue-collar jobs and then to treat all workers as if they are blue-collar workers has become a prescription for disaster.

The problem, then, is that the professional worker, who has made both the blue-collar worker and the organization man obsolete, continues to be treated as if it is still 1945. While professionals have an edge on the knowledge curve and, therefore, influence, and managers are now the equivalent of co-workers, the cultural biases of organizations insist on treating management as if it still has the power. The result is the donnybrook we see and the reason why the *six silent killers* are thriving. Management valiantly attempts to exercise control and cannot, so influence falls between the chairs.

Color-Blind Approach to Managing Professional Workers

Modern technology is responsible for creating the professional worker. It is now the organization's job to get inside these workers' heads and to manage them in a way which serves their needs and the requirements of organization. Management sees white-collar workers (professionals) in blue-collar terms. How could it be otherwise?

Blue-collar workers are conditioned to expect to be managed. Professionals expect to manage themselves. Professional workers cannot be managed. The nature of their work is primarily qualitative, not quantitative; subjective, not objective; symbolic more than substantive; informational rather than product-oriented; and more abstract than concrete. The workplace culture and the structure of the organization are more critical to success than ever before. In the current competitive world, if these workers do not respond to challenges promptly and effectively, business can suffer. Therein lies the critical difference between blue-collar workers and professionals.

When the nature of the business is stable, routine, and predictable, blue-collar workers have responded positively to the formalized nature of QCC problem-solving. Definite production standards exist, with discrete performance criteria with which to gauge performance. Small groups of workers meet regularly to solve work-related problems. The problems they solve relate to climatic factors—more light in working areas, less noise, or more privacy from other operations—and procedural considerations—more visuals in blueprints, better gauges, or better quality raw material. It is the nature of their work to deal with things, and so they think in terms of things.

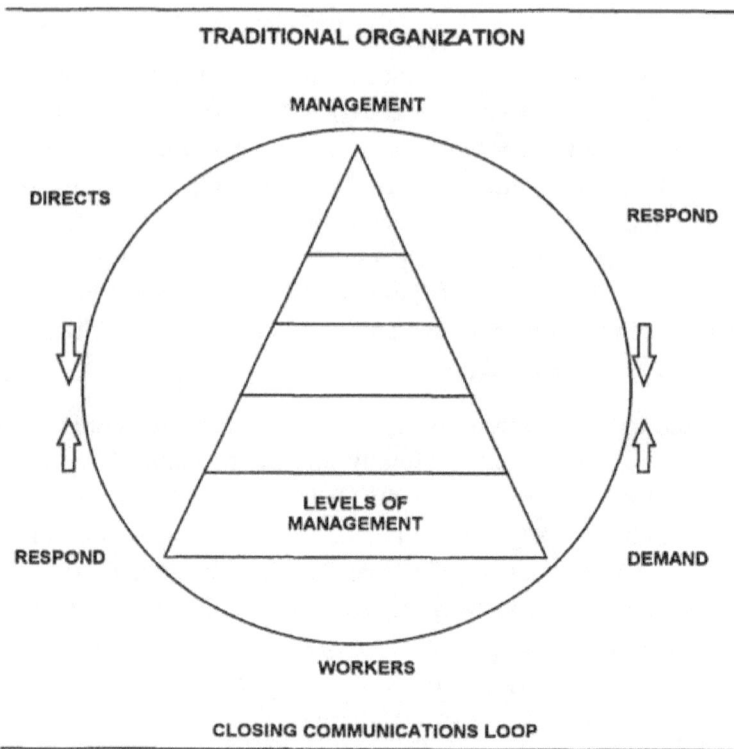

TRADITIONAL ORGANIZATION

Work, in the case of professionals, is an integration of thinking and doing, which is often complex. The work they perform is more specialized and personalized and is situationally controlled. Not only are the thinking and doing integrated, but the managing and performing are as well. Managers and professionals are part of the same team, partners with differing skills but a common objective.

Thinking is the critical mass of work today, as doing was in the past. Thinking becomes a problem when position power takes precedence over knowledge power, when the approach to work is not consistent with its demands. You cannot preach quality in one breath and practice expediency in the next, nor can formality take precedence over informality. The mechanistic mind-set, which set the precedence in the past, now gives way to the organic.

The organization is not a fine-tuned clock of many discrete parts, but a single organism with multidimensional, interdependent, integrated, and simultaneously supportive functions. Moreover, the archaic problem-solving formula of linear logic, cause and effect analysis, and concrete data that are popular in QCCs is not sufficient for today's problems. QCCs were designed as a voluntary system of worker participation, giving workers the opportunity to contribute to the decision-making process. J. M. Juran has observed such efforts directed at solving the trivial many problems and not the vital few. Juran states that only 15 percent improvement can be effected if blue-collar workers are 100 percent successful. This leaves 85 percent of the problem untouched, which Juran sees as only germane to management and professionals. Juran and W. Edwards Deming introduced the team concept to the Japanese in the late 1950s.

More remarkable is the fact that Joseph Scanlon introduced this same concept to Empire Steel and Tin Plate Company in Mansfield, Ohio, in 1932.[49]*The Scanlon Plan* was responsible for saving the company from bankruptcy by promoting union and management cooperation. This teaming was aimed at reducing costs and improving quality. The wholehearted cooperation which ensued was instrumental in Empire Steel's turning the financial corner. The plan also included profit sharing with all employees. The Scanlon Plan hoped to establish a free-enterprise system in which every worker could become a capitalist. The cultural bias of the organization, however, doomed this innovative idea. Once Empire Steel was back on its financial feet, it went back to managing and operating as if nothing had changed.

This still happens. A General Motors assembly plant in the Van Nuys area of Los Angeles instituted the Japanese approach to the team concept in 1987. Three years later, an incident indicated how badly it was failing. Reporter Barry Stavro of the *Los Angeles Times* (January 28, 1990) tells this story:

It was only one of the 3,000 or so parts that go into a new Chevrolet Camaro or Pontiac Firebird. But for Larry Barker, a welder. . . one part summed up all that is wrong with the way GM builds cars. One night last fall Barker, along with the rest of the shift, was sent home early after GM ran out of a reinforcement panel that is welded next to the wheel wells near the motor compartment. . . The panels came in pairs—one for the right side, one for the left side—and when the plant ran out of panels for one side, the assembly line stopped. A night shift supervisor came down and actually took one of the panels from the other (wrong) side and literally tried beating it into place with a hammer and then welding it. The Rube Goldberg fix-it took so long, Barker said, that GM decided "it wasn't worth it, so then they sent us home." If the wrong part could have been forced into place faster, they probably would have run the assembly line.[50]

What is important about this story is that GM immediately put into place procedures to prevent this from happening again. But procedures do not replace a mind-set. The Saturn automobile, produced by GM, demonstrates how a quality product is possible in a workplace culture if the mind-set is totally committed to quality, whatever the circumstances. Workers at Saturn plants have the right to stop the assembly line and fix the problem. This is part of GM's continuous improvement plan to make better cars. It works when it is practiced, and it is practiced when the workplace culture supports the company philosophy.

The team concept didn't prepare the workers at the Van Nuys plant for trying to force a wrong part into an automobile, but the lingering management style did. "There's a difference between having a part a little wrong, and beating one into place with a hammer," Barker confided. "They want quality, and they want you to be proud of what you're building. How can you when you see stuff like that?" Such confusion creates cynicism, and cynicism leads to the *six silent killers*. At the Van Nuys plant on a typical day, 17 percent of the workforce are no shows. The team concept and the drive for quality are a joke to them. Morale is poor. Workers want to believe in what they do. They want to be able to stop the assembly line and fix what is wrong. This gives them pride in what they do. Workers also want to be cross-trained to do different things, which breaks the routine and monotony. Barker confesses sadly, "Management is too busy keeping the line moving."[51]

Professionals are even more cynical of such devices. They see themselves being expected to function in a one-dimensional world when the demands of work are multidimensional and being buried in information with little opportunity to have input into conceptual designs. Information overload is a common problem, but professionals have ideas on how to handle it. These ideas are foreign to management, because it is not privy to the subtleties of their work. The challenge is to find a way to integrate professionals and managers—with diverse talents and complex personalities—into effective teams. Attacking the trivial many with blistering energy at the expense of the vital few problems is a reflection of obsessive compulsive behavior.

Vanishing blue-collar workers are not the problem. They have seen their jobs disappear and their lives ruined, believing in a system that no longer exists, a system which regarded them as interchangeable parts in a complex machine. Education, training, orientation, and continuing support are now essential components to them in the new world of work. Blue-collar workers were never considered shareholders in the sense that Scanlon dreamed. This lesson has not been lost on professionals. These workers, however, lack the maturity to take hold of their new opportunity. They want the power and authority denied them before, but with the comfort and security they have always enjoyed. Power and influence will continue to elude them if they do not accept the responsibility and consequences of their actions.

Silent Killer No. 6: *Malicious Obedience*

Examples are withholding information that is critical to the success of an operation; hiding information required by colleagues to perform their jobs; giving false information; doing precisely what instructed to do even when one knows it is wrong; circulating disinformation about the company, colleagues, or superiors which frustrates the organization from its purpose; playing games of divide and conquer; talking behind people's backs; inciting distrust by spreading rumors; toying with colleagues' natural suspicions; and misusing company property, all while having the appearance of doing nothing wrong. Malicious obedience is aimed at punishing and thwarting the efforts of others. It is the most insidious of the silent killers.

Take malicious obedience as reported by David Brand in *Time* (February 1, 1988).[52] Laurie Bernstein, 30, started work at a small Southern law firm, getting distinctly icy treatment from the only other woman lawyer on the staff. When Bernstein was given one of her female colleagues' cases to handle, resentment turned to spite. She discovered, to her frustration, she was not given the court documents and other important papers needed to handle the case. Late one evening, she accidentally uncovered them hidden in the other woman's mailbox. Ms. Sabotage was severely reprimanded. "I felt terrible," recalls Bernstein. "I expected a camaraderie to emerge between us as the only two female lawyers at the firm. Quite the opposite occurred."

Malicious obedience is not exclusively a feminine complaint. Men have been doing this to each other for centuries in their roles as principal breadwinners. Now women are equally involved in the competitive jungle of making a living. What authors Luise Eichenbaum and Susie Orbach write about in *Between Women: Love, Envy and Competition in Women's Friendship* (1988) applies as readily to men.[53] With promotions stalling, amalgamation of job categories, and management opportunities disappearing, professional workers have become known to turn their considerable skills on placing land mines in the way of each other. This irrational behavior is fueled by fear, hysteria, and rumor, yet professionals have far more opportunity than ever before. Cooperating with co-workers is the key to job satisfaction, morale, and greater job security. Even so, more professionals are falling on their own swords exercising malicious obedience.

The idea of malicious obedience is so repugnant that many choose to be unaware that it is in their arsenal of competitive warfare. It is far more common than most would like to admit, and chances are many of us have practiced it on occasion. The word "malicious" describes the intent, while "obedient" describes how the behavior appears. Malicious obedience is a paralyzing emotional trap in which the perpetrator becomes the victim of his own experience. With such a venomous mind-set, the perpetrator cannot clearly define his situation and moves blindly in a fog of malicious contempt. His frame of reference is clouded by competitive zeal, envy, jealousy, or self-hatred. What protects the person from malicious obedience are emotional maturity and healthy self-reliance.

These buffers come into play when we accept ourselves as we are and others as we find them. We don't own other people's problems. We realize there is plenty of space for us in the universe. We don't become defensive because we haven't made the progress we would like. Instead, we maintain a sense of humor about what we're doing with what we have. We don't compare ourselves or our progress with where others are. We realize if we haven't made the progress we want, it is because we haven't needed to. It wasn't as important as we would like to believe. We don't play games with ourselves. We are aware of ourselves as we are, accepting in that awareness, choosing (or not choosing) to act on that awareness to change (or not change) our circumstances. We know, after all, it is up to us to make our own way, that the only freedom and joy in living is to seek opportunity and move away from repressive dependence, which is the domain of malicious obedience.

What goads the maliciously obedient person is the game of success and failure, appreciation and ingratitude, inclusion and exclusion. It is not easy to make the correct inference as to what goads the maliciously obedient, for success to one is failure to another. The truly maliciously obedient person is evil, but such a person represents only a small segment of this silent killer. The real carriers of the venom are people who are neither too malicious nor obedient, but passively indifferent. They operate mainly on automatic pilot.

These people have little understanding of the severe consequences of their behavior. They operate from spite. They have been wronged, and they must hurt back. This urge is fueled more by impulse than conscious desire to destroy. "I don't get angry," they coo, "I get even." Vengeance is a corrosive disease, but so is indifference. With indifference, we encounter the personification of disrespect and disengagement. To wit: secretaries in a high-tech company use computer-aided design (CAD) computers as word processors rather than personal computers. The cost of the CAD computers is ten times that of the PCs. If they are doing this in ignorance, it is one thing. If they know the relative cost, it is *malicious obedience*. If an engineer observes the secretaries doing general correspondence on these computers and does nothing, this is also *malicious obedience*. If the section supervisor is aware of what is going on but chooses to do nothing because he doesn't want to cause alarm and draw attention to the budget, it is *malicious obedience*. If the director is complacent because the program is a "cost plus" program with the government footing the bill, it is *malicious obedience*.

This situation might appear hypothetical, but it is in fact true. It wasn't until the situation reached the vice president of operations that something was done. *Malicious obedience* was practiced at all levels below him. What happened to the offending parties who had cost the customer tens of thousands of dollars? Nothing. Was the customer informed of the wrongdoing and reimbursed? What do you think?

Malicious obedience grows out of a contempt for the civilized needs of others and a scornful disregard for the interdependent nature of all things. Companies need workers, and workers need companies. Sometimes this simple declarative truth is lost in the emotions of the moment. It doesn't take much for an employee to feel a right to malicious obedience. *Working Women* (September 24, 1996) carried a survey of cancer survivors who worked while undergoing treatment.[54] According to the article, employees with cancer are fired or laid off five times as often as others. Those who keep their jobs, the article continued, are often stripped of important duties by supervisors who believe the treatment will slow the worker down. Such information feeds malicious obedience because the rumor mill carries the implicit dread far beyond the scope of this article.

Many readers are too young to remember Ralph Nader's frontal attack on General Motors for what he believed was a cavalier disregard for automotive safety. This young lawyer wrote a book about the dangers of driving a Corvair automobile, *Unsafe At Any Speed* (1956), which caused GM to go ballistic.[55] GM's first response to the accusation was neither to verify nor refute the claim. GM sought to compromise Mr. Nader by invading his privacy and, hopefully, to discover some scandalous deviltry. When no shameful activity was uncovered, GM became obsessed with Nader and compulsive in its strategy to deal with him. The result was that Nader grew to national prominence while GM looked ridiculous. Nader was an independent contractor who felt a responsibility to set the record straight. This is the opposite of malicious obedience.

When a manager is operating on a tight budget, scrambling for breathing room and feeling compelled to make his numbers creatively, he practices malicious obedience. The Chrysler executives who rolled back the odometers on 60,000 automobiles were maliciously obedient. They were guilty of knowingly doing something that hurt their customers. Anyone who was aware of the activity and failed to report it was also guilty. The Watergate cover-up was a classic example of malicious obedience, with every level of the executive branch—all the way to the presidency—arrogantly disregarding ethics and common sense. Similarly, the Iran/Contra scandal was incomprehensible to most Americans, who could not conceive of their government selling arms to terrorists—to a nation that had held Americans hostage for more than three agonizing years.

Holding Americans hostage gave the terrorists a paralyzing grip on the American psyche. As with the Great Depression, this rekindled the psychological fixation of helplessness in the face of adversity and of innocence in the face of doubt. To learn that the American government was a partner with these criminals was more than many could fathom. In order to cope, many American workers have become hardened to duplicity, chicanery, and bad faith. This is evident in how they are reacting to the Whitewater investigation. "Why wouldn't President Clinton and the First Lady be involved in that exposé? After all, they are politicians, right?"

Malicious obedience often starts with surprising innocence and builds to spiteful deception, climaxing in consequences clearly out of control. Lt. Col. Oliver North, with his steel-hammer commitment to following orders, saw any means as justifying the end. Patriotic zeal was shielded behind the American flag. North grew to epic proportions on television as the American people, failing to see his behavior for what it was, malicious obedience, became captivated by his ramrod confidence as he appeared before the Senate's Iran/Contra Hearings. Elevated to epic hero, North was forgiven, for the moment, on a wave of patriotic emotion. But in 1994, when he ran for a senate seat in Virginia, the emotion had faded, and he was defeated.

Shakespeare's Iago in the Tragedy of *Othello*

Malicious obedience has intrigued man for centuries. William Shakespeare froze this deception in the character of Iago in the tragedy of *Othello, The Moor of Venice* (1622).[56] Othello is a good man who struggles with good and evil in his soul. Iago, the villain, perhaps the most sadistically evil character in all literature, is maliciously obedient. On the surface, he is an obedient and dedicated liege to Othello, but in his heart he is a malicious viper. The tragedy takes place shortly after Ensign Iago is passed over for promotion in favor of Cassio as Othello's chief of staff. What follows is an intricate pattern of skullduggery in which Iago means to settle the score.

Like most men of an evil heart, Iago makes it his business to know Othello's vulnerability. He knows that Othello is hopelessly in love with his wife, Desdemona, and is intensely jealous, keeping a diabolical register of Othello's possessive looks on his wife and his obsessive attention to her. Iago has noted that Cassio, too, loves Desdemona, but that his love is pure and innocent and no threat to Othello. Taking these delectable circumstances to heart, he schemes. Iago tells Cassio that Desdemona loves him and not Othello. He arranges a meeting of Cassio with Desdemona to confirm the truth of this. Desdemona is ignorant of the purpose of the meeting, nor has Cassio any intention of presuming that it is so. Cassio agrees to meet Desdemona when and where Iago has scheduled the rendezvous. While they are talking, Iago brings Othello in full view of the pair but too far to hear the conversation. Iago whispers into his ear vague innuendoes as to what they might be saying.

Afterwards, on a regular basis, Iago makes references to the meeting and asks questions of Othello in a manner meant to cause him to wonder if Desdemona has been intimate with Cassio. Once the seed is planted in Othello's jealous heart, Iago exploits the doubt. Othello questions Desdemona's fidelity by wondering after her most innocent comments or movements. Anxiety mounts while treachery smolders. When Othello complains to Desdemona of a headache, she offers to bind his head with her handkerchief, Othello's first gift to her. Later, she inadvertently drops it, only to have Emilia, Iago's wife, pick it up. The opportunity nearly blinds Iago with joy. He seizes the handkerchief from his wife and deftly hides it in Cassio's room.

When Othello finally asks Iago for proof of Desdemona's unfaithfulness, threatening to kill him if he cannot, Iago states with great calm that he has such evidence. He claims only that day he slept in Cassio's room and overheard Cassio speak sweet words of Desdemona in his sleep. Moreover, in his presence, Cassio wiped his beard with a handkerchief which was not unlike the one Othello had once given to Desdemona. With the evidence at hand, overcome by passion and madness, Othello vows revenge. He orders Iago to kill Cassio, appointing the ensign as his new chief of staff, while he goes on to smother Desdemona to death in her sleep. Learning too late of Iago's treachery, mad with grief over what he has done, Othello plunges a dagger into his own heart.

Profile of the Maliciously Obedient Person

Shakespeare's kind of malicious obedience is a whispered presence in most washrooms, company cafeterias, local eateries, social hangouts, board rooms, and dinner tables across the globe. Psychologically, the maliciously obedient, whatever their age, are not satisfied. They don't know why they are not satisfied, but they know it is not their fault. They don't expect anything to last—not love, work, family, or life. They are in it for right now, and everybody is on their own. It amuses them when serious people ask them their opinion. The fact is they don't think. They scheme—how to get what they want from whomever with the smallest risk and inconvenience to themselves. They lie, cheat, steal, deny, ignore, covet, or confiscate if they think they can get away with it. There has been so little uplifting grace to their time, they rationalize, that they don't need a conscience or a soul to ponder. Economically, they come from every class and every segment of society.

Malicious obedience is democratic. They are more clever than wise, but consistently bright. They are more prominent among professional ranks than blue-collar workers because the majority of the latter still believe. The maliciously obedient have long ago given up belief and are in it for what they can get. Politically, they cover the spectrum, but not in the sense of a party or ideology. Malicious obedience is a scheming strategy. It requires the cunning of a politician and the heart of an executioner.

The maliciously obedient are as likely as not to be narrow-minded, intolerant, self-pitying, extroverted, politically sophisticated, and materialistic. Few can escape its pull if the circumstances are right. So, labels offer few clues as to the maliciously obedient. They think more than they feel, act more than react, operate more on a scheming strategy than automatic pilot—precisely the reverse of other passive silent killers. Malicious obedience can be seen as a crippling disease of an otherwise resourceful population. That is why it is so damaging to the organization.

Identifying the Six Silent Killers before they take hold

What makes this problem so difficult to deal with is that it is endemic to our existence. Two things drive us: one is fear and the other is desire. While we are going to school and developing our personalities, we are programmed daily by peers, parents, teachers, preachers, friends, and relatives as to what is important and what is not. This conscious stimulation we absorb or fend off because we encounter it directly. Less obvious but equally constant is the subliminal bombardment of television, radio, and the Internet, which support or refute our ethnicity and its rites and rituals of passage.

The predominant characteristic of our conditioning is to please others, invariably at the expense of pleasing ourselves. Many find this a "catch-22"—our greatest desire is to please while our greatest fear is to fail to please. In an effort to please everyone, we end up pleasing no one, especially ourselves. Without

292

knowing it and before we can express it in words, we find ourselves a victim of circumstances not of our choosing, existing but not living, and exercising someone else's agenda, not our own. We are bitter without having a reason. Angry without having a cause. We go to school because we have to, we go to church for the same reason, and we take this mind-set to the job. The cumulative effect of always living up to what others expect skews our behavior toward the negative, expecting to be disappointed, exploited, defiled, taken for granted, or worst of all, ignored. Nowhere do we find a place for pleasing ourselves. We are told that pleasing ourselves is selfish and being selfish is a cultural curse. So, we lie.

The war between desire and fear rages on silently in the shadows of our mind with our real self being hidden from the eyes of others. Without consciously desiring it, we find ourselves seeking solace in schemes beyond the accepted. Without a carefully worked out plan, we become the instrument of the *six silent killers*. There are several discernible signs of this social debility. The most discernible is that the social character of our personality appears to change as our desires and fears conflict. When our fears become our desires, we are no longer in control. We:

- *Dress differently or appear careless about our appearance for the first time.*
- *Avoid long-time friends, no longer share lunch with co-workers, or always find an excuse to be left alone.*
- *Begin to curse, to flower our speech with colorful, earthy expletives, or to tell dirty jokes to shock others, when previously we didn't swear or listen to such stories.*
- *Take up smoking, drinking, or start doing drugs, or if we have stopped, we start again.*
- *Put down people absent from the group, bad-mouth the company or our manager.*
- *Attempt to convince others to be deviant with us or to violate established norms.*
- *Become promiscuous after being considered just this side of a prude.*
- *Gain or lose weight dramatically.*
- *Lose interest in what before were consuming interests.*
- *Become especially careless with money as opposed to being miserly before.*

- *Are given to spontaneous and inappropriate eruptions of rage without provocation.*
- *Become especially talkative or quiet—both abnormal behaviors for us.*
- *Lose long-time friends and don't seem to mind.*
- *Commence to hang out with those considered losers.*
- *Stop going to church if a church-goer.*
- *Start lying a lot, which was not characteristic of us before.*
- *Bad-mouth our mate, if married; extend the same to family and friends.*
- *Show an inclination to cruelty uncharacteristic before, especially to animals.*
- *Let the quality of our work break down with little consent.*
- *Become argumentative about nothing.*
- *Start missing work.*
- *Become accident prone.*
- *Develop credit problems.*
- *Become a supervisor's pet project to save us.*

If you can see yourself in some of these behaviors, don't be surprised. They are common to most of us at one time or another. The conflict that desire and fear can generate can go beyond frustration to draw us into a web of self-defeat. The way "in" to this behavior is alone, and the way "out" is alone as well. What we will now show is how workplace culture and its cultural infrastructure sponsor comfort and complacency. This cultural conditioning produces dependency that is as repressive as any prison. It also sponsors the immaturity necessary for the *six silent killers* to breed. Without intending to, this places workers in suspended adolescence from cradle to grave. Prevention of the *six silent killers,* as you shall see, is a monumental task.

References

1. Henrik Ibsen, *Peer Gynt* (Act IV, Scene 13) in *Works of Henrik Ibsen,* Vol. 1 (New York: Scribner's, 1911), pp. 228–229. This play is about the human *will.* Our *will* is broken up into specific wishes, wants, desires, and appetites. For Peer Gynt, the basic drive of that *will* is a will-to-power. In the scene alluded to here, Begriffenfeldt seeks to make Peer "Lord of the Lunatic Asylum." As Peer sinks down into the mire, a wreath of straw is pressed on his brow, as "Monarch of the Madhouse." This chapter on the *six silent killers* shows parallels to this as the reality of our times which make this unsettling.

2. W. W. Rostow, "To Compete, Americans Must First Cooperate," *Minneapolis Star Tribune,* March 16, 1987, Commentary section, 1. Note also: Michael Elliott writes, "American Competitiveness Is Out of Style," *International Herald Tribune,* February 23, 1987, Opinion section, 1.

3. Willard and Marguerite Beecher, *Beyond Success and Failure* (New York: Pocket Books, 1966), pp. 56–65.

4. Erich Fromm, *Beyond the Chains of Illusion* (New York: Simon & Schuster, 1962), p. 41.

5. Ibid., p. 41.

6. Ellen Goodman, "Once-Rebellious Baby Boomers Dread Their Kids' Q&A," *The Tampa Tribune,* September 15, 1996, Commentary section, 6.

7. Karl Zinsmeister (American Enterprise Institute), *The Tampa Tribune,* April 10, 1980, Nation/World, 18.

8. Daniel T. Rodgers, "Work Ethic Has Long Been Resisted," *The Tampa Tribune,* October 4, 1981, 4-C, This article draws heavily from the work of Robert and Helen Lynd and their classic 1920s study of Muncie, an Indiana factory town, made famous in their study *Middletown* (1959).

9. John Strohmeyer, *Crisis in Bethlehem: Big Steel's Struggle to Survive* (New York: Penguin Paperbacks, 1987). He writes, *"They had practically every benefit you could think of, including 13-week paid vacations every five years for the senior half of the workforce. Anybody on the outside could see this would not possibly last; that the bubble was going to burst; that these people had really negotiated themselves into a corner and had; that in effect, crippled the goose that was laying the golden egg."*

10. Lance Morrow, "What Is the Point of Working?" *Time,* May 11, 1981, 93–94.

11. James O'Toole, "The Meanings of Work," *The Tampa Tribune,* September 6, 1981, 4-C.

12. Studs Terkel, *Working: People Talk About What They Do All Day and How They Feel About What They Do* (New York: Avon Books, 1972), p. xiii.

13. Edward Tenner, *Why Things Bite Back: Technology and Revenge of Unintended Consequences* (New York: Knopf, 1996).

14. Karen Cherry, "FiloFax Feeds a Trend," (study by Priority Management Systems, Inc.), *St. Petersburg Times,* January 20, 1990, Business, 1.

15. *The Complete Essays and Other Writings of Ralph Waldo Emerson* (New York: The Modem Library, 1950), p. 145.

16. Marvin Harris, *Why Things Don't Work: The Anthropology of Daily Life* (New York: Touchstone Books, 1987). The author wonders if America is dying of a broken part. He sees change as the culprit as disparate aspects of change form an unintended coherent pattern of poor performance.

17. "Give Me Liberty And. . . " unpublished play by Eugene O'Neill as reported in *Time* (Source: Alan Valentine, *Age of Conformity,* p. 95).

18. Jim Henderson, "Young, Rich—and Deep in Debt," *USA Today,* March 31, 1983, Business, 1.

19. Michael A. Hiltzik, "As Boesky Sings, Evidence Trebles," *International Herald Tribune,* December 16, 1987, Business/Finance, 1.

20. Alexander Cockburn "Of Cocaine, Capitalism and the Martyred DeLorean," *The Wall Street Journal,* October 28, 1982, 31.

21. Craig R. Waters' comments appeared in the DeLorean cover story for *Inc. Magazine,* April 1983.

22. Columnist Joseph Kraft is quoted in the Cockburn piece, stating that "high rollers are on the loose. Greed at the top has been systematized and even sanctified."

23. Kevin Phillips, "Hart's Withdrawal Gives the Republicans a Boost Against 'Seven Dwarfs,'" *Los Angeles Times,* May 15, 1987, Op-Ed, 33. The seven dwarfs alluded to were Governor Michael Dukakis of Massachusetts, the Reverend Jesse Jackson, Representative Richard Gephardt of Missouri, Senator Joseph R. Biden, Jr. of Delaware, Senator Paul Simon of Illinois, Senator Albert Gore, Jr. of Tennessee, and former Governor Bruce Babbitt of Arizona.

24. William van den Heuvel, "When the Other Woman Wasn't a Flaw," *New York Times,* May 11, 1987, 30. Heuvel writes, "A reporter approaches Mr. Willkie after his nomination and told him that he had information that he was living with a woman other than his wife. 'Yes,' Mr. Willkie reportedly replied. 'I am in love with another woman—and I don't intend to apologize for that or to pretend that it isn't so. If you print this story, my campaign for the presidency is

probably over. But that is your decision. I have made mine.'" Obviously the story was never published.

25. "European Press Has a Field Day," *USA Today,* May 30-June 1, 1987, Washington/World section, 4. Ben Franklin, JFK, and FDR were mentioned as great philanderers in a piece appearing in Brussels' conservative *Libre Belgique.*

26. A. M. Rosenthal, "Gary Hart Ought to Know Who Shot Down Gary Hart," *International Herald Tribune,* May 12, 1987, Op-Ed, 4.

27. Gregory Katz, "Rice Skirts Questions on Hart, Says He'll 'Survive,'" *USA Today,* June 20, 1987, 1.

28. David Maraniss, "To His Friends, Hart Was Often Reluctant to Tell It 'Straight,'" *International Herald Tribune.* May 9–10, 1987, Op-Ed. 10.

29. Garry Wills, "A Tale of Two Cities," *The New York Review,* October 3, 1996, p. 22.

30. Martin Walker, *The President We Deserve: Bill Clinton, His Rise, Falls, and Comebacks* (New York: Crown Books, 1996), p. 217.

31. Wills, op. cit., p. 22.

32. Richard A. Knox, "Medical Fraud: Rise & Fall of a Medical Legend— Former Co-workers Are Left in the Rubble of Dr. Darsee's Discredited Research," *Boston Globe,* May 23, 1983, pp. 46–48.

33. William Butler Yeats, *Bartlett's Familiar Quotations.* No. 22 (Boston: Little Brown, 1992), p. 599.

34. Richard N. Ostling et al., "TV's Unholy Row: A Sex-and-Money Scandal Tarnishes Electronic Evangelism," *Time,* April 6, 1987, 38–43.

35. Andrew L. Yarrow, "Jessica, Donna, Fawn and Fame," *International Herald Tribune,* September 29, 1987, 13.

36. Timothy McQuay and Jack Kelley, "IRS Says Bakker's Took PTL Funds for their Own Use," *USA Today,* June 6–8, 1987, featured story.

37. An insight into President Nixon's reckless abandon passive defensiveness is last section of *The Memoirs of Richard Nixon: The Presidency 1973–1974* (New York: Grosset & Dunlap, 1978) pp. 761–1090, compared with Bob Woodward and Carl Berstein, *The Final Days* (New York: Simon and Schuster, 1976).

38. John Dean, *Blind Ambition* (New York: Simon & Schuster, 1979).

39. Saul W. Gellerman, "Why Good Managers Make Bad Ethical Choices," *Leaders of Humanity* (New York: Center for International Leadership, Bell South Management Institute, 1986).

40. Ibid.

41. Ibid.

42. Lally Weymouth, "Has Chrysler Been Saved?" *Parade Magazine,* cover story, September 12, 1982.

43. Philip Greer and Myron Kandel, "Chrysler's Miracle: Iacocca Doesn't Merit All the Credit," *USA Today,* August 30, 1982, 13.

44. Howie Kurtz and Warren Brown, "Chrysler Named in Indictment on Odometer Fraud," *International Herald Tribune,* June 25, 1987, 11.

45. The Associated Press, "Chrysler Defends Practice: Says All Makers Take Free Ride," *International Herald Tribune,* June 26, 1987, 11.

46. Rollo May, *The Meaning of Anxiety* (New York: W. W. Norton, 1977), p. 113.

47. Michael D. Lemonick, "The New Miracle (Redux Regimen) Drug?" *Time,* September 23, 1996, 60–67. Update: Christine Gonnan writes in *Time,* "Redux on the Ropes," June 23, 1997, p. 47: ". . . bad news, bad luck and too high hopes add up to disappointing sales for last year's hot new diet pill."

48. National Institute on Drug Abuse. Research Triangle Survey, *The Tampa Tribune,* January 15, 1989, Commentary section, 1-C.

49. Sandra Salmans *(New York Times),* "Procter & Gamble Exorcising Devilish Rumors: P&G Gossip—'In the Beginning, God Made the Tree. When Did Satan Get Charmin?'" *The Tampa Tribune-Times,* August 1, 1982, 2-E. Note: We see demonstrated here corporate obsessive compulsiveness which is constantly repeated with unintended consequences. Take the obstreperous attempt of the *Southern Baptist Convention* (June 1997), the largest Protestant denomination in the United States, to have its 16 million members boycott *Disney Enterprises.* The corporate complaint here is that Disney lets gay and lesbian groups have the same run of *Disney World* and *Disneyland* as other groups; that the company gives partners of homosexual employment the same benefits it gives the spouses of heterosexual ones; and that ABC-TV (which Disney owns) let "Ellen" (DeGeneres) out of the closet in her weekly situation comedy. Generally

speaking, corporate obsessive compulsiveness has the same impact that it has on individuals, which is a negative if not an embarrassing one.

50. Lee Iacocca, *Iacocca* (New York: Bantam Books, 1984), pp. 120–121.

51. Lawrence Peter and Raymond Hall, *The Peter Principle: Why Things Always Go Wrong* (New York: Morrow, 1969).

52. Page Smith, *Killing the Spirit: Higher Education in America* (New York: Penguin Books, 1990), pp. 177–198.

53. John Kenneth Galbraith, *The Anatomy of Power* (Boston: Houghton Mifflin, 1983), pp. 44–46, 48, 59, 62, 63.

54. Edward Wolff, *Top Heavy: The Increasing Inequality of Wealth in America and What Can Be Done About It* (New York: W.W. Norton, 1996), pp. 32–45.

55. J. M. Juran, "Product Quality—A Prescription for the West," *Management Review.* June & July 1981; "International Significance of the QC Circle Movement," *Quality Progress,* November 1980, 18–21.

56. Myron Tribus, "Deming's Way," *Mechanical Engineering,* January 1988, 26–30. Deming's famous 14 points are: (1) create consistency and continuity of purpose; (2) refuse to allow commonly accepted levels of delay for mistakes, defective material, and defective workmanship; (3) eliminate the need for and dependence upon mass inspection; (4) reduce the number of suppliers—buy on statistical evidence, not price; (5) search continually for problems in the system and seek ways to improve it; (6) institute modern methods of training using statistics; (7) focus supervision on helping people do a better job—provide the tools and techniques for people to have pride in workmanship; (8) eliminate fear—encourage two-way communication; (9) break down barriers between departments—encourage problem-solving through teamwork; (10) eliminate the use of numerical goals, slogans, and posters for the workforce; (11) use statistical methods for continuing improvements of quality and productivity and eliminate all standards prescribing numerical quotas; (12) remove barriers to pride of workmanship; (13) institute a vigorous program of education and training to keep people abreast of new developments in materials, methods, and technologies; and (14) clearly define management's permanent commitment to quality and productivity.

57. Genichi Taguchi, *Introduction to Quality Engineering: Designing Quality into Products and Processes* (White Plains, NY: Unipub/Quality Resources, 1986).

58. William H. Whyte, Jr., *The Organization Man* (New York: Simon & Schuster, 1956), p. 53.

59. John Kenneth Galbraith, *Money: Where It Came, Where It Went* (Boston: Houghton Mifflin, 1975), pp. 268–283.

60. "Sony Chairman's Commencement Address," *Wharton School of Management Review,* June, 1990, 16.

61. John Kenneth Galbraith, *The Culture of Contentment* (Boston: Houghton Mifflin, 1992), pp. 154–165. Galbraith writes of what might be called "incipient catastrophe" in Chapter 13, "The Reckoning."

62. Peter Drucker, "World in Flux: Drucker Dissects Global Change," *Time,* April 7, 1986, 48.

63. Drucker, op. cit. By reference to the "symbolic economy" is meant that money, credit, and capital no longer are tightly bound to the real economy of produced goods, services, and trade.

64. Frederick G. Lesieur, *The Scanlon Plan: A Frontier in Labor Management Cooperation* (Boston: MIT Press, 1964).

65. Barry Stavro, *Los Angeles Tunes,* as reported in the *St. Petersburg Times,* January 28, 1990, Business/Finance, 1.

66. Ibid.

67. David Brand, "Love, Envy, and Competition in Women's Friendships," *Time,* February 1, 1988, 56.

68. Luise Eichenbaum and Susie Orbach, *Between Women* (New York: Viking, 1988), p. 133.

69. Judie Glave (The Associated Press), "You Can't Do That," *The Tampa Tribune,* September 25, 1996, featured story. From *Working Women,* September 24, 1996, featured story, 1.

70. Ralph Nader, *Unsafe at Any Speed* (New York: Grossman, 1965).

71. William Shakespeare, *The Tragedy of Othello: The Moor of Venice* (New Haven, CT: Yale University Press, 1961).

The Taboo Against
Being Your Own Best Friend

We are all authors of our own footprints in the sand, heroes of the novels inscribed in our hearts. Everyone's life without exception, is sacred, unique, scripted high drama, played out before an audience of one, with but one actor on stage. The sooner we realize this the more quickly we overcome the bondage of loneliness and find the true friendship with ourselves.

James R. Fisher, Jr., "Fragments of a Philosophy"

If the body is in pain, one of the first things to look for is infection; if the soul is in pain, we might look for lack of friendship. Friendship creates the cosmologies in which we live, and if we do not have a cultivated world made through the conversations and exchanges of friendship, we will necessarily feel detached, unmoored and unplaced, Like so many things of the soul, we may believe that friendship is tangential to life, an added boon, or an accessory. But if we were to take Epicurus, Ficino, Thomas More, Emily Dickinson, and many other writers at their word, we would realize that friendship is a necessity."

—Thomas Moore, Soul Mates (1994)

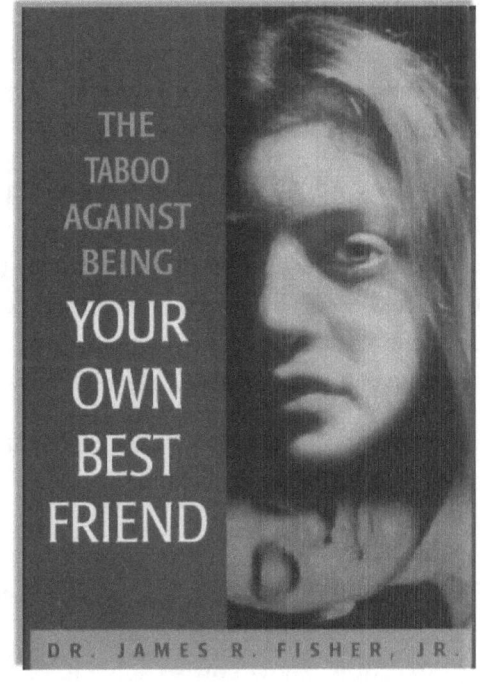

"The Almighty is presumed to pass His judgments and dole out His penalties to individuals, which allows us to suppose that nations are spared painful sessions with the Recording Angel. But if ours is ever so summoned, we may suppose that the inquiry into its cardinal sins might begin with the question: And why, America, did you, in your arrogance, teach so many of your children to hate themselves?'"

—Murray Kempton, New York Review (1995)

Introduction—To Have A Friend, You Must Be A Friend, Starting With Yourself!

Throwing Off the Chains

No greater taboo exists than the one that prevents us from being our own best friend. Tragically, instead of cultivating loyalty, trust and belief in ourselves, we elevate the opinions of others above our own; trust experts rather than cherishing our own experience; search for heroes to worship, rather than celebrating our own lives. We yearn for outside approval, while it is within us.

Widely, we are counseled about the critical importance of self-knowledge, while popular culture incessantly promotes self-indulgence. Self-help books feed this self-indulgence by the devious ploy of inferring that personal progress comes at the expense of self-rejection. This rejection feeds self-doubt. Ironically, the more self-conscious we are, the less genuine we are with ourselves, eventually leading to a desperate search for self, by avoiding personal self-responsibility.

How many people do you know who are obsessed with self-improvement schemes that have actually achieved positive change?

False Prophets

When we hit a bump in the road, when things go awry, in our personal and professional life, there will be an army of friends and acquaintances who know what the problem is, know how to solve it, or more likely, know the right party for us to consult to fix us.

We listen, flattered by the attention, often following the advice given, unhappily, and seldom with satisfactory results. This is not because the advice is simply bad, or that our advisers have devious motives. More likely, the advice is their presumptuous projections of their own demons onto us, along with certain remedies they have devised

302

to wrestle with theirs. These demons simply aren't our demons; we are not like that other person much as we may think we are.

Even professionals in the counseling business get lazy and assume that our situations are exactly like others they have handled. Television psychologists are a prominent example. Making an instant analysis of a person's situation, on limited data, in a short broadcast, they represent more of a threat to that unfortunate person and the naive viewing audience than could possibly be calculated.

I do not mean to discount the importance of the examined life, for without such an examination, life is not worth living. Yet, what we must not do is unquestioningly accept arguments that the issues, the problems, the trauma, the perturbations, the embarrassments, the guilt, the anger, the doubt, the confusion, and the fear that reside within the individual's labyrinth, in the recesses of the mind, are sacred topography only navigable by experts.

If personal issues are weighing on an individual, definitely, a concerted effort to bring them out into the open is needed, not always an externally directed effort however. One of the amazing miracles of life is that once these demons leave the hidden confines of our acquired self (i.e., personality), and come into the light of day, they never seem as intimidating as they were before, lurking in the recesses of our psyches.

We have all heard the admonition, "You are your own worst enemy." The irony is the person who makes this judgment thinks they know us better than we know ourselves, and usually suffers from the same malady.

In many ways, our culture teaches us self-loathing; to scorn ourselves for what are normal emotions; inclinations of a fully human being. We are all imperfect but possess vast potential. Yet, we cannot begin to tap that potential by rejecting what we are, or purporting to be something we are not.

Granting Acceptance

Tolerance, our magnanimous acceptance of others, is not born without a similar magnanimity towards ourselves. Tolerance is born of self-acceptance. Invariably, what we despise in others are the very things we despise about ourselves. Hence, as we learn to accept ourselves, as we are, warts and all, we begin to accept others as we find them.

Genuine love of others is a gift we share, once we find in our hearts the ability to love ourselves. Curiously, the process doesn't seem to work in reverse, although it is preached to us that way. Similarly, there is no such a thing as the ideal job, the perfect vocation or profession that ensures our happiness. Once we comprehend that happiness is choosing to be happy with "who we are" and "what we do." love of being results. It's a form of gratitude.

There is no monetary threshold that guarantees happiness, no level of education or intellectual enlightenment, no status or credentials. When the worker and work become one, inseparable, with no discernible parts, love is manifest.

Virtual You

In the past, work drove deeds, now deeds drive work. We live in the Information Age, an electronic age that links us abstractedly to ourselves, as well as to everyone else. Our bodies and minds float across invisible circuits that have reduced us to sound bites and pixels. It makes the human alienation of the original Industrial Revolution seem as nothing compared to what is now happening in the Post-Industrial Revolution.

Complexity has become a bad word, because it threatens our control. It finds us in a state of panic, disoriented, denying the existence of problems we cannot control. Yet, we can't sit still. We can't handle quiet. We must have noise. We must have some device in our hands texting or tweeting, or talking, or checking our e-mail. We simply must be busy! Metaphorically, we have one foot planted firmly on the accelerator, the other on the brake, wasting gas and burning rubber, yet standing still. We are not happy campers. We have lost our moral compass; we have lost our way; exceeded our capacity to adapt, and we are vulnerable.

Chaos is the new normal, caused by continuing lay-offs, plant closings, shifting work requirements and deteriorating human relationships. In some ways it appears we have an undeclared war against ourselves. Multiple realities appear to exist simultaneously. Everything is precisely as it seems, and exactly the opposite.

Unhappily, we have turned to conspicuous consumption for therapy, the favored palliative of an anxious era. Contradictions are something we ought to confront, not avoid. At the moment contradictions are the grist of the new reality mill, where nothing is either/or but "either" and "or." Regrettably, popular culture merely dishes up over-simplifications, salves for a life-threatening wound, unrelenting complexity. We go along.

It would be funny, if it weren't so tragic. We're so very good at deluding ourselves.

Self-Deception

We show a different face to different people, and still a different face to ourselves. It is in this duplicity that self-hatred dwells. As much as we may think we loathe others (some pursue loathing as a career) nothing compares to self-loathing.

Words are meaningless when they fail to aid us in accepting ourselves as we are and others as we find them. Money is not the root of all evil; money is the illusion of security. We think if I have enough money:

No one can hurt me

I will have security

I need never to be alone, never grow old

I need never be afraid, never worry

The paradox is that people with too little or too much money invariably have similar problems. Next the most pressing quandary is that of time.

Time, That Great Foe...Not!

Time, chronological time, is constantly portrayed as an enemy to conquer, when that is absurd. We have a drive to "become happy" when happiness is a state of mind, not a destination. We postpone enjoying life until we retire, but once we do, we can think only of work, which lives on in our minds.

Psychological time relates to now, what we are doing now, not what we did, or are planning to do in the future.

If we are watching too much television, it is now time that we should watch less. If we are addicted to our iPad or iPhone, it is now time that we set them aside, not later. Being reminded that time is flying reveals the mind is dead to its own longings. To change a habit or behavior has little to do with chronological time but everything to do with psychological time. That is why smokers who quit cold turkey are less likely to resume smoking than those that use a patch or quit one-step-at-a-time. Subliminal stimuli bombard our subconscious throughout the day with artificial wants that we translate into legitimate needs. There is a good chance we are playing out someone else's agenda as most of us dress and behave alike, reacting in a consistent norm to those constant subliminal stimuli.

Were we only to pause a moment we would realize we come into the world alone and we leave the world alone. What transpires between the coming and the going is our own individual affair as we are in the constant company of ourselves.

Meet Your New Best Friend

We are all authors of our own footprints in the sand, heroes of the novels inscribed in our hearts. Everyone's life, without exception, is sacred, unique, unscripted high drama, played out before an audience of one with but one actor on stage. The sooner we realize this the more quickly we overcome the bondage of loneliness and find true friendship with ourselves.

Life is not a journey absent of struggle, pain, fear, disappointment or discouragement. When we embrace life and confront its challenges, we escape a prison of mind, and the cage of an imposed existence. We are not completely free, but we are freer, having made friends with the most important person in the world, our self.

With that step behind us, we are primed for our journey together, through this chaotic era that is common to us all.

James R. Fisher, Jr., Ph.D.

The United States of Anxiety (USA)

"Have you reckon'd a thousand acres much? Have you reckon'd the earth much?

Have you practis'd so long to learn to read?

Have you felt so proud to get at the meaning of poems?

Stop this day and night with me and you shall possess the origin of all poems

You shall possess the good of the earth and sun, (there are millions of suns left),

You shall no longer take things at second or third hand, nor look through the eyes of the dead, nor feed on the spectres in books,

You shall not look through my eyes either, nor take things from me,
you shall listen to all sides and filter them from your self.

—Walt Whitman, Song of Myself (*Leaves of Grass*)

"I shall tell you a great secret, my friend. Do not wait for the last judgment,
it takes place every day.

—Albert Camus, Nobel Laureate and author of *The Plague*

The difference between today and yesterday is we "flaunt our stuff" rather than apologize for the hubris. We see the world through different prisms. That is the reality we will staunchly defend, a reality different to other reference prisms. This is not insincere or dishonest, but it can lead to misunderstandings. When we have clashes of cultures, we witness the clashes of prisms. An obsession with prisms leads to inescapable tension, which finds the individual the enemy of his own society. It places him in an impossible double blind. If the individual acquiesces, and conforms to societal prisms without understanding why, he suffers the loss of personal freedom and identity. If the individual parks his prism at the door, and views life without discernment, he suffers societal disaffection. He can't win for losing.

A civil society is committed, to use Isaiah Berlin's famous distinction, to "negative liberty," or freedom from interference rather than "positive liberty," where the arbitrary powers of government restrict such freedom. For example, Americans carry the right to bear arms to the point of absurdity with more guns in the hands of citizens than there are citizens. Many of these guns are sophisticated military style weapons of war. Then there are mega-corporations with price-fixing against the law yet these corporations operate essentially as monopolies.

Early in 2013, at Sandyhook Elementary in Newtown, Connecticut, twenty elementary school children and six teachers were gunned down by a deranged youth. In the wake of this tragedy, the cry was immediate to restrict the "right to bear arms," which is provided under the Second Amendment of the Constitution. Vice President Joe Biden headed a taskforce to impose more exacting vetting processes in the sale of guns.

"Positive freedom" is designed to protect citizens from themselves and their basic instincts, which was the function of this task force. The clash between "positive" and "negative" freedom is another example of the clash of prisms. What "positive freedom" guarantees is a set of negative checks and balances. Amendments to the Constitution are essentially negative and therefore aspects of "positive freedom."

Were it not for the First Amendment, freedom of speech, for example, "the moral majority" would shut down the porno shops in a heartbeat. Liberty in a civil society could not be otherwise. No group of citizens could ever agree, in principle, on what positive freedoms to advocate, beyond the protection of the liberties of individual citizens. Society offers no salvation, only protection. Sometimes the citizen misunderstands who is meant to be in control. The individual is free to pursue his own private vision of paradise or hell on earth. A possible remedy to societal madness is offered in Walt Whitman's *Song of Myself*:

Has any one supposed it lucky to be born?

I hasten to inform him or her it is just as lucky to die, and I know it.

I pass death with the dying and birth with the new-wash'd babe, and am not contain'd between my hat and boots,

And peruse manifold objects, no two alike and every one good,

The earth good and the stars good, and their adjuncts all good. I am not an earth nor an adjunct of an earth,

I am the mate and companion of people, all just as immortal and fathomless as myself,

(They do not know how immortal, but I know.)

Whitman showed no hesitation in being his own best friend. It was his entrée to being friends with all men, and with the universe. His redemption was in an intimate and meaningful relationship with self. If we manage that, life will not be chosen over death, but life and death will be part of our immortality. Love will not be chosen over hate, but like the lion laying down with the lamb, they will be bedfellows. Eros will not be chosen over Thanatos, but mirth and melancholy will be part of the same celebration.

A reporter with AIDS sees people with the disease quite differently from other terminally ill patients if he views life through an AIDS prism. AIDS patients will be seen as larger-than-life martyr heroes. News embarrassing to those so afflicted will be left out. Healthy people, the AIDS journalist may feel, should give awards to those with AIDS who lead productive lives. But seeing life through such a prism fails to detect the inherent self-pity to such advocacy. Meanwhile, it is likely that such a reporter will maintain he is a journalist, not an advocate, the tic of a prism viewer.

Society, recoiling in guilt, complies with the reporter's slanted story by dedicating more research dollars to AIDS research than to many other diseases which are more life threatening. For example, breast cancer kills tens of thousands more women every year than does AIDS. At least with AIDS, we know the disease is closely related to lifestyle, the sharing of needles for intravenous application of designer drugs and promiscuous sex, especially homosexual relations.

Experts have said repeatedly that a radical change in lifestyle could reduce AIDS to manageable levels, and ultimately render the disease extinct.

To put the AIDS prism in perspective, according to the U.S. Public Health Service, the government spent $2 billion in 1995 on AIDS research and prevention, 2.7 billion, if you include funds earmarked for treatment. That compared to $800 million allocated for heart disease. Yet AIDS caused the death of less than 2 percent of Americans in 1995, while heart disease was responsible for more than 33 percent. Moreover, in the past decade, AIDS has killed 300,000 Americans, while deaths to heart related diseases amount to that number every 20 weeks. Put otherwise, the government spends 3.5 times more money on AIDS than on heart disease, which kills 18 times as many people. In 1994, 40,000 people died of AIDS in the United States, which is appalling, but that number is fewer than the number who died of diabetes, fewer than the number who died of pneumonia and flu, fewer than the number who died of cancer, fewer, in fact, than the number who died of cancer every month. Yet, largely because of celebrity hype, more federal money is spent to fight AIDS than to fight any of these other diseases.

This isn't new. In 1992, the Associated Press calculated that the U.S. government spent about $79,000 for every American who died of AIDS, as against only $7,300 for every death from cervical cancer, $6,300 for diabetes, $2,800 for breast cancer, $800 for prostate cancer, and $600 for stroke. "There is more money going into AIDS," states Dr. David Denhardt, chairman of biological sciences at Rutgers University, "than any rational distribution would come up with." This is indicative of how powerful the AIDS prism is in today's American society. AIDS is simple to avoid. Unlike most cancers, unlike muscular dystrophy, unlike Lou Gehrig's disease, unlike schizophrenia, unlike diabetes, unlike Alzheimer's, AIDS is caused by willful behavior that most people know is not good for them.

The cavalier disregard for safe sex is a case of fatalism viewed through the AIDS's prism. Some persist stubbornly to live in suspended adolescence. This is especially true of the twenty something set. In a Boston survey of 1,841 gay and bisexual men, four out of ten younger than 23 report at least one instance of unprotected intercourse during the previous six months. About 20 percent of all persons with AIDS are between ages 20 and 29. Given the long latency between infection and onset of the disease, many are infected as teenagers. What complicates this dark picture further is that medical research indicates, according to The New England Journal of Medicine, there is no such thing as "safe sex." Latex condoms have been shown to be osmotically porous. Molecules of the AIDS virus, therefore, are able to pass through the latex fiber to contaminate the sex partner. This is a prescription for fiscal anarchy. Ultimately, we not only get what we deserve; we deserve what we get. Polls provide no buffer to this reality.

Politics have become entangled in modernity's web. We reside in a culture, which is characterized by resentment and disenchantment. During the last quarter century there has been a profound shift in people's underlying assumptions and attitudes. For most of human history, it was implicitly understood that life was a strenuous pilgrimage of which struggle was an important part. We were meant to endure, and to live honorably.

Today, the prevailing view is that we have a constitutional right to a life free from struggle and hardship. Freedom, prosperity and a free public education are no longer treated as the privileges they are but considered God given rights.

Society sends the message that a life of comfort and ease are preconditions for civic contentment and human happiness. As a result, we have a complacent society, laid out in suspended adolescence, unaware and unconcerned of the dangers looming over the horizon.

Today, Americans live in the most affluent country, during the most comfortable period in human history with a standard of living inconceivable 50 years ago. And what do we hear but a chorus of complaints? Anomie (self-estrangement) is in. We have everything and nothing at all.

Fewer and fewer people are willing to accept the vicissitudes of life. Government is now expected to meet the public's unmet needs—material, emotional, even spiritual — as if we had returned to the Garden of Eden. But paradise this is not. It is closer to hell on earth.

Politics-as-therapy was not what the Founders had in mind. They were realists in a world filled with danger. They looked into the heart of the colonists and saw the good, but they also saw the evil. The checks and balances of our constitutional democracy was not an accidental design. Struggle is what has made us great. Ergo, our founding fathers would be deeply disturbed by the adolescent whining of Americans today.

Government overreach has sapped our self-reliance. It has driven the collective soul out of the community. People once looked first to themselves, to their faith, their families, and their communities for identity and support. Today they look to the state for provisions, and for meaning.

The American people have traveled a long road from healthy skepticism of too much government, to a deep and corrosive cynicism regarding their capacity to self-govern. They are overwhelmed by the complexities of modernity, demonstrating an insatiable appetite for easy answers to complex questions. Consequently, we are now edging our way toward a crisis in representative democracy. But it is a crisis of our own making.

As this book was being prepared in its final form, the Federal Building in Oklahoma City, Oklahoma was bombed (April 19, 1995) with 168 men, women and children killed, and millions of dollars' worth of damage to surrounding buildings. Quite predictably, rising from the prism of simplicity, the cry was for Federal legislation to be drafted to give the F.B.I., D.E.A. and A.T.F. more discretionary authority to invade the privacy of American citizens "for their own good."

This would mean the authority to tap our phones or look at our credit-card records with impunity. Robert Wright of Time magazine (May 15, 1995) puts this in true perspective: "What Do 168 Deaths Justify?" Wright points out that 38,000 Americans are killed every year by guns, over 40,000 die on our roads, yet suddenly Americans feel at risk when a single bombing kills 168 people. He writes:

> *"The fact remains that a single explosion scares people more than the background noise of highway deaths. Proposed antiterrorist laws are in some sense aimed less at averting future deaths than at averting the ensuing fear."*

Terrorists know the psychology of fear. It forces most of us to gravitate to the prism of simplicity. Philip G. Plotica, a Time magazine reader (May 22, 1995), writes, "For those concerned over the erosion of personal freedoms, forget it.

311

We've already lost the most basic one of all: freedom from fear." He speaks, I sense, for the majority and his voice sounds rational, but isn't.

Viewing society through the prism of family values develops a darkened rainbow of enchanting shades. Illegitimacy is not simply an African-American problem, but a societal one. Some take comfort to see it as a minority issue. Actually, the climbing rate of illegitimacy for all races is disturbing. The problem generates many proposed solutions. Since more than two-thirds of births to African-American women are out of wedlock, some feel the answer resides in the inducement of African-American men to father and parent their children. Were it only so simple.

Several years ago I gained some insight into the black man's dilemma. While in Kingston, Jamaica on business, I attended an evening Catholic mass. The Bishop of Jamaica was the celebrant. The church was filled to capacity with black women and a handful of black men. My associate and I were the only whites in attendance. The bishop's sermon was directed at the problem of illegitimacy in Jamaica.

> *"When a man can only sense the dignity of his manhood through his loins," the bishop said, "he will celebrate that fact by spreading his seed to the greatest number. It is not a question with him of either morality or responsibility. It is a question of self-authentication. His seed tells him he is a man. Don't blame him. Blame society for minimizing his options. Blame society for not giving him the opportunity to express himself in meaningful work, to find his identity in what he does. As long as the black man does not have the equivalent status of his white brother, he will behave as we see him. This is not because he is inherently evil. It is because his goodness is not allowed to express itself."*

Through the prism of Generation X, where many have been their own parents, there is a sense of abandonment. This arises in part from the broken promises of parental love, which resonate with a generation of children who have several combinations of parents, or no parents at all. Entertainers who appeal to this generation are often survivors of difficult childhoods themselves, such as Janet Jackson, Michael Jackson, Richard Pryor, Jodie Foster and Bridget Fonda.

This post-baby boomer generation feels bitter, even disgust with what previous generations have presented as legacy:

- A crippling national debt,
- An anemic economy with fiscal uncertainty,
- A spoiled environment,

- An entrenched underclass with social fragmentation,
- A covert hostility to uncommon sexual preferences,
- A deterioration of public education,
- The false god of diversity,
- The acquiescence to mob rule in the inner city.
- The shrinking job opportunity for traditional blue and white-collar occupations.
- A punishing self-estrangement.

This generation expresses its bitterness in popular music, such as Natalie Merchant's "Eat for Two," which decries teen pregnancy, while "What's the Matter Here?" sounds off about child abuse. "Dust Bowl" chronicles rural poverty, while "Poison in the Well" bemoans toxic waste. Merchant's "Blind Man's Zoo" strives for a metaphor of the times.

No solutions are proposed. Generation X's predecessors had a mania for solutions. It does not. Instead, it is stymied, traumatized. Perhaps it is not prepared to inherit an imperfect world that previous generations took for granted. It seems to cry, "Why me?" It has reasons to be skeptical.

The Importance of Disobedience

"Of Man's first disobedience, and the fruit Of that forbidden tree, whose mortal taste Brought death into the world, and all our woe, With loss of Eden, till one greater Man Restore us, and regain the blissful seat, Sing, heav'nly Muse."

—John Milton (*Paradise Lost*)

"Wherever there is authority,
There is a natural inclination to disobedience."

—Thomas Haliburton, Nova Scotia humorist

The solution to a society at war with itself is revealed in a much misunderstood concept, disobedience. There is a time to obey and there is a time to disobey. Before we attain status as an individual, while we are in the process of being molded into a person, it is a time in our culture to obey. But to discover our own identity, to understand what we are about and why we exist for the future, it is necessary, even prudent, to disobey. Most disobey to unshackle themselves from the conditioning process of The System at some point in their lives. The splendidly perfect child may not find the courage until middle age. Generally, however, the process happens quite naturally during late adolescence. Society has never found the measure of understanding this natural disturbance to deal with disobedience properly, choosing instead to give the conduct an assortment of negative connotations and to see it explicitly in shameful terms.

The System is not a sinister force designed to corrupt the individual. The System is society's institutional acculturation process, the total impact of conditioning that shapes us into the person we become. This conditioning starts from the moment we are born, long before we have any conscious say in the matter. We are squeezed and pinched, pushed and prodded into what eventually and hopefully becomes a human being.

314

Experts note the remarkable importance of touching in our early physical and psychological development. Research shows babies held for long periods of time become healthy faster. Human touch also demonstrates long range psychological benefits. Babies who enjoy constant human touch during their nursing or formula feeding period are more affectionate and gregarious, as they get older. A husband or wife cold to the touch probably had little to do with the creation of this disposition. The same is true of the neighborhood's outlaws. Love in the form of touching is powerful medicine to the human spirit. It appears critical to development as a human being. There is no substitute for the warmth of human caring.

Touching is an uncommon practice with children of today's generation. Society is characterized as insensitive. Touching and holding take time and patience. Time impacts the schedule of a hedonistic culture; time which most are unwilling to sacrifice. Substituted for this lack of touching are things, material possessions. It is no accident that unloved children turn into consumer crazed adults, for they equate possession of things with love. Therapy for them is a new toy, a relational gadget, which they can show off to the envy of others. But it never works. Love is priceless and no amount of having can ever be substituted for genuine caring.

The answer tells us who is in control. What follows is a journey into our society and us as individuals. It is a bumpy ride so fasten your seat belt.

When people start to entertain their own thoughts, begin to sense the quality of their own hearts, experience the conflict between what they are told and what they uncover for themselves, we have the making of disobedience. This disobedience is both healthy and necessary. It is the only path to maturity. Disobedience is the route to personal identity as an individual. It establishes a human being as a person and not as a clone of others. Without disobedience, individuals never become persons wholly on their own terms and in their own right. They attempt instead to live up to the expectations of others. Not only is this impossible, it can prevent a person from becoming all that person could become. The German poet Johann Wolfgang von Goethe put it best:

"If you treat an individual as he is, he will stay as he is. But if you treat him as if he were what he ought to be and could be, he will become what he ought to be and could be."

This takes giving yourself the benefit of the doubt. It means seeing yourself the person you would like to become, and then being a friend to that person in a supportive and encouraging manner. The kindness you show yourself when it counts, the tolerance you display when you fall short of the mark, and the love you demonstrate when there is no love about will ensure you become that person.

Disobedience usually manifests itself at puberty. With the constant assault of the senses via television, radio, newsprint and now the Internet and its social connections, it can happen earlier. If anything, this acceleration has thrown the individual and society off course.

Still, at this stage, it can be controlled and guided through the headstrong know it all mind set of youth to an agreeable conclusion, not necessarily through secondary processes such as family support, counseling and education, but more likely through the primary role of the individual finding it within himself to be his own best friend. Without self-acceptance during this traumatic period of chaos, doubt, confusion and rejection, the individual is unlikely to negotiate the no man's land of disobedience and arrive safely on the other side to maturity. Instead, the individual is apt to spend most of his days in suspended adolescence, a puppet to a titular authority. Before a person can show genuine kindness to another person, he must first be able to show kindness to himself.

The disobedient person, with the courage to accept the responsibility of the condition, recognizes the primacy of The System. He first attempts to find himself within society and to bend the rules to accommodate his developing awareness and personal belief and value system. Outright rebellion is the Court of Last Resort. Unable to find meaning and measure for himself in The System, he goes to the extreme.

Rebellion views traditional values and beliefs as either unfounded or irrelevant. This is sophistic, but such an individual is too committed to "throwing the baby out with the bath water" to sense anything but his own existence. Life is senseless as experienced and therefore everything beyond the self "sucks." Keep this differentiation in mind. Disobedience—rebellion remain pivotal as we continue in development, and both have their function in the person who will ultimately reach maturity. The first signs of change are traumatic for parents and the child, but inevitable.

Mary was a single parent of a thirteen-year-old daughter. Mary worked in an electronics firm as an assembler. She was proud of her daughter who was tall for her age, beautiful and a high achiever. One day Mary broke into uncontrollable sobs at her workstation. When her supervisor tried to console her, she displayed erratic behavior. She became abusive of the supervisor and went into an incoherent tirade, ending with "Why don't you mind your own business?"

Totally perplexed, the supervisor sent her to the company psychologist. "She is one of my best workers," the supervisor said, "what has gotten into her, I don't know, but she is not herself. Help her if you can. She is good people."

The first thing Mary asked when she met with the psychologist was, "Can I smoke?" The psychologist smiled. Mary knew it was against company policy. "If you must, yes," he said.

"Now, may I ask you a question?" An icebreaker is often the most critical stage.

Mary looked away, grabbed a pack of cigarettes from her purse, jammed the cigarette hard on the desk, then like a hairy armed bouncer, lit it, took a deep drag, then looked defiantly at the psychologist, as she blew smoke over his head. "It depends," she said.

"Fair enough," he replied. He pretended to be looking through her file, which he had read already. "Do you like working here?"

"Yes."

"Do you like your work?"

"Yes."

"Do you like your supervisor?"

"I thought you were going to ask one question. That is three," she said studying him.

He put his right hand over his heart, "I plead guilty as charged." She broke into a guarded smile. "Yes, I like my boss. She's a gem."

"So, I think we can assume this is not work related. This is personal." He waited for her reply. Her look expressed volumes. There was hurt in her eyes. Real pain. Still, she said nothing. He waited. It was obvious she was torn between defensiveness and disclosure. Could she trust him?

"It's Champagne, my daughter," she said finally. She then went on to describe her daughter in the most glowing terms, a conscientious honor student, churchgoer, always punctual, never lies or talks back, always polite, always tells where she is going, popular but 'not yet boy crazy like her girlfriends,' tidy, industrious and so on. She sang her daughter's praise for twenty minutes. Her face was aglow as she expressed her maternal pride. She stopped suddenly, breaking into tears. The psychologist gave her a tissue. She thanked him, wiped her eyes, the tissue black with mascara.

"I don't know what to do. I am at my wit's end." She then sobbed, clenching and re-clenching her fists, as her supervisor had described.

As she continued to sob, the psychologist remained composed, quietly waiting, making no attempt to move on. The catharsis seemed to exhaust her, but also to relax her. She was ready to tell the rest of her story.

Champagne was not coming home after school. She was lying about where she had been; not going to church; staying out past curfew (Her mother had an 11:00 p.m. curfew); being seen with boys. Her room was a mess. She failed to make the honor roll in the first two grading periods of the year, a first! She skipped school and hid a letter of suspension from the principal that was mailed to her mother. Cigarettes were found in her purse. She denied they belonged to her, denied ever smoking. Now she was even talking back to her mother.

"So what do I do, doctor?" she said defiantly. "I understand you have all the answers."

"What seems to be the problem?" the psychologist said without sarcasm. "What I have. . ." He didn't get any further.

"What seems to be the problem?" she screamed. "What the freaking hell seems to be the problem?" she repeated hysterically. "You've got to be joking?" Her face an expression of disbelief, coated with anger.

"No," he repeated.

"Buster! You know what? You beat all!" She grabbed her purse, spun around in her chair and nearly leaped to the door. All the time she was shaking her head, expletives leaking out of her hair.

"Wait!" he said. "Please! Wait!" he continued in a quiet voice. "I've listened to you. Right? You owe it to me to hear me out." She hesitated, turned back. "Please!" he said again. She slumped into the chair, looked at her watch. "You've got two minutes!"

He smiled. "I'll hurry," he said, letting her know she was in charge. That was a good sign. "What I hear," he began, "is your fear. I also sense your love for your daughter. She is your life. You want for her all the things that you have been denied.

318

You also want to save her from the hurt and pain you've experienced." Mary rummaged through her purse for another cigarette. She was not going anywhere. Her eyes were downcast, fixed on her lap as if doing penance. She smoked furtively, picking off the tobacco from her lips. She was enveloped in a cloud of smoke.

"It is hard for us to realize it sometimes," he continued, "but what made you the person I see is that experience. Your daughter is taking those first precarious steps we all must take to become a person. Up to now she has been a windup doll, a robot, a machine . . . ."

He studied her. There was doubt expressed in her sad eyes, but she was listening. "She was your machine," he added, "and you provided all the meaning to that machine. None of this was hers."

"Now she is struggling to become a person in her own right, no longer your or anyone else's machine. She is struggling to find out whom that person is. Identity is a horrendous problem to her. She will experiment. She will test. She will flirt with danger. She lives in her head. She dreams. She fantasizes. She romanticizes her experiences. She embraces danger everyday but sees herself immortal."

Mary bolted upright with these words. The psychologist decided to go forward more gently.

"She will change her dress. Use cosmetics. Change her hair. Her nails. Her language. Yes, perhaps even her name and certainly her behavior. Be a tease. Fantasize she is a party girl. Life is her laboratory. She may even get a tattoo for she is flirting with the idea of a more glamorous persona. This is common.

"She will also start to question things, like the value of school, going to church, of working for a living, her relationships. All this is normal, healthy. Also necessary. You smoke. She will try it. If you drink, she will try that, too.

"On the other hand, if you neither smoke nor drink, no guarantee she won't experiment with them. None. There are no guarantees at all at this stage, just as there were none when you were young. Youth is precarious, exciting, enchanting, and dangerous. But the dangers are so great today and so final in consequence, that the need for vigilance is real. Your concern is important to her. No doubt. She wants you to worry. She wants you to care. She wants to know there is someone who loves her when she finds it difficult to love herself.

"What your daughter needs now is not a mother, but a friend, a confidante. A mother's love got her to this point. She must find a way to cross the barrier to love, respect and trust herself, to be equal to the challenges ahead without you looking over her shoulder.

"She needs you now as her best friend. She needs that person in whom she can confide and not be judged, who will tell her the things happening to her are part of life, not to be feared. She needs to know her best friend has been there before and understands.

"Tell her she is okay, so she can tell herself that, too. A friend doesn't have to be perfect. Indeed, perfection is not what a person expects from a friend, but understanding and support when she feels less than perfect.

"A friend makes no attempt to make her daughter into a Mother Teresa or the Blessed Virgin Mother. A best friend helps to understand the dancing hormones in her child's body, to accept the anguish in her young heart, to appreciate her possibilities without surrendering her will. A best friend helps her deal with her fears and not be afraid to love. Love and fear are constant throbs in her young heart. Confusing. Tempting. Exciting. Scary.

"Give her a little slack. Not too much. Just a little. When she screws up, let her know you know. Knowing she is not getting away with anything is an important kind of punishment.

"Tell her always, no matter what, that you love her. She needs to hear this in order to love herself. Express your disappointment, too, but show her that being disappointed is not the end of the world. Help her to learn to love herself despite her imperfections. Make it clear you are always there for her. This will help her learn to be there for herself. Linus in the Peanuts cartoon is not the only one who needs a blanket to feel safe. We all do.

"You are still her teacher, but the education is now daughter centered, no longer mother centered. Disappointed as you may be, she needs to be more disappointed. There is no leverage in saying, 'How could you do this to me after all I've done for you?' That is mother centered. Say instead, 'Champagne, how could you do this to yourself?' Disappointment is the most fitting punishment.

"Control of behavior must move from your eyes to hers, from your center to her center. Once established, flirting with danger will have less and less appeal. You are showing her by being her best friend how she can learn to be her own best friend. It is what you really want, isn't it?"

"Yes," she replied weakly. "I want so to be the perfect mother," wiping her eyes. "I'm not, you know," wondering if the psychologist could see through her.

"Is that what you heard me say?" he asked. She shook her head. "No."

"Good," he continued. "Perfect we're not. It is much better to be human. Better to like ourselves as we are." She rose. "Can I come again?" He nodded affirmatively. "It won't be easy," she confessed. He nodded again. As she opened the door, she turned back, "Is fear more powerful than love?"

"You tell me," he answered. "I don't think so," she replied hesitantly, and then smiling, "I think I'm going to find out."

"You'll be fine," he said as she left. And she was. Her daughter, four years later, graduated from high school with honors.

When disobedience happens much later, say as a mid-life crisis, it is beyond damage control. Severe traumatic shock reverberates throughout all connecting links of the older individual, from the family, job and profession to socio-economic status, and affiliations. It is a natural disaster that could be avoided if someone paid attention.

Dr. Peter Grary, 39, was a partner in a thriving medical clinic in the Southwest. He was married and the father of two children, six and nine. Dr. Grary was a quiet man, dedicated to his family, on solid terms financially and with no apparent hang-ups. Regarding the latter, his colleagues often came to him for advice. He was considered the ideal physician, easily the most popular doctor in the clinic. What everyone missed is that he had no support system for himself, only for others. It was as if he had no problems. A mistake.

Dr. Grary usually took his lunch at his desk. One day he departed from this ritual, telling his partners that he was going out to eat. Asked when he might be expected back, he shrugged his shoulders. "Eventually" he said without smiling.

On the surface, no one thought twice about it, but upon reflection, it was strange. He never came back. No one has heard from him in twenty years. His wife and children never recovered. The children, now adults, are obsessed to find their father. Foul play was suspected, and then ruled out by police. They failed to uncover any leads to indicate this or otherwise. Dr. Grary simply vanished.

What is most shocking about Dr. Grary's story is not his disappearance, but how routine it has become. Thousands of professionals repeat this behavior every year under similar mystifying circumstances. Not long ago, a dentist in Dallas turned up after a decade's absence. His explanation, 'he had to get away.' The pressures of conforming to a herd mentality eventually demands relief. Runaway children have always been a problem. Now, runaway adults are joining them as a popular form of late blooming disobedience.

No matter when it occurs, the seeds of discontent are planted early. Deny them if you will, one day The Wild Thing demands reckoning. Much as we have the tendency to lie to others to get through the day, studies show the average person lies at least sixty-nine times daily, and to himself at least ten times that number.

Denial is The Big Lie. Surprisingly, to complain constantly keeps many in harness, and disobedience more or less at bay. Ventilation through complaint postpones precipitous behavior indefinitely. Complaining for many becomes an end in itself. To do something about it, whatever it may be, seldom enters the complainer's mind. Their objective is to dump The Wild Thing (the seeds of their discontent) on others and let them carry the monkey. Taking action is never part of the drill.

No one complains more than sailors at sea. Once I was at sea for nearly two months during the British bombing of the Suez Canal in 1956. Sixty days without coming ashore is a lifetime of incarceration to a sailor. My ship was the Flag Ship of the Sixth Fleet, U.S.S. Salem (CA-139), a heavy cruiser stationed in the Mediterranean during this Middle East crisis with 1,400 men aboard.

As the days mounted into weeks, and the weeks literally into months, complaining grew to an art form. One division attempted to squash the scuttlebutt by establishing a policy whereby unsavory remarks were subject to a Captain's Mast, a form of punishment, which could involve loss of rating or worse.

Up to that point, there was no destructive behavior to either persons or property, just a lot of bitching. Once that humiliating policy was posted, it was as if a pin pricked the pent up rage aboard. All hell broke loose, everywhere! Tempers flared, fights broke out, compartments were damaged, fires were set, and bedlam was the byword. The crew was out-of-control. Spontaneous human combustion was the product of this idiocy.

Within the hour after the Captain rescinded this policy, order was restored. It was like dousing an uncontrollable fire with a miraculous fire repellent. The P.A. announcement was greeted with cheers as the ship quietly settled down from chaos to order. The message convinced the crew their Captain understood them. It was a short statement. No homilies. The Captain acknowledged the error in judgment while recognizing our sea weariness. He also confessed he suffered similarly. A reprieve was granted for all but the most violent perpetrators. It taught me a lesson:

- Deny the reality of human nature and you let loose the rage of the caged animal. Accept the reality of human nature and deal with it from that vantage point, and reason will eventually quiet its restless spirit, even in the face of mounting tension and certain adversity.

What triggers our minds to finally say, "Enough already!" is impossible to determine. It could be a cumulative effect, like a pressure cooker, which eventually blows its lid. What prevents many from blowing their lid is they find someone to talk to, someone to hear them out. A responsive ear is disarmingly seductive. It attracts people to each other more than glamorous appearance, sexual appeal, money, or even common interests. We all need someone with empathic understanding. It helps us to deal with our pent up angers and imagined fears.

Moreover, we seek the approval of significant others for we have an inclination to question ourselves, to be hypercritical of what we think and do. Being either defensive or dogmatic is indicative of this tendency. It is the reason we hide so much of ourselves from others and ourselves. A symphony goes on in our heads, "If you only knew me as the fraud that 1 am, you would never like me." Something gnaws at our conscience, a struggle between our Ideal Self (what others tell us we ought to be), and our Real Self (what we actually are). This dichotomy makes us feel an impostor compelled to boast to others of our accomplishments, while belittling them to ourselves. As if this were not enough torment, we exaggerate the accomplishments of others compared to our own, throwing us into perpetual depression.

We waffle, like a lost soul, looking for someone to give us permission to accept ourselves as we are, a permission we find impossible to give ourselves. We search for someone to say, "Hey, you're okay!" and mean it. Such approval gives us the right to approve of ourselves. How much simpler if we could do that ourselves.

The lack of an empathetic ear is what drives most marriages into the divorce courts. The problem is the partners fail to find acceptance at home. They look for it elsewhere.

Friends are shocked when beautiful people meant for each other, with everything going for them, get divorced.

Immediately, gossip commences. Sex, it must be a problem, right? Wrong. Sex is a distraction from the obvious. Sex has little to do with devotion to marriage. Sex is as available as chewing gum, so why marry for great sex? Marriage is an emotional investment and psychological commitment, the knowing and accepting of each other as he or she is, not as he or she should be.

Marriage is only meaningful to mature adults. What happens as the body deteriorates is that the spiritual investment pays dividends, as two people become psychologically one. This mutual support system is where devotion resides and the will to prevail as a couple lives.

Preoccupation with the body and its imperfections is the luxury of adolescence, not maturity. Those who argue otherwise are likely suspended in adolescence. They have avoided the necessary steps to maturity, which call for disobedience and self-discovery.

Instead many are married and still looking and living a fantasy of "what might have been." They are adults as mischievous children.

Husbands and wives openly advertise in newspapers for lovers. Potential adulterers are now more bold and brazen than ever. These two-timers, however, might be more comfortable on a psychoanalytical couch than in bed. When middle-age men go messing around, they are looking for reassurance of their potency as much as for someone to make them feel wonderful. Middle—age women of the same persuasion are looking for reaffirmation as desirable mates.

Most men and women who wander from the marriage bed don't expect to get trapped and upend their lives. They just want to put a little excitement into them, and therefore expect their assignations to be considered as outpatient therapy.

We are condemned to die from birth. Aging is a given and a reminder that life is only a temporary experience. This fatalism penetrated our complacent spirit with the splitting of the atom. Journalist Norman Cousins writes in Modern Man Is Obsolete (1945):

> "The beginning of the Atomic Age has brought less hope than fear. It is a primitive fear, the fear of the unknown, the fear of forces man can neither channel nor comprehend ... it is the fear of irrational death."

The obsession with sex can be traced to Hiroshima and August 6, 1945 when a new age was born. It marked the violent death of one stage of man's history and the plaintive beginning of another. Death, not life, fear, not courage has frozen society in suspended adolescence. The German novelist Gunter Grass captures this in the character of Oskar Matzebath, a self-willed dwarf who refuses to grow up. The Tin Drum (1964) is a mock-epic novel of a world in upheaval in which values are inverted and indistinguishable, where the tragic is at the same time the comic.

The modern world displays the same refusal to grow up. We see it when happiness is sought in a wrinkle-free-body. The faces of people are changing, and bodies, too. They are submitting their bodies to the pain of cosmetic and reconstructive surgery for as little as $2,000 per procedure.

Incredibly, in the United States, alone, there is one plastic surgeon for every 50,000 citizens. Their clientele go under the knife for no other reason than to look good. Many television commentators have their body parts shifted hither and yon.

Take pesky television journalist Geraldo Rivera. A few years ago he flaunted his corrective surgery on his show when he had some fat transplanted from his buttocks to smooth out wrinkles in his forehead. This was followed by having his eyes "done" (a. k. a. wrinkle removal) via state-of-the-art plastic surgery. Rivera is not alone in this madness to pretend the clock is not moving. Here are typical types of surgery, circa 1995:

- *Top Five Procedures in U.S.A. for men:*
- *Nose reshaping*
- *Eyelifts*
- *Liposuctions*
- *Breast reduction (Yes, for men!)*
- *Dermabrasion*
- *Top Five Procedures in U.S.A. for women:*
- *Eyelifts*
- *Liposuctions*
- *Collagen injections/Facelifts*
- *Nose reshaping*

The genius of Hugh Hefner and his Playboy enterprises is apparent. Hefner understood and exploited 20th century madness for profit. He did this with a simple formula, called his Playboy Philosophy:

- *Arousal of prurient interests with skilled airbrush photography concealing female imperfections. Look, no wrinkles!*
- *Reconstructive female anatomy with cosmetic surgery to complete the illusion.*
- *A steady diet of sexual fantasy, which makes no demands on men, no need to perform, no need to compare, no chance of rejection, combined with a chimerical illusion of power and money to quiet men's fears of irrational death.*
- *A cynical dismissal of the cerebral for the physical, looking good taking precedence over thinking clearly, and the fictive world being substituted for reality.*

And it worked! Hefner didn't create this narcissistic vulnerability. He simply was alone in seeing clearly "what is." He understood a sexual menu fools the head and rules the heart. Lust, he saw in the post WWII world, replaces romantic love for those afraid to either love or be loved. He saw modern man in a state of paradoxical panic: needing sex, but being terrified of domesticity. Hefner perceived correctly that men want women to love them, but back off when they do.

Incredibly, society now accepts irresponsible males, their insouciant suspension in juvenility, and even approves of their cosmetic surgery. The irrational is now the rationale for a youth-conscious society. Where dressing well for business was once a given, now business people frantically have their eyelids or chins lifted to maintain a competitive edge in the business world. Youthfulness, it is argued, is particularly important in sales and advertising. No one can afford to get old! Or at least look old! Hefner believes in his own Playboy Philosophy for at the age of 87 he married again in 2013 to a 27-year-old beauty because he could and bought her a $5 million home that was hers as long as she was loyal to their wedding vows. The man wants it both ways, and can afford to get it.

The post WWII world created a curious paradox: modern man as a charming misogynist who sees marriage as a commitment to Hell, but also as his only salvation.

The lifelines of family and marriage are seen as potential prisons. Hefner's antihero is a disturbing character to watch as he escapes into fantasy seeing women as sex objects, on the one hand, and as adversaries on the other. Sex wars and class wars are subtly interwoven into gender politics. This disguises unhappiness behind a veil of hearty good cheer.

Meanwhile, not unlike Hefner himself, this modern lothario reluctantly gets married, and has a family, even though convinced that it will all end in misery, but still realizing there is one thing sadder than connecting badly with another person, and that is not connecting at all.

Sexual fantasy has a lightning rod reputation but the staying power of a firecracker. It is mostly a head game unwittingly championed by psychoanalysts, the contemporary version of Dr. Etiquette. It is the role of the shrink to advise us on our best sexual behavior in the interest of improving our internal manners. This is variously called maturity, or mental health or a decentered self.

Psychoanalysis has become the science of the sensible passion and prudent fantasy. How it got on this detour is hard to say, but it aims to make people more comfortable being the strangers they are. Should psychoanalysis make too much sense, it turns into the exact symptom it is trying to cure, obsessive compulsiveness. There is nothing like sexual fantasy for making a mockery of virtue, which is self-knowing. Eroticism invades our lives and is seldom in accord with our presumed standards. We are vulnerable to the oddest things, and the best of us are constantly on the brink of ruin, because of this obsession. So a word to the wise, take note the danger of scandal or making a fool of ourselves is always near at hand.

In this enigmatic age, the complexity of sexuality is intrinsically conflicting because when we talk about sex we don't know what we're talking about. People are more interested in sexual identity than in having good sex. This whole explosion in sexual preoccupation finds we have made the rules without knowing what the game is, and the irony is the rules are there to stop us from finding out.

Wanting to be defined by our sexuality may only be symptomatic of our wanting to be defined. Given the ambivalence of this obsession, drifting between masochism and narcissism, sadism and asceticism, the unconscious, as Freud describes it, always has a blurring effect. This creates a commercial opportunity for the pawnshops of the prurient, because our sexuality has becomes that thing that makes identity both necessary and impossible.

We get lost in our sexual fantasies and we want to know where we are when the knowing is not even in the equation. Sexuality may be the modern cure for class distinction, rather than the other way around.

The sex industry is an aberration, good at self-promotion, taking credit for outrage, especially as maker or destroyer of marriage. Notice love is not even considered in the spirited athleticism of conjugal bonding. Pornography is an invention of the modern era that dates back to the 16th century.

Should you think our obsession with comparisons and quantifications, or our fascination with quantity and quality is new you would be wrong. How many inches? How many times? How many positions? How many partners? Italian poet Pietro Aretino's Postures (1524), the first widely circulated work of Renaissance pornography, featured an engraved display of 16 sexual positions. Don Giovanni's boast of 1003 Spanish conquests is a priapic tribute to *The Age of Enlightenment's* notion of *l'homme machine.* This industry is not new; nor is the promotional myth that without "good sex" most couples will eventually have affairs. Indeed, sex sells even if it is selling lemons!

Affairs are real, but their popularity is exaggerated. Those buying the myth, however, make it a self—fulfilling prophecy. Affairs, incidentally, are not a form of disobedience leading to maturity. Quite the contrary. They are but another form of immaturity in the guise of compliance that leads to ritualistic conformity, the herd mentality of the mythmakers. Men are made to feel impotent if not at least thinking of an affair; if not acting out the nervous tics and mannerisms of their class stereotype.

What triggers affairs? Many things. Perhaps it is more a need to dominate, to feel a sense of power over another, than to satisfy a sexual need, more a matter of pride, to overcome the age-old anxiety of the male inch-war, necessitating the need to register a conquest. Remember, the heart rules the head but "The Child" dominates the heart: If the heart and the head are not on speaking terms, the libido or Id rules the Ego.

- The Id has no conscience, is impulsive and pleasure seeking. It is The Child in the full—grown but immature person.

- The Ego is level headed, logical and deals with the consequences of reality. The Ego is The Adult in the grown—up. The Ego, however, can be suppressed with flattery or depressed with controlled substances (drugs, alcohol), so as to release the Id as its free child—consequences then no longer matter.

The mantra of the psychosexual therapist is "Good sex saves everything!" These enchanters see salvation through orgasm. It is a shell game. It is the opposite of intimacy. The human body is but a way station on route to the mind and heart, where intimacy resides. These therapists appeal to The Child, not The Adult.

The adult understands it takes work, suffering, responsibility and struggle to realize intimacy. It has little to do with sexual performance or gargantuan genitalia (The truth is the ten-inch penis is very rare. The average man's pride and joy is 4" rising to 5" to 7" when fully erect.). The Parent in us worries about such things while The Child in us is lost in its play.

Automobiles are the quintessential phallic symbol of our times. Listen to sex therapists and you think of automobiles:

- *Well lubricated;*
- *Warm up (before getting into gear);*
- *Pressure points;*
- *Tune up;*
- *All gauges working;*
- *Older models don't have the same acceleration, be patient;*
- *Take on the road and try out before buying;*
- *Good fit;*
- *Beware! Fresh paint and scent of newness can throw you off as to age;*
- *No qualms turning old model in for new;*
- *Change is good for the soul!*

This population was first thought to be heavily concentrated in a few large cities such as San Francisco and New York City, but skeptics insisted homosexuality was more pervasive. To determine the validity of this claim, scientists prefer a sample of some 20,000 or more. This required the financial support of the Congressional Finance Committee of the US Senate. The late Senator Jesse Helms, self-appointed "watchdog of American morals" squashed such financing.

Obviously, even with all this new information about our sexuality, we still have considerable difficulty relating to each other. Apparently, the remedy is too simple. The three magic words to a meaningful relationship are not "I Love you," but talk, talk, talk. As long as we confront each other with what is bothering us, there is a chance to purposeful relationships. The key is frequent but polite confrontation, not infrequent but violent clashes. Surface politeness and obedience is not healthy. It is mockery.

Anxiety is a luxury of a self-indulgent culture. It is a culture that has time on its hands. Instead of focusing on living, to experience the pleasures that cost nothing, the anxious take themselves too seriously and life not seriously enough. They are constantly on the go, too impatient to stop and ask themselves, "Why the hurry? Why the worry?" They worry about what others think, of fitting in and being included. This leaves little time to enjoy the moment or to think for themselves. Life is not much fun without a focus or a plan.

Herein lies the anxiety: to have a goal suggests action, which means to take risks, to embrace pain and endure struggle. Instead, many resort to planning for planning sake. Planning is an end in itself for they want no struggle, only comfort and security. This finds them:

- Too obedient, too compliant, too ready to buy into what others say is best for them, too willing to surrender their freedoms to the promise of a painless existence, too eager to give others the benefit of the doubt but not themselves, too anxious to believe what others have to sell and not what they themselves have to say

The narcotic, plenty, is the culprit. Too many have had too much, too soon. Few seem willing to fight for what they believe in and even fewer take responsibility for their problems. "Put life on a credit card and max it out!" is a common cry, which has symbolic implications. Many state governments encourage this. Bankruptcy laws allow debtors to walk away from financial obligation with painless consequences. This reinforces suspended adolescence while the rest of society carries the note.

Disobedience is in our nature. Human history began with an act of disobedience in the Garden of Eden, and it is unlikely it will end without an act of disobedience. When we disobey for personal principle, it leads to social justice. Not only does disobedience ensure our personal freedom, but also it gives the stress of existence a safety valve. This prevents life from becoming a pressure cooker. With this safety valve, anger can be a constructive motivator. Without this safety valve, anger turns inward and leads to debilitating depression.

There is no pain greater than depression, no world riper for human combustion. Nothing is more dangerous to an individual than an angry mind turned inward. With frightening regularity, we are seeing senseless acts of violence perpetrated by supposedly harmless people. We read about them in the newspapers or see them described on television, and say, "How sad!" Chances are they don't touch our lives. They happen to other people out there, but not always.

When my children were teenagers, there was a young man from the neighborhood who came by occasionally. He was intense, but quiet, well-mannered and polite. He completed his studies at the university and took a position in the Tampa Bay area. He was in his early thirties. I had lost track of him.

Imagine my shock when this young man walked into the insurance company, for which he worked, at lunchtime, shot and killed four people, wounding several others. He then went to a city park, shot and killed himself. His employer, a short while before, had fired him for poor performance — incomplete staff work, and failure to show up for work.

Many theories are offered to explain such horrifying behavior. He must have felt terribly alone, depressed beyond comprehension. Clinical depression is a treatable condition. With the proper support system, and qualified therapy, full recovery is possible. Without it, a person may become a time bomb ready to explode, possibly leading to suicide or genocide.

My wonder is how this young man saw himself before that final act: the victim or victor; the puppet or one in charge; the cheated or the cheater; the violated or the spoiled brat; having nothing to lose or willing to lose everything? He must have been in excruciating pain to manifest such cowardice, the taking of innocent lives.

The young man grew physically mature, earning a college degree, but he never grew up emotionally. He never accepted the suffering and responsibility of adulthood. He couldn't have known or liked himself very much. Worse yet, his tragedy haunts us as copycats continue to repeat this senseless violence from the arbitrary killing of several at a West Coast MacDonald's, to killing co-workers at a busy post office, to randomly killing a shopping center throng, to the hate crime killing of six innocent commuters by a crazed gunman on the Long Island Rail Road in late 1993, to the taking of 168 lives in the Oklahoma City Federal Building bombing. This tragic and seemingly chronic behavior continues unabated. We read about these things as if far removed from anyone we know. I once thought that, too.

If disobedience is avoided, the individual is likely to be frozen in suspended adolescence, the emotional maturity of a thirteen-year-old. At such a level of maturity, it is impossible to be an effective problem solver with the complexities of modern life, either on a personal or professional level.

Immaturity is a societal disorder, sad to say, that is consistent with society's programming. Print journalism, television and films appeal to a juvenile mindset. They exploit our basic instincts, which have an appetite for the sensational, but fail to expand our consciousness. They perpetuate the same programming with which they had been inculcated without conscience. The media is the most conforming group of society instead of being the cutting edge of change that it could be front-page prominence is given to the serial killer once apprehended. Common fare is then to immortalize the miscreant in hard cover, and capture his non-life in television psychodrama. Out in the hinterland, defective minds watch and dream of their moment of infamy via an irrational killing spree. How lost to our times are the words of English author Thomas Babington Macaulay, "The measure of a man's real character is what he would do if he knew he would never be found out."

The media and entertainment industry are not to blame. They give us what we want, not what we need. The common denominator of immaturity is pervasive in industry, commerce, education and government. Those in charge subscribe to K.I.S.S. (Keep It Simple Stupid) and "If it ain't broke, don't fix it!" The charter of the work force is to behave, not think, to submit, not challenge, to manage crises, not prevent them. Management creates crises, programs workers to solve them, and then praises itself, completing the folly. It is the principal route to a successful career in the United States of Anxiety.

Society produces the culture it sponsors. The culture it now sponsors discourages citizens to grow up and take charge. The more society does for its citizens the less they need do for themselves. Social planners know it is easier to control citizens in subservience than to develop them in self-sufficiency.

A point is reached when this no longer holds true. We have reached that point of diminishing returns. Society experiences identical problems to those experienced by the individual: that is, neither society nor the individual can have it both ways. Society cannot have a responsible, responsive, accountable and productive citizenry if people are not encouraged to grow up.

Growing up requires stretching the mind, body and spirit. It means forever challenging the system (status quo), generation after generation. It means accepting risk, pain, failure, suffering and struggle as part of the price of maturity. On the other hand, immaturity engenders: thoughtless behavior, cover-up, passive behavior, martyrdom (victim complex), whimpering dependency and learned helplessness. It also provokes lethargy, pettiness, temper tantrums, outrage and hypersensitivity (political correctitude).

Which behaviors do we most frequently see at home, in the workplace, on our college campuses, in the oak—lined halls of government, business and industry, in the sanctuaries of the religious? In my experience, it is these behaviors just described.

It would seem society is morally disintegrating, but is it anyone's fault? If no one is to blame; no one is guilty; right?

- John Hinckley shot President Ronald Reagan and blamed it on the movie, Taxi Driver (1976). In the film, cabbie Travis Bickle (Robert De Niro) harbors inexpressible frustration until he finds a girl (Cybil Sheperd), who becomes his reason to live and inspires him to kill. Jodie Foster, a child-woman in the film, became Hinckley's obsession. What inspired this fantasy to turn him into an assassin like cabbie Bickle in the film is known only to his therapist.

- Teenagers kill or maim themselves imitating something stupid they see in the television movie, The Program (1993). In that film the hero, a college quarterback, tries to prove grace under pressure by lying down in the middle of a busy highway flipping through a magazine as trucks swerve to avoid him. An 18-year-old boy does this in rural Pennsylvania and is killed. Is it television's fault, or the boy's?

- A grieving mother blames the teenage MTV's madcap cartoon, Beavis & Butt—Head, when her child sets fire to their home, killing his sister. No one questions how television was more of a parent than she was.

- Michael Miliken steals millions with junk bonds on Wall Street. He blames it on the tenor of the times. Society awards him, once he serves his prison time in a gentleman's prison, by giving him a faculty position at UCLA.

- The Menendez brothers kill their parents in cold blood while they are sleeping. Their defense is that the fault lies with their parents. They claim to have been physically abused as children, a claim which of course could not be corroborated, as the accused parents were dead.

- Reginald Denny is nearly beaten to death in East Los Angeles during the 1992 riots. We're asked to accept that he was in the wrong place at the wrong time and no one was really trying to hurt him. Besides, everyone else was rioting and doing bad stuff then, too.

None of these people take responsibility for their actions. It is always someone else's fault. How different it was when President Harry S. Truman had a plaque on his desk some 70 years ago, which read, "The Buck Stops Here!" Today, like a hot potato, the buck never stops getting passed around or kicked down the road.

A model for explaining arrested development identifies paternalism (The Parenting Syndrome) with The Superego, The Parent in our make—up. This dictates the moral tone of society, what Freud referred to as the Morality Principle. The (restless) Child is the Id, the animal spirit, which is consumed with Freud's Pleasure Principle. The Adult or Ego looks at the irrational world with a rational eye and is concerned with the Reality Principle. This struggle might be likened to this:

A patriarchal society is reluctant to allow The Adult to show its face for fear The Parent will lose control. Control is everything to The Parent. Therefore, The Parent prefers to appeal to The Child in deference to The Adult. "People act like children," The Parent insists, "so they must be treated like children."

How often have we heard that patronizing statement? Parents, teachers, employers, and the religious repeat it every day. It promotes dependence and keeps the majority forever immature and in their place.

Visit the workplace anywhere and you are likely to hear something like this: "Give workers more pay, more freedom to control their work, more support and better tools to do the job, and you still need management (The Parent) to see that the work gets done." If true, it is only because management gets what it expects.

 Management has gravitated to a parenting role. Although obviously not intended, it was inevitable since workers were made management dependent and programmed to be reactive to detailed instructions rather than proactive by taking the initiative and ownership of what they did. In the 21st century and the Information Age this puts the worker and the workplace at a considerable disadvantage. Management, in that sense, is anachronistic. Self-starting and self-managing adults now need to replace the role of traditional management.

Nobel Laureate physicist Richard Feynman had a father who advised his son, "Have no respect whatsoever for authority; forget who said it and instead look at what he starts with, where he ends up, and ask yourself, 'Is it reasonable?'"

Dr. Feynman's father groomed his son to have a mind of his own. He gave his son guidance into adulthood so his son might discover his own essence. Feynman was a young scientist on The Manhattan Project that gave us the atomic bomb to end World

War II. He did original work in quantum electrodynamics for which he earned the Nobel Prize for Physics, and it was he who solved the mystery of The Challenger Shuttle disaster with his 0-ring ice-water demonstration. Read his biography, *Genius* by James Gleick (1992) and you see how management, throughout his career, attempted to kill his spirit, but failed for the self-reliance taught to him by his father.

What a difference a parent makes when it leaves paternalism aside! Dr. Feynman's father, Melville, a Jewish immigrant from Minsk, Byelorussia, had a practical, vivid appreciation of science. He once explained to his son that a dinosaur twenty—five feet high with a head six feet across, if standing in the front yard, would almost be able to get his head through the second—floor window. Melville Feynman sold police uniforms and automobile polish without notable success. But he was a most successful friend, coach and instructor for his young prodigy.

To give some sense of Feynman's achievements, his work has been compared in significance with that of Albert Einstein and Isaac Newton. At Caltech, without consulting books, he slowly built an entire edifice of physics. It was the physical world as he saw and understood it.

Graduate students and other professors came to listen to his Caltech Lectures. Eventually, they became the three—volume Feynman Lectures on Physics, which can be found on the bookshelves of almost every professional physicist in the world. They are considered a triumph of human thought with a place in the history of Western culture alongside Aristotle's Collected Works, Descartes' Principles of Philosophy, and Newton's Principia. It all started with a father, who peddled for a living, but challenged his son, and then allowed him to soar.

Management, like most parents, however, demonstrates little patience with those who challenge its authority. Mature adults are likely to have a take charge attitude and to be disinclined to give deference to such authority if it negatively impacts the job.

Conventional authority sees this as insubordination. It is actually healthy disobedience. Defiance is often a cry to understand, to be convinced, and to see the reasonableness of the proposition. The days of accepting things on blind faith are over. "Why," is the central word in the new vocabulary.

Management often sees itself as the benign parent, the head of the family, even Santa Claus if you will, exercising the role of the generous parent through entitlements. Fear & favor are however manipulative devices to maintain control. Giving or withholding favors is an operational practice but not how management sees itself.

Mature adults have little interest in favors or favoritism. Work is the grist of their mill, not politics; performance the focus of their efforts, not personalities; real challenge is their drive, not counterfeit activities; contribution their litmus test, not being seen as safe hires; an equitable distribution of company funds on the basis of merit, not a bogus performance appraisal system that hands out merit increases as if giving candy to babies.

Anthony O'Reilly, C.E.O. of H.J. Heinz, received $75,085,000 in 1991, or about $300,000 every working day, $37,500 every working hour. Had he been running something in Japan, he would have been paid about $400,000 and received about as much again in fringe benefits. The next ten American executives received at least $11,000,000, while twelve hundred directors of Wall Street firms earned (on average) $1.1 million in 1991.

To put this issue in perspective, in 1989 the richest 1 percent of American families owned 36.2 percent of the nation's private wealth, 5 percent more than they did six years before. The next 9 percent owned about the same, while the remaining 90 percent together owned a trillion dollars ($1,000,000,000) less than the richest 1 percent.

This extremism has become known as "the 1 percent" and led to the "Occupy Wall Street" movement to demonstrate the other 99 percent was no longer awestruck by the popes of this civil religion.

What this means is that a redistribution of wealth is not possible until collective self-negation is destroyed. Once it is destroyed, tolerance for nonsensical compensation packages to executives will be the first to be challenged. No doubt mature adult workers are threatening to the existing infrastructure and management's status quo:

Mature adults take control. They organize resources and create appropriate strategies. They make decisions without protocol. They avoid politics and are not interested in pumping up their resumes. They do nothing for show. They echo the sentiments of Melville Feynman, "look at what you start with and where you end up."

Diversion tactics will not distract them. Nor do they accept the myth that without executive leadership the company would fold. Mature adult workers know the strength of the company is its people. They have had enough of executive posturing:

- Planning for planning sake;
- Training for training sake,
- Voodoo marketing for the sake of cover up.

Nor do mature adult workers believe in the mantra do everything right the first time. This is impossible and sponsors cheating. They prefer to focus on strategic thinking and doing the right things well, and not worrying about making an impression. Their energy is directed at the 20 percent "right things" that make 80 percent of the difference.

Management, as we know it, has no choice but to let go of workers as reactive dependent children. When capitalism flourished at the turn of the last century, and the capitalists created a management elite to run things, no one expected management to become so entrenched that it could not be controlled. As it exists today, it is the single most intractable obstacle to increased productivity, profit and success.

Workers are an important part of the future. Public and private enterprise cannot solve its economic and cultural challenges without workers and managers taking hold in a new distribution of economic and psychic energy.

Since biblical times, The Critical Parent has ruled. Society remains skewed towards that programming or stasis even in the 21st century. This is apparent when kowtowing engineers seem like babbling children when it comes to protecting their self-interests. They are polite and obedient, compliant if still always complaining, but unable to extricate themselves from dependency or counter dependency status. A cultural cleansing is underway:

Tens of thousands of managers and other white-collar professionals are joining the hundreds of thousands of blue-collar workers who have already lost their jobs. This will accelerate. By the middle of the 21st century, unless or until there is a radical correction, these numbers will soar into the millions.

The Mega Corporation is dead. Rand Corporation's senior social scientist, Francis Fukuyama, writes in *Foreign Affair* (1995):

> *"In sharp contrast to the first half of the twentieth century, when most people believed industrial modernity required gigantic enterprises, the fashion today has swung in the opposite direction, toward the belief that small is beautiful."*

The purpose of large corporations is to exploit economics of scale in sectors that are capital-intensive, involve complex manufacturing processes, or require extensive distribution networks. Small companies, on the other hand, tend to be better at organizing more labor-intensive activities and cluster in sectors demanding flexibility, innovativeness, and speed in decision-making. A global economy and the rapid advance of Third World countries find the Mega Corporation cannot support the white elephant it has created. That said we have yet to fully appreciate how the Internet and this electronic age will change the disposition of work, workers and the workplace.

The Mega Corporation is stumbling blindly, trying to save itself from itself. Still, it moves to its inexorable fate with the conceit General Custer demonstrated at Little Bighorn.

Some may refute this claim pointing out the stunning mergers of such corporations as Walt Disney Enterprises with Capital Cities/ ABC Broadcasting Group, General Electric with NBC, SONY with Columbia Pictures, or the continuing antics of Rupert Murdock, he of the deep financial pockets, or of Ted Turner, he of the cash—poor, but content—rich CNN. Then there are the greedy for partners of Times Warner, Viacom, TCI and MCA.

Just as frightening dinosaurs once dominated the earth, mega corporations are now approach networking overload in a desperate attempt to remain viable.

Mega compensation is the last bastion of an anachronism as the carpetbagger mentality dominates the corporate workplace, which could be a harbinger of its selective demise. However, in the short run, as corporations shrink, top executive compensation goes through the stratosphere. This is possible due to downsizing, and the voodoo creative financing and mythical bookkeeping of such mergers. Meanwhile, lawyers do very well as they collect a fee every step of the way on the buy-outs and takeovers.

Fad, fantasy and fanfare fill the air. Teaming is the newest deception. The idea is an attractive one, that working together produces increased morale and greater productivity. This is not a new idea, but a repackaging of the group norm to offset the threat of individualism.

The infrastructure that supports teams has not changed as the basic working culture has not changed, which means it is an idea superimposed on an anachronistic foundation. Therefore, teaming is a bogus enterprise. Teaming in a Parenting infrastructure represents a collaboration of weakness because it fails to sponsor adult take-charge individualistic behavior. Obviously teaming registers some improvement, but:

- Does it address the core problems?
- Does it encourage adult thinking and adult behavior?
- Is there less preoccupation with moralizing about competition?
- Is the focus more on customer requirements or internal politics, policies and procedures?
- Do workers or do managers call most of the shots?
- Are workers self—starters, organizers and controllers of their activities?
- Are decisions made at the level of consequences?
- Are promotions and incentives built around the team or the individual?
- If the team succeeds or fails is the outcome shared equally among its members?

- Is the atmosphere informal with meetings conducted on an ad hoc rather than formal scheduling basis?

- Is protocol on the basis of the problem and who has the expertise rather than position power, credentials or who has seniority?

- Has executive compensation come into line with that of working professionals? If there is a bonus system, is it the same formula used for team members as executives?

- What financial sign off authority does the team have?

- Is the business growing from internal performance and external acumen?

Increased productivity is not growth and therefore a faulty standard. Production is a function of expanding business, not efficiency. The two, productivity and production are not synonymous. The major fault here is the belief that the great task of management is purely technical; that administrative change, or innovative approaches (like teaming) will resolve entrenched systemic distress in the organization. It will not, and it does not.

Visit the classroom anywhere and you will find teachers differ little with their cousins in industry and commerce, and even less so with the religious. "What would these (workers, children, parishioners, citizens) do without our direction," they cry in unison, "who would protect them from themselves?"

Parenting as a socio-economic construct generates only one thing, dependent children. We have a society of children who propagate a society of spoiled brats as children and the beat goes on!

Young people today, by actual survey, are willing to give up everything, including their freedom, for guaranteed medical benefits, job security and a life without pain. Little interest is shown in learning. There is a plague of classroom cheating. In a recent survey of high school students, 80 percent confessed to cheating. The students surveyed were "A" students, high achievers, members of *"Who's Who Among High School Students"* (1994). These high achievers are into earning grades, not learning the material. They admit to preferring to read summaries rather than assigned books. They are not in charge of their lives; their lives are in charge of them. They are moving to the ethical beat established by societal default. As adults, they will continue to behave as children and they will continue to cheat. The adult euphemisms for this behavior is being enterprising, not cheating.

The child-man has a propensity for pleasure seeking. Pleasure seeking is normal, but pleasure in what? Is it something fleeting or sustaining to life? The classroom is now a place to survive, not a place to revel in the pleasure of learning. There is no pleasure that sustains us that does not have its price in pain. There is no free lunch.

Pain and pleasure are opposite sides of the same coin, as are good and evil, love and hate, success and failure, happiness and sadness. No great ecstasy escapes depression. Great defeats accompany great triumphs. Comedy and tragedy are made of the same substance. The funniest people in public are often much less funny people in private. That is the way it is. The Reality Principle establishes the adult ego state. This state recognizes and deals with things as they are, not as they should be.

The mind of a child sees only one side of the coin and is confused and terrified by the other. The mind of a parent sees both sides and judges one good and the other, bad. The mind of an adult sees both sides, makes no judgment, and deals with the side that turns up as aptly as possible.

As the child reaches the age of an adult but remains averse to embrace adulthood, it copes by denying the other side, and often is blind-sided by that denial. Take the person who drinks "because it is part of my job to be sociable." This may hide the fact that he drinks compulsively to cover his shyness, his insecurity, or his inability to deal with the accompanying stress. One day he finds himself an alcoholic because of this denial.

Mickey Mantle, the baseball great, thought he would die young, and so he lived a hard and fast life. No male in his family lived past the age of 41. Both his father and grandfather died of Hodgkin's disease. Years after passing this milestone, he joked to friends, "If I'd known I was going to live this long, I'd have taken better care of myself." His triumph over a family history of early death does not overshadow the self-destructive lifestyle that required a liver transplant at age, 63, complicated by hepatitis and pancreatic cancer.

The "live hard and die young" attitude is prevalent today among many young people in both affluent and poorer neighborhoods. Their lifestyle reflects a sullen fatalism that manifests itself in drug and alcohol abuse, poor performance in school, crime and no planning for the future. The pseudo-suicidal path "The Mick" took. It cost this ballplayer his life two months after the liver transplant. This hero fell with little impact. Reckless fatalism remains the fuzzy thinking of the adolescent mind reluctant to take life seriously.

Society sponsors this confusion. There is a frantic search for feeling, meaning, purpose, and a reason for living for the future, but without the fundamentals to bring that about, which are self-awareness and self-acceptance. Everyone is the course of a lifetime is likely to experience pain and suffering, struggle and disappointment, embarrassment and humiliation.

The mature adult is able to embrace these watershed moments, because that is precisely what they are, and soar, while the rebel without a cause retreats from such moments flattened by them into remorse and self-pity. He escapes into booze or some other behavior to underscore his discontent.

Disobedience is necessary to be your own best friend, while rebellion is the route to being your own worst enemy. Such a mind has been misdirected from knowing and loving itself by a patriarchal society. Parenting never produced a single adult in history. Adulthood is generated by treating each other not as a child, not as a parent, but as an adult. It is that simple, but simplicity is not the problem. Cultural conditioning and blindness is.

Universal adulthood has never been required before. When society messed up, the consequences were not cosmic. Now they are. It is essential that society have adults to run it, people of maturity who can face and deal with reality sensibly. Since society won't do this on its own, disobedience is required, disobedience that may lead to a radical transformation of the system. We appear to be moving in that direction at some speed.

Corporate Sin

Leaderless Leaders & Dissonant Workers

Corporate Conundrum of Leaderless Leadership

We all feel it. There is something fundamentally wrong in the workplace, wrong between workers and management. Mainly, despite lofty expectations, the new and growing majority class of workers has failed to achieve lift-off. As a whole, professional workers have failed to assert themselves with conviction. Sadly, this enormously capable segment of the workforce seems content to linger in the bosom of comfort; more concerned with protecting positions, than forging careers; more focused on the reaping than the sowing; more fascinated with the present than excited about the future.

James R. Fisher, Jr.

Frustratingly, professionals have shown little inclination to self-manage. They do complain, however, and often with reason, but seldom with any purpose in mind, seldom with conviction. Instead, professionals have shown they highly esteem the traditional hierarchies of corporations, being obsessed with climbing the corporate ladder for the promise of power and prestige.

What they fail to see, however, is that these relics of position power are about to vanish. Traditional management methods and structures, although pervasive, are now obsolete. In the context of a professional workforce, industrial age management techniques are old technology. Unfortunately, when professionals aspire to be managers, they abandon their own province of expertise, and enter a realm where the essential tools and methods of their discipline, their craft, are superfluous and potentially a handicap.

Assigning the Blame

We could throw the blame on managers for creating this problem; management methods specifically, and we would be right; partly right that is. And, most people would not argue. But that would be letting professional workers off the hook. We would be saying, in essence, that professional workers are allowed to forego personal and professional obligations the moment they become employees. That is, each day as he or she walks through the office door to work, miraculously, a professional worker transforms from responsible adult, to obedient child. We cannot, in conscience, condone such a deliberate renunciation of obligation.

Where Professionals Go Wrong

As the management track dissolves into a phantom ladder, managers continue to be paid more than professionals. This unsettles professional workers, who seem not to know what to do about it. So, they wait, indefinitely, to be rescued by a miraculous paradigm shift at no cost to themselves. The result:

Personality becomes a mere selling device. Friendship becomes contacts. The urge to improve deteriorates to mere acquisitiveness. Money becomes the measure of accomplishment. So much intellectual energy is devoted to outward market research that there is none left for inner observation. The language of commerce obliterates the vocabulary of morality.

David Brooks, *On Paradise Drive: How We Live Now (And Always Have) in the Future Tense* (2004)

The function of work has changed, yet the structures around work remain the same. Inevitably, seeds of dissatisfaction are sown, provoking frustration. Like a crippled giant unable to walk, legions of professionals seemingly cannot find their legs. They possess the necessary skills, but not the courage to become self-directed, to stand on their own two feet. They are a product of outmoded human programming and they remain externally directed rather than self-directed, passive rather than engaged. Pathetically, they look to others for solutions they alone possess. The new reality is that professionals must strive to enhance their talents, and in doing so, enrich their places of work.

In tandem with this problem, companies are struggling in a state of insecurity, wandering in a new wilderness. In business, there are no guarantees anymore, if there ever were. Nevertheless, certainties are still sought, while this irrational rhetoric persists, which merely adds to the confusion.

The Delicate Balance of Purposeful Work

We are a corporatist society and, accordingly, the waste of human capital and individual talent, in total, is a grave *corporate sin*. It is the reason for this book. Corporations, on the whole, do not understand how to leverage or develop their people, to maximize human potential and thus maximize their own. What is required is nothing less than a revolution with creative, courageous leaders acting as architects of healthy, supportive work cultures. At the outset, corporate leaders, managers and directors, must:

(1) Reject the notion that there is a single ideal corporate workplace culture. Suspend the outside search for the model workplace culture. It doesn't exist;

2) Devote energy and talents to the business of creating a beneficial work culture;

(3) Accept that the impetus for change invariably comes from the trenches not from mahogany row. People on the front lines have less to lose, and therefore are eager for change;

(4) Realize that people near the top, corporate executives, feel they have everything to lose by surrendering the status quo;

(5) Appreciate that we are in the midst of a quiet revolution in which not only the color of workers' collars is changing, but also the complexion of the individual and collective will;

(6) Understand the key to purposeful performance is a *Culture of Contribution*; adults, not obedient children directing the activities of work; their work;

(7) View the pursuit of the optimal work environment as a work in progress characterized by ongoing change, experimentation and adaptation; not a remedial program or a fixed goal;

345

(8) Admit that management fumbled the ball by vigorously defending the status quo and business as usual practices, disconnecting from reality and respectful engagement.

Although disturbances representing systemic change naturally bubble up from the bottom, the professed architects of change invariably emerge at the top. *Since gridlock and stalemate are the bitter fruit of top-down change initiatives, Corporate Sin, the wasting of professional talent, continues unabated.*

Historical Context

When the twentieth century dawned, ninety percent of workers were employed in agriculture. The working guilds of craftsmen and artisans were still very much in place. Work was primarily in small groups with no hierarchy, position power or remote authority. Hand tools were used to make finished products. The collaborative corporate model was not yet in evidence. Job descriptions and role identity had to await the arrival of social engineers to create the nomenclature.

As the *Industrial Revolution* was about to take off with rail, plane and ship transportation connecting markets near and far, the world was exploding with new inventions among which were the radio, telephone, airplane, motion picture, automobile and electric power plant. Industrial centers were hastily created in urban areas hungry for bodies to run their factories causing a rapid shift of workers from the farm to the city.

In 1914, *World War I* broke out in Europe. This fueled a new iteration of technological development. *The Panama Canal* was finished and opened. Robert Goddard successfully launched a liquid oxygen and gasoline rocket. Weapons of war became more sophisticated with German submarines and Allied attack planes and battleships. Sir Arthur Stanley Eddington founded theoretical astrophysics. David Wark Griffith turned motion pictures from a curiosity into a viable new industry with *"The Birth of a Nation."* Alexander Graham Bell developed instant communications, making the first transcontinental telephone call from New York City to San Francisco to Dr. Thomas A. Watson with the message, "Mr. Watson, are you there?"

Education was changing, too, with the new curriculum ideas of John Dewey. He encouraged students to be independent thinkers and problem solvers rather than rote learners. Albert Einstein published his theory of relativity. Even food preparation was changing. Clarence Birdseye invented the freezing and packaging of fresh foods, and called the products, "Birds Eye." Farming was changing as well with the gasoline-powered tractor replacing the oxen driven plow.

In the wake of the "Great War" meant to end all wars, inconceivable prosperity turned into reckless indulgence against a backdrop of pervasive cynicism. Artists and writers, portraying themselves as members of the *"Lost Generation,"* proclaimed the death of culture while flappers and their beaus embraced the *"Roaring Twenties,"* dancing to the *Charleston* all night to a *Jazz Age* beat. That is, until the party ended in 1929 with the stock market crash on *Wall Street,* reverberating around the world, triggering *The Great Depression.*

Against this backdrop, a new business class was emerging. Small guilds of tool and die makers, fixture manufacturers, machine shop operators, and electrical component makers were merging into larger enterprises. They spawned corporations such as General Motors, Ford Motor, General Electric, Western Electric, Westinghouse, and American Telephone & Telegraph. These companies were financed with common stock issued to private investors who became absentee owners with no direct connection to company operations. Enter the *management class.*

Few former guild operators would emerge in control of operations as Henry Ford and Thomas Edison did. Managers were hired to oversee operations and *Boards of Directors* were created to set company policies. Workers were introduced to a new concept of repetitive "piece work." This would turn into the assembly line of mass production refined by Henry Ford in the manufacture of his Model T and Model A Ford.

Once wealth creators such as John D. Rockefeller, Andrew Carnegie, Henry Ford and Thomas Edison stepped away from daily operations, executives in management roles, often members of the family, replaced them. These executives were employees, the same as all workers, family members or not, but quickly gravitated to the psychological identity of owners. To be fair, this was true to a point as part of executive compensation was in company stock. In contrast to this mentality, although 80 percent of employees are likely to own company stock today, few think of themselves as owners.

With the worldwide *Great Depression of the 1930s*, everyone suffered from the economic collapse, but none more than the poor. They had been forced into cities to work in factories isolating them from the land. Now, they were without jobs, no longer having farm properties to call home. Millions wandered the country with their families looking for work. John Steinbeck captures their plight in *The Grapes of Wrath* (1939), a powerful indictment of capitalistic society highlighting the dangerous chasm between the rich and the poor.

Even employed workers were likely to live in hovels in city slums. Children as young as eight worked alongside adults in factories. Working conditions were horrific. Serious accidents and even deaths on the job were common. Workers had no medical benefits, unemployment compensation, or recourse to sue their employers. They were the working poor, the underclass, and came to see themselves as society's victims.

Labor unions evolved with workers participating in walkouts and manning picket lines. A terrifying period followed. During the 1930s, confrontations between thugs hired to protect company interests clashed with union workers to blacken society. This led to much bloodshed, which is hidden in the footnotes of history books.

The growing interdependence of the nations of the world was apparent as economic chaos swept the globe. The resulting societal turbulence proved fertile soil for capitalistic fascism in Germany and the rise to power of Adolf Hitler in 1933. The 1930s ended with Germany invading Poland unleashing History's greatest conflict, *World War II*. It was not America's war until a surprise attack.

On December 7, 1941, the naval and air forces of the *Empire of Japan* launched a surprise attack on the United States at Pearl Harbor in Honolulu. Four battleships were sunk including the Arizona, four more disabled, eleven other ships were sunk, 188 aircraft were destroyed on the ground, and 2,330 servicemen and women and 100 civilians were killed. A slumbering giant became aroused.

The combination of America's manpower, management acumen, technology, natural resources, economic wealth and common commitment would produce tanks, planes, ships and weapons faster and in greater volume than all the Allies and Axis Powers combined. It was America's and American management's finest hour.

Hence, World War II established the management class, as we know it today. It took pride in the critical role it played in the war. Once victory was declared, management it felt a license to exercise its muscle.

Management gurus surfaced dispensing corporate blueprints that defined the corporation as an entity housed in a central authority dispatching directives to divisions spread across the land to submit to corporate demands to the letter.

This rational ordering model treated workers as things to be managed, not people to be led. This model was exceedingly successful during and immediately following World War II. Management's position power and hierarchical authority now controlled recruiting, hiring, promoting and firing with few if any challenges.

A set of standardized management tools followed, designed to maintain this control and efficiency:

(1) Management by Objectives (MBOs)

(2) Strategic Planning

(3) Performance Appraisal

Management by Objectives (MBOs) was a process of dividing and subdividing objectives among departments and divisions until every operation had a slice of the same objective pie. Collating the results followed, and voila! We met our goal! Not quite.

MBOs worked much better on paper than in purposeful performance. It didn't matter. It was a ritualistic exercise that gave managers a sense of being in control sharing in the big picture. Besides, business was good to great.

Strategic planning, another time-consuming ritualistic practice, often proved wide of the mark, but mid-course corrections was a luxury management took for granted.

Performance Appraisal was the third staple in this toolkit, a process meant to enhance performance through continuous worker development. Unfortunately, it drifted off that track to be a conference on compensation and merit pay.

MBOs, strategic planning and performance appraisals were solid control mechanisms as long as people behaved as manageable profit making centers and not as persons to be led.

Everything changed in 1970. It was then that the *Vietnam War* hit the consciousness of young people, who in mass rejected the war, as well as the *managed society* that sponsored and orchestrated it.

This disenfranchised segment of society stopped that war. Nothing has ever been the same since. Management's tools lost their luster and relevance but continued to be employed as if nothing had changed. Protests of the war had been overt. Protests in the workplace continued to be covert. Unfortunately, this led to the *Corporate Leaderless Leadership Syndrome* because:

> *The structure of work determines the function of work. The function of work establishes the workplace culture. The workplace culture seeds the dominant behavior in the workplace. Management is the architect of this delicate balance.*

So, it falls to executive vision, leadership and competence as to whether an organization is purposeful or flounders. Modern workers have a passion for work when it is designed for success. Conversely, they are apathetic when it is not. Purposeful work is not a matter of serendipity nor does it happen in a vacuum. It is a question of executive purpose and leadership. There is far too much evidence this reality is not perceived.

> *Six Silent Killers: Management's Greatest Challenge* (1998)

Any organization has 15 percent of *hard chargers* and 15 percent of *foot draggers* with the other 70 percent *middle-of-the-road followers* or "safe hirers," doing what told to do but little more.

The corporate toolkit may have worked 50-years ago, but it no longer works today. Incredibly, few dispute this, but still there is little movement to change, or inclination to buck the trend.

Interventions

During the 1942-1945 wartime period, where less than 10 percent of American workers were college trained, and less than 50 percent high school graduates, where workers were dependent on management for direction, where decision making was indisputably an exclusive managerial right, and where position power trumped knowledge power, workers jumped through hoops even if the hoops bordered on the ridiculous.

Workers were treated as children and expected to act like children, as managers were the only grown-ups. Workers shied away from challenging the authority of even of the lowest supervisor, or indeed, of ever going over that supervisor's head to lodge a complaint. The way to stay out of trouble was to keep your head down.

The boom continued through the 1950s and 1960s, then the calamitous 1970s came. The United States was losing the war in *Vietnam*; American markets were declining in electronic parts, computers, glassware, televisions, microwaves, and finally, automobiles. Japan, South Korea and Singapore were making quality products that were cheaper and more reliably than those made in the US.

Panic set in, as corporations looked desperately for answers. They studied South East Asia competition only to discover they were using American quality control technology, expertise that fit nicely into Asian group oriented cultures, but had been essentially ignored by American companies.

A period of schizophrenia followed. First, there was a wild dash to superimpose the Asian success model on Americans without recognizing the clash between group and individualistic norms. Secondly, blue-collar workers dominated the Asian workforce whereas they did not in the American workplace. By 1980, already, American professionals outnumbered four to one every Asian professional.

The 20 percent of American workers who were blue-collar responded to this intervention as they did to *Elton Mayo's intervention in 1927 at the Hawthorne Works at the Western Electric Company in Chicago*. The workers were flattered for the attention. Fast-forward to the 1980s and these workers didn't mind the problem solving being confined to cosmetic change (e.g., workstation design, reducing noise, changing lighting). This was not the case with professionals who saw this attention as "by the numbers" rote exercises.

A stream of interventions followed: *Total Quality Management, Quality Control Circles, Quality of Work, Quality of Work Life, Total Employee Involvement,* and *Participative Empowerment Management*. Essentially, nothing changed.

These were programs. *Quality is a process*, a mindset that depends on the integrity of the supportive structure. This was not developed. So, everything drifted to a freeze framed of 1945 nostalgia, which only compounded worker frustration.

That said, work has changed dramatically from brawn to brainpower, and workers have changed intellectually with this. Now, *knowledge workers* occupy 90 percent of the critical mass in high tech industries. Yet, with the exception of these industries, most workplace cultures remain in cadence with the distant past.

Given this scenario, professionals complain about how things are instead of realizing they have the capacity to change them, still looking to the company for relief of their anxieties as dependent children and still behaving as dissonant workers.

Management is not leadership. It has opted for pyramid climbing by always campaigning for the next position never having time to do the job paid to do. Now that the pyramid is collapsing and with it its position power, the workplace has become dysfunctional to the extreme. Why, then, should there be any surprise when those that climb to the top cannot lead?

Leadership combines vision and values with resolve and power.

Henry Ford and Thomas Edison demonstrated leadership inconspicuously and quietly.

Ford didn't invent the automobile or the assembly line. He used both to create the working middle class that could afford to buy his automobile by using the assembly line to make the vehicles cheaply.

Edison didn't invent the light bulb but created the first practical incandescent light. Whereas others confined their efforts to laboratory applications of light bulbs, he concentrated on its commercial use in homes and businesses by mass-producing long-lasting light bulbs. A system of generating and distributing electricity followed, which led to the establishment of the first electric utility in the world at the Pearl Street Station in New York City.

Ford and Edison were known as something of curmudgeons and hardly charismatic figures. Leadership with them wasn't an act but a behavior.

What is construed as leadership today is a managerial process of refining what is known with little interest in venturing into the unknown. As such, it is obsessed with competition and therefore imitative, which is unimaginative, predictable and myopic. Trapped in this habit of mind, this often leads to corporate fraud and malfeasance with those in leadership roles using their positions unseemly. This is not new. Machiavelli wrote about it 500-years ago.

Who created these sybarites? Society did. Who structured organizations to spawn them? Society did that as well. Who is society? We are. Top executive pay has skyrocketed from 100 to as much as 1,000 times that of the average worker. This happens when leadership fails to rise in Ford-Edison fashion from the bottom of the tree.

This is truly unfortunate as companies as late as 1975 still weren't tarnished by runaway executive compensation, as ethical standards were high and maintained with few exceptions. Everything seemed to unravel with compensation going crazy in the cyberspace era. Lost has been true leadership, as no one seems in charge with everyone's head down in some electronic distraction.

Professional Workers

Information technology has transformed knowledge workers into a breed apart, as work, workers and the workplace have been made redundant with no efficacious model to replace this vestigial organ. Central corporate control with its phalanx of electronic tributaries is also redundant as is its management. This dinosaur is a relic now fit for the museum.

A possible antidote is guided autonomy of workers in a more natural setting where cooperation and trust and connection materialize by sponsors without hidden agendas.

It is passé for workers to be simply polite, obedient, docile, uncritical, submissive, apologetic and dependent, with no voice in the decision-making. No longer can we afford for workers to be switched-off and passive on the job and proactive off the job. No longer can we afford for them to behave as children at work and adults at home.

Executives protest, "Why can't workers behave as adults? We give them everything!" Not true.

Professionals are seldom treated as either adults or equals, when they are often more than equal to those in charge. To add insult to injury, professionals are monitored, tracked, and watched with surveillance cameras and computer monitors, plainly indicating they are not trusted, not respected and not accepted as colleagues. Professionals are deliberately pitted against each other for pay increases and promotion as well as for perks, driving them into passive-resistant behavior.

Managers have created a system that predictably brings out the worst in professionals. While they are the soul of the machine, executives run off with the proceeds, as if that is the most natural thing to do.

It took the first half of the twentieth century for management to flourish and the second half of the century for management, as we know it, to move perilously close to extinction.

Management acumen at mid-century was deemed leadership, when it was clearly a survival strategy. Even at its apogee, it misread workers as being interested only in a paycheck, motivated only by self-interest. Work has always been the workers true interest, professionals in particular. The work is the reward.

James R. Fisher, Jr., Ph.D.

CORPORATE LEADERLESS LEADERS

More books are written on leadership than any other subject with the possible exception of mystery novels and romances. The symbols of leadership are everywhere while leadership is practiced nowhere. It doesn't take a genius to downsize, merge, reengineer, streamline, or whatever else you want to call the mania of the moment.[1]

Obsession is everywhere, but especially in corpocracy. *HYPE* (Harvard, Yale, and Princeton Elitism) is the order of the day, but it has little to do with either leadership or followership. *HYPE* inculcates context into a winning style with a nod to content. *HYPE* sounds good so it must be good! *HYPE* professors write books on the "competitive edge" after the competitive advantage is lost, but no one seems to mind. The university community is as much a good ole boy and good ole girl network as the corporate world.

Where is leadership in the media? Several anxious moments followed once the O.J. Simpson soap opera came to an inconclusive end, only to be refilled with the gonadal ambiguities of a sitting president, which set the stage for the grandest of soap operas, *the Impeachment Trial of the President of the United States*, only to be followed by the ludicrous custody battle over the six-year-old Cuban refugee Elian Gonzalez, and the beat goes on. Media doesn't seem able to get above the trivia story line of a Harlequin Romance.

Where is leadership in the church? There is not a church in existence that is not constantly fighting scandals. The church experiences all of the excesses of the corporation because it is saddled with the same megalomania being more interested in protecting its image than dealing honestly with its mission, more in the practice of deceit than truth-telling.[2]

Where is leadership in science and technology? Does anyone in science wonder about the consequences of its discoveries? And if it does, what do scientists do about it? Do technologists who turn science into "Toys of the Mind" register concern about the impact of these distractions on society? One day in this 21st century 12 billion souls will be walking on this planet. That is nearly double the world's population today. We have long passed the stage of a sane world. What will it be like then? Does anyone know? Does anyone care?

Corporate leaderless leadership is skewed to special interests. Here pragmatics take precedence over passion. Thus we have a dichotomy between those who do with a passionate point of view, and those who are governed by polls. Corporate leaderless leaders are vulnerable because they can be bought or frightened into action. They have no moral center, no moral compass, and thus they cannot find their way. *This is the essence of corporate sin.*

Killing the Spirit

Something is missing in work. Everyone knows it. It isn't the pay. It isn't the working conditions. It isn't even management. Management, as we know it, is quietly disappearing. So what is it? The spirit is being driven out of work. Work is no longer fun. Work is no longer good for the soul, no longer *had "love made visible."* Kahlil Gibran writes:

And if you cannot work with love but only with distaste, it is better that you should leave your work and sit at the gate of the temple and take alms of those who work with joy.[3]

Not only has work become more mechanical, it has become more nonsensical. Most work is the *non-doing doing of non-thing* things, or make-work. Work is no longer mainly by the sweat of the brow, but the merry dance of the *"little gray cells."* To exercise these little gray cells, work needs to be treated as creatively as play. Otherwise, work leads to stress, burnout and ultimately, moral and physical collapse.

Even the ethics of work have changed. What once was considered work – working hard and being loyal like a good little Boy or Girl Scout – is now obsolete. Working smart is the order of the day. Compliance is not enough. The command and control dictates of management are dinosaurs, no longer sufficient to meet the changing and accelerating demands of the market place. In fact, management as practiced gets in the way of productive work.

Even if it takes more brains than brawn, there still is a problem. Work has lost its poetry. Work is like a dime store novel. It has gotten a bad name. Companies are making the workplace more like a playground for kids. Adults have been shrunken to the emotional equivalent of adolescence and fixated there.

As a consequence, workers have gravitated to *learned helplessness* and *irresponsibility.* Most workers are *suspended in terminal adolescence* whining about how bad they have it, when they've never had it so good.[4] They berate their bosses and the company with a *"woe-is-me"* helplessness while they're too self-indulgent to realize they have the power.[5]

There is a good chance you're one of these *dissonant workers*! If so, you're likely to be suffering from one addiction or another to cover your numbing frustration. Meanwhile, the economic landscape is painted with optimism. *"Can't be anything wrong,"* you say, *"look at the GDP? The United States is going great guns, right?"* If this is so, why don't you have a happy face? [6]

Obviously, the present economic climate is impressive. So what? The figures tells another story. Pareto still reigns supreme.[7] It is very likely that 80 percent of your effectiveness comes from 20 percent of your effort. Put another way, 80 percent of the productive work in your workplace is most likely accomplished by 20 percent of the workers. It doesn't stop there.

The way you work, and your attitude towards what you do, spills over into what you are, and how you behave in society. You are not a separate entity from your work. You are your work. Chances are you don't know what to do with yourself when you're not working, so you fill the void with white noise.

Unconscious Incompetence

Do you have too much time on your hands? If so, your life revolves around nonsense that is called "normal," making you an unhappy camper. In a word, you've lost your moral compass and thus your way. When you've lost your place and can't find your space, you are apt to blame it on everything but the cause. It is your cultural conditioning. You have been molded into the helpless toad you are, dependent on forces outside yourself of which you are not aware.

Yet you are your culture, and your culture is serving you poorly.

What is your culture? Culture is everything that bombards your senses from the time you wake until you go to sleep, day in and day out. It's your collective values, or your *collective unconscious.* It dictates the way you behave without thinking.

Things function the way they are structured to perform. It is the structure of work, which defines the function of work, which creates the workplace culture, which in turn dictates behavior – like a house of tumbling cards. Culture is the way you behave on automatic pilot. It is that silent hand that gently pushes you into action or inaction as if you were a robot.

Once, the family provided this cultural mechanism, assisted by the church, but no longer. The family is lost. The church is confused. Together, they are as lost and confused as you are. Consequently, your culture has a migraine and is pushing you right into the arms of dissonance. You don't agree? Good, *go against the grain* and prove me wrong. Don't pull out a book and quote some myths. Don't squirrel yourself away in the library and find comfort with some dead authors. Look to your own life. How much of your history can you see through those rose colored glasses?

Make up your mind to take control. Don't wait for someone else to make it up for you. My hope is that you will prick your ambivalence. My aim is to force you to think. My ambition is for you to take a stand as an owner, not as a renter.

You have been programmed to believe what is best for you. This robs you of your own point of view. Life is short and can be sweet. It is well to remember that. Life gives no guarantees. Few will remember you when you're gone. This is your show, your opportunity to *"work with joy."*

What you think is likely to be second hand information – impressions from a popular press, television programming, your favorite pundit or guru, a charismatic politician, firebrand preacher, or any number of other impressionistic wizards. The irony is that your saviors are as lost as you are. Listen to yourself. Do you sound like them? Have you been too busy to think, wonder, and take control of your life?

Nobody knows for sure. That's the key. Certainty has been lost to doubt. Nothing is taken on face value. The paradox is the more educated you are the less certain. That is why intellectual arrogance is so pervasive. Intellectuals need an audience to reassure themselves. They want to define you without an iota of thought on your part. Knowledge has become the greatest trap of personal enslavement. Don't ever confuse knowledge with wisdom.

Do you challenge this? When someone puts you on the defensive, do you hide behind a knowledge barrier, or do you play a racial or religious card? If you don't, you are the exception.

Insincerity has ruled too long. Deceitful behavior is endemic to everything. My beat is the corporation and therefore my focus. Insincerity extends from corporations to communities, from sacred institutions to profane associations. The *dissonance of workers* and *leaderless leadership* of managers reflect the times. My sense is you have had enough of the gamesmanship. It is time to *go against the grain and take charge of your work and your life.* If you feel the same way, welcome aboard! You are about to ride the Fisher express.

Please leave your toys behind. This is a grown-up call. It is time to take responsibility and deal with it.

References

1. James R. Fisher, Jr., "Leaderless Leadership," *Executive Excellence*, November 1998, p. 5.

2. Garry Wills, *Papal Sin: Structure of Deceit*, Simon & Schuster, 2000.

3. Kahlil Gibran, *The Prophet*, Alford A. Knopf, 1972, p. 28.

4. Dora L. Costa, "Inequality of income no longer means a fair number of households go hungry," *The Tampa Tribune*, July 23, 2000.

5. Visit www.faceintel.com. You will get the impression Intel workers have no power.

6. American psychologist after brooding for years on human anxiety are now into a "happiness revolt": "Think Positive," *The Tampa Tribune*, July 9, 2000.

7. Vilfredo Pareto (1848-1923) gave us the 80/20 rule.

Corporate Leaderless Leadership in a Society Without a Moral Compass

Nothing is more expensive than a start.

Friedrich Nietzsche (1844-1900)
German Philosopher

A new moral principle is emerging which holds that the only authority deserving one's allegiance is that which is freely and knowingly granted by the led to the leader in response to, and in proportion to, the clearly evident servant nature of the leader.

Robert K. Greenleaf, *Servant Leadership: A Journey into the Nature of Legitimate Power and Greatness* (1977)

Soren Kierkegaard, so the story goes, once had a large bundle of laundry, bracing himself to carry it through the streets of Copenhagen, searching desperately for a cleaning establishment. Finally, he saw a shop window displaying several signs, among them was one in bold letters, *"Laundry done here!"* With great relief, he pushed his way through the door and dumped his load on the counter, only to register confusion on the part of the storeowner. "You do do laundry here?" Kierkegaard asked. The store owner shook his head, "No, dear sir, we don't. We make signs."

Leadership, like sex, never goes out of style as a subject of compelling interest. The Internet is replete with websites devoted to the subject. Like the sign maker, the symbols of leadership are everywhere while leadership is practiced nowhere.

People worry if Wall Street can maintain a bull market. Yet while the Dow Jones Industrials soar to new levels, more than 50 percent of the stocks on the big board have been going south for years. Nobody notices because nobody is paying attention. Affluence is the narcotic, which feeds the need for more, while the real world is irrelevant. You would think that money makes the world go round, but it does not. It is *passion* that does.

Obsession with symbols doesn't start or stop with Wall Street. It is everywhere. Between 80 and 90 percent of Ivy League students are alleged to receive "A's" as a matter of routine. They apparently don't even have to show up for class, just be able to pay their fees. This has been going on for years, according to several distinguished journalists and scholars, but is this leadership? [1]

Where's the Leadership?

Where is leadership in the media? Anyone inclined to listen to the pontificating of Ted Koppel, the hand wrenching interviews of Larry King, or the army of lawyers who have become media stars on sixty channels, has wandered into Watergate revisited and Kierkegaard's sign company.

Where is leadership in the church? Religion is no longer the opium of the people. Nor is religion sanctuary for the lost. The American Roman Catholic Church, for example, has had to come up with more than a billion dollars to deal with suits against its priests for pedophilia and sexual abuse. It is mentioned here because Catholicism is the single largest denomination in America. Other churches are forced to deal with similar scandals. Indeed, this institution experiences all the excesses of corporate society because it is laden with the same American disease, *corpocracy*. [2]

If you doubt this, find me a happy church that is declining in membership and revenue. The church, like society in general, is in the throes of entropy, or rotting from within. Napoleon, who knew something about leadership states:

"There are only two forces in the world, the sword and the spirit. In the long run, the sword will always be conquered by the spirit."

If you define spirit as passion, it doesn't take much reflection to see the American spirit is in trouble. We seem to have lost or misplaced our passion.

Where is leadership in science and technology? Does anyone in science wonder about the consequences of their findings? And if they do, what do they do about them? Einstein admitted having misgivings about his role in the creation of nuclear fission. His philosophical reflection states this in graphic terms:

"All our lauded technological progress – our very civilization – is like the ax in the hand of the pathological criminal." [3]

Leaderless leaders have no center. They operate on expediency. My sense is that you may have forgotten what gave you your passion. *Leadership* is related to passion, which is your spiritual drive. Leadership is also about *followership* for it is never better than the quality of its followers. And followers are always waiting for someone else to show them the way, someone else to take control. But leadership doesn't work that way.

You cannot separate the leader from the follower. They are connected. They are part of the same whole. A leader is a complete follower before being a leader. It could be no other way. How else would the leader know where the followers want to go?

We have become obsessed with escape, be that escape in work, beauty, celebrity, power, money, sex, youth, dominance, or whatever. The narcotic of temporary refuge always drives escape. This is the habitat of the confused and the adolescent, of the dreamers afraid to dream, of people afraid to grow up and face their bankrupt lives. Addiction is the norm in a society without a moral compass. We are all addicted to something.

Leadership doesn't start with a significant other. Leadership starts with you. Leadership is your moral compass, which indicates clear readings of north, south, east and west. You know your leadership dial is working by the simple tests in everyday life. It starts with the home, which is a microcosm of the world-at-large. What you learn at home by design or default prepares you for the world. There is no point in blaming your parents for what they lack, or for their wrong mindedness if that be the case. You have a mind, free will, and perceptive tools. You have the equipment to be a learner. With a passion for learning, school is always in and you get a report card every day.

Happiness is not a condition. It is your choice to make. You don't seek happiness. You create happiness out of life. Where you are, what you are is where you expect to be. It is where you chose to be. If you put pleasure before pain, harmony before struggle, comfort before contribution, you won't find yourself too far from where you started. There is no point in blaming your teachers. Education is not a function of teacher excellence, but of the passion and quality of your curiosity. Nor is there any point in blaming your priest, rabbi or minister for what you cannot find in your place of worship. The temple of your essence is in the crucible of your will.

God didn't write the *good books*. Men wrote them. These men may claim the authority of God's inspiration, but they are still men. Obviously, if you are a believer, the words of these books are sacred. This is a personal matter. A leader knows this. A leader also knows that the wages of sin relate heavily to the waste of human potential, and attempts to provide a broad umbrella for both faith and purpose, taking comfort in the words of George Bernard Shaw: *"There is but one religion, only one hundred versions of it."*

The venerated prophets once walked the earth and envisioned the God of their minds. Out of this came Judaism, Christianity, Islam, and many others. Each religion represents a mask of God.[4] Yet religion has often carried out the most inhumane treatment of others in the name of religion. It is not enough to preach brotherly love, but to practice it as well.

If you are truly spiritually alive, you will strive to become whole. Wholeness guides you toward helping others to find their wholeness. You will not be afraid of your human nature, nor of the diverse and conflicting expressions of that nature. Although the mission of religion is to make us whole, it often divides the mind from the body, the spirit from the soul, creating a *divided self,* which is very much on display today.[5] *When you truly accept yourself as you are, and others as you find them, you will be kind and caring.* Others who believe differently than you do will not be threatening. Once you make peace with your own character flaws, you will become more tolerant of the flaws you find in others.

Belief in the truest sense is a stop sign. There is no motivation to go further. You declare, "I have found the answer." Perhaps. But it need not be the answer for others. It reminds me of the fellow who was looking for Tampa. Tired and discouraged, he got to Tallahassee, which was hilly and land locked, and called it "Tampa," even though Tampa was hardly hilly, further south, and on the Gulf of Mexico. Imagine if he had true believers following him. They would have to agree that they had found Tampa, or be ostracized from the group. If this seems ludicrous, this is the problem with religious dogma.

To strengthen your mind, solace is found in lifetime learning, or conversely, little satisfaction is realized in arrogant knowing.[6] You, as a learner, will derive no pleasure in punishing others with your knowledge. Instead, you will encourage them to be learners, too. On the other hand, you will not be intimidated by the pedigree of thinkers, or be duped by people who feign compassion when they clearly have none. You will take their dishonesty and manipulative skills for what they are, psychological enslavement, and have none of it.

When anyone claims authority, be it in religion or science, philosophy or art, or whatever, you will remain cautiously dubious. You will process the information in terms of what you know to be true in your own experience.

With associates, you will listen and learn. Moreover, you will embrace your resistance to criticism. You will not be afraid to surround yourself with persons of differing perspectives and experiences. These people enlarge the parameters of your own views and strengthen your mind.

You will recognize that there is an instinctual monitor within you, which intuitively protects you from acting stupidly. The problem is not that the monitor is faulty. The problem is that most people fail to heed its intuitive instruction. This monitor separates safety from danger, good company from bad, sense from nonsense.

You will always listen to this inner voice and be honest to its commands. You will not be driven by flattery, applause, coin, or compliment. You will be your own person, a comfortable outsider to the frenetic pace of hurrying insiders going nowhere.

You will remain in no relationship or job which does not make you feel fully human. To be fully human, you need respect, appreciation, recognition, and acceptance as the person you are. A set of principles comes before friendship, as there is no possibility of true friendship without an ethical integrity.

What I have just spelled out is derived from my own experience. It may not match yours, but it might prove helpful as you discover the leader in you. Our great leaders used a similar device in their careers. *Thomas Jefferson* composed his own bible to speak to his spirit. *Benjamin Franklin* created his own science as an amateur to feed his curiosity. *Abraham Lincoln* found most of his inspiration in intuitive meditations. A melancholy man, he was often on the brink of despair. The irony is that the *Civil War* gave him the theater to save himself by saving the nation. To his great frustration, however, Lincoln discovered most of his generals lacked leadership, being more concerned with protocol and ceremony than combat engagement. It forced him to take command of the battlefield by resurrecting an over-the-hill *Ulysses S. Grant* with a drinking problem, and the renegade spirit of *William Tecumseh Sherman* to do his bidding. For this audacity, the nation was preserved.

Henry Ford, a bicycle mechanic, celebrated for the invention of the automobile, was responsible for a far more compelling creation. He invented the working middle class by instituting the pay scale of $5 per day when most workers didn't make $5 a week. He was acting out of self-interest as Ford workers could now afford to buy his model A's and T's.

Thomas Edison, remembered best for inventing the electric light bulb, had a more impressive vision. He invented the public utility, which commercialized his invention. Both Ford and Edison were grammar school dropouts but had passion and visionary leadership in their bones.

Leadership involves the capacity to see and the ability to serve. If you are looking for leadership, look for the passionate individual. *Harry S. Truman* and *Ronald Reagan* were not giant intellects. Passion can make a modest intellectual engine soar as if it were brilliant. Eric Hoffer pursues this theme in *The Passionate State of Mind* (1955):

There is in most passions a shrinking away from ourselves. The passionate pursuer has all the earmarks of the fugitive. Passions usually have their roots in that which is blemished, crippled, incomplete and insecure within us. The passionate attitude is less a response to stimuli from without than an emanation of an inner dissatisfaction.[7]

Truman never went to college but he defined the post WWII world. Reagan attended small Eureka College in Illinois, and rose from a minor Hollywood celebrity to see the dismantling of the Cold War and the disintegration of the Soviet Union. What these two presidents had in common was passion for what they believed in and a clear vision of what they were about, uncomplicated by intellectual folderol.

Leadership always starts with the individual and often in the most modest of circumstances. The passionate mind of the 16th century monk, Martin Luther, took on the mighty Papacy of Rome and changed the course of Christianity, and gave birth to capitalism.

These men, and many more like them, created a world consistent with their passions and in many cases, that world eventually became ours.

Leadership is seldom identified with an upper case "L," or with the elite. It is usually the elite, however, who eventually assume the role of leadership. Leadership rises out of passion before that passion has taken a clear form. The Reverend Martin Luther King, Jr. stumbled into leading the *Civil Rights Movement.* He wasn't at all the instigator of this movement, or even the initial spokesman for it. His role evolved haphazardly. Yet he was indeed a leader, and as he acquired his voice, and vision, the tidal wave of history swept him into prominence. Leadership is displayed in the lower case before it becomes the upper case as Eric Hoffer points out:

The exceptional adaptability of the human species is chiefly a peculiarity of its weak. The difficult and risky task of meeting and mastering the new – whether it be the settlement of new lands or the initiation of new ways of life – is not undertaken by the vanguard of a society but by its rear. It is the misfits, failures, fugitives, outcasts and their like who are among the first to grapple with the new. Only when, after a clumsy and wasteful struggle, they have somehow bound and tamed the unknown do their betters move in and take charge. The plunge into the new is often an escape from a familiar pattern that is untenable and unpleasant. It is the weak who strain their ears for a new word, clutch at every promise and rally around a savior and a redeemer. The role the unfit play in human affairs should make us pause whenever we are prompted to see man as a mere animal and not a being of an order apart.[8]

Leadership embodies the management of change. When momentum drives us forward without leadership, chaos is our destiny. How else can we explain the pollution of our minds, bodies, and spirits? The air is not fit to breathe, the water to drink, the food to eat, and now our cars aren't safe to drive. The land we cultivate is poisoned with the ignorance of our soul.

Leadership comes from within, not from without, from individuals, not from groups. Leadership is seldom popular when it first challenges the familiar. Leadership invokes change and threatens the comfortable and the powerful. Leadership always requires a radical change in mentality from the certain to the uncertain; a structural change in the way the world is viewed and understood. Leadership requires the individual *go against the grain,* knowing full well that for it he might invite the enmity of his fellow man.

References

1. *Thomas Sewell, Inside American Education: The Decline, The Deception, The Dogma, Free Press, 1993.*
2. *Corpocracy: The Corporate American Disease.* See page 38 of this volume.
3. *Jerry Mayer & John P. Holms, Bite-Size Einstein, St. Martin Press, 1996, p. 35*
4. *Robert A. Segal, Joseph Campbell, "The Mask of God," A Meridian Book, 1997, pp. 72-152.*
5. *C. G. Jung, The Undiscovered Self, Mentor Book, 1958.*
6. *Charles D. Hayes, Self-University: The Price of Tuition is the Desire to Learn. Your Degree Is A Better Life, Autodidactic Press, 1992.*
7. *Eric Hoffer, A Passionate State of Mind, Perennial Books, 1955, p. 7.*

8.   Ibid. p. 51.

Culture Against the Worker

The average American has learned to put in place of his inner self a high and rising standard of living, because technological drivenness can survive as a cultural configuration only if the drive toward a higher standard of living becomes internalized; only if it becomes a moral law, a kind of conscience.

Jules Henry, *Culture Against Man* (1963)
American Sociologist

P. T. Barnum, the American showman, was convinced *"a fool is born every minute."* In modern parlance the same appears to hold true every nanosecond. You could make allowances for this if it were primarily out of ignorance. It is harder to justify when the best brains on the planet are caught in praise of folly. Still, there are distinguished voices that are meant to warn us.

Dr. William Joy, chief scientist of *Sun Microsystems*, writes in *Wired* magazine (April 2000) that the future doesn't need us anymore. He envisions a future where smart machines are capable of replicating themselves, and populating the world as science fiction becomes reality. Interviewed on PBS's *The Newshour with Jim Lehrer,* he confessed that the technology he helped to develop could eventually enslave its creators.[1] Watching Dr. Joy in all his seriousness, I thought of a world infested with Mary Shelley's *Frankenstein monsters.*[2] Chilling, to be sure. Farfetched? As this is being written, Drs. Jordan Pollack and Hod Lipson of *Brandeis University* have just announced that they have created the *First robot* that reproduces itself, almost entirely without human help or expertise.[3]

No one has any idea where technology will lead, not even the most astute scientists. Technology tampers with the human mind and creates confusion with the human heart. More disturbing still, technology contaminates the innocence of the human soul. While you delight in your computers, cell phones, hand held digital devices and laptops, oblivious to the people around you; your soul shrinks with a certain agoraphobia. You are in a cage of your own making.

367

People don't talk to each other anymore. They don't look at each other. Their cell phones are sealed to their ears as if part of their anatomy. Standing in a checkout line at the supermarket, driving along the Interstate, walking through the mall, sitting quietly in the library, theater, church, or classroom, cell phones go off like nervous coughs to knowing stares. Alpha, Beta, and Gamma rays bombard your sensibilities from cell phones, computer monitors, and television screens to laptops, from hand held digital devices to beepers, from ghetto blasters to surveillance cameras, from electronic eyes in retail outlets to x-ray machines at airports. No one knows what harm these technological wonders do to the *little gray cells* in our brains, or to the complex genetic biochemistry of our bodies.

We go with the flow just as people did a half century ago when told that nuclear bomb testing was safe. You weren't alive then? Well, I was. I lost my father to the then rare bone disease called *multiple myeloma*. He died three days after his 50th birthday. It was not a pretty death. He wasted away barely weighing fifty pounds. I wondered then if it had anything to do with nuclear testing. More people are dying of this disease today for which there is no cure. Sam Walton of Wal-Mart fame died of multiple myeloma. His billions couldn't save him.

Our inclination may be to make sport of this. That is what we do in our culture when something disagreeable assails our senses. It is much easier to do that than to take action. That is why the *Dilbert* cartoon is so popular. *Dilbert's* invectives count on our passivity and our inclination to make sport of our fears. *Dilbert* laughs at the stupidity of management, the duplicity of corporate life without our having to do anything about it, but laugh with him. We can remain in the innocence of denial, seeing others caught in this web of chicanery, but of course, not ourselves. We like to think we have a sense of humor, when what we have is a perverse sense of dread. Anything that will distract us from this awareness is welcomed relief. *Dilbert* fits the bill.

Recently, a woman standing beside me in the crowded cable car at *Tampa International Airport*, which connects passengers to the main terminal, concludes her conversation on her cell phone.

"Isn't that crazy?" she says with a smile. I have no idea what she is talking about. She points to her cell phone.

"Nobody's home. Just had a conversation with myself." I still look puzzled. "With my message machine," she laughs, "until the machine cut me off." *Not crazy, lady, more like ridiculous.*

"Have you ever wondered what that thing might do to your brain?" I asked with a touch of sarcasm. Obviously, I don't have a cell phone. Although I can see the advantage to having one for an emergency. Otherwise, I find them a nuisance. She is in the process of dialing another number when she is suddenly aware that I have been talking.

"What?" she says with a startled look.

"Damage," I point to my head. "Ever wonder what it might do to your brain?"

We are now at the main terminal, the doors open, and people push as if running from a fire. She steps off with an accusative look, hands on hips.

"What about my brain?"

"I just wondered what damage that thing might do to it. That's all."

"You're kidding, right?"

"No, I'm not."

"Well, mister, the FDA wouldn't allow cell phones to be used if they were harmful. Of course," she added sarcastically, "I'm sure you know that."

"That's what they said 50 years ago about nuclear testing."

"Well, I wasn't around then, was I? So I'll have to take your word for it." With that she was gone, again talking animatedly on her cell phone as she escalates down to baggage. The irony is now I cannot live without my iPhone.

The Blurring of the Real

Workers as consumers are oblivious to safety. It is not their responsibility. As they accept there is God in heaven, they accept government has their best interests at heart. It is even most surreal. Workers as consumers forget that government is a human institution and therefore as flawed as they are. It isn't so much that workers are trusting of government as they are preoccupied with toys of distraction, oblivious to the government's whirling desultory impact on their lives.

Listening to this woman put me in mind of a television production. I fully expected someone to yell, "Cut, print and wrap!" It was so much like a spoof of reality.

369

Great writers of the 20th century tried hard to get our attention to the absurdity of our ways. Read *Nausea* (1938) by Jean Paul Sartre, *The Plague* (1947) by Albert Camus, and *Waiting for Godot* (1952) by Samuel Beckett. These writers, all Nobel Prize Laureates, focus on the irrationality of our times.[4] Most remarkable, although action is negligible, and development of character of only passing concern, these works express the lingering anxieties that still haunt most workers as they move into the 21st century.

Antonine Roquentin in *Nausea* lives in an increasingly imaginary world feeling a terrible loneliness. He begins to have a series of disturbing psychological experiences, which he terms "nausea" (Sartre's term for the *absurd*). He feels there is something new about commonplace articles; even his hands seem to take on new aspects, to have an existence of their own. His super self-consciousness separates him further and further from the reality of his experience.

Dr. Bernard Rieux, a young physician in *The Plague,* searches for meaning while dealing with a frightful plague, and finds an answer to "Why are we here?" Fighting the plague, he learns that human contact is important for everyone. For himself, he is content to help man fight against disease and pain. He welcomes the plague as the instrument to give meaning to his otherwise meaningless life. Without the plague, he feels he would be like everyone else, lost, confused and self-pitying.

Vladimir and Estragon, two tramps in *Waiting for Godot,* are continually aware of pain, hunger, and cold, yet joke about these things, while doing nothing about them. It never occurs to them that some action might alleviate their deprivation. They vacillate between hope and despair. They are obsessed by uncertainty. Their lives, and Beckett infers all modern life, are caught between blind persistence and seeming hopelessness. And so the two tramps refuse to be destroyed while they wait for *godot* (God?) to deliver them from their condition.

Close to death, Beckett was asked in 1989 if he had found anything worthwhile on his journey through life. He answered, "Precious little. And for bad measure, I watched both my parents die." [5] One hears in this authentic note the deep melancholy that afflicted Beckett from the beginning to the end. He refused to be a hypocrite. Like Sartre and Camus, he unflinchingly addressed the world's anguished soul and fleeting innocence. While others calibrated the wondrous achievements of the 20th century, Beckett could see only irrevocable loss with modern man moving away from beauty and light and into his tragic cage:

There then all this time where never till then and so far as he could see in every direction when he raised his head and opened his eyes no danger or hope as the case might be of his ever getting out of it.

Was he then now to press on regardless now in one direction and now in another or on the other hand stir no more as the case might be that is as that missing word might be which if to warn such as sad or bad for example then of course in spite of all the one and if the reverse then of course the other that is stir no more.

Such and much more such the hubbub in his mind so-called till nothing left from deep within but only ever fainter oh to end. No matter how no matter where. Time and grief and self so-called. Oh all to end.[6]

Beckett is not interested in absurdity for absurdity's sake, but means to convey the meaninglessness of our ways, how the absurd has become the norm, and how the absurd manages to sound as if truth personified.

Alexis de Tocqueville, more than 150 years ago, considered Americans empty-headed, in mortal dread of being different than their neighbors, and lopsidedly preoccupied with making money and obtaining material enjoyments.[7] He found us sunk in personal pleasures and so frightened of having a deviant opinion that he wrote:

When I survey this countless multitude of being, shaped in each other's likenesses, among whom nothing rises and nothing falls, the sight of such universal uniformity saddens and chills me, and I am tempted to regret that form of (aristocratic) society, which has ceased to be.[8]

Indeed, today absurdity sounds like virtue, a monument to logic. Even using a cellular phone like a *"Toy of the Mind"* is normal behavior, a triumph of technology. Meanwhile, entire communities in America have become sinkholes of despair, rife with crime, violence, illegitimacy, illiteracy, poverty, homelessness, disease and chaos. Ambushed by free-floating anxiety, workers everywhere have lost touch with touch.

Just at that moment along comes television's *"Who wants to be a millionaire?"* and hits a cultural nerve, and not just for the free-lunch crowd. If this were not absurd enough, professional wrestler, Jesse Ventura, the loud, swaggering elected governor of the *State of Minnesota* becomes a national figure, while he and many of his wrestling mates produce best-selling *non-book books*. Not to be outdone, Regis Philbin, the monochromatically dressed host of the millionaire game show, merchandises his own apparel with Philliops-Van Heusen shirts and ties. Projected 2000-year sales: $50 million.

American culture rotates on an absurd axis of constant discovery and exploitation of hidden cravings. There is no middle ground between the needs of the caveman and the cravings of the spaceman. It reminds me of the zoo. The animals are entertainers. They are the show and we are the audience. Jesse understands this. So does Regis. They perform like clever monkeys in a cage, and we make them rich celebrities for their clever swinging.

Meanwhile, self-denial seems nowhere in sight as heaven has been detached from society, and we have been detached from ourselves. Not only are we spectators to Jesse and Regis, but we are uninvolved in work and uninvolved with others. We use the coffee break at work to cope with this hopelessness and treat it as our on-the-job therapy. We use the beer after work as psychotherapy for coping with pending emotional collisions at home. Is it any wonder that the breathtaking success of American capitalism leaves many of us anxious, hostile, confused, and even violent?

Fear, the Condiment of Choice

American workers have become clowns in everyday dress. Hateful of people of difference, of looking for reasons outside themselves for working a job where they are not appreciated, losing a job when they have done nothing wrong, having a failed relationship, and not being what they think they should be, they strike blindly at shadows as did Beckett's two tramps. They mirror their enemies. They gossip. They blackball. They retreat into their cave of despair. They give vent to homophobia, belligerence, racism, and fear. They become their own worst enemy.

The American culture is a driven culture. The driver is fear. Take away fear of competition, fear of failure, fear of lost markets, fear of humiliation, fear of becoming old, fear of becoming obsolete, fear of not being needed, and most of us would likely collapse like a jelly fish. Fear is our skeletal system. It holds us upright. Fear in many ways is America's most important product.

Fear as a product has given media a new role. When workers look for answers to their plight outside themselves by comparing and competing, imitating and envying, media are there as obliging definers. Media give workers what they want and expect. Media tighten the worker's psychological blindfold by reinforcing all his hopes and despairs. Media has become a packager of insulating biases selling this packaging like cold cuts at the supermarket. And media know we are far more interested in how the cold cuts taste than how they are prepared.

Included in media's condiments are books, articles, interviews, and assessments that keep reinforcing in our minds that as a workers we are strong, fearless, purposeful, alert, skillful, responsible, industrious, and the envy of the world.[9] What media neglect is that as workers we are as likely to be weak, fearful, ambivalent, lethargic, inept, irresponsible, indolent, and needy waiting for *godot*.

Obviously, fear is necessary for survival. But when it pervades to excess, it loses its function and magnifies our self-ignorance. We see this in our attitude toward diversity, differences, and change. We operate robotically, and become fixated in indifference. If there is a philosophical system at work in the 21st century, it is not existentialism. It is advertisement.

Advertisement deliberately creates needs to permit our culture to continue. We demonstrate our patriotism by buying to excess with unhinged glee. The tension of uncertainty that boom may become bust has little to do with need but everything to do with want. Our anxieties float on a sea of want.

American workers don't like looking in the mirror. But if they do, they see only a reflection of their outer shell – the inner self, the engine of the soul, which lies beyond the depths of the mirror.

Workers and a Reality Check

Workers believe in the American dream. They believe America is the land of unlimited opportunity even as they see it shrinking. When failures occur, as they increasingly do, blame is the game. Workers' failures must be a lack of preparation, skill, and initiative, along with a pinch of greed and indifference. Those are standard failures. But at a more subtle level, something else pops up. Failure plays now against the inept elements of a schizophrenic society that judges disturbances as simply distortions in a sane system. No one wants to suggest that the American soul has been damaged by a sick society. So it is virtually impossible to discover what is killing the spirit of American workers.

We like to think if you fix the distortions – drug addiction, obesity, pornography, illiteracy, illegitimacy, violence – everything will fall into place. Politicians pull these nonsense strings and nothing changes. Corporate executives take a cue from them and launch large interventions into quality, empowerment, and streamlining and nothing changes. Panic drives them to downsizing or to a mania for mergers. No one talks about limits, of a shrinking economic pie, or of a spiritual collapse. Hope rides on the wings of despair.

Workers have allowed themselves to be persuaded by the *godot* of management (leaderless leadership) that their destiny is secure, that the world is being remade into America's image and likeness and that the world can't wait to become a McDonald's franchise. Workers, without reflection, embrace this warped vision of a "Golden Age" yet to come. They tie their hopes to the *godot* of science, which promises them cures for their vices without the necessity of any behavioral change. Optimism governs the soul of workers, but she never governs wisely.

Workers see economic parity as their birthright. As such, they see themselves rightly sharing in an ever-expanding economic pie. They seldom stop to ponder this absurdity. It never happened before and is unlikely to happen in the future. The distribution of wealth in America has not changed dramatically since the 18th century. During the *American Revolution*, 40 percent of the wealth was controlled by 10 percent of the population. On the eve of the *Civil War*, 70 percent of America's resources were still controlled by 10 percent of its citizens. Industrialization had an even more devastating impact. In the first decade of the 20th century, 60 percent of this nation's wealth was controlled by 2 percent of the people, while the bottom 65 percent controlled but 5 percent of the nation's wealth. Since *World War II*, the top 20 percent has controlled 40 percent, while the bottom 40 percent has controlled less than 6 percent. Although American workers benefited with an unprecedented share of the economic pie immediately following *World War II*, between 1968 and 1981, real wages for the average American worker actually declined 20 percent. The cushion of comfort provided by post *WWII* demands around the world for American products has all but disappeared. America's best customers have become its greatest competitors. For example, in 1947, American workers produced 60 percent of the world's industrial goods. Today that figure is closer to 30 percent. Manufactured goods such as automobiles, agricultural machinery, and telecommunication equipment have declined as much as 30 to 50 percent. There is little promise that the *Information Highway* and the *Internet* are America's exclusive terrain, nor that America will miraculously recapture its lost momentum.[10]

Workers insist in the belief that they live in a classless society. Class has always separated Americans from each other, socially, politically, economically, culturally, and professionally. It is one of the myths that we cherish. Decreasing economic mobility, however, is increasingly emphasizing class lines, primarily as it relates to education. In the face of this, most workers are tired of social climbing, tired of explaining their individual failure, and even more tired of their *leaderless leadership* which incessantly explains what it cannot do rather than what it can and will do. Tired as they are they still cower from reality, seeking refuge under the canopy of denial.

Workers cannot accept that there is a limit to an economic boom; that everything in life oscillates between extremes. Meanwhile, they allow politicians to exploit their ambivalence. Both political parties assure American workers that the boom is not over. The rhetoric is the same. The assumptions are identical. Workers might as well be blindfolded to pin their vote on the tail of the donkey or the elephant.[11]

The *common good*, the radical idea upon which this *Republic* was founded, is missing, replaced in both parties by majority interest. Polling controls the mind of government, and by extension, the apathy of the governed. Workers fail to see how their disinterest in the political process first fosters then breeds *leaderless leadership,* placing their social and economic wellbeing in permanent jeopardy. Badly misled by corporate bosses as well as political leaders, workers have been conditioned to see the whole in terms of the part becoming mesmerized by special needs: e.g., high school graduates who cannot read (education); joblessness that plagues urban ghettos (poverty); 50 million Americans are without medical insurance (health care). These are legitimate concerns, but the solution is not to throw money at them and hope it sticks. It never does. You don't feed fish to the hungry. You show them how to fish. Workers forget that their success is because they pulled themselves up by the bootstraps and made something of their lives.

Maniacal ethnocentrism is a common American addiction. Despite little evidence to support it, American workers revel in the conviction that they are the greatest. This addiction brings out the *Renaissance man* in a few, but the fascist out in the many. American workers are primed for fascism, for a quick solution to crime, violence, economic turmoil, and social unrest, which excludes their involvement.[12] Caught between two colossi, one of which has no heart and the other no head, they are primed for sacrificing their freedom for the promise of peace. Already, their bodies are sustained on tasteless food, their minds freeze framed before television screens or computer monitors, while they listen to white noise masquerading as music as they robotically talk about automobiles, their health, the weather, sex, or what they would like to do if they could afford it.

Workers favor computers in the classroom, the earlier the better. First graders have computers; many even have electronic calculators. Yet, 8, 10, or 12 years later, these same students cannot do their multiplication tables, long or short division, fractions, and cannot balance a check book. They don't know the parts of speech, and cannot diagram a simple sentence. They don't know a gerund from a participle, and cannot spell 200 common words, while reading at what is designated as the dull normal level.

This is painfully illustrated every year when more than a million skilled workers are imported to work in industry and commerce because American students-as-workers are ill prepared. What is even more amazing is that these imported students, with English their second or third language, are often more expressive and have a better command of their adopted language than their American co-workers.

Technologists promised to make America a more educated society, a society that would lead to greater harmony. The exact opposite seems to be the case, as technology becomes increasingly user friendly. Futurists Arthur C. Clarke, James Martin, and Loy Singleton assure us that hand-held computer tutors will revolutionize education worldwide. It sounds wonderful. But learning is more a social than a mechanistic function. Even psychologist Carl Rogers is caught up in this technological blitz. He sees high-tech communications as the key to his person-centered education, and the promise of a new dawn of enlightenment. Rogers predicts global competition will be replaced by cooperation, accompanied by respect for others and mutual helpfulness. Again it sounds wonderful. History suggests otherwise.

Human history throughout its recorded volumes has changed little. Man is inclined to hoard, bully, to exploit weaknesses, frustrate purpose, divide and conquer. Tons of food have been sent to the starving poor in Somalia and Ethiopia, never to reach the intended, because of these human tendencies.

These prominent voices seem plagued with the same feeble myths workers crave to believe. Mythology as hope does not beget courage or compassion. The suggestion that the distribution of sophisticated technology and the manifestation of altered states of awareness is a linear connection is not realistic. Indeed, there is no substitute for love, but love is not imprinted on wire circuit memory boards.

Workers often confuse rights with *privileges.* Nobody owes anyone anything including a living. Nor, as author Charles D. Hayes insists, an education is not something you get but something you take.[13] Preparation for life is your business, nobody else's. And therefore, it is your responsibility. A public school education is one of the great privileges of American citizenship. This remarkable privilege gives an ordinary person a chance at being someone doing something. No one came from lower down in the food chain than I did. But thanks to my mother, who pounded into me the privilege of being educated "free," I have been able to hold my own with those born to wealth, and yes, privilege. As I have said often, everyone gets a report card every day of his or her life and therefore school is never out. Being in a learning mode gives you, whatever your circumstances, an opportunity to expand your consciousness and tap your inherent potential.

Public school education is a 20th century American phenomenon and an astonishing privilege of modern society. Education has little to do with rights. Treated as a right, education is sure to be abused. Students take the idiotic stance that they are doing society a favor by conscientiously attending classes and becoming educated. So they fight the idea of being educated. What we obtain too cheaply we esteem too lightly.

When students complete twelve years of public education, at virtually no cost to them, and are unable to read or comprehend these words here, they have failed, and have enslaved themselves to a life sentence of victimization. They can blame their failure on "the system," on their ethnicity, religion, family, or poverty, but the fact remains students are ultimately responsible for what they become.

Professor John H. McWhorter makes this clear in his new book, *Losing the Race: Self-Sabotage in Black America (2000)*. Although initially a supporter of affirmative action, Professor McWhorter now regards it as having outlived its usefulness and has become counterproductive.[14] He claims the main harm it has done to blacks is to reduce the incentive to do their best.

Often malcontents have told me along my life's journey that they have had few *"great"* teachers, implying that being poor students *"was not their fault."* I made many of my mediocre teachers better, and some even great. I did this by bringing out their passion and spiritual commitment to learning. Amazingly, I can remember the names of every teacher from kindergarten through high school, if not through college and graduate school. I believe this to be so because the foundation of learning is during our most impressionable years. This is when we are most ready to learn. Because school was always a privilege, I was able to take an ordinary intellect and breathe life into it. I never got bogged down with the nature-nurture debate.

Learning for me didn't stop there. I often found myself the teacher to other students. At lunchtime in high school, I would help others with word problems in algebra and geometry, or conceptual ideas in English literature, history and science. Being a teacher of others made me a better student. It did this by clarifying my own mind of what I had learned.

More than fifty years ago I was in the sixth grade at St. Patrick's Catholic Elementary in Clinton, Iowa. As I was writing this, I got a letter from my teacher, Sister Pauline Logsdon, who is still teaching. I share this with you because it illustrates school is never out for work that is love made visible:

June 11, 2000

Dear Jim,

*As a lad you were very talented, determined and above all – loving. I remember how you walked home with your mother arms about each other. We **noticed** that in an era when boys didn't dare show much affection publicly. I was so proud of you and still am with ever more reason.*

I, too, picked up several Master's and did my doctorate in gifted education. All my life I thought bright children had to be quiet and let others recite, although they needed as much love and attention as any child. I am delighted with this work.

If we teachers could only hear what miracles our students perform but we seldom do. You are a very special case in many ways.

Love,

Sister Pauline

Sister Pauline was a new nun when I had her in the sixth grade with a cherubic smile and an ego-free innocence in her eyes. She is still teaching, still growing, still working, and it has little to do with recognition or reward. It is simply a love affair with learning. And learning is the life of the mind for the worker.

References

1. *The Newshour with Jim Lehrer: an interview with Dr. William Joy, PBS May 10, 2000.*
2. *Reference to Mary Shelley's gothic novel Frankenstein (1831).*
3. *Kenneth Chang (The New York Times), "Scientists create I Robot that reproduces," The Tampa Tribune, August 31, 2000.*
4. *John Paul Sartre declined the Nobel Prize for Literature, 1964.*

5. John Banville, "The Painful Comedy of Samuel Beckett," The New York Review, November 14, 1996, p. 24.

6. Ibid. p. 29.

7. Jules Henry, Culture Against Man, Vintage Books, 1963, p. 5.

8. Alexis de Tocqueville, Democracy in America (Vol. 2), 1901, p. 825.

9. A worker once challenged me on my assumptions, waving a copy of Juliet B. Schor's The Overworked American, Basic Books, 1991.

10. Jeffrey Madrick, The End of Affluence: The Causes and Consequences of America's Economic Dilemma, Random House; also Madrick's "The Cost of Living: A New Myth," New York Review, March 6, 1997, pp. 19-24; "In the Shadow of Prosperity," New York Review, September 21, 1995, pp. 13-17.

11. Lewis H. Lapham, Imperial Masquerade, Grove Weidenfeld, 1990.

12. To keep these terms straight, a capitalist believes the means of production should be privately owned; a socialist believes the government should own the means of production; and a fascist believes the government should control the means of production.

13. Charles D. Hayes, Proving You're Qualified: Strategies for Competent People without College Degrees, Autodidactic Press, 1995.

14. John H. McWhorter, Losing the Race: Self-Sabotage in Black America, Free Press, 2000. Professor McWhorter admits he never went "all out" to do his best in high school because he knew it wouldn't be necessary in order to win admission to a first rate school.

Corporate Conundrum of Dissonant Followership

The road to leadership is through following. The true leader then is the compleate follower with the vision to take followers where they want to go.

James Macgregor Burns, *Leadership* (1978)

Workers Suspended in Terminal Adolescence

That sir which serves and seeks for gain,

And follows but for form,

Will pack when it begins to rain,

And leave thee in the storm.

William Shakespeare, *King Lear*

American workers are addicted to a lingering dependence. But are they to blame? Could it be their programming, their culture? Can a capitalistic system tolerate, indeed, sustain its advantage with mature workers, who are self-determined, self-directed, self-reliant, self-motivated, and self-pleasing? Or are such qualities as immaturity, self-indulgence, self-denial, and feigned innocence essential to keep the American work force edgy? It is doubtful that a liberal democracy can produce a stable labor force, indeed, that it would want to. The wonder is why we try.

American workers take pride in their lack of sophistication. Consequently, many are not far removed from being intellectual barbarians who breed banality. Yet, American workers as a group drink and smoke far less than either Europeans or Orientals. On the other hand, they eat more fast foods than both of them combined. Ergo, it is no accident that at least 50 percent of American workers are overweight and under-exercised. Nor is it a stretch to conclude that the average American worker is a self-indulgent child who refuses to grow up. Obsessed with age and the need to be "cool," workers imitate their kids in their juvenility. This radicalism extends to tattooing and piercing their bodies to be in sync with this collective carnage, and following their kids' fashion trends, while at the same time, spending tons on ointments to deny the ravages of progressive aging. This once was the domain of the idle rich. Now it is the pleasure mode of idle minds across the socio-economic sphere.

The problem is that American workers can no longer play dumb and wax innocent. They can't claim ignorance and blame society for their cultural malaise. They are not only products of this sick society, but its collective architects. Minds that can make technology soar are not minds without the capacity for self-mastery. The plunge into chaos has been a gratuitous retreat into self-indulgence. Instead of changing their ways and taking matters into their own hands, American workers have allowed themselves to be treated as interchangeable parts in a giant machine (the American economy), gravitating to the pathetic role of victims of circumstances.

Massive redundancy exercises, plant closings, and plant relocations, reengineering, streamlining, and whatever other euphemistic terminology is invented to explain corpocracy's impulsive behavior, these corporate actions fail to improve workers' attentiveness to their vulnerability. American workers have all the power and they act as if they have none. They could stop this manic drift with a simple statement, *"Hell, no, I won't go!"* Even in the year 2000, people still count for more than robots, that is, if they can see themselves as counting more.

American workers are so programmed to a machine mentality that machines control them, and management acts precisely like a machine of no living parts. The ambience of their world not only applies in the material sense, but in the spiritual sense as well. Philosophy, art, music, literature, and science are so mechanistic today as to require little wondering. Effort, attachment and opinion turn on mechanistic reflection. Even the idea of religious redemption is a hiccup phenomenon, a 2000-year iteration that just might not be what the doctor ordered.[1]

Souls of stainless steel may not easily corrode but they provide little solace to pristine innocence. Novelist Sinclair Lewis addressed oppressive standardization in *Main Street* (1920). He envisioned intellectual complacency killing the moral fiber of the community, and by extension its spirit:

It is contentment. . . the contentment of the quiet dead. . . it is slavery self-sought and self-defeated. It is dullness made God . . . . A savorless people, gulping tasteless food, and sitting afterward, coatless and thoughtless, listening to mechanical music, saying mechanical things about the excellence of Ford automobiles, and viewing themselves as the greatest race in the world.[2]

American workers have been co-conspirators in their own delusion. They have allowed themselves to believe that they work principally for money, that money is the spiritual coin upon which their universe rotates. Not true says Robert E. Lane professor emeritus at Yale University in *The Loss of Happiness in Market Democracies* (2000). He finds the correlation between income and the level of happiness is close to zero in advanced societies. It is even sometimes a negative (the richer, the unhappier). With a correlation between level of income and happiness between 0.12 and 0.18, the United States is near the bottom of the list of materialist nations. To most Americans, factors other than income are overwhelmingly more important in explaining happiness. Moreover, as American workers' material prosperity increases, the gap between income and satisfaction with their lives seems to widen. Predictably, money has its most positive effect on the poor, but once a person has achieved a minimal standard of living, the level of income has almost nothing to do with happiness.[3]

For the majority, spirituality and close relationships, rather than money, are the keys to happiness. Indeed, Lane concludes one stands a better chance of achieving a satisfactory life by spiritual development and spending time with family and friends than by striving for higher income. He points out that in the United States, as people get richer, the probability of divorce increases dramatically.

Lane quotes a cross-national study of mental depression which found that in advanced societies, such as the United States, there is a rising tide of major depression, an illness most marked among those under 40. Moreover, he observes teenage suicides have increased in recent decades, especially in the United States, reinforcing the idea that companionship and spiritual development are part of our biological endowment. *We need each other more than we need money.* By ignoring our biological and spiritual programmed needs, and substituting artificial material needs, we risk physical and mental distress.

Yet the primacy of most American workers is to fulfill economic needs. This justifies their selling of themselves and their integrity to the highest bidder. The twisted ethics of this apparently never crosses their minds. Instead, they get on the mindless treadmill of consuming more than they can afford and then doing the nervous dance to their creditors to the beat of *"the check is in the mail."*

But, alas, economics is not enough. Being well heeled financially does not make for happy campers. Nor does it lead to a state of physical, moral, and spiritual fulfillment. Quite the contrary. It leads instead to a state of suspended juvenility, to whining about unhappy troubles, which too often translates into panic.

Many American workers are in *"the Prison of Panic called NOW!"* – See it now, have it now, feel it now, be it now! Most of our notions of happiness arise from the culture in which we grew up, and thus our discontent. Modern society with its sound bites, media blitzes and endless advertisements, bombards us constantly with manipulative subliminal ads instilling in us the obsession that we must possess designer jeans and sneakers or the biggest SUV or we cannot regard ourselves as being happy.

Pleasure is an addiction. Pain is to be avoided. To explore whether happiness might be induced by a change in brain chemistry, we try Prozac only to find ourselves more lethargic and irritable than ever. Envy is the game and delayed gratification is not for American workers. Planning for the future is a bore. Such workers behave as if the boom will last forever, while consumed with the nerve-racking doubt that it won't.[4]

American workers, especially those employed by the industrial giants of the old economy, have been given everything but the kitchen sink in the last quarter century.[5] But those of the holistic school of management feel even these concessions are not enough.[6] Companies must do everything, and anything to hold valuable workers. It has pushed spoiled brats deeper into adolescence where some will remain terminally dependent to the end of their employment.

The adage that we learn from our mistakes doesn't necessarily hold true here. For the past half-century management has been willing to exchange entitlements for retaining power and control. It worked reasonably well when American workers didn't mind being patronized and compared to *"pig iron."* Frederick Winslow Taylor, the industrial engineer whose invention of *"scientific management"* promised to revolutionize American industry, is largely forgotten. Taylor was once linked with Thomas Edison and Henry Ford as one of the great American industrial innovators. Often quoted is this dictum from his *The Principles of Scientific Management* (1911):

. . . one of the very first requirements for man who is fit to handle pig iron as a regular occupation is that he shall be so stupid and so phlegmatic that he more nearly resembles an ox than any other type.[7]

Not surprisingly, even among the few who remember his work today, it is difficult to find anyone who would dare endorse this characterization. Still, even if speedy Freddie is no longer intellectually fashionable, his doctrine still haunts the American work culture. Taylor's biographer Robert Kanigel observes:

Taylor bequeathed a clockwork world of tasks timed to the hundred of a minute, of standardized factories, machines, women and men. He helped instill in us the fierce, unholy obsession with time, order, productivity, and efficiency that marks our age. Foreign visitors to America often remark on the rushed, breathless quality of our lives. Taylor – whose life, from 1856 to 1915, almost exactly coincided with the Industrial Revolution at its height – helped make us that way.[8]

Taylor's draconian schemes in their entirety were actually adopted by only about 1 percent of all industrial workers at the zenith of his popularity, but the psychic force of his ideas captured the American mindset then as now. The crucial element of Taylor's system was the aggressive effort by management to gain control over technical knowledge connected with work. This still dominates American labor relations even in this era of "post-industrial" methods of shared decision-making and flexible work arrangements (to increase workers' satisfaction and, thereby, company profits). Taylor's basic division of responsibility between expert managers and worker-drones survives even if anachronistic and atavistic. The poison of an idea has many lives.

Consider this against the fact that workers, not managers, are the critical mass today. Management knows this and is trying to buy time by being sucked into the scheme of "holistic management" or what is called a "humanistic approach to management." It didn't work in the 1960s, 1970s, 1980s, 1990s, and it won't work now.

It has never worked because it detached workers from the reality of their experience, and placed the burden of their existence outside themselves. In a word it spawned the victim complex.

When workers depend on forces outside themselves to solve work and relational problems, they freeze-frame themselves in permanent adolescence. Workers of such a mindset throw in, "free of charge," their sacred identity as individuals. Conditioned, as they are, they cannot see past their noses. Short-term gain at long-term expense is the rule of the day. The shadow of speedy Freddie still looms over them.

American workers like being taken care of, trusting their employers to do the heavy lifting to stay competitive. They don't like to be reminded that what goes up inevitably comes down; that the good is likely to be accompanied with something distasteful; that pleasure does not come without pain; and that comfort does not come without some price.

Now many of these same workers, who have been complete passengers in life, leaving the driving to others, who didn't pay much attention in school, and went along for the ride, believing the good times were here to stay, are out of work, under qualified, or have obsolescent skills for an informational economy. They are jobless, powerless, and victimized, and they feel they have done nothing wrong. They are passively waiting for their employer, the government, and the church to extricate them from this dilemma with miracle relief. They are waiting for *godot*.

What complicates the problem further is that workers have convinced themselves that they "can't afford" to go back to school, or "can't afford" to swallow their pride and take a job at 50 percent of their previous income. Yet, when circumstances dictate, they find they can live on a lot less, and can sacrifice lifestyle without penalty. Indeed, often they find they are happier than ever before. Less is more. And any work is better than no work.

Work for an American is as important as breathing. It has little to do with how much you make, but how much pleasure you derive in the doing. The most satisfaction in work is a consequent of doing something that serves someone else. Without satisfying work, there is little sense of self. And without this sense, an American is lost.

Yet Americans love to complain about how hard they work, how they are under appreciated, under paid, and overworked. They forget that no one is holding a gun to their heads. Workers can quit and move on. But that takes individual responsibility, self-reliance, and risk. It takes an adult mentality, which they have never developed. So, instead they wait to be fired, for the plant to close and move elsewhere, or for the technology to change and make them redundant. Then they have an excuse to be a victim, and an opportunity to blame someone else for their lot in life.

The chronic problem with American workers today is working hard rather than working smart. This is because they are primarily knowers rather than learners. They learn a skill and then bleed it to death, or they go to school forever, and then punish people with their knowledge. In either case they fail to be students of what they do. This is shown by their inclination to be tellers rather than listeners, to measure their productivity in terms of quantity (number of hours-spent doing) rather than quality (meaningful results). They are also bent on doing everything right the first time. This leads to the tactical error of cheating to produce such results, rather than concentrating on the 10 percent right things, which make 90 percent of the difference.

American workers, like Faust, have sold their soul for comfort and have become complacent. And like Faust, they now want to buy it back at bargain basement prices. Look inside all the self-help books, the obsessive quest for self-esteem, identity, and personal recognition and what do you find? You find a working population with a consuming drive for a second chance.

Money hasn't been the answer. Material wellbeing hasn't provided spiritual contentment. Spiritual deprivation is the engine of the worker revolution, not economic parity. American workers gave up their power for thirty pieces of silver, and now they want to buy it back.

Seduced by money, workers are always paid a dollar more an hour than they believe they can afford to quit, and move on. This keeps the lid on their lips, and their spirits in the cage. The irony is that they have all the power, and could take control of their collective lives and destinies. But they are too involved in escapism to see this fact.

Companies are going down the tubes because workers are withholding valuable information. Sometimes this is for spite (malicious obedience). Often it is because it is considered career threatening to disagree with the boss, even when the boss is blatantly wrong. Failure of workers to openly express themselves is a failure of the culture to support sincerity. Everybody loses. All because the company sponsors compliance and calls it cooperation, failing to realize that compliance is always coercive, while cooperation is always voluntary.

When workers are afraid to challenge authority when it is wrong, their inclination is to express their anger and frustration subversively. They go to ground. They whine about their plight to each other, sabotage operations, take bogus sick leave, participate in work slowdowns, or become the equivalent of social termites. They destroy the infrastructure silently and unobtrusively, only to have the damage discovered when it is too late for damage control.

These workers treat their job as if it is the enemy and a separate reality from themselves. Few, if any, think of *going against the grain* and expressing their grievances formally and politely to management as they occur. You might expect this constructive counterattack from mature adults, individuals who want to understand why management is behaving as it is so that they may get on with their work.

Management is not the enemy. Management is as lost and confused as any worker. It is a time of new circumstances, and systems have yet to be developed that are congruent with the needs of the organization. Answers are not apt to be found in academia or consultants. Experts are always there to exploit the confusion to their advantage, while academia invents obtuse language to cover its ignorance. They have no answers. Nor are there *"excellent companies"* to model and imitate. Senior management has no choice but to become involved in the heavy lifting, company by company.

It is pointless to search for the ideal answers to working situation. Workers and managers must first defined the problem in concert and create a working model for their particular operation. This is not a time for cynicism or an adolescent mindset. More than a trillion dollars is lost every year with the attitude: *"Get as much as you can while the getting is good. Stick it to them (bosses) before they stick it to you. Let management solve it. They get the big bucks!"* Every dime workers squander "with such an attitude" in passive disruptive behavior robs them and kills their possibilities. They are always the big loser!

There isn't a workplace, in my experience, in which a conspiracy of silence doesn't damage operations. Even the most dedicated workers do not want to be considered snitches. Nor do they want to worry about profits and cash flow problems, or the company's shrinking market share. They conveniently play ignorant of escalating costs of material, the unreliability of designs, or any problems relating to the health of the company. *"That's not my problem! That's management's."* Not anymore!

Such concerns are no longer outside the purview of the average worker. Workers are important members of the operational team. They can no longer play naïve. Companies, industries, markets and jobs can disappear before you can say *"Uncle Sam"* with such an attitude. Selective naiveté does not beget security for anyone.

One of the amazing myths of management, which now haunts it, is the idea that management is different than workers. Managers, even the CEO, are employees of the company. In the technical sense managers are no more owners than workers are. Put another way, workers have every right to claim themselves as owners the same as managers. The problem is that workers see themselves as renters. They believe and behave like renters. Managers see themselves as owners. They believe and behave like owners.

Management is essentially a 20th century phenomenon, which has been reified into a belief system. Workers, with little foresight, empowered managers to be their caregivers and caretakers, indeed, their surrogate parents. Once this die was cast it reversed the normal developmental process from dependent child to carefree adolescent to responsible adult. Workers settled into terminal adolescence without experiencing the carefree nature of it. Once employed, they were expected to be polite, obedient, punctual, reactive, conforming and submissive to authority.

Reminiscent of the 19th century family, workers were expected to participate at the economic dinner table, but to be seen and not heard, to do and not think. This suspension in adolescence grew into counter dependency on the company for their total well-being. This was the experience, for example, of assemblers at the automotive plants of Detroit, generation after generation, until the last decades of the 20th century. It was a welfare system under the guise of lifetime employment.

As a youth visiting relatives in Detroit, many of my friends there had grandfathers and grandmothers, fathers and mothers working in these automotive plants. My friends expected that they, too, would one day spend their lives in similar work. When Japan, Inc. started eating this industry's lunch in the 1970s and 1980s, the honeymoon ended. Tens of thousands lost their jobs never to again experience the standard of living that their extended families once enjoyed. More pitiful still, many of these displaced workers are waiting for the glory days to return to Detroit. They envision themselves as once again being the envy of the American working class.

Workers gave up control of their destiny for the promise of security. A guaranteed job is only possible for companies to provide in the best of times. Since *World War II*, American workers have increasingly luxuriated in a climate of sublime comfort and subservient dependence. They now feel that they have been betrayed, and they have been, but not by their employers. Workers have betrayed themselves. They have been thinking with their head in the sand.

Now these same workers "think" they want their power back, of course, without the concomitant responsibilities of that power. Workers want the perks of power, along with the welfarism that they have come to enjoy. They want empowerment, not accountability, with the buck still stopping with management. *"Let management handle it!"* They want power without risk, pain, or consequence. If they foul up, they still want the biweekly paycheck. They yearn to continue to live in dreamland, and to enjoy their fun and games as if nothing has changed.

What workers don't seem to understand is that management is not in a position to empower them. Management no longer has the power. Power, or more precisely control, is in the domain of doing. Doing requires special knowledge. Workers, not managers, have such knowledge. Managers and knowledge workers, at best, can only be partners. Management no longer is in charge. And that means, quite sadly, nobody is.

Workers must step up to the plate and take their chances. They can't have it both ways. They can't play the victim and expect to be the victor. They can't project the blame if things go wrong. They can't picket and whine to the media in self-pity for the wrongs they endure. The 20th century free lunch is over.

Workers and managers are all connected. Workers have no choice but to get off their asses and take charge of their lives. There is bound to be struggle ahead with a steep emotional and intellectual learning curve. Cosmetic changes will not suffice. Passive resistance is already killing the golden goose. It is time for workers to fish or cut bait.

Professional athletes now share the wealth of their prowess. Before, athletes were given chump change for their exploits, that is, until Curt Flood came along. Flood was an excellent major league baseball player who refused to accept a trade. He refused to see himself as chattel that owners could arbitrarily treat as they liked. He considered himself to have collective bargaining rights as a player. His courageous stand cost him his career, but now, thanks to him, all professional athletes share in the wealth of their exploits. Where are the Curt Floods in commerce and industry? Who has the courage to *go against the grain* and change the course of history? Maybe it is you reading this.

In any case the whole empowerment movement is counterfeit. What is more important is accountability. Empowerment without accountability is bogus. The sooner it is realized the sooner a strategy can be adopted to recover the lost momentum of organization. Management has no intention of giving up power if it can avoid it. Management is anachronistic and doesn't want to face this fact. Why should it? It continues to play MONOPOLY with real money and with the lives of real workers. It will continue to do so until someone has the courage to say, *"Hell no, I won't go!"* as Curt Flood did.

Obviously, American workers are not ready for such a confrontation. Power demands attributes missing in their programmed make-up. Workers have been culturally weaned from self-responsibility and programmed into *learned helplessness* and *no responsibility.* Attributes of accountability, grace under pressure, inclination to take risks, accept blame, endure failure, believe in themselves when no one else does, listen to the rhythm of their own heart, do their best when no credit is likely to come their way, and be driven by the will to serve rather than by the willful need for money are obviously in short supply if not missing entirely.

Power demands other things as well. There is considerable difference between a guaranteed paycheck every two weeks, and worrying about the survival of the company 24 hours a day. Power demands thinking like an owner, not a renter. If you say many managers don't know the *owner's manual,* you would be right. Countless managers are pleasers, more interested in making an impression than a difference, more driven by their personality than their performance. They spend most of their time campaigning for the next promotion. Their dream, as envisioned by Lewis H. Clapham in *The Wish for Kings* (1993), is to win the lottery of becoming the CEO with all its hidden perks. These aspirants know they are not being measured by their achievements but by the weight of their connections and the number of levels below them in the table of organization.[9]

Managers have traditionally been power brokers, but never power barons. They are going through a similar metamorphoses to that of workers. Now, if the company doesn't perform well on Wall Street, CEOs and senior managers will experience the same hook that baseball managers have come to expect if they don't make the playoffs.

Even so, many managers and workers still treat the future as an illusion with denial the hammer of indifference. They think the present quandary will correct itself as if by osmosis – that they need do nothing differently. Managers, especially, refuse to see the handwriting on the wall. Senior management senses, however, something is awry. So they turn to consultants to solve the predicament.

Consultants are the curse of our times. They are the witch doctors of the age, the explainers and simplifiers of massive operational and behavioral problems in euphemistic terms. They are the court jesters. The answers are never with the consultant. The answers are always with the people in the organization. The problem is that no one listens to the people. Consultants are hired, talk to the people, and then translate what the people say into euphemistic terms and cosmetic interventions. Recommendations are made that are non-threatening to those in charge and are neither critical nor an embarrassment to the leadership.

One reading the consultant's report would think that the client – always management, never the organization – is running nothing less than a tight ship. Nothing changes. Workers grow more cynical. And management dodges the bullet one more time. Typically, the company sinks further into dysfunction.[10]

The irony is that most companies have 90 percent of the people needed to turn their business around. They don't have to merge, downsize, reengineer, streamline, reorganize or relocate. They simply have to find a way to get workers and managers responsive to the needs of the company without feeling intimidated or in jeopardy of losing their jobs. The expertise and answers are always there. What is missing is the mechanism to exercise this advantage to the company's benefit.

The problem with consultants is that they attack the problem from the outside, and they are never there for damage control. Consultants invariably fabricate a new "we/they" polarity by looking for solutions at the expense of one group or another. They address disenchantment with cosmetic surgery, which is likely to be iatrogenic, with the cure worse than the disease. If an intervention fails to touch the soul of workers and managers alike, it is an exercise in futility.

For the past quarter century there has been an obsession with quality without a fundamental structural or functional change of work. Quality is a commendable goal. Who could argue against quality? The problem is the obsession with quality at the expense of everything else. Quality is not a product. Quality is a process and a mindset. A process cannot be sustained on a faulty foundation. And the foundation is the workplace culture. It is not a fad, not a program, nor is quality the pursuit of national recognition such as the *Malcolm Baldridge Award*.

Establish a mindset of quality and everything else will fall into place. The problem, though, is that mindset is the product of the structure and function of work. There is an axiom, which always holds true:

If workers believe in an idea, whether it is a good or bad idea, it will succeed. Likewise, if they fail to believe in an idea, no matter how sound it is, the idea will fail. A mindset is that powerful.

This suggests that it is not prudent to attempt to radicalize workers' thinking, but to understand this thinking and to build on its foundation. The premise is to make workers part of the problem so that they will buy into the solution. This is unlikely to happen unless the structure and function of work are changed.

Companies would do well to be cautionary. Workers have been programmed to be reactive. To make them proactive requires reprogramming. Reprogramming requires structures and functions be modified to support such efforts. Workers as thinkers are far removed from the strategic thinking of the company. They are usually the last to find out. Then they are asked, *"What do you think?"* Consequently, they are used to sitting in the bleachers and watching as spectators to the decision making process. Now times are different and their contribution is critical to success.

Senior management cannot *will* cultural change to happen. It has to develop a cultural strategy, become totally involved in the implementation of that strategy, be there when it starts to fall apart, then modify it with the same problem solving dedication that fiscal policy enjoys.

Order is first established in the worker one person at a time before any behavioral change is manifested in the company-at-large. Change the man from a passive person to an active participant with a social conscience, involved in self-management, and you change the company. This demands more than simply changing the worker's mind. It requires the creation of a radically different mentality, a different mindset. Anything less is an irrational aberration that fails to touch, much less change anything.

Workers, when they are young, are compliant, amorphous, and like silly putty, can be shaped into many forms. But once their programming hardens into an attitude, it is difficult if not impossible to recast. Many workers have been programmed to build psychic castles of sand, drifting through life lost in confusion, obsessively dependent. Others have been molded into self-responsible adults. Trigger words of *"lifetime employment," "social security," "universal health coverage,"* or other holistic nomenclature can result in workers forgetting their spiritual underpinning of self-responsibility.

These trigger words spell comfort and lead to complacency. Workers are always ready to barter their souls for material satisfaction. Getting can easily block out their natural inclination to giving. It can also result in spiritual deprivation making them always needy.

Workers and managers, owners and customers are all part of a common cloth. Worker power is not only a national issue but also a global fact. If workers continue to insist on being suspended in adolescence, allowing others less competent to solve company problems, employment is bound to be meaningless and companies are destined to swallow each other whole, until the beast is so large it cannot support itself. Remember the dinosaurs.

It is time for workers, like late blooming roses, to come to grips with reality. Otherwise, adolescence won't be a phase of development, but a terminal state.

References

1. David Van Biema, "The Search for Jesus. The Gospel Truth?" (Cover Story), Time, April 8, 1996, pp. 52-59.
2. Sinclair Lewis, Main Street, Harcourt Brace, 1950.
3. Robert E. Lane, The Loss of Happiness in Market Democracies, Yale University Press, 2000.
4. Mark Kingwell, In Pursuit of Happiness: Better Living from Plato to Prozac, Crown, 2000.
5. John Strohmeyer, Crisis in Bethlehem, Adler & Adler, 1986.
6. Cheryl Comeau-Kirschner and Louisa Wah, "Holistic Management: A new millennium calls for a new approach to employee management.

Welcome to the age of holistic management," *Management Review*, December 1999.

7. Fredrick Winslow Taylor, *The Principles of Scientific Management*, W. W. Norton & Co., 1911, p. 59.
8. Robert Kanigel, *The One Best Way: Frederick Winslow Taylor and the Enigma of Efficiency*, Viking, 1997.
9. Lewis H. Lapham, *The Wish for Kings*, Grove Press, 1993.
10. The consultant's role in organizational development (OD) is to be physician to the organization in the same manner as the medical practitioner is physician to the individual.

Corporate Management
Architects of a Failed System

We are scarcely ever interested in the performance of a communication-engineering machine for a single input. To function adequately it must give satisfactory performance for a whole class of inputs, and this means a statistically satisfactory performance for the class of inputs, which it is statistically expected to receive.

N. Wiener, *Cybernetics: or Control and Communication*
in the Animal and the Machine (1948).

Wierner's basic research into robotics was to find ways to make robotics behave. He realized that to find a heuristic program with robotics is not guaranteed to yield the "right" or sought after results every time. Failure is part of success. What concerns the engineer with his robots is whether mis-performance is a telling one, or not:

(1) Does it reveal something about a pattern of systematic weakness likely to recur?

(2) Does it reveal an inappropriate and inauspicious linking between sorts of circumstances and sorts of reactions?

(3) Is this sort of thing apt to happen again, or was it due to the coincidental convergence of fundamentally independent factors highly unlikely to reoccur?

Alas, were corporate managers only wise enough to apply the same systemic thinking to the management of workers that is applied to robotics! True, even robotics display certain aberrancies. But this is nothing compared to the aberrancies of people with emotions. People are different. Yet, the same logic might apply.

Engineers have the concept of "don't care" when it is rational to ignore the results. They focus on the rule rather than the exception. They don't waste time with doubt. Too often senior corporate management focuses on the exception rather than the rule. It is the squeaky wheel that gets the grease, while it is the engine that needs the attention. The soul is the engine of the work force. So, what is the problem?

Corporate management has a lopsided education. It is well schooled in finance and commerce, engineering and logistics, science and technology, but fatally ignorant of culture and people as persons.

Workplace culture defines behavior, and behavior determines whether a company is to succeed or fail. Unfortunately, all too often corporate management allows itself to get caught up in cosmetic interventions (*Quality of Work, Quality of Worklife, Quality of Management, Quality Circles, Empowerment, Leadership Style, Sensitivity Training, Total Employee Involvement*, et al), while failing to deal with fundamental cultural issues (workers' spirit, will to work, quest to learn new things, creative commitment, self-management, ethical conduct, character, confidence, competence, et al), or the cultural foundation of a high performance workplace.

Complaints are bound to fester at the bottom of the organization when management ignores the culture. These complaints pass through several filters. Each filter interprets the complaints in its own best interests. No one wants to be the messenger who gets killed. So what is eventually understood to be the case, seldom is.

Corporate management knows it cannot trust its accountants and auditors to give an accurate picture of the financial health of the company without its painstaking attention to fiscal details. To lead effectively, it believes it must have complete command of the financial situation. Likewise, it should not trust human resources to create, monitor, and manage the workplace culture without its total involvement in the exercise. Otherwise, the silent implosion of human effort can occur all around without anyone the wiser until the walls collapse and the ceiling caves in. This catastrophe is happening with increasing frequency as diverse company cultures are merged into new entities.[1] When cultures merge, the problems encountered can be as instant as whiplash. It is like mixing oil and water and wondering why there is separation.

Cultural Arrogance: the Anatomy of Disaster

Danka Business Systems, a Tampa Bay company, started out quite modestly in 1977 as a storefront operation. From this base, it grew into a global company of $3 billion. The company grew by scores of mergers and acquisitions as well as creative marketing and executive leadership. But Danka was to hit a snag when it acquired the troubled *Eastman Kodak* copier division in September

1996. The acquisition of *Eastman Kodak* doubled both Danka's size and sales force. Its employee rolls jumped to 20,000. The critical snag was not finance, it was cultural arrogance.

Danka leadership, which was sailing along without any concern about coral reefs, ran into one when it attempted to superimpose its workplace culture on the Kodak sales force without a strategy or sounding out policy. It assumed that what was good enough for Danka employees was good enough for Kodak, like it or lump it! Danka proceeded to convert the Kodak sales people from their Kodak salary-based compensation plan to Danka's commission-based compensation plan. If this were not unsettling enough, Danka decided to reclassify the Kodak marketing and sales jobs to an entirely new system. This double-whammy cultural shock failed to cause the Kodak people to rebel. Instead, they decided simply to drag their feet. They hid in the *six silent killers* and punished operations without anyone able to detect the damage until it was much too late.[2] Sales and profits plunged, and with them the price of Danka stock. From a high of $50 a share on August 1, 1997, Danka plunged to a low of $2.75 on October 9, 1998, then rebound to about $12 in early 2000, only to plunge, once again, below $2 in late 2000.[3]

Two brazen policies led to this fall: (1) the Kodak people's compensation plan was summarily changed with only their perfunctory participation; (2) Kodak jobs were reclassified to weed out the weak producers. These two policies were an affront to the dignity and pride of the Kodak workers, and crushed their spirits before they could blend in with their new partners. The question I am often asked is how did Danka rectify the situation? It didn't. Danka fired its co-founder Dan Doyle. At the price that shares are selling for today in late 2000, it is apparent that little learning has taken place.

Yet *Danka Business Systems* is small potatoes compared to another deal supposedly made in heaven – the merger of Citicorp with Travelers Group, Inc. to form Citigroup. This $50 billion merger, however, displays the same cultural arrogance. When the merger was approved in April 1998, everyone was touting it as an ideal fit. The consumer businesses – Citibank's credit cards and Travelers' insurance – quickly meshed. But trouble soon started to brew.

Citibank cultivated close relationships with 1,700 multinational companies. Salomon Smith Barney of Travelers specialized in serving non-investment-grade companies with loans and securities underwriting. But there were areas of overlap and confusion. What side of the new company, for instance, would handle loan underwriting for companies needing complex financing? Additionally, the unions of the two operations had sharply different styles and cultures.

Citibank's relationship bankers are proud of their globetrotting but conservative image. Citibank's goal: promote Citibank as a brand name recognizable everywhere. Travelers' Salomon Smith Barney culture is more entrepreneurial. Its executives stay more focused on serving clients than pushing its brand names.

Consequently, when these two discrete cultures merged, fractures started as serious rifts, then progressed to turf wars and ultimately led to personality assassinations. This found its way into some stock price fluctuation, but no precipitous decline. What did Citigroup do to stem the tide? It fired Jamie Dimon, 42, president of Citigroup on November 1, 1998, only six months after the merger.

For Danka, Citigroup, and others like them, I fear, the recriminations are just beginning. People problems are at the core of their difficulties but culture is apparently a foreign language to corporate management. People drive culture and culture drives behavior. Sigmund Freud had this to say about culture in *Civilization and Its Discontents* (1961):

It seems certain that we do not feel comfortable in our present day civilization, but it is very difficult to form an opinion whether and in what degree men of an earlier age felt happier and what part their cultural conditions played in the matter. We shall always tend to consider people's distress objectively – that is, to place ourselves, with our own wants and sensibilities in their conditions, and then to examine what occasions we should find in them for experiencing happiness or unhappiness. This method of looking at things, which seems objective because it ignores the variations in subjective sensibility, is, of course, the most subjective possible. . . .[4]

Freud placed a high value on man's problem solving ability, not only as problems related to nature, but problem related to himself as well. This has obviously been ignored here.

People are not just born into a family or community or peer group. They are born into a culture, which programs certain values, beliefs and expectations. This influence begins at birth and affects nearly every interaction and experience. Culture becomes part of people's geography, which they carry wherever they go for the rest of their lives. They bring it to school, to work, to all their associations. Meanwhile, schools, companies, and communities with which they become associated have discrete cultures of their own. These corporate cultures, like people's individual cultures, evolve over time into a distinct but often-silent authority, which directs behavior to accepted norms. Cultural shift and cultural shock are bound to be experienced throughout the life of workers as they move from one set of circumstances to another. These experiences can be very unsettling and may result in counterproductive behavior, not because these workers are bad people, but because there has been no strategy, no effort to assimilate them into the new environment.

Corporate management must be cognizant of these factors, as the problems encountered in the merging of cultures give no warning. Distinct differences must not only be acknowledged but also dealt with directly. The best way to approach this challenge is to make the people involved part of the problem so that they might buy into the solution.

People cannot be treated as things to be managed but must be seen as partners dedicated to making the merger succeed. Too often assumptions are made in the interest of expediency as diverse cultures merge into a new entity. The focus is on what should be done to workers without their involvement in the process. Such draconian measures always fail.

Workers are not two-dimensional, but complex and multidimensional. A company's cultural strategy must be as sophisticated as its business strategy if success is the goal. Otherwise, the chances of success are like shooting dice.

Architectural Flaws to the Workplace

It is time corporate management admits, when it comes to issues of culture, that it is flying by the seat of its pants. It is time that it gets inside failed approaches of the past to bringing workers on board, and to realize that workers will respond enthusiastically to its involvement. There are three crucial flaws to the present work climate:

(1) Most workers, whether they be professional or blue-collar, are suspended in adolescence, displaying the emotional maturity of mere children. These workers have failed to grow up and seize the moment as mature adults, when it is mature adults that are needed to deal with the challenges of the times.

(2) Workers come into the workplace as knowers rather than learners, tellers rather than listeners. This is the fault of an education system designed for an industrial economy, not the *Information Age*. Formal education fails to produce creative thinkers and innovative problem solvers because education is mainly a passive experience. Education attempts to reify knowledge as cumulative

information rather than conceptual understanding. Consequently, workers know a lot of things but the things they know serve them better as "Toys of the Mind" than as tools.

(3) Workers give the impression that they are obsessed with control. True, they want to do their "own thing" but they don't want to take any risks or suffer any consequences in the doing. They want it both ways, "their cake and eat it, too." They have little sense of the demands of responsibility and shy away from accountability.

Workers as Children

Mature adults accept reality. They see problems as opportunities. There is little inclination to determine *"who is wrong"* because their focus is always on *"what is wrong?"* Nor are mature adults obsessed with *"what should be"* or *"what has been,"* or even *"what is going to be,"* but *"what is needed to be done, now!"* They are pragmatists and realists.

What industrial society has created in the workplace, in the main, are dependent children who look on management as their surrogate parents. The double irony is that these workers-as-children refuse to grow up, while the workplace culture stubbornly defends the culture that makes them remain suspended in adolescence.

Closer examination of the emotional mentality of these workers reveals them to have the disposition, inclination, collective identity, and impulsive rashness of children. You see this when they sue for higher wages, better benefits, and greater opportunity. They put the responsibility for the problem solving on the back of management, only expressing their complaints in broad generic terms, not in specific remedies tied to increased productivity, improved profitability, and greater market share. It never dawns on them that *"they are the company,"* that the company can never be greater than their collective contribution. Yet they know in their bones, even if they will deny it if challenged, that 80 percent of the effective work done in their shop is done by 20 percent of the workers.

These workers don't want the facts. They want satisfaction the way a child wants a new toy and isn't interested in how much it costs. They want more and they want it now. They are past the stage of rational negotiation. They have been molly-coddled since birth and see no reason to change the programming.

Missing in this emotional baggage that they carry is the realization that feelings are facts, and nothing changes until they change themselves. They feel.

They don't think. Feelings could aid thinking, like hunches bring about intuitive insight, but with them, feelings flood the gates so that they see little clearly, leastwise their own self-deception.

Workers as Knowers

Most workers learn a skill, a craft, or a profession in some kind of formal setting, then expect to coast for the next forty years. Physicians are as guilty of this as pipe fitters. This indolence was tolerated in an industrial economy, but not now. Today school is never out and life-long learning is the key to everything. More than 80 percent of the new jobs today did not exist a decade ago. The challenge of every job is to keep current with the latest information.

Knowers have a tendency to punish others with their special knowledge. Learners are always open to new data and experience. They welcome constructive criticism because they want to improve their skills. Knowers are apologists. Learners are thinkers.

Knowers are inattentive to what is happening around them, and are victims of cognitive dissonance, that is, the translating of everything experienced into what is already known and fits their natural biases.

Knowers love gurus, pundits, armchair scholars, and high priests of science and religion that wallow in obfuscation and reinforce their information seeking mentalities. It allows knowers to fit the magic of their elbow pronouncements to the memes of their minds.[5]

That is the irony of knowers. They identify themselves with these journeymen knowers who make a living telling people what to think, feel, value, and believe to be true. Often these journeymen knowers wallow in the same confusion, giving expression to their own inherent doubt. It is a case of the blind leading the blind with no one the wiser.

Workers and Control

Few workers realize the best way to control anything is to "let go" of it. The opposite of control is to be obsessed with it, and therefore the prisoner of chaos. The more workers attempt to control their nature, for example, the more nature controls them. They fight their addictions – eating, drinking, gambling, cheating, lying, stealing, and womanizing – only to be more possessed of these demons. It never occurs to *admit* what they are, *accept* why they are that way, and *deal* with how they are but kindly.

Self-contempt is not the answer. It only compounds the obsession. A better stratagem is to be one's own best friend, to seek and enjoy one's own company, and by this device learn to say "no" to those who would corrupt. But as Murray Kempton writes, that is more easily said than done:

The Almighty is presumed to pass His judgments and dole out His penalties to individuals, which allows us to suppose that nations are spared painful sessions with the Recording Angel. But if ours is ever so summoned, we may suppose that the inquiry into its cardinal sins might begin with the question: "And why, America, did you, in your arrogance, teach so many of your children to hate themselves?" [6]

It is equally true in the general as in the particular. Corporate management would do well to realize this. Set systems in place and let workers evolve creatively and independently of management constraints and the results are likely to prove exceptional. Self-control doesn't occur in a vacuum. Self-control comes from looking kindly on one's little failures, and profiting from them. Likewise, workers would do well to accept themselves as they are and others as they find them, which implies accepting their pestering demons as well as their guardian angels; their doubts as well as their certainties; their failures as well as their successes; their pains as well as their pleasures.

Western man has delighted in the conquest of the natural world, and for it, we have pollution, decadence, disease, and depression. Western man has treated nature as a separate entity to self, as if man is not an earthling but an intruder. The divided self extends to man's self-contempt. It is as if the enemy of man's nature must be subdued and conquered. It is the 2,000-year-old idea that man is inherently evil, and must be mastered to be good.

Notice how little attention media give to man's goodness; how much to man's inclination to evil. Television news and newspapers are devoted to chronicling corruption, chicanery, duplicity, rape, murder, and man's incessant fall from grace. Yet 99 percent of the people listening to or reading these reports are good people. They have been, however, systematically programmed to doubt that others share such goodness. So, viewers and readers alike are vicariously entertained with the misdeeds of others, which is called *news*.

And so workers are out-of-control. How could it be otherwise? The controller and the controlled are always one and the same. Unfortunately, corporate management has embraced the philosophy that workers must be managed, motivated, manipulated, and mobilized as if the controller (management) and the controlled (workers) are separate entities. Management sees itself less vain, less dependent, more in charge. Were this only so.

As a wedge has been driven between the mind and the body by Western philosophy and religion, between nature and man, is it any wonder that management should operate in any other way? Division and compartmentalization are the practice of management, while management celebrates the rhetoric of connection. Leaderless leadership is on display and the product is dissonant workers.

Viewed in the particular, the more workers attempt to control their passions the less they control them, the more they are victims to their excesses. Deeds, not words, make the difference.

Control remains a maddening pursuit, which fractures, segments, and isolates. Obsession with control leads to chaos, not order. But apparently workers, programmed to respond mechanistically, cannot think otherwise. A mechanistic mentality thinks in terms of separation into component parts, not in their connection. Mechanistic man avoids conflict and searches for harmony, failing to realize that managed conflict is the glue that holds workers to work and to each other.

Mechanistic man would find it strange to suggest that he think with his whole body, not simply his mind. Yet thinking is not isolated to the mind, but to the heart and soul as well.

We live in the scientific age where science is the new religion. Unfortunately, it is becoming as dogmatic as any religion ever was. Science insists in objective truth, in value-free analysis, in reified quantitative validation. There is no room for magic. Man no longer has convictions. He only has opinions. Yet man is a subjective, not an objective being, with a natural bias as a reflection of his cultural conditioning. It is qualitative, not quantitative validation that renders the most meaning to him.

Virtually everything in human experience is connected and related to everything else – subject to object, object to subject, cause to effect, and effect to cause, the abstract to the concrete, and the concrete to the abstract. The connecting lines are invisible as if by magic.

Consequently, the problems workers solve are the problems workers create. Resolving problems in the particular always generates problems in the general, and vice versa. Often the solution to the problem is worse than the problem because the problem solver is enslaved exclusively to linear logic and cause and effect analysis when problems are never one-dimensional.

Moreover, circular logic differs little with the rodent in the cage frantically spinning the treadmill wheel and going nowhere. Chronic problems, however, can be isolated and dealt with if only workers would get off the treadmill and observe them. Problems can be resolved only when controlled practices are suspended, chronic problems defined, and systems put in place to deal with them.

This requires that corporate management change the structure and function of work to more effectively support this new orientation. Unfortunately, *"letting go" of* circular logic is unfathomable to the mechanistic mind.

What Workers Think, They Become!

If workers feel they have no real stake in what they do; if they are programmed to react as renters rather than as owners; if the work they do is mainly bogus and done because it has always been done that way; then it follows they will hardly consider themselves genuine or their work important. They will behave as "things" doing things, and no more.

On the other hand, place a worker firmly in reality and in charge of what he does and such a worker will move toward mature effort. He will more likely develop relevant skills and be adaptable to change as the needs arise. For being more confident and competent, this worker will be happier and more productive. A healthy disposition is on equally good terms with sorrow and disappointment because maturity sees these inseparable from joy. Pleasure is also seen as having a natural connection to pain; success to failure; certainty to doubt; clarity to confusion. The mature worker accepts imperfection as a human condition, while not apologizing for a drive toward perfectibility.

Happiness is not something searched for but something chosen. The mature worker chooses to be happy *going against the grain* of what might otherwise pull him into depression. This worker realizes happiness, like everything else, has its peaks and valleys, as good and bad days are part of experience. With this perspective, a happy, healthy worker is unlikely to psychologically or physically abuse his mates, project blame, commit suicide or homicide, become deviant or criminal. A healthy, happy worker is humble and a law abider on and off the job. This worker is not likely to covet either his company's or his neighbor's property.

Since society has failed to produce this worker, and because such a worker is so critical to a company's success today, the job has fallen on corporate management.

Blueprint for Corporate Management

For American workers, life revolves around work, not leisure. Since this is so, and since it is unlikely to change for many years, it puts a tremendous cultural burden on employers to develop workers in a way that not only serves the company, but that serves society as well. The way to leverage workers' energy and to develop their positive mindset is through the appropriate workplace culture. To that end, senior management might consider this agenda:

(1) *Recognize that there is no idealistic corporate culture.*

The cultural climate in America is not the same as in Europe. Nor is the workplace culture in General Motor's operations in Indiana the same as GMs' operations in Detroit. Moreover, in a specific GM plant, the culture in production is not the same as it is in engineering, or administration. All differ. All are unique to their respective histories and cultural biases respective of the groups within and between them. Yet there is a dominant American culture that differs with that of Japan, China, and elsewhere, as there is a predominant culture in GM, which differs with that at GE, AT&T, or other companies. Workplace culture is a combination of micro and macro cultures within and between entities and must be understood in such terms.

(2) *You don't search for the appropriate workplace culture. You create the culture.*

Tom Peters and Robert Waterman found that out. Many of the companies they profiled in their bestselling book *In Search of Excellence* (1982) eventually fell on hard times.[7] One can only imagine what happened to imitators of these select companies.

(3) *The drive for change invariably comes from the foundation of the company, seldom from the top.*

People at the bottom have little to lose with the status quo, whereas those at the top have everything to lose. Well within the bowels of the company is where methods, policies and procedures, work rules and job descriptions began to frustrate productive work. A company, like an individual, can become sick, confused, and debilitated, and yet not want to go to the doctor. Yet, increasingly, it is unable to deal with its internal stress and external accelerating demands. One day it collapses from fatigue and its very survival is in jeopardy.

This was the case in the 1970s, when companies were finding they were having cash flow problems, losing market share, while their employee costs for absenteeism, sick leave and health care were soaring. What did most companies do? They conducted employee surveys in which they asked workers touchy-feely questions about working conditions and supervision. What companies didn't do is ask workers how they might improve productivity, reduce costs, and make job training more relevant to current operational needs. Workers obediently responded to the questionnaires with touchy-feely answers. They didn't volunteer answers to questions not asked. Amongst themselves, workers would talk about these things, but would seldom share them with management. *"Why bother,"* they would say, *"management never listens anyway!"*

In any event these workers were not conditioned to see being persuasive as part of their role. Obviously, there were suggestion programs. Most workers are cynical of these programs and see them as another example of benign paternalism. Programmed to go with the flow, workers traditionally wait fatalistically for the other shoe to fall. Now, at a time when we need their brains more than ever, many are overwhelmed with information, and too traumatized to act.

(4) *We are in the midst of a quiet revolution in which not only the color of the collar of workers is changing, but the whole complexity of collective enterprise is changing as well.*

The command and control philosophy of the hierarchical organization is giving way to worker-manager interdependence. The *span of control* of the traditional organization is giving way to the *span of relationships.* Intracompany competition is giving way to interdepartmental cooperation, where workers act more as learners than knowers, listeners than tellers, as customer-friendly partners than functional adversaries, with finesse preferred to aggression and intimidation.

Indeed prudent companies are moving away from the muscular arrogance of the masculine paradigm to what might be called the *feminine paradigm,* where intuition and lateral thinking complement

405

cognition and vertical thinking. Answers to the company's dilemma can be found as they rest with their people. When companies turn to their people for answers rather than consultants, they experience a synergy that is beyond comprehension. This represents a revolutionary change and the rebirth of the company's collective spirit.

(5) *The key to everything is the Culture of Contribution.*

This is not a program but a process. It represents a mindset change. It is appropriate for the times because work, workers and demands of the workplace are changing. It is appropriate for management because the chemistry of technology is changing at a maddening rate and there must be a simultaneous climatic cultural change to meet this challenge. Much is written about the shift from brawn to brains, from doing to thinking, from management as surrogate parent to partnership with workers.

But if you look more closely at companies, you see little has actually changed other than rhetoric. There is still preferred parking for executives versus mass parking for workers; perks for executives that aren't available to workers; while workstations, cubicles and office space still have the feel of an earlier age with the executive offices antiseptically removed a safe distance from the work at hand. The organizational chart still retain the appearance of pyramid even if behavior fails to follow that impression. The *Culture of Contribution* is symbolic and operates like an invisible hand throughout the company. Outmoded practices thwart its authenticity and discourage it from taking root. You create a *Culture of Contribution* when you seek to meet both the mission of the company and the needs of the workers.[8]

(6) *It is apparent that corporate management doesn't get it.*

Corporate management has been receptive to change as long as change didn't cost too much, produced quick, tangible results, didn't disrupt normal operations, didn't require too much of corporate management's time, and could provide easily measured quantitative results. Management didn't want to hear that cultural change at first involves one step forward and two steps back for an extended period of time. Once the momentum catches hold, however, it takes a quantum leap forward beyond what anyone could imagine.

On balance then, cultural change is a waste of everyone's time if corporate management is not on board and totally involved in its implementation. Commitment is not enough. It requires no less diligence than managing fiscal policy. The healthy financial status of the company is due to this diligence. Likewise, managing the cultural life of the company ensures that behavior will be in sync with productivity projections, which in turn ensures the prosperity of the company.

Even though disruption and the need for change come from the bottom, the architects of change must always come from the top. So far that is not the case, and therefore it must be concluded that corporate management remains architect of a failed system.

References

1. James R. Fisher, Jr., "Merging Cultures," *Executive Excellence, April 1999, p. 12.*

2. James R. Fisher, Jr., *Six Silent Killers: Management's Greatest Challenge, St. Lucie Press, 1998.*

3. *Danka Business Systems leadership was further caught off guard when customers demanded digital copiers as opposed to analog equipment.*

4. *Sigmund Freud, Civilization and Its Discontent,* W. W. Norton, *1961, p. 41.*

5. *Richard Dawkins, The Selfish Gene, 1976.*

6. *Murray Kempton, "Home of the Brave," The New York Review, April 20, 1995, p. 66.*

7. Business Week (Cover Story): *"Who's Excellent Now?" November 5, 1984.*

8. James R. Fisher, Jr., *"A Culture of Contribution," Executive Excellence, January 1997, p. 16.* See problem in establishing this by referencing the schematic in this volume on page 78.

Post World War Spoiled Brat Generation
& Its Children
Are Not Happy Campers!

This is the true joy in life, the being used for a purpose recognized by yourself as a mighty one; the being thoroughly worn out before you are thrown on the scrap heap; the being a force of Nature instead of a feverish selfish little clod of ailments and grievances complaining that the world will not devote itself to making you happy. And also the only real tragedy in life is the being used by personally minded men for purposes, which you recognize to be, base.

George Bernard Shaw (1856-1950)
Irish dramatist, essayist and critic

Most workers within my experience are not happy campers. They can be making $100,000, $200,000 or more and yet they feel in a cage not of their making. They complain a good deal of the time. Neither their luxurious homes in the suburbs with lawn and garden service, nannies and maids, nor sympathetic neighbors of like circumstance and disposition can put a happy smile on their brave faces.

These workers routinely have membership in opulent country clubs with little time to make use of the facilities. They belong because they are expected to belong. Status drivenness fails to lessen their unhappiness. Discontent is transformed into a kind of pressing exigency. Play is work. Health is a war. They must excel. They must beat the odds.

These workers punish their bodies in iron men and women contests, diets, and give up all vices. There is no sanctuary, no peace. Everything is up-tempo, go-go! Professional relationships are tense, marriages strained, parent-child relationships in shambles. They pay psychotherapists to listen to them because their friends won't or can't. Their friends are saddled with the same problems and are cracking under similar nervous strain. Psychotherapists send them off to psychiatrists where they attain the most fashionable anti-depressant prescription drug of the moment. Others seek shelter in an AA group or one of its imitators. Life is lived in quiet desperation shored up by the belief that as affluent Americans they are the envy of the free world.

Now if affluent Americans are not happy campers, why is there such a mad rush to imitate their dyspeptic ways?

Perhaps unhappiness **is** the American way. Americans seem driven by envy. Bertrand Russell submitted that envy was the basis of democracy because *"no one should have something that someone else does not."* So we pursue more and more pleasure and material goods, but this type of happiness seems fleeting at best.[1] We can never keep up with the Jones.

It seems to matter little whether workers are surviving on unemployment checks or managing six and seven figure incomes. Unhappiness appears democratic. Americans hold melancholia in common. Studies indicate that 60 percent of high achievers feel they have sacrificed too much in pursuit of material rewards. But do they ask for a *"time out"*? Do they get off the bus? No, they complain while continuing to raise the bar of achievement. They search for fulfillment in a world turned upside down. Social researcher Daniel Yankelovich in *New Rules* (1981) writes:

A sweeping, irreversible Cultural Revolution is transforming the rules that once guided American life. In place of the traditional ethic of self-denial and sacrifice, we now find an ethic that denies people nothing. At the core of the revolution is a contradiction between goals of self-fulfillment seekers and their means. Our culture and our economy are on opposite courses: while the culture calls for freedom, the economy calls for constraint. The most ardent seekers of self-fulfillment fallaciously view the self as an endless series of gratifiable needs and desires.[2]

Meanwhile, they complain in self-pity that they have sacrificed their identity and wasted precious years, and for what? Yet they can't seem to do anything about it. They feel trapped. After all, what would happen to the nation's *Gross Domestic Product*, the *National Trade Deficit*, if they were to drop off or tune out?

Americans have a fuzzy way of projecting their surreal impact on socio-economic indicators, which let them off the hook. They con themselves into thinking that making tons of money, while being increasingly unhappy, is their patriotic duty. They convince themselves they couldn't change courses even if they wanted to. Their families (translated: their spoiled brats and pampered mates) are dependent upon them to make this huge salary.

Yet to attempt to do for others what they might better do for themselves is to weaken their resolve and diminish them as persons. People feel better about themselves when they are carrying their own weight, and aren't obliged to take handouts.

The real reason these unhappy campers don't get off the bus is that they are addicted to a lifestyle and its feeding frenzy. It is all they know, or all they want to know. What would people think if they stopped the bus and got off? Chances are they don't want to think about that. Nor do they want to face the possible aggravation at home should they slow down. Besides, work is the happiest excuse they have for staying away.

Much of the unhappiness of American workers is tied to pleasing others rather than pleasing themselves, to doing what others expect or believe important for them to do. They are so caught up in this pleasing business that they don't have a clue as to what actually turns them on. They have never stopped to consider that happy possibility.

Many corporate managers have admitted to me that they put on a front of being cool, in charge, rational, when most of the time they are actually flying by the seat of their pants. Moreover, they put on a stoic face to criticism while thinking of measuring the criticizer for a straitjacket. It is axiomatic: the higher a person climbs up the organizational ladder the more self-conscious and sensitive they are to all nuances that might penetrate their deceptive shield. Unfortunate is the messenger that fails to realize this.

Therein lies a double irony. Workers in the bosom of the company think corporate management is impervious to their inflammatory salvos. What they fail to realize is that people at every organizational level crave acceptance; like to think that they are being appreciated; thought to be doing a good job. Everyone lusts for recognition, and covets approval so that they may in turn accept and approve of themselves.

Workers at opposite ends of the food chain are more alike than different. They are equally tense about the possibility that others may uncover the folly of their ways; similarly preoccupied with comparing and competing; and inordinately concerned with how others might see them. As incredible as it might seem, they both are consumed with the belief that they carry the burden of the world on their shoulders, while traumatized with the doubt that they are equal to the task. In a word, American workers across the board take themselves far too seriously and life which is fleeting not seriously enough.

American Workers Like None Other!

The American imperial system of commerce is guilty of a stunning paradox. There are the "haves" and "have nots," to be sure, but it is hard to tell them emotionally apart. American workers at every level tend to be dull witted, humorless, culturally impoverished, shamelessly self-indulgent, and as interesting to talk to as reading the want ads in the newspaper.

American workers don't believe in stretching their minds, but in stretching their pocket books. When they exercise, they have to have personal trainers goad them on to work out, or they must compete in triathlon contests to combat their eating disorders to sculpt their bodies beautiful. Exercise bulimia is a real concern for many Americans.[3]

Good health is the rhetoric but peripheral to physical fitness. Being in shape is a matter of comparing and competing. So, most Americans say, *"Why bother?"* and go the other way. They turn their attention to being fanatical spectator fans, making young men and women incredibly rich for hitting, carrying or throwing some kind of a ball. Meanwhile, they sit, watch, eat and drink putting on such girth as to be the most overweight nation in the world.

Programmed to react, not act; to complain, not communicate, they identify with celebrities and hard charging athletes as if it were they "out there paying the price," as they like to put it. John Rocker, a pitcher for the *Atlanta Braves*, got himself into a lot of trouble in the 2000 season by describing his contempt for the subway fans of the *New York Mets*. Rocker made some nasty remarks to *Sports Illustrated* magazine about immigrants, AIDS victims and people who differed from him. "Unpleasant stuff," as psychiatrist-columnist Charles Krauthammer says, *"though in truth, not terribly different from your average rant at a redneck bar."*[4] It wasn't pretty what he said, nor was it right, but it illustrated the fans sensitivity to celebrity approval. They inadvertently made this relief pitcher with a loose tongue and a malevolent heart into more than a baseball player.

Most fans are workers who don't want to look at themselves in the mirror but through a looking glass, which shows them to be the svelte and stunning reflection of their heroes. They work a job, but is it the job they wish to do? Chances are it is not. So, they escape this question in the fanaticism of spectator sport. There they can identify and fantasize through the exploits of others. They can roar with approval when their heroes do well, or boo to the top of their lungs when they fail. Meanwhile, work is a necessary evil where they prefer to vegetate than to think. Once off the job, a cadre of celebrities fills their vacant heads and carries them forward.

The problem with this is that happiness is not a passive process. It is an active choice. Happiness is tied to self-fulfillment, not money, but most American workers believe they work only for money. The energy, enthusiasm, anger, fight, and combative spirit that they display defending their sports heroes slip from their consciousness once they enter the workplace. Their zest and spirit is left at home in the closet, along with their game face and togs, until the next battle of their heroes. Workers believe it is dangerous to wonder aloud, to think combatively amongst their peers, to wax eloquent about work or to intellectually challenge their superiors. The stigmata of being different would surely isolate them from the group. Yet all this is forgotten once they put on their team's colors and leave their wimpish self on the closet floor.

Alexis de Tocqueville, whom Americans love to quote, actually saw American democracy spawning mediocrity. He could see no place for intellectual elitism to flourish, as the brilliant, the idiosyncratic, and the genius, as well as the party pooper, held themselves in check for fear of disapproval. That was 1832.

Today, with all the marvels of technology we have round-the-clock celebrity watch. Great homage is paid to pop idols. In the lifetimes of the iconoclastic American physicist Richard Feynman and the highbrow British philosopher Isaiah Berlin so little exposure was their lot that most readers won't recognize their names. Both went *against the grain* in their chosen fields.

Feynman was a great mathematician who performed magic in science. Architect of quantum theories of physics, *enfant terrible* of the atomic bomb project, caustic critic of the space shuttle commission, and *Nobel Laureate*, he gave physicists a new way to describe the interactions of subatomic particles. Originality was his obsession. Never content with what he knew or with what others knew, he unceasingly questioned scientific truths.

Berlin was a British don by way of Latvia, where he was born. His major contribution to philosophy was his subversive idea of *value-pluralism,* which runs against the dominant Western traditions, secular and religious, which avow an ultimate harmony of values. Berlin finds no evidence of an ideal universal culture, economic or political system, which can be founded on rational choice. Each culture is unique to itself and diverse from every other culture, and Berlin adds, *"We should be thankful for it."*[5]

Should you think I am singling out a special class of American workers, think again. It has been my experience that:

(1) Most college professors read little more than the general public.

Check their class notes. Most are ancient. If class notes are less than ten years old, you're dealing with a neophyte. Tenure is a communal disease leading to intellectual incompetence.

(2) Doctors are not incompetent. Doctors are simply poor self-managers and planners, if not exhausted students.

Medicine is changing so rapidly that prescription drugs and their applications are quickly outdated. That doesn't stop many doctors from prescribing and treating their patients as if it were the days when they first graduated from medical school, which might be 10, 15, 20 or more years ago.

(3) This would suggest that psychiatrists are essentially blindfolded psycho pharmacists.

This problem is even more pronounced with psychiatrists. They prescribe antidepressants that have been approved by the FDA with little sense of their psychophysical impact on their patients. Moreover, psychiatry, which is esteemed by laymen, is close to quackery in practice. Psychiatrists have less training in psychology than psychologists do, and we know how locked into psychobabble they are. The fact is psychiatry plays *"Russian roulette"* with human physiology, often prescribing drugs that have an adverse effect on their patients causing them to become ill and disoriented. Modern medicine, as it learns more about the workings of the human brain, admits to having previously operated much in the dark.[6]

(4) Most engineers have engines for brains and see everything in terms of the mechanics of "things," with little patience or appreciation regarding the impact their designs might have on human beings.

Can anyone justify the metamorphoses of the automobile to the SUV? It is ugly, a gas-guzzler, a polluter extraordinary, and turns like a Sherman tank. Engineers would reengineer the social system to look like an SUV and claim it one of the wonders of the world. To them, there is no soul, only discrete parts that follow cybernetics.

(5) The virus of the age is science. It contaminates everything.

Yet American workers worship science as a god. Did monotheism ever reach so deep into the soul of man? For every problem science solves it seems to create two new problems. Most modern diseases are gifts of science as earlier diseases have mutated to new forms. Disease has always been with man, and man is living longer in America and other developed countries of the world than before. But does it follow that living longer is necessarily a precondition to living wiser or happier? [7] My wonder is where genetic engineering will take us. For whatever scientists discover, technology gurus will turn it into a commercial product without a moment's reflection or hesitation.

(6) Anyone who has had the sad experience of being embroiled in litigation knows that they might have better represented themselves than their hired counsel.

We have more attorneys than medical doctors. Lawyers are running America. Their lawsuits are setting policy on guns, tobacco and HMOs. *Time* magazine asks the rhetorical question, *"Who elected them?"* Of course they elected themselves and swarm into our lives like a locust storm.[8] The plethora of attorneys is a reflection of our mistrust of each other. In most major cities there is an attorney for practically every household. If this sounds preposterous, consider Washington, DC. Here the ratio balloons to one attorney for every four citizens.

(7) The book publishing business symbolizes a cultural paradox.

Most American workers don't read a single book a year once they complete their formal education. Yet, thanks to electronic books and every-reader-a-writer, this promises to soar above 100,000 new titles in 2000, and possibly double or triple that in 2001. Who reads these books? Good question. Probably there are more books published than serious readers. So besides writers reading their own books, it is doubtful that many others do. Now, there are exceptions. J.K. Rowling's fourth book in the "Harry Potter" series (*Harry Potter and the Goblet of Fire* 2000) is a children's book of some 734 pages. It is a publishing phenomenon. Nearly 400,000 advance copies were sold by Amazon.com weeks before the publishing date of July 8, 2000. In the United States 3.8 million copies and 1.2 million copies in Great Britain were produced in the first printing, a record. Obviously, this author is reaching her readers. But what about the more than 50 percent of Americans who read so poorly they cannot read the labels on food and drugs? What complicates this picture further is that few Europeans and Asians admit to reading American authors outside their field of interest.

"Making it" is the theme song of most American workers. This extends from workers in the trenches to corporate executives, from academics to health care

414

specialists, from scientists to technologists, from politicians to clerics. They are all enamored of power. So operating as courtiers to power is a precondition to making it, which makes ass kissing an occupational necessity. It is the main ingredient to the successful executive career, the tenured professor, the HMO doctor, the grant-funded scientist, the corporate engineer, the elected official, and the diocesan priest. The fawning sycophant knows that obsequious discretion far outweighs either brains or bold thinking. On the contrary, *"making it"* in America is a game of connections. Being amenable to the boss, be he or she the CEO, CFO, COO, or the friendly supervisor, still cuts it. A superior's mind might be as light as air and twice as dense, but that person is the courtier's ticket to the good life.

"Making it" is a system geared to mediocrity. Everybody knows it. And no one does anything about it if they can help it. They are too busy exploiting it to their advantage. The system is built on replicating what is known and what worked before. And what is known is dressed up in what is expected. To depart from this formula is to do so at your own peril.

Vive la difference!

Bill Gates of Microsoft is considered a genius because he is the richest man in the world. He is the richest man in the world because he wasn't greedy when IBM asked him to develop software for them, which became MS/DOS. Others were approached before Microsoft, but they thought it was a splendid opportunity to gouge IBM, and of course the rest is history.

Since the reader may not be familiar with the story, it is one which bears repeating. It illustrates the wisdom of *going against the grain.* The time is 1980. IBM is preparing to launch its first personal computer. At the time IBM enjoyed a clear leadership in the world market for large computers, a position it had maintained since the dawn of the computer age after WWII.

By 1980 IBM decided it could no longer ignore the personal computer market. *Apple Computer* and other companies were demonstrating the market's extraordinary potential. IBM rushed to put together a system that could be based on existing components and technology instead of considering a complete reengineering of its mammoth *System 360.*

System 360 offered much more computing power for the price than competing machines from Burroughs and UNIVAC. *"Instead of raising the prices in traditional monopolist style,"* wrote Charles Ferguson and Charles Morris in their book *Computer Wars* (1980), *"IBM typically forced widespread price-cutting through the industry, always following up its initial offerings with a steady stream of new technology breakthroughs . . . IBM's leadership was based not on controlling a technology but on exploiting it better than anyone else."*[9]

Microsoft would remember this lesson and use this strategy to its advantage.

It is at this point that things got interesting. The best candidate to produce IBM's operating system in its first computer was a small company called *Digital Research.* But IBM could not come to an agreement with Gary Kildall, the engineer who was head of Digital. Kildall missed his golden opportunity by choosing that day to go flying in his private plane. Kildall's wife, Dorothy McEwen, in any case, normally handled business negotiations for *Digital Research.* She was there to meet with the IBM representatives – and to reject the terms offered as being too one-sided in IBM's favor. Her main objection was to the *"nondisclosure"* agreement required by IBM, which would, as she saw it, have allowed IBM to hear all about *Digital Research's* products and plans and then go out and duplicate them on its own.

Microsoft was of another mind. It saw advantages to accepting IBM's terms rather than disadvantages. Besides, it was IBM! Microsoft looked on the operating-system contract as a vehicle that would allow it to sell its real products – *the programming languages that it was developing.* So late in 1980 IBM signed the agreement that would eventually launch Bill Gates and his partners Paul Allen and Steve Ballmer into the stratosphere of multi-billionaires. IBM went looking for Kildall and ended up with Gates.[10]

Gates learned quickly. Microsoft mirrored the business strategy of IBM and took a chapter from the Japanese, and didn't waste time acquiring technology that already existed. Microsoft bought the rights to what was called the *"Quick and Dirty Operating System"* or QDOS (which became MS/DOS) from *Seattle Computer.* Microsoft first paid $25,000 for non-exclusive rights and then another $50,000 for exclusive rights. In 1986 Microsoft paid *Seattle Computer* $1 million to settle a dispute over rights to DOS.

After this start, Microsoft shrewdly eliminated all rivals in the operating system business, and established DOS and Windows. Then it went on to solidify its market control in a manner after IBM's strategy for marketing *System 360* in 1964. Unfortunately, by 1980 "Big Blue" was eroding as Microsoft was soaring.[11] IBM couldn't let go of its fixation on the large computer business and essentially gave Microsoft a free ride into changing the face of American industry. There is a lesson in here for everyone.[12]

Microsoft perhaps epitomizes the times more for what it is not rather than for what it is. It is not, for example, an innovative company, but an exploitative one. Metaphorically speaking, Microsoft is not a leopard without spots, but a snake without fangs. Microsoft is the child playing adult games and doing so without recrimination. Bill Gates, himself, has the head of a mischievous child on a man's body, so why should his company differ?

Entrepreneurs, such as Gates and others, know that most workers fail to see themselves as part of the problem and therefore outside the solution. People have ideas on how to improve, indeed, how to radically change operations to be more productive, but they don't entertain them. Those are decisions for management, for people who are not afraid to take risks, such as the Bill Gates of the world, "No skin off their teeth!"

The biggest difference between Bill Gates and most workers is not brains but brashness. He is not afraid to please himself, not afraid to be the maverick, not afraid to break convention. One attribute of Bill Gates that is repeated again and again is that he isn't into wasting his or anyone else's time. If he couldn't find what he needed, in school for instance, he created it out of his own experience. In that sense Gates reflects the philosophy of Emerson, which is to value direct experience rather than external authority and tradition.

You can't be timid and be an entrepreneur. You can't sit on the sidelines and complain about *"what if"* and expect the world to get better. You can't be a fatalist and say *"Life, do with me what thou wilt."* You can't be a paid robot and non-thinker, and expect to be always outside *Harm's Way*.

This indictment of passivity embraced IBM in 1980 and it has never recovered from it since. But it extends as much to lily fingered professionals as it does to grubby gloved blue-collar workers who remain fixated on what they have and are afraid to venture beyond it.

What holds most workers back?

Workers are passive for reason. Workers know when they think for themselves, take a stand, *go against the grain,* or fail to go along with the silent majority, all hell breaks loose. Or at least that is what they have convinced themselves will happen.

Workers don't want to be labeled *"trouble makers."* Heaven forbid that they be considered a maverick or eccentric. It is so important to fit, to support the prevailing norm, to ape the stance and echo the sentiments of the majority. It is equally important to be well liked, to be included, to be "one of the guys," even if being in such company *goes against the grain* of everything a worker considers important. The prison of conformity is the residence of the paid robot. Its walls are constructed of the fear of humiliation; the fear of being demoted; the fear of missing a pay raise increase; and the fear of being rejected by the group.

A worker who thinks for himself, and has a high need to meet his own expressed needs is likely to be subjected to a psychic campaign of duress. The individual who is self-confident intimidates conformists. They feel a need to strike back. The self-confident person is not invited to participate on the department's soft ball team; is excluded from the lunch crowd; is not copied on departmental e-mails; is not notified of scheduled meeting changes; and is constantly harassed by put downs and kidding. If this fails to make the impact desired, the maverick is treated as if invisible. The tormentors ultimately get their wish. The person retreats into his shell or quits.

Upstarts are the first casualties of downsizing. The majority observes this and cowers in waxed compliance. They assume the role of the victim. Even the best workers work only at about 40 percent of their capacity. They don't know this because they are too busy working hard rather than smart, too busy doing what has always been done rather than identifying chronic problems and resolving them. Unconscious terror and resentment boil beneath the surface. Workers' energy is consumed in watching their backside, and wondering when the other shoe will fall rather than focusing on productive work.

Cynical management rules in the vague world of innuendo where workers are thought to be different. Workers and managers are a common breed. Cynical management holds to the idea that workers are children because they behave as children, and therefore need to be managed and treated as children. It never occurs to management that it has created the culture that has produced dependent and counter dependent workers. Cynical management has also seen workers move away from the philosophy of the *"common good"* to the idea of *"personhood."*

Personhood has evolved over time as workers have increasingly detached themselves from intimacy with family, friends, church, school, community, and the workplace. Once a wedge was driven between them and these institutions, workers went forward as a *divided self.* Then a peculiar thing happened.

Electrifying progress thwarted the normal maturation process from adolescence to adulthood. Americans became obsessed with wealth building, but strangely, without the accumulation of wealth. Albeit the poorest savers amongst advanced technical societies, wealth became the wedge between the spiritual and material world, between the *common good* and *personhood*.

Personhood evolved as children were weaned on television as babysitter and a diet of McDonalds, learning along the way to play the guilt card. Parents responded by providing them with every material comfort imaginable, which still failed to satisfy their spiritual needs. As a result, children have matured bereft of spiritual sensitivity explaining their rejection of the *common good*: that is, *"The idea that what is good enough for my family, my church, my school, my community, my company, my country is good enough for me."* These children who have rejected this creed want more, and they want it now!

Self-indulgent child-adults vote for self-determination, but oddly without self-responsibility. They want their cake and eat it, too – the right to think, believe, behave, live and work as they please. They seek a world of pleasure without pain or consequence, a world in which they need never grow up. When their plants close and their workplaces turn into eyesores; when their communities dry up and there is precious little work for anyone, whom do they blame? Not themselves!

These workers are a product of *learned helplessness* and *irresponsibility*. This absolves them from any taint of collusion in their own tragic circumstance. These child-adults, these spoiled brats, are not happy campers and have no moral compass. They see themselves as victims forced to take the brunt of circumstances on their chins – *"Woe is me!"* they cry. They conveniently forget that they always went with the flow, kept their noses clean, never challenged their bosses, ignored the company's decline, took comfort in saying *"That's the way the ball bounces,"* until there was no bounce left.

Management acted as their surrogate parents, and provided them with all the comforts of home. Moreover, the company stepped in and provided them with so many entitlement toys that it was as if they had never left home. Submerged in pervasive adolescence, is it any wonder workers behave as they do today?

American workers of the past two generations fail to see that they are the company and without them there is no company; there are no products or services, no markets, nothing at all. Conversely, when these same workers fail to perform; when they look the other way when peers gouge the company; when they focus on what they can get, not give, there is no sustainable way for the company to survive. Workers have literally killed their spirit, and in doing so, the viable spirit of the company.

In that same vein, when workers fail to fight for their jobs, fight for competence and contribution, fight for market share, fight for fiscal security, fight for their professional dignity, they are not only wimps they are children who have failed to make the transition into adulthood.

Workers of a Different Mindset – Mature Adults!

Our American culture has played the innocent card too long – that of the youngest international kid on the block, the pampered ethnocentric ugly American, the waste maker. The whole life of the mind – the world of art, literature, music, politics, science, religion, and philosophy – holds little interest to most American workers. They are too busy making a living. There is an exception. These are the *mature adult workers*, a breed apart.

Mature adult workers question decisions of management because they know it is their work where the rubber hits the road. They know corporate management is too remote to clearly understand the requirements of work. They also know that their direct management passes what they say through several filters before it reaches these decision-makers. So they act. It is their philosophy that it is easier to ask forgiveness than permission. They put their special knowledge to work at the level of consequences, and accept the accountability that goes with it.

Mature adult workers are not afraid to question company aberrations such as its obsession with schedule at the expense of quality, outdated production practices, red tape, or anything else that may impact negatively on their work. If the company has a philosophy of *"not losing"* rather than growing the business, they want to know why – convince me! They pay attention to the company's philosophy, whatever it is, and demand an explanation when policy takes precedence over it. They are not in the habit of waiting for the other shoe to fall. Instead, they are ready with suggestions on how to avoid that happening.

Mature adult workers are not interested in something for nothing. They know entitlement programs cost money. They know that the company pampers its employees to hold them. But they also know entitlements don't motivate. Their real income and benefits have declined over time. So they say, *"Let's end the charade. Treat us as partners. Get us involved in the design of work. We know what works and what doesn't. End the patronizing. Give us a chance to truly feel this is our company. Show us the money. That motivates!"*

Mature adult workers don't need to be micromanaged, don't need to be praised as if schoolchildren. They know their worth. What they need is real work, real objectives. They need to be stretched. They say, *"Give us the assignment, its parameters, due date, and get out of our way!"* Then they add, *"Measure us on what we do, not some arbitrary scale cooked up by HR or some consultant."* They resent the patronizing twaddle of performance appraisal.[13] Everyone knows it's a joke. They see themselves as self-managers.

Meaningless slogans, campaigns, fads and copycat programs turn off mature adult workers. *"What worked across the street,"* they say, *"should stay there. It ain't us and we ain't it. Let's create something that's consistent with what we are."* They question the wisdom of empowerment programs when all they see around them is powerlessness and the lack of accountability. Nor are they fond of being herded off to quality meetings as if quality were high church. They don't need convincing; don't need to be treated as if in grammar school. They know quality is essential. It is the rhetoric of quality that isn't.

Mature adult workers have little patience with executive gamesmanship. They see this gamesmanship on display with the frantic quest for national quality awards. They see it also in the pep rallies on teamwork as if work could be accomplished in any other way. They say, *"If quality is the orthodox religion, let's start practicing and quit preaching quality. Let's not reduce teamwork to a kid's pajama party."*

Mature adult workers address the *"right things"* because they know that is where the gold is. They treat the mantra, *"Do it right the first time,"* as a meaningless jingle. They are strategic doers focusing on the 20 percent vital few problems that make 80 percent of the difference in operations. They make no excuse for avoiding the trivial many problems. They ask, *"Do you need to be efficient or effective?"* Those needing to be efficient are consumed with 80 percent of the problems, which have only a 20 percent or less impact on the bottom line. They can get excited about doing the right things especially when they see the results. It gives them a sense of pride and accomplishment and spurs them on to greater performance.

Mature adult workers do value symbols and rituals, which connect them to the company's history. After all, they are devoting their blood, sweat and tears to making the company successful. They are suspect of rhetoric. They are builders and see themselves sharing in the symbols and rituals with builders of the past.

Mature adult workers have no interest in working hard, but only in working smart. They are performers, not personalities. Work for work's sake has no appeal to them. They focus on the chronic problems in the process and correct them rather than have the same undesirable outcomes replicated, *ad infinitum*.

Mature adult workers know that conflict and disagreement are normal fare, and that passionate workers are sure at times to disagree, often heatedly. They don't need to be best friends to work effectively together. They know that conflict can be managed and resolved equitably if the focus is on the disagreement and not on the disagreeing person. Congeniality is nice at dinner parties but unrealistic in a thriving work climate. They accept the fact that risk, uncertainty, and failure are often the price of success.

Mature adult workers are annoyed with cosmetic change; change that takes executives off the hot seat by real or imagined crises. They know that crisis management is management that solves problems it creates, and then congratulates itself for the effort. It sees cosmetic driven solutions naïve and counterproductive. Mature adult workers know that defining the problem is hard work; that it takes time; and that it is not always easy, but it is the only way to raise the bar on performance.

Why does adolescence still have a hold on workers' minds?

Mature adult workers are of course threatening to the status quo of the company. They are not necessarily polite, obedient, obsequious, conforming, punctual and loyal as children are expected to be. They have a *high need to please themselves* and have confidence in their own judgment. They don't take anything on the authority of others if it fails to make sense to them. They are self-directed, self-managed, self-reliant and self-responsible.

Companies applaud the idea of maturity but sponsor and promote immaturity into their workers. Why?

Companies want their people to behave, not to think; to do, not to question why; to appreciate, not find fault with operations. The emphasis is always on being *other-directed* rather than *self-directed*. Companies think they must put a fire under their people rather than a fire in them. There is always the unspoken fear that people will not behave as they should behave if they are self-motivated and become self-satisfied.

From being reared at home, to attending school, to taking a job, from paying homage to church and state, from birth to death, workers are expected to behave as disciplined children. Home and school teach children to conform to authority. The workplace is defined and managed to conform to a similar authority. The tenets of religious faith are written to capture the attention of starry-eyed children, while government could not demonstrate a lower opinion of the prospects of its citizens' self-regulation.

Companies in particular and society in general are afraid of *mature adult workers;* afraid of the madness that adulthood demands. *Mature adult workers* see the madness of things much more clearly than by those who claim to be sane. *Mature adult workers* see companies running from their challenges by downsizing or merging in a frantic madness to survive. They preach empowerment and practice archaic management and autocratic rule.

Moreover, society professes the sanctity of man and Christian love while it breeds new forms of violence, crime and neglect in its bosom. Love no longer recreates itself. Self-hatred is pervasive. Why is this so? [14]

Whether symptomatic of the problem or the cause, we do know baby boomers and Generation X (and Y) remain spoiled brats and not happy campers. They remain children in a world, which demands adults. A paternalistic society prefers indulgent children to unmanageable adults. With *mature adult workers*, control no longer resides in the parent-figure as overlord, but in the mind and heart of workers.

The agony of the times is that these pampered children have become parents, which means no one is in control. They bully their children as they have been bullied, but their children realize they have no heart for the bullying. Therefore, they can do as they please which of course fails to please them at all. These mischievous offspring as workers feign helplessness, as did their parents, and for it, like them, they behave as if suspended in adolescence. Society's redemption cannot depend on them. It rests with *mature adult workers* who, unfortunately, are the exception rather than the rule.

Even if the mission of society suddenly became dedicated to the creation of an adult work force, it would most likely take the better part of a century to realize the change in culture. Cultural conditioning is that ingrained.

Workers are programmed to be self-negating with a compelling need to conform to group norms; to avoid conflict and confrontation; to comply with arbitrary standards; and to look for answers outside themselves. For most workers it would be as impossible for them to behave differently, as it would be for them to defy gravity and fly. The most damning epitaph of the present work force, however, is this: *They seem to be at their very best only when the going is good.*

Then, There is "Now!"

Given these challenges, the reality is that we live in *Corporate America* in an age defined by capitalism, globalization and technology. While politicians in Washington, DC take center stage, it is the icons in the wings that are calling the shots: the entrepreneurs, technologists and business leaders. Mark Zuckerberg and Jeff Bezos, et. al., are off stage but occupy the symbolic iconic center of power once exclusively the domain of industrialists and politicians.

Meanwhile, millennials and centennials fall into line with *Corporate America* armed with their impressive professional credentials and comfortable affluence, not giving a toss one way or the other about the shenanigans going on with Wall Street power brokers and politicians in the nation's capital who are on center stage. They are into their own "cloud."

In a survey, the *Higher Education Research Institute* (HERI) asked incoming freshmen to American colleges and universities if they considered developing a philosophy of life. In 1967, 86 percent responded it was "essential to very important" them to do so. By 2013, this had plummeted to 45 percent. In other words, they were into and all about "Now!"

David Brooks captured the essence of this in the cover story for *The Atlantic* (April 2001), claiming young men and women of America's future elite work their laptops to the bone, rarely question authority, and happily accept their positions at the top of the heap as part of the natural order of life. He writes:

At the top of the meritocratic ladder we have in America a generation of students who are extraordinarily bright, morally earnest, and incredibly industrious. They like to study and socialize in groups. They create and join organizations with great enthusiasm. They are responsible, safety-conscious and mature. They feel no compelling need to rebel – not even a hint of one. They not only defer to authority, they admire it. "Alienation" is a word one almost never hears from them. They regard the universe as beneficent, orderly, and meaningful. At the schools and colleges where the next leadership class is being bred, one finds not angry revolutionaries, despondent slackers, or dark cynics but the Organization Kid.

Some 57 years earlier (1956), William H. Whyte published *The Organization Man*. The man he describes has abandoned his individualism and a personal life to blend into the demands of the corporation for which he works. He is an uncomplicated man who puts the organization before his family and friends, forsaking any secret desires to be a totally committed well-meaning organization man.

During this same post-World War II period, novelist Sloan Wilson wrote a novel about the "organization man" titled *"The Man in the Gray Flannel Suit"* (1955). It was made into a popular film of the same name in 1956. Sloan's story is of a suburban father and husband haunted by his memories of World War II, including a wartime romance with an Italian village girl named Maria, which resulted in an illegitimate son he has never seen. Pressed by his unhappy wife to get a higher-paying job, he becomes an "organization man," floundering in confusion lost in his secret identity.

It is significant – 1945 to 2019 – that this period has given us the *"Organization Man"* and now the *"Organization Kid"* with neither of them moving off the dime of Corporate America's 1945 nostalgia. Meanwhile, the majority of Americans who have little in common with either the "Organization Man" or the "Organization Kid" wait to be rescued.

References

1. Teresa Brandt, *"Happiness remains elusive,"* The Tampa Tribune, Commentary (Books), August 6, 2000, p. 4.
2. Daniel Yankelovich, New Rules, Random House, 1981, p. 163.
3. John Stenzler, *"Few treatments for men facing eating disorders,"* The Tampa Tribune, April 23, 2000.
4. Charles Krauthammer, *"You don't send a bigot to a shrink,"* The Tampa Tribune, Nation/World section, November 19, 1996, p. 11.
5. James Gleick, Genius: The Life and Science of Richard Feynman, Pantheon Books, 1992.
6. Steven Pinker, How the Mind Works, W. W. Norton & Co., Chapter Three: *"Revenge of the Nerds,"* 1997.
7. Time (Special Issue), *"Beyond 2000, November 8, 1999. Issue asks provocative questions such as will we still need to have sex.*
8. Adam Cohen, *"Are Lawyers Running America?"* Time, July 17, 2000, pp. 22-27.
9. Charles H. Ferguson, Charles R. Morris, Computer Wars: How the West can Win in a Post-IBM World, Times Books, 1994.
10. Stephen Manes and Paul Anderson, Gates: How Microsoft's Mogul Reinvented an Industry and Made Himself the Richest Man in the World, Touchstone/Simon & Schuster, 1994.
11. Paul Carroll, Big Blues: The Unmaking of IBM, Crown, 1994.

12. James Fellows, *"The Computer Wars," The New York Review,* March 24, 1994, pp. 34-41.

13. Diane Stafford, *Kansas City Star, "Why employee appraisals so often miss the mark," The Tampa Tribune,* Commentary Section, August 7, 2000, p. 9.

14. Peter Gay, *The Cultivation of Hatred,* W. W. Norton & Co., 1993.

AFTERWORD

Dr. James Fisher, "Jim" to me, has been observing, studying, dissecting, theorizing and writing about American corporations for over four decades. Like the *Dilbert* cartoon, any employee reading Jim's works will immediately say, "That's my company!! He has been studying MY COMPANY!!" I've been with the same organization for forty-one years, and the accuracy of his assessments are uncanny, almost as if he has the whole place wired.

THE POST MODERN WORKER EXPOSED is the distillation of Jim's life's work. The knowledge density of this work is profound, the espresso version if you will. The reader should come prepared to think and be intellectually stimulated.

Jim's perspective has always been from that of the worker. As I stand at the end of my career, I am convinced that human organizations exist to serve the interests of those who run them; not the stakeholders, not the workers. As Jim points out, the workers could have the power, but I believe they don't want it. More specifically, the workers do not want to become what they must become to succeed in the palatine political games that go with the pursuit of organizational power. They'd rather have a comfortable life and be true to their own values.

Decades of focus on education over experience have created a tremendous thinking imbalance favoring the hypothetical over the pragmatic. We are all marching lock step (perhaps staggering) into the Age of the Absurd. It will be for those who come behind us to sort it out. Perhaps Jim's work will give them a solid starting point to move forward.

Eric Michael Rodts, an executive and international consultant with Honeywell, Inc.

ACKNOWLEDGEMENTS

Were it not for my wife Betty this modest writing career—which has extended through our 31 years of marriage—could not have proceeded. Thank you, my love, Beautiful Betty.

Likewise, it would be impossible to thank the many great authors I have read over the years who have helped me to form my thoughts and ideas into words from my empirical experience. And, I would not have found these authors unless the good Sisters of St. Francis at St. Patrick's School had not taught me to love reading, to embrace the English language and to follow my passions.

Then there are the organized team sports in which I participated. In elementary, high school and college these formative experiences wrought me into the adult I would later become. Athletics taught me discipline and punctuality. Among other things, I learned to commit myself wholly to practice; to accept criticism from coaches and teammates; to take success gracefully, disappointment philosophically and failure in stride; while playing within the rules and subduing my own temper.

Above all, it is work and workplaces that taught me the most. It is hard for me to precisely identify why I have enjoyed so much every job I have ever had—from bagging groceries and stocking shelves at the A&P Supermarket as a boy; working five summers as a laborer at a chemical processing plant, between semesters at university. If not for that particular summer job, college graduation would not have taken place for me. Each job was my laboratory, where I was the subject of study, the lab rat. My responses to the stimuli at work taught me the principles I now apply in my writing. These jobs, of course, took place while I was still a student in primary, secondary, college and finally graduate school.

Then there are the job experiences of my chosen careers. These include being on active duty for the United States Navy in the Mediterranean on the Flag Ship of the Sixth Fleet, the USS Salem (CA-139); being a R&D chemist for a chemical company; then a chemical sales engineer for another chemical company for ten years, eventually an international corporate executive; taking a two-year sabbatical in my mid-thirties to read and write, publishing one book, trying to make sense of my life; then going back to graduate school for six years moving out of the hard sciences and into the soft sciences—consulting and acting as an adjunct professor for several colleges and universities; then joining a hi-tech company as an industrial psychologist, and again rising to an international executive. Now, for the past thirty plus years, I've devoted myself to writing, some books, some articles, all stimulated by work and workplaces, drawn from personal working experience since I was a boy.

Finally, I must mention my mentor and friend, author William L. Livingston IV, an engineer, and an inventor with over 100 patents. Bill has generously shared his own wisdom and wit with me over decades, while venturing far beyond my own comprehension. He too continues to write.

And one last thank-you to George Daly, up in sunny Alberta Canada, in Calgary. George has held my hand through one IT jam after another, as I struggled with these books. Thanks George. I couldn't have done it without you.

To all these people and organizations, I offer a river of gratitude. They have shaped me into the person I am today, motivated me and enabled me to share what I have learned with this and coming generations. Humbly, I thank you.

Note on the Author

Social psychologist James R. Fisher, Jr., Ph.D., sees himself as a peripatetic philosopher intrigued with the eclectic imagery of his time, which he reports on dutifully in terms of his own empirical experience in this genre through a score of books.

www.ingramcontent.com/pod-product-compliance
Lightning Source LLC
Chambersburg PA
CBHW061333280526
45784CB00001B/2